THE CLASSICAL FOUNDATIONS OF
THE AMERICAN CONSTITUTION

The Framers of the American Constitution were substantially influenced by ancient history and classical political theory, as exemplified by their education, the availability of classical readings, and their inculcation in classical republican values. This book explores how the Framing generation deployed classical learning to develop many of the essential structural aspects of the Constitution: federalism, separation of powers, a bicameral legislature, independent courts, and the war-making and foreign relations powers. Also examined are very contemporary constitutional debates for which there were classical inspirations, including: sovereign immunity, executive privilege, line-item vetoes, and the electoral college. Combining techniques of intellectual history, classical studies, and constitutional interpretation, this book makes a unique contribution to our understanding of contemporary constitutionalism.

David J. Bederman is a professor of law at Emory University's School of Law in Atlanta, Georgia. After earning an undergraduate degree from Princeton University in international affairs (with highest honors), he went on to receive a M.Sc. in marine affairs at the London School of Economics. Professor Bederman read law at the University of Virginia, and, after graduating, clerked with the Hon. Charles E. Wiggins, judge of the U.S. Court of Appeals for the Ninth Circuit.

Professor Bederman's academic and professional career has focused on international law and its practical impact on American government. He has written extensively on the influence of ancient legal traditions on contemporary law and politics. In addition to holding a diploma from The Hague Academy of International Law, as well as a Ph.D. in law from the University of London, he has served as a legal advisor at the Iran-U.S. Claims Tribunal in The Hague. He is a member of the Board of Editors of the *American Journal of International Law*. After a stint in private practice with the Washington, D.C., firm of Covington & Burling, he accepted his current teaching appointment at Emory University School of Law. He has been a visiting professor at the University of Virginia and New York University law schools. In 2001, he was appointed as a Fulbright Distinguished Chair for Canada, lecturing on international and constitutional law at Osgoode Hall Law School, in Toronto.

THE CLASSICAL FOUNDATIONS OF THE AMERICAN CONSTITUTION

PREVAILING WISDOM

David J. Bederman

Emory University School of Law

CAMBRIDGE
UNIVERSITY PRESS

CAMBRIDGE UNIVERSITY PRESS

Cambridge, New York, Melbourne, Madrid, Cape Town, Singapore, São Paulo, Delhi

Cambridge University Press
32 Avenue of the Americas, New York, NY 10013-2473, USA

www.cambridge.org
Information on this title: www.cambridge.org/9780521885362

First published 2008

Printed in the United States of America

A catalog record for this publication is available from the British Library.

Library of Congress Cataloging in Publication Data
Bederman, David J.
The Classical foundations of the American Constitution : prevailing wisdom /
David J. Bederman.
p.   cm.
Includes bibliographical references and index.
ISBN 978-0-521-88536-2 (hbk.)
1. United States – Politics and government – 1783–1789.   2. United States – Intellectual life –
18th century.   3. Political science – Greece – Rome – History.   4. Constitutional history –
United States.   5. United States. Constitution.   I. Title.
JK116.B43   2008
342.7302′4–dc22   2007026964

ISBN   978-0-521-88536-2 hardback

For Paideia and all my teachers

What chiefly attracts and chiefly benefits students of history is just this – the study of causes and the consequent power of choosing what is best in each case. Now the chief cause of success or the reverse in all matters is the form of a state's constitution; for springing from this, as from a fountain-head, all designs and plans of action not only originate, but reach their consummation.

Polybius, *The Histories*, vi.2.8–10

CONTENTS

PREFACE

OUR RECEIVED WISDOM IS THAT THE FRAMERS OF THE UNITED States Constitution were pragmatists, not theorists. Just as importantly, we have come to believe that the American Revolution and the subsequent creation of the American republic marked a definitive break from previous political models and truths, that it well and truly began a modern mode of government of the people, for the people, and by the people. Indeed, some have gone so far to suggest that the Founders knew they were making "a new kind of society that produces a new kind of human being. That human being – confident, self-reliant, tolerant, generous, future-oriented – is a vast improvement over the wretched, servile, fatalistic, and intolerant human being that traditional societies have always produced."[1] In short, the political story of the Founding has been turned into the ultimate morality play.

I intend to question this radical and revolutionary construct of the Framing by suggesting a simple, but subversive, idea: that the members of the Framing generation were as much influenced by the political values and experiences of classical antiquity as they were by Enlightenment liberal philosophy and by the exigencies of the struggle against Great Britain. Even more pertinently, I intend to show here that the Framers' use of ancient history (perhaps even more than their reading of classical philosophy) informed their decisions in drafting the Constitution of the United States. More than merely suffusing their general political theories, my thesis is that ancient history guided, in many material respects, the fashioning of the most basic features of our government. Such organizational elements I will call here the "structural Constitution," as distinct from the provisions of our national charter that grants rights to individuals, groups, or civil society in general.[2] Foremost among the enduring aspects of the structural Constitution are the federal scheme, which allocates authority amongst the national and state governments; bicameralism in Congress; the separation of powers among the legislative, executive, and judicial branches; the provision of a strong and vigorous presidency; and the constraint of the war-making and foreign relations powers of the national government. Together these elements define a constitutionalism of limited, but effective, government. Each – as I will argue here – had its roots in classical antiquity, antecedents that the Framers were well aware of and that they fashioned for their own instrumental ends in creating the American republic.

I am mindful in writing this book that I am wading into treacherous intellectual waters. Perhaps no political subject has been given as much attention as the *mentalité* of the Framers and the consequent impact on the Constitution and their historic legacy. Nor has the subject of the Framing generation's inculcation in classical learning gone unnoticed, and it is appropriate for me to reflect at the outset of this project on the significant contributions made to this subject by previous writers. Even with the rediscovery in the 1960s of the influence of republicanism on the Framers,[3] "the extent to which Americans' republican sensibilities derived from Roman [and other ancient] models has often been overlooked by modern scholars whose interests and training lie elsewhere."[4]

Most illustrative of this dismissal of the classical tradition in the framing of the Constitution is this gracious passage from Bernard Bailyn's towering work, *The Ideological Origins of the American Revolution*: "The classics of the ancient world are everywhere in the literature of the Revolution, but they are illustrative, not determinative, of thought. They contributed a vivid vocabulary but not the logic or grammar of thought, a universally respected personification but not the source of political and social beliefs."[5] Or, as Russell Kirk put the matter: "America's political *institutions* owe next to nothing to the ancient world – although American modes of *thinking* about politics were indeed influenced, two centuries ago, by Greek and Roman philosophers long dead."[6] But perhaps Clinton Rossiter put the sharpest point on the proposition: "Most [American revolutionary and early republic] authors used the ancient Greeks for window dressing.... Americans would have believed just as vigorously in public morality had Cato and the Gracchi never lived."[7] Central to this vision of the intellectual basis of the Founding was the primacy of Enlightenment rationalism and political pragmatism over all competing influences, whether classical antiquity, the common law, or Protestant theology.[8] Indeed, it may be properly suggested that the contemporary dismissal of the Framing's classical debts is attributable to either a willful refusal to recognize that the Framers had a very different cultural construct than we have today, or that it is somehow improvident to believe that they were motivated by anything other than Enlightenment ideals.[9] And although one might err in believing that ancient history provided direct and linear inspiration for the Framers' political judgments in crafting the Constitution,[10] it would be safer to give the classical tradition its due.

The crux of this book's approach to intellectual history is to take the Framers at face value in their speeches and writings – to let them speak for themselves (sometimes at great length, given the rhetorical styles of their day[11]) when they make use of classical idioms to explain and amplify the political considerations in drafting the Constitution. This does not mean that we are obliged to assume that the Framing generation had a perfect understanding of ancient history. Indeed, they did not. One of the contributions that this book hopes to make is to assess – based on modern archaeology, philology, and historiography – the actual operation of the constitutions of ancient polities and republics and thereby better appreciate how the Framers used and abused the historical evidence then at their disposal. For some writers on this subject, the classics are merely a window onto the intellect of the Framers; for them, the underlying ancient history really does not – and cannot – matter. I prefer to reverse the polarity of this assumption and evaluate the ancient tradition of constitution-making in its own right while considering the practical impact that tradition has had on American constitutional practice.

The last significant confession that has to be made at the outset of this book is that it comes from the mind of an academic lawyer. Although the intellectual history charted here is significant, it does not exist for its own sake. Rather, as someone who has combined the disciplines of law and classics in previous volumes,[12] my preoccupation is with the impact of classical philosophy and ancient history on constitutional text and doctrine. And although the first part of this book is concerned with making the (relatively easy) case of demonstrating the classical predilections of the Framing generation (in Chapter 1) and the impact of ancient political models on the Framers (Chapter 2), the balance of this book quickly turns to more lawyerly pursuits.

In the Chapters 3 and 4, my objective is to chart a *terra incognitae* in the legal literature: the Framers' original intent – as based on their use of ancient history – in drafting various textual provisions of the structural constitution. Although the dangers of originalism in constitutional interpretation are notorious,[13] I am willing to accept for the purposes of writing this book that it remains a potent, if not the preeminent, approach to constitutional discourse in the United States. In pursuing this mission, I intend to look at two sets of constitutional controversies. The first (considered

in Chapter 3) is the central and defining structural issues of the Constitutional Convention of 1787 and the state ratification conventions that
followed: the allocation of authority between the federal union and the
states; the construction of the deliberative senate, energetic executive, and
safeguarding judiciary; and the concerns over the war and foreign relations
power of the new nation. The second set of issues (addressed in Chapter 4)
is torn from the headlines of today's constitutional debates: the sovereign
immunity enjoyed by the states in our federal union, executive privileges
exercised by the presidency, the executive branch's insistence on a line-item
veto, and the continued use of the electoral college in presidential votes.

At stake in the revival of the ancient tradition of government in the constitutional debates of 1787 and today is nothing less than a common vision
of republican government. And although, throughout this book, I refer to
the Framing generation and a classical tradition, I am mindful that neither
is a monolithic and homogenous concept. Rather, there is a set of values and
concerns that are implicated in the way that the Framers employed ancient
history in the making of the structural Constitution. This book continues
the superb intellectual historiography on this subject by adding a lawyerly
sensibility on modern constitutionalism, as well as a classicist's concern for
fidelity to the truths imparted by ancient history.

I incurred many debts in writing this book. Among them are those to
my colleagues at many universities, including Thomas C. Arthur, Curtis A.
Bradley, Christopher L. Eisgruber, Martin S. Flaherty, Michael J. Gerhardt,
Marc Miller, Polly J. Price, Michael Ramsey, Robert Schapiro, and M. N. S.
Sellers. All errors and omissions remain my own, despite the best efforts
of these fine scholars and friends. I wish to particularly thank the staff of
the Emory Law Library, and especially my colleague Will Haines for all
his assistance in gathering sources for this book. I am also grateful to my
editor at Cambridge University Press, John Berger, without whose gentle
encouragement this project would not have been brought to fruition. As
always, without the support and sacrifices of my family this book would not
have been possible.

ABBREVIATIONS

AHR	*American History Review*
AJLH	*American Journal of Legal History*
AJP	*American Journal of Philology*
Art. Confed.	Articles of Confederation (1781)
CAF	THE COMPLETE ANTI-FEDERALIST (Herbert J. Storing, ed., Chicago: University of Chicago Press, 1981)
CJ	*Classical Journal*
CQ	*Classical Quarterly*
Cont. Cong.	JOURNALS OF THE CONTINENTAL CONGRESS, 1774–1789 (Worthington C. Ford et al., eds., Washington, DC: 1904–1937)
Elliot	Jonathan Elliot, THE DEBATES IN THE SEVERAL STATES CONVENTIONS ON THE ADOPTION OF THE FEDERAL CONSTITUTION (Washington, DC, 1854)
Farrand	Max Farrand, RECORDS OF THE FEDERAL CONVENTION OF 1787 (New Haven; Yale University Press, 1937)
Federalist	THE FEDERALIST PAPERS (Clinton Rossiter, ed., 1961)
GRBS	*Greek, Roman, and Byzantine Studies*
JHI	*Journal of the History of Ideas*
JRS	*Journal of Roman Studies*
RIDA	*Revue Internationale des Droits de l'Antiquité*
U.S. Const.	Constitution of the United States (1787)
WMQ	*William and Mary Quarterly*

ONE

THE FRAMERS' CLASSICAL EDUCATION
AND WORLD VIEW

CLASSICAL ANTIQUITY MOLDED THE LEGAL EXPECTATIONS OF THE Framers of the American Constitution, and guided their legal judgment in the actual structuring of the checks and balances of that national charter. As with any proposition of intellectual history, this one requires a proof in several stages. The first step is a demonstration of the classical propensities of the Framing generation. This chapter accomplishes that by assessing the way in which the Framers and their contemporaries acquired a classical education. But it is not enough to understand how the Framing generation learned Latin and Greek, studied classical texts, used classical references in their social discourse, and assumed classical modes of argument in their political debates. Rather, one must also consider the values that classical education imparted to American leaders involved with the Constitution's drafting in 1787 and subsequent ratification.

For starters, I need to be clear about what I mean when I refer to the "Framing generation." Wishing to be as broadly inclusive as is sensible, that group must include not only the individuals who were present in Philadelphia as delegates to the Constitutional Convention in the summer of 1787, but also those involved, formally or informally, in the subsequent ratification debates that occurred in the states in the months following. Even more significantly, the Framing generation needs to be extended back in time to include prominent thinkers and leaders of the colonial period, as well as the patriots who launched and fought the American Revolution (1775–1783), and who held the country together during the Articles of Confederation period (1778–1788). Given the nature of civil society in the American colonies and states of this period, the Framing generation must include all participants in the political life of the times, not just elected representatives and politicians. Pamphleteers, ministers, and social leaders have as much claim to inclusion in the Framing generation as those who signed their names to the draft Constitution or who subsequently lent their assent to its ratification.

Nevertheless, one cannot be too apologetic about the elite nature of the social and intellectual history that is to be charted here. Although the general population of the American colonies (and then states) were among the best educated and literate in the world at that time,[1] that certainly did not mean that all participated in political councils on an equal footing. The voices that will be heard throughout this book are uniformly those of white, propertied men. And although a searching review of the sociology of the leadership caste of the Framing generation is beyond the scope of this book,[2] one cannot forget the unique conditions that gave raise to such a large and able cadre of individuals who assumed positions of authority during the time of the consideration and ratification of the Constitution. Although they may not have completely or faithfully reflected the People to whom the Constitution was addressed,[3] they nonetheless perceived of themselves as pursuing the People's business and as the instrument of the commonwealth.

Another note of explanation needs to be made about the classical tradition that is the subject of this book's analysis. Although the nature and extent of the classicism that the Framing generation appreciated will be gradually revealed here, it has to be realized at the outset that a classical tradition was strictly bounded by a set of conventions. For example, classicism was understood to be limited to Latin and Greek sources. Although the early American experience with the classical tradition was an intellectual continuation of Renaissance learning, it did not necessarily share the broader interests of contemporary European thinkers.[4] Except among a handful of divines or theologians, interest in Biblical philology, including the study of Hebrew and other ancient near Eastern languages, was rare. There was an accepted notion of a classical canon of works, and little effort was made to expand or refine that core of works, either through critical cross-reading of texts or by archaeological and inscriptional inquiry (which was just beginning to emerge as a method of classicism in Europe by the end of the eighteenth century). The Framing generation thus tended to accept classical texts at face value.

Another significant limitation on the classical tradition embraced by Americans at the time of the Revolution and the framing of the Constitution was its emphasis on history in political discourse. While, for example, Greek drama and Roman poetry exercised a substantial influence on artistic forms in Europe from the late Middle Ages on, we see less evidence of that in the roughhewn cultural life of the colonies and new republic. The one exception was the use of classical architectural devices, and this was closely connected with the political aspirations of the new country and its leadership, as Charles and Mary Beard noted:

> Through the architecture of the republican age, the political note rang with startling intonations. In casting off monarchy and established church, the patriot Fathers, like their emulative contemporaries, the leaders of the French republic, returned in their dreams, their oratory, and their architecture to the glories of republican Greece and Rome – to the simple columns, roofs, porticoes, and straight lines of early Mediterranean structures. Nothing seemed more appropriate. The ornate elaboration of renaissance Gothic appeared out of place in a country that was republican in politics, practical in its interests, and tinged, at least, with democracy.[5]

So, one of the significant themes of the early American engagement with a classical tradition was its political instrumentalism. Classicism was less a private intellectual pursuit than a public affirmation of a set of social values. How classical learning was transmitted to the Framing generation, and the values it inculcated, will be considered in the remainder of this chapter.

A. MODES OF CLASSICAL EDUCATION AND EXPRESSION

The classical training of the Framing generation has been the subject of exceptionally able recent scholarship.[6] My task here is to generally review the ways and means of classical education in the American colonies and new republic of the latter half of the eighteenth century, while particularly emphasizing the role of the classics in legal education and legal practice for attorneys. Additionally, it is important to understand the leading sources for the Framing generation's knowledge of classical history and its consequent political lessons. Finally, it is worth examining the specific educational experiences and intellectual engagements of particular members of the Framing generation with classical antiquity. The purpose of this exposition is not strictly to offer proof of the undoubted influence of classicism on the mindset of the Framing generation – what Carl Richard calls the "classical conditioning of the Founders"[7] – but also to begin the process of understanding those aspects of classical antiquity that were later to find themselves incorporated into the very fabric of the structural Constitution itself.

1. Classicism and the Early American Educational System. Following English models, the core of colonial primary educational systems was the study of Latin and Greek languages and literatures, as well as classical antiquities, even to the exclusion of English language studies.[8] Colonial American grammar schools, particularly those associated with the handful of universities, prescribed a vigorously classical education. For example, the trustees of the College of William and Mary dictated for its grammar school that "as for the Rudiments and Grammars, the Classick Authors of each Tongue, let them teach the same Books which by Law or Custom are used in the Schools of England."[9] This extended throughout the colonies, for only the poorest of areas did not maintain a grammar school.[10] There were some exceptions to this iron rule of a classical curriculum for grammar schools, and the only apparent innovations at some institutions was the introduction of instruction on commercial subjects for boys intending to enter business.[11] The ideal of a well-rounded education – a Greek concept of *paideia*[12] – was notably absent in early America.

So for nearly the course of a young man's[13] primary education at grammar school, which began at age 8 and continued for up to 7 years,[14] schoolmasters "required young scholars to display their knowledge of Latin and Greek [and] they exercised their charges in the classics – and little else."[15] And as Noah Webster observed, "The minds of youth are perpetually led to the history of Greece and Rome or to Great Britain; boys are constantly repeating the declamations of Demosthenes and Cicero or debates upon some political question in the British Parliament."[16] Instruction in the classics was nearly a full-time occupation for young students, lasting almost the entirety of school days. And, indeed, the modes of classical instruction at this primary level of education hardly changed during the colonial and early republic periods.[17]

Students were required to memorize Latin grammatical rules, and then to translate basic Latin texts into English both through sight-reading and then by formal written expositions. To complete the process, these translations were then rendered back in the original Latin, although usually in a different tense.[18] As a student progressed, so, of course, did the difficulty of the Latin texts. Within a few years, Attic Greek was introduced to the student. Although there was substantial pedagogic criticism of the colonial educational system's preoccupation with memorization, translation exercises, and rote learning,[19] the effect was to produce young men who could not only read Latin and Greek, but who could also (to a surprising degree) speak it in an almost conversational way. This helps to explain the way in which Latin (and, to a lesser degree, Greek) phrases were used in published political commentary or in deliberative debates, often without translation. Given the nature of these conversations, it was naturally assumed (although erroneously in some instances) that all of the participants had the same fluency in classical languages, as acquired from primary education.

This is not to say, however, that the quality of classical instruction in grammar schools was high in the American colonies and in the early republic. By all contemporary accounts, it was not.[20] Part of the problem was the lack of training of schoolmasters and difficulties in retention. For all but the most elite schools, teachers were recruited from the ranks of recent college graduates. These individuals were often serving as teachers in a provisional capacity, waiting only to take their master's degree in divinity to begin a career in the ministry, or to begin reading law in an attorney's office.[21] And that described the schoolmasters who had ambition; many teachers bordered on the incompetent. It was later observed of some classical instructors in North Carolina: "if they have diplomas in their hands, [they] must be confessed to have more Latin in their hands than in their heads."[22]

And if all of that were not enough to discourage most young students of the classics, there was the nearly universal association of Greek and Latin with corporal punishment meted out by zealous, and on occasion, sadistic, schoolmasters.[23] Failure to properly respond to a locution in class, a single mis-step in the declension of a Latin word, or a faulty translation of a passage, could bring on a swift flogging at the hands of an instructor. Such was the widespread nature of this phenomenon that it became its own literary trope, what with writers like Richard Steele, Samuel Johnson, and Henry Fielding lamenting the abuses they suffered at the hands of their schoolmasters.[24] Edward Gibbon succinctly said that "by the common methods of discipline, at the expense of many tears and some blood, I purchased the knowledge of Latin syntax."[25]

Carl Richard is, nonetheless, right to observe that "[i]t is quite remarkable that the association of Greek and Latin with physical punishment so rarely left a lasting distaste for the classics."[26] Josiah Quincy (1744–1775), a leading figure at the time of the Revolution, managed to overcome the brutalization he suffered at the hands of his schoolmaster for his failure to master Latin grammar at age six. "But when I began upon Nepos, Caesar, and Virgil, my repugnance of the classics ceased," Quincy later reminisced; and the beatings were likewise curtailed.[27] There were clear exceptions to the rule of the rod. Ezekiel Cheever (1614–1708) was eulogized by Cotton Mather as the leading schoolmaster of seventeenth-century New England. He not only taught "Latin without tears," he also quite literally wrote the book on the subject. His primer on Latin grammar stayed in print until 1838.[28]

Individual members of the Framing generation often had outstanding classical instruction. The Reverend James Maury taught Thomas Jefferson (who was well-prepared for admission to The College of William and Mary by 1760), and was known to have said that "an Acquaintance with the Languages anciently spoken in Greece and Italy, is necessary, absolutely necessary, for those who wish to make any reputable Figure in Divinity, Medicine or Law."[29] Donald Robertson's boarding school near Dunkirk, Virginia, had as pupils George Rogers Clark, John Tyler (father of the later president), and James Madison. Robertson, somewhat exceptionally for the period, also instructed students in the French language. Nathan Tisdale's boarding school in Lebanon, Connecticut, was among the largest in the colonies and new republic, drawing nearly eighty pupils a year. Samuel Moody's Dummer Academy was also rated as providing a superior education, and he contributed more than a quarter of Harvard's entering class each year. Tisdale and Moody were also known for their aversion to corporal punishment, so the alumni of their schools tended not only to highly regard their classical education but also to genuinely revere their teachers.[30]

Much of the rigor of early American primary education in the classics was attributable to the entrance requirements of the indigenous universities of the period. Of course, a relatively small percentage of grammar school boys went on to college. Even at the time of the Declaration of Independence, only about one American in a thousand had attended college, and in the period from 1745–1763 the total number of graduates produced was little more than three thousand.[31] One of the reasons for these minuscule numbers – aside from the expense of college education and the opportunity costs of foregoing an early apprenticeship into the many trades – was the entry requirements.

All nine colleges in the colonies (as of 1776) – Harvard, William and Mary, Yale, New Jersey (Princeton), Philadelphia (University of Pennsylvania), King's (Columbia), Rhode Island (Brown), Queen's (Rutgers), and Dartmouth – had strikingly similar entry requirements, virtually unchanged since the early 1600s. Harvard's entry rules from 1655 demanded reading proficiency of "ordinary" Latin texts, including Cicero and Virgil, from the leading teaching volumes, and dictated that an applicant "Can readily make and speak or write true Latin prose and has skill in making verse, and is competently grounded in the Greek language, so as to be able to construe and grammatically to resolve ordinary Greek."[32] Yale's regulations from 1745 and Columbia's ordinances from 1755 both required extemporaneous reading ability of selected works from Cicero, Virgil's *Aeneid*, and the Greek Testament, as well as a working knowledge of arithmetic.[33] When Thomas Jefferson was planning the curriculum of the University of Virginia in the 1820s, he "scrupulously insisted . . . that no youth can be admitted . . . unless he can read with facility Virgil, Horace, Xenophon, and Homer: unless he is able to convert a page of English at sight into Latin: unless he can demonstrate any proposition at sight in the first six books of Euclid, and show an acquaintance with cubic and quadratic equations."[34] Those among the Framers that attended college were certainly not exempted from these requirements. When John Adams matriculated at Harvard in the 1750s, John Jay at King's College in 1760, and Alexander Hamilton at King's in 1774, they were closely examined in their Latin and Greek.[35]

Nor is there any real doubt that the leaders of the Framing generation were, to a large degree, college-educated. Of the fifty-six members of the Continental Congress that deliberated the Declaration of Independence, twenty-seven had college backgrounds (including eight with Harvard degrees). At the Constitutional Convention in Philadelphia in 1787, twenty-three of thirty-nine signers had baccalaureates (nine of them from one school, the College of New Jersey (now Princeton)).[36] Other representatives at these political conclaves, without possessing an American college degree, may have had equivalent educational experience overseas or with home schooling or self-study.

It is no surprise, then, that one of the most significant intellectual figures in the early republic was the Rev. John Witherspoon (1723–1794), president of the College of New Jersey from 1768 to 1794. A Scotsman, with a degree from Edinburgh in 1739 (with a heavy emphasis not only on classics but moral philosophy), he was enthusiastically recruited to lead the Presbyterian college by Benjamin Rush. He quickly made America his home and began to exercise extraordinary, if not charismatic, influence. Aside from his own brilliant political career (signer of the Declaration, member of the New Jersey provincial legislature and the Continental Congress), it has been estimated that his graduates included ten cabinet officers, twenty-one senators, thirty-nine congressmen, twelve governors, thirty judges (including three on the U.S. Supreme Court), and fifty members of state legislatures. Even after accounting for substantial duplications in officeholding, this is an astonishing figure, especially considering that it includes the likes of James Madison and Aaron Burr.[37] Witherspoon was praised by even those who had no affiliation with his college. John Adams said that he had "*wutt* [wit] and sense and taste."[38]

And, make no mistake, Witherspoon was adamant that classicism was the core of higher education: "The remains of the ancients are the standard of taste," he noted at his first commencement address. Moreover, "A man is not, even at this time, called or considered a scholar unless he is acquainted in some degree with the ancient languages, particularly the Greek and the Latin," study which is necessary "to fit young men for serving their country in public stations."[39] Witherspoon rigorously prescribed Princeton's curriculum upon his arrival: "First year: Latin, Greek, classical antiquities, and rhetoric; second year: one ancient language, geography, philosophy, mathematics; third year: language, mathematics, natural and moral philosophy; final year: higher classics, mathematics, natural and moral philosophy, history, literary criticism, and French, if desired."[40] And if all of this was not enough to put a classical imprint on his graduates, then there was Witherspoon's senior lectures, in which he managed to combine classical history and moral philosophy and relate it to the burning political issues of the day. He discoursed on the proper modes of oratory. He opined on whether the institutions of Greek city-states had relevance to the government of large provinces, an issue that would later prove crucial in considering the Constitution. He speculated "Some states are formed to subsist by sobriety and parsimony, as the Lacadaemonians [Spartans] ... Public spirit in others, as in Greece, ancient Rome, and Britain."[41] "What [Witherspoon] desired was the *spoudaiotes* (earnestness) of the classical thinkers, studied and then applied to contemporary life."[42]

The curricula at other American colonial colleges adhered largely to classical models.[43] Although King's College made a half-hearted attempt in the 1750s to broaden the course of instruction to include "the Arts of ... surveying and navigation, of Geography and History, of Husbandry, Commerce and Government, and in the knowledge of all Nature ... " it is by no means clear that this represented a trend in American education of the time.[44] It is true that the College of Philadelphia did establish a medical school in the early 1700s (the first in the colonies), and that faculty and students at Yale and Harvard pursued laboratory work in the pure sciences and engineering, but these are undoubtedly the modern liberal exception to the classical rule. Yet relief from the unremitting emphasis on classical reading could be found in the library collections of colonial colleges. Theological works accounted for nearly half of the library holdings (undoubtedly because of the religious affiliations of these institutions and their role in training ministers), with the remainder of subjects sprinkled between history, belle lettres, science, and philosophy.[45] Public booksellers had apparently even less cause to stock classical subjects.[46]

Perhaps even more strikingly, the nature of extracurricular activities at American colleges did more to reinforce the classical education that students were receiving at the feet of their instructors. Regularly scheduled and impromptu debates in Latin were a constant feature of student life.[47] Student literary societies flourished at the colonial colleges. At Yale were established the Linonian Society and the Brothers in Unity. At Princeton, the Cliosophic Society was founded in 1765 (by Aaron Burr), and four years later the American Whig Society was established by James Madison (they exist to this day as the nation's oldest college political, literary and debating society). During the eighteenth century and most of the nineteenth century, they were the major focus of student life at Princeton outside of the classroom, fulfilling the students' social needs as well as providing educational opportunities that were not part of the college curriculum. The societies provided fora for public speaking and creative writing, as well as access to extensive libraries for their members. The rivalry between the societies was very intense, and it was forbidden for members of one society to join the other society or even to enter the other's building. Members of Whig and Clio were given pseudonyms upon initiation, and most selected classical personages as their monikers.[48]

To the extent that the American college experience was an immersion in classicism, few seemed to complain. As Robert Middlekauff explained, "men in colonial New England rarely questioned the value of this curriculum. . . . Whether or not they knew Latin and Greek, most New Englanders respected the intellectual excellence the classics upheld. . . . Even the poorest country parson could testify that a college degree raised a man's status, and all recognized that the path to the professions lay through a liberal education."[49] Classically trained college men received societal approbation as well as access to all the learned professions: medicine, ministry, and law. Dr. Robert Saunders at a commencement address at William and Mary informed students that "you have separated yourselves from the throng who grope in the night of ignorance, scarcely conscious of the possession of intellect," and that as graduates they were "entitled to that homage which the awakened intellect universally commands."[50]

2. Classicism in Legal Education and Law Practice. Before proceeding to consider the leading classical sources for the Framing generation, it is worth noting some aspects of graduate education in the American colonies and new republic, particularly as related to legal education and law practice. Baccalaureate degrees did not end the formal education of a handful of students in America. Those desiring to go on to positions in the ministry (in almost all American denominations) were required to attain a master's degree. After waiting a refectory period of three years, a candidate could present to his college faculty a set of *quaestiones* on an appropriate subject, the precursor of what would today be regarded as the master's thesis. *Quaestiones* were a feature of graduate studies at Oxford University, and the very name implied a species of discourse derived from Roman rhetorical forms of

Cicero and Quintilian.[51] In early colonial times, *quaestio* tended to be tests of technical, logical reasoning, and the topics selected were often aridly religious or philosophical.

As time went on, however, the subjects chosen were overtly political. For example, Samuel Adams's (1722–1803) thesis oration, delivered in Latin in 1743, considered, "Whether it be Lawful to Resist the Supreme Magistrate, if the Commonwealth Cannot be Otherwise Preserved?" It is no surprise that Adams took the affirmative in that address.[52] John Adams's 1758 Harvard thesis addressed whether civil government originates from the consent of the governed.[53] After the Stamp Act Crisis of 1765, many theses attempted to apply the precepts of Aristotle, Cicero, and Polybius to issues of the impending imperial crisis and Revolution. A Brown graduate of 1769 opposed taxation without representation, and another from the same college in 1773 questioned whether "the American colonists have the same rights as inhabitants of Great Britain?"[54] As reflected in graduate education, classicism was often seen as a vehicle for polemicism and robust political debate. Whether it was in spoken oratory, contentious disquisitions, or in formal and stylized *quaestio* or theses, the same styles of argument that would be used by students would later be employed as officials, delegates, or pamphleteers.

Legal education proceeded under slightly different premises, but was no less influenced by classicism. The paradigm of training for the bar in colonial America and the new republic was a college education followed by a few years work in a law office as a clerk under the close tutelage of a practicing attorney.[55] The general rule followed throughout the country was that a man could only be called to the bar after five years of apprenticeship, but that a one or two-year allowance would be made for college graduates.[56] Generally speaking, the majority of attorneys admitted to practice in the early republic had college degrees. For statistics kept in Massachusetts and Maine from 1760 to 1840, 71 percent or 1859 of 2618 trained lawyers had baccalaureate degrees.[57] That meant that the majority of practicing lawyers in America had already confronted and embraced the classical tradition in their formal studies.

During this period, an ideal legal education was regarded as consisting of three parts: practical training, theoretical knowledge, and a general education contributing to accurate reasoning, effective expression, and moral improvement.[58] Practical training was obviously accomplished in the day-to-day drudgery that the master lawyer managed to devise for his clerk. Copying pleadings was a common teaching tool, as was the drawing of standard writs and instruments (including wills and contracts).[59] Theoretical knowledge of the law was often derived by reading reported decisions of courts in England and colonial tribunals. But this case law was often undigested and uncategorized, so additional treatises were consulted, such as Matthew Hale's *History of the Common Law* (first published in 1713), and William Blackstone's extraordinarily influential *Commentaries on the Laws of England* (1765–1769).[60] Prior to Blackstone's appearance, the leading treatise was undoubtedly Edward Coke's *Institutes* glossing Littleton (1628).[61]

But English sources were not exclusively followed in legal education. William Blackstone, for example, called on common lawyers to study the "fountains" of English law, through "the customs of Britons and Germans, as recorded by Caesar and Tacitus."[62] There was also a strong Romanist tradition for civil law studies from Europe, and it was generally regarded as necessary for any working library to have either Justinian's *Corpus Juris* (which included the *Institutes*, as a primer, as well as the *Digest*) in the original Latin, or a reliable English gloss, such as Thomas Wood's *New Institute of the Imperial or Civil Law* (published in 1704). John Adams had both in his law library collection.[63] Other civilian texts, many of which were available only in Latin (or, more infrequently, in French), were Hugo Grotius's classic work, *On the Rights of War and Peace* (De Jure Belli ac Pacis) (first published in 1625, and translated in the edition by Barbeyrac in 1720), Jean Domat's *The Civil Law in Its Natural Order* (folio published in 1777), and Samuel Pufendorf's *Law of Nature and Nations* (first appeared in 1688; Barbeyrac edition of 1702).[64] All of these works heavily relied on classical sources for their exposition of the doctrines of international law, as well as their precepts of natural law.[65] These civilian writers – and the classical authorities they relied upon and expounded – were given great weight, even in the insular, common law tradition of England and the colonies.[66] Reading lists for lawyers-in-training – including one drafted by Thomas Jefferson in 1821 – traditionally included these civil law and classical materials.[67] Some later legal scholars maintained that making references to civilian sources was a means to "maintain the social exclusivity of the legal profession, to cement its cultural and political status, and to give the patina of authority to their legal arguments."[68] The attraction of historically derived natural law may have been an attribute of the familiarity and comfort that colonial and new republic lawyers had with the classical tradition.

The emphasis on scholarly understandings of law as practiced in America also gave rise to the phenomenon of instructors being appointed at colonial colleges to lecture on the subject.[69] George Wythe – Thomas Jefferson's legal mentor and the leading judge of Virginia – received an appointment to the professorship of "law and police" at William and Mary in 1779, where he served until 1800, to be succeeded by Henry St. George Tucker.[70] In August 1790, James Wilson, a Scots emigre educated at St. Andrews University, was appointed as the first professor of law at the University of Philadelphia. Wilson was a signer of the Declaration, as well as attending the Constitutional Convention. He later served as a Justice of the U.S. Supreme Court. In 1793, the trustees of Columbia College appointed James Kent (1763–1847) as its first law professor. In addition to serving as Chancellor in New York, he was the author of the first American law treatise, *Commentaries on American Law*, which while self-consciously modeled on Blackstone's effort was quite innovative in its handling of a number of subjects.[71]

The objective of instructing in legal reasoning and advocacy was also part-and-parcel of training young men for positions of leadership in American society. Legal training was viewed by James Wilson as a way "to furnish a rational and useful entertainment to gentlemen of all professions, and in particular to assist in forming the Legislator, the Merchant, and the Lawyer."[72] An advertisement for law lectures at King's College was aimed at moral and intellectual improvement, to wit: "all virtuous Habits, and all such useful Knowledge as may render [students] creditable to their Families and Friends, Ornaments to their Country, and useful to the Publick Weal in their Generations."[73] And although lectures in moral philosophy were often better attended than those on purely legal topics, the connection between the two realms was clearly understood.[74] Besides, members of the legal profession were often leaders in other fields of intellectual pursuit. As Robert Ferguson noted, lawyers "furnished half the literary critics of the day, controlled literary journals, and supplied most of the membership of *belle lettres* societies."[75] Needless to say, lawyers comprised a majority of the men who signed the Declaration of Independence and the Constitution.[76]

3. Techniques of Classicism by the Framing Generation. Before considering the classical experiences of individual members of the Framing generation, and also reflecting on the values derived from classical reading, it is important to consider the particular methods of classical scholarship employed in colonial America and the early republic. Whereas Gilbert Chinard has famously observed that "most of the men who made a name for themselves during the revolutionary era were no mean classical scholars,"[77] one might legitimately wish to distinguish the exercise of reading and immersion in the classics from active scholarship and the generation of truly new ideas and insights about classical texts and subjects. The truth was that there were major impediments to the development of true classical scholarship in America. These are worth noting now because these limitations later reflected on the lessons drawn by the Framing generation on issues related to the drafting and ratification of the Constitution.

One of these constraints was the nature of classical texts available in late-eighteenth-century America. Latin and Greek texts in their original versions were often corrupted. Errors and omissions often crept into works undetected, and the science of classical philology and the close, technical reading of classical texts were only beginning in Europe at this time. Students engaged in the learning of Latin and Greek were aware of these textual defects, and Princeton trustee Robert Finley writing in 1815 observed that they gleefully and "incessantly harassed [their teachers in order] to have the classical text examined, and the existing errors exposed and corrected. . . . and, besides, the student, always ready to impute difficulty to inaccuracy and to suspend his efforts till doubt is removed, finds his diligence in application and independent exercise of thought much impaired."[78] Additionally, some American versions of classical texts omitted salacious passages, and, in deference to prevailing religious views embraced in some communities, those sections that too vigorously expounded polytheistic ideas were excised.[79] In short, some of the texts over which American students labored for years were hopelessly compromised.

It is no surprise, therefore, that members of the Framing generation so heavily relied upon translations into English of the classics. Despite the protestations of such figures as Thomas Jefferson – who always counseled that classical texts must be read and appreciated in the original[80] – most followed the example of John Adams, who preferred to find quality English versions of classical texts, but also have the original version handy to check disputed or doubtful passages.[81] The truth was, that despite the intensive and rigorous training that many had received as youths in Latin and Greek, most Americans preferred later, as adults, to read the classics in translation.[82] In this respect, they were little different from their English counterparts, or, for that matter, other colonial societies.[83] This phenomenon of reading the classics outside of their original drew a faint sort of praise from Samuel Miller, writing in 1803, calling eighteenth-century America "the Age of Translations," and commenting on their widespread use, "particularly within the last sixty or seventy years."[84] Even so, in published discourse, many Greek and Latin texts were left untranslated, on the assumption that educated readers would either have enough recall of school-taught classics, or could consult a dictionary or an English translation.[85]

The Framing generation also used a variety of secondary sources to inform their knowledge of classical antiquity. Montesquieu's *Esprit des Lois (The Spirit of the Laws)* (1748) is certainly the most-referenced gloss on classical history mentioned by the Framers. James Madison noted in *Federalist* 47 that "[t]he oracle who is always consulted and cited on this subject [ancient modes of government], is the celebrated Montesquieu."[86]   Other secondary works on ancient history used in colonial America and the new republic included the Abbé Millot's *Elements de l'histoire générale, ancienne et moderne* (published between 1772 and 1783), the Abbé de Mably's *Observations sur l'Histoire de la Grèce* (1766), Charles Rollin's 13-volume *Histoire ancienne des Égyptiens, des Carthaginois, des Assyriens, des Babyloniens, des Mèdes, des Perses, des Macédoniens, des Grecs* (published between 1730–38), Montesquieu's *Considerations on the Causes of the Greatness of the Romans and their Decline* (1734), Conyers Middleton's *A Treatise on The Roman Senate* (1747), Edward Wortley Montagu's, *Reflections on the Rise and Fall of the Ancient Republics adapted to the present state of Great Britain* (1759), David Hume's *Essays* (1777), and Adam Ferguson's *History of the Progress and Termination of the Roman Republic* (1783).[87] Additionally, Joseph Addison's play *Cato, A Tragedy* (1713), was a staple of the American colonial stage.

The availability of these secondary works on ancient history should not suggest, however, that classical historiography was very far advanced by the late eighteenth century, for it was not. Archaeology as a tool for understanding the past was virtually unheard of, and until Napoleon's expedition to Egypt in the last days of the century there was no systematic effort made to unearth the historical past and subject it to contemporary investigation. Likewise, few attempts had been endeavored to collect Greek and Latin inscriptions, often notices that were memorialized in stone and exhibited in public spaces that are today a significant source of information for classicists about the dating of ancient events and the proper reading of documents. Most of the scholarship of ancient events was thus dependent on literary sources, the canon of ancient writings that had managed to survive to modern times in a relatively uncorrupted condition. However two important works of ancient political theory – Aristotle's *Constitution of the Athenians* and Cicero's *De Re Publica* – were largely unavailable to the Framing generation, for the simple reason that they had not yet been rediscovered in their complete manuscript forms, and thus had not been widely published.[88] As George A. Kennedy has observed: "By the mid-eighteenth century, the great rush for classical knowledge which marked the Renaissance had worn for itself a well trodden but narrow path. The scientific impulse for historical veracity of the nineteenth century had not yet emerged. The classics were what they were: a common body of material, commonly used, or misused, by educated men for their own purposes."[89]

Now it is important to briefly discuss the leading classical writers that the Framing generation relied on for purposes of their political discussions. The full range of classical writing appreciated in colonial America and the new republic is beyond the discussion here, and has, moreover, been the subject of excellent scholarly commentary.[90] As has already been observed, the Framing generation read Greek plays and Latin poetry,[91] but tended not to derive their social thinking from those sources, preferring to cite historians, moral writers, and political writers of antiquity. The point now is to introduce the classical materials that will figure most prominently in the narratives that will follow in this book about the political philosophy underlying American constitutionalism and the drafting of particular provisions in the Constitution.

Starting first with classical writers in Greek, the Framing generation particularly prized the works of Plato, Aristotle, Thucydides, Polybius, and Plutarch, in that rising order of esteem. One might have expected that revolutionary Americans would have been distrustful of Plato's dialogues, given their profound distrust of democracy and their conservative political bent. Thomas Jefferson deplored "the whimsies, puerilities, and unintelligible jargon"[92] used by Plato. John Adams – never one to mince words – was even more direct, saying that his "disappointment was very great, my astonishment was greater, and my disgust shocking"[93] at Plato's *Republic*. But other revolutionaries, including Jonathan Mayhew (1720–1766),[94] credited Plato with introducing ideas of "civil liberty."[95] By way of contrast, Aristotle's *Politics* was regarded as more utilitarian than Plato's abstract speculations, and was also the subject of at least one authoritative English translation, by William Ellis, published in 1778. Aristotle's tripartite division of constitutional government between monarchical, aristocratic, and democratic forms[96] was obviously influential. Moreover, Americans of the Framing generation would have received Aristotle – although with substantial skepticism, revision, and rethinking – through other great works of Enlightenment thinking, including Machiavelli's *Discourses on Livy* (1531), Hobbe's *Leviathan* (1651), Locke's *Essay on Government* (1690), Montesquieu's *Spirit of the Laws* (1748), and David Hume's *Enquiry Concerning the Principles of Morals* (1777).[97] And although Adams sharply disagreed with Aristotle's conclusions on citizenship and the natural inequality of men, he did endorse his views on the rule of law.[98]

Ancient historians were highly prized by the Framing generation. As Meyer Reinhold has said, the Framers "ransacked" the ancient historical canon but treated these sources "as an historically undifferentiated pool of information [from which] they extracted what they looked upon as timeless verities."[99] Benjamin Franklin wrote in 1749 that "if history be made a constant part of [students'] reading, such as the translations of Greek and Roman historians . . . may not almost all kinds of useful knowledge be that way introduced to advantage.... ”[100] Thomas Jefferson, in his proposed 1779 "Bill for the More General Diffusion of Knowledge," would have legislatively prescribed the study of Greek and Roman histories for the better safeguarding of republican liberties. In these respects, Americans were as infatuated with classical history texts as were their French revolutionary contemporaries.[101]

Among Greek histories, Thucydides was read in the colonies and the early republic period, and although his account of the Peloponnesian War was not so widely regarded as other works, it was considered a standard Greek history (unlike Herodotus and Xenophon who are rarely mentioned in the literature of this period).[102] Thucydides was, however, a special favorite of John Adams who, although he once called him a "nervous historian,"[103] praised him to his son, John Quincy, in these terms: "There is no history . . . better adapted to useful purpose than that of Thucydides. . . . You will find it full of instruction to the orator, the statesman, the general, as well as to the historian and the philosopher."[104]

But among the Greek historians, Polybius was probably the most-referenced in the Framing generation, although more for his political philosophy (which borrowed from Plato and Aristotle, but which was more gracious toward republican ideals) and his accounts of the Roman constitution at the time of Rome's expansion against Carthage and Greece. Polybius' political theory of the "mixed constitution," as mediated through Machiavelli (1469–1527) and Montesquieu (1689–1755), was positively crucial to the Framer's sense of checks and balances or separation of powers,[105] one of the subjects of the next Chapter. Polybius also espoused an alluring theory of the rise and fall of nations, commenting on the strengths and weaknesses of militaristic Sparta, democratic Athens, and republican Rome. His was a history that resonated with the fall of empires and the rise of republics; in short, the political world of the Framing generation.[106] Not only was Polybius cited extensively by John Adams in his *Defence of the Constitutions of Government of the United States of America* (1787),[107] but also by James Monroe on the floor of the Virginia Constitutional Ratifying Convention of 1788.[108]

Unquestionably the most influential Greek work in colonial America and the early republic was Plutarch's *Lives* and *Morals*. It is not only as a recent Plutarch biographer noted that they "are among the most formative books of western civilization,"[109] but also that his gallery of Greek and Roman personages, and his direct moralizing about "the evils of arbitrary government and the glory of opposing tyranny,"[110] would have a special resonance among American revolutionaries.[111] After all, Plutarch himself noted that "I am writing not history but biographies . . . Using history as a mirror, I try somehow to improve my own life by modeling it upon virtues of the men I write about."[112] It is no surprise, therefore, that Plutarch became the standard text in an educational system that self-consciously desired to build character and raise the moral standards of young men. With no understatement or irony, Cotton Mather called him "the incomparable Plutarch."[113] Benjamin Franklin could recall that Plutarch inculcated his first love for general reading.[114] And while John Adams and Thomas Jefferson rarely cited Plutarch in their writings,[115] he was a favorite of other members of the Framing generation, most notably Alexander Hamilton and James Madison and references to Plutarch figure prominently in *The Federalist* and their other polemic writings.[116]

Among the Latin writers, the histories of Livy, Sallust (*Jugurthine War, Conspiracy of Catiline*), and Tacitus (the *Annals* and *Germania*, especially) are most prominently featured. Livy's *History of Rome* (available in a Boston-published version from 1788) was celebrated for its history of the virtuous Roman republic and for its strong moral tone. Appian's *The Civil Wars*, dealing with the last years of the Roman republic, was occasionally consulted. Less widely available, and also less well-regarded for its historical accuracy, was Dionysius of Halicarnassus' *Roman Antiquities*. Even more than Livy, Sallust and Tacitus were seen as "polished and perfect Roman historians," as John Adams noted.[117] "Both were avidly read by early Americans because both treated historical crises as moral issues, provided a quarry of sententious maxims, assailed tyranny, and placed emphasis on moral decay in a sick society, the one [Sallust] at the end of the [Roman] Republic, the other [Tacitus] during the early Empire."[118] Although Sallust had a justified reputation for appealing to the prurient interests of schoolboys, Tacitus was regarded as the deeper political thinker.[119] In 1808, Jefferson would write to his granddaughter, Anne Cary Bankhead, with the sage exhortation "I like very much your choice of books for your winter's reading.... Tacitus I consider the first writer in the world without a single exception. His book is a compound of history and morality of which we have no other example."[120]

That leaves Cicero (also referred to by the Framing generation as Tully) as the leading Latin author used and consulted by the Framing generation. Cicero, along with Seneca's and Lucan's moral writings,[121] was seen as the epitome of oratorical accomplishment, the commitment to liberty against tyranny, and the leading of a moral life. John Adams wrote in 1778 that "As all the ages of the world have not produced a greater statesman and philosopher united than Cicero, his authority should have great weight."[122] James Wilson and Thomas Jefferson were more circumspect in their praise, however. Wilson could only abide Cicero after making "very considerable grains of allowance."[123] Jefferson could not understand Cicero's praise of Plato, although he conceded that Cicero was "able, learned, laborious, practised in the business of the world, and honest. He could not be the dupe of mere style, of which he was himself the first master of the world."[124] Cicero's orations were often held-up as models of courtroom or legislative rhetoric, although Jefferson (somewhat in tension with his later remarks) noted that "I doubt if there is a man in the world who can now read any of his orations through but as a piece of task-work."[125] Likewise, Cicero's epistles were esteemed as a model of letter writing and moral perseverence against tyranny. Cicero's most famous philosophical works for colonial and early republic America were *De Officiis* (*The Offices*), and the *Tusculan Disputations*, both of which were available in highly accurate translations, and were regarded as significant expansions on Aristotle's theories of constitutional government and separation of powers.[126] Indeed, Cicero's political works were among the first to be subject to translations by American scholars, including James Logan (1674–1751), who possessed the largest and finest collection of classical writings in colonial America.[127]

As will be seen in the balance of this book, it is often quite difficult to characterize the Framing generation's use of classical sources in particular contexts. There is no question, for example, that classical citations were used as an affectation, a literary flourish to demonstrate the erudition of the writer or speaker.[128] As Charles Mullett observed in his groundbreaking article, the occasional appearance of "the window-dressing value of classical writers and incidents ... was not to be scorned as merely ornamental."[129] Modern scholars, such as George Kennedy, have sought to categorize the use of the Framers' classicism into a number of broad technical devices. "Specific" influences were often manifested in the members of the Framing generation's use of particular details of ancient history to make a specific point, and will be closely examined in Chapters 3 and 4 of this book. What Kennedy referred to as "general influences" included the making, "often without explicit reference to ancient texts, of ideas, conceptions, of values of the Greeks and Romans, particularly those relating to the nature of man and society,"[130] and these will be considered in the remainder of this chapter and in Chapter 2.

What Kennedy refers to as "formal" classical influences extended to more subtle and structural elements of the Framers' use of ancient history – whether it be in the adoption of classicized pseudonyms, or of ancient epistolary or oratorical devices. The prose style of *The Federalist Papers* (composed of individual letters, written under the name "Publius," by James Madison, Alexander Hamilton, and John Jay) have been likened to Ciceronian models, as interpreted by Augustan-era English pamphleteers, including that of Joseph Addison.[131] As open political letters, many numbers of *The Federalist* share an affinity with Demosthenian speech-making: the rhetorical climax occurs in the middle of the piece, after an exposition of a problem and before a refutation of opposing views.[132] Although Hamilton was known to write more plainly than either Madison or Jay, Madison was regarded as being the more relentlessly logical of the trio: "Occasionally the personality of the individual breaks through the veneer of Publius. Jay is perhaps given more to antithesis than the others; a great deal of the least colorful part of the argumentation is by Hamilton, but he is capable of writing passionately. He uses most of the classical figures, and he is the only one of the writers to follow the classical convention of inserting a speech into the narrative.... Madison seems the most varied of the stylists, and though not an especially passionate man, he appears more given to passionate rhetoric than Hamilton."[133]

As for their use of classical sources, Douglass Adair noted that Hamilton "was not scholarly in his approach to politics; his use of history was that of a propagandist citing examples from the past in order to make the debater's point rather than to establish historical truth. Madison's treatment of Greek confederacies [particularly in *Federalist* numbers 38, 45, and 63] was based on widely gathered material from all the available authorities carefully cross-checked and qualified before being synthesized in a rich and suggestive study. Hamilton's research consisted in superficially extracting bits of Demosthenes and a hasty reading of Plutarch."[134] For these reasons, the direct classical allusions in *The Federalist* are predominantly Greek (by nearly a margin of two-to-one). Although this is somewhat misleading (after all, Polybius and Plutarch wrote in Greek on Roman historical subjects), it does indicate the interest of the Framers in Greek city-states as a model for the American colonies. Nevertheless, Roman examples, especially in the constitution of the Senate and the fashioning of executive power, are prevalent.[135]

Another example of the systematic use of classical references, and illustrative of the integration of classicism in law practice at the time of the Framing generation, is in their proliferation in judicial opinions. To take two sets of materials – George Wythe's decisions as Chancellor of the Virginia High Court of Chancery in the late 1700s and the opinions issued by the United States Supreme Court in its first decade of operation (1790–1800) – is to conclude that classical references were intended to serve important purposes in legal decision making. Although George Wythe (1726–1806) had no college degree, nor any formal education, he had a high degree of fluency in both Latin and Greek, apparently acquired on his mother's knee. As a law professor, Wythe tutored Jefferson, James Monroe (1758–1831), John Marshall (1755–1835), and Henry Clay.[136] Thomas Jefferson later referred to Wythe as "the best Latin and Greek scholar in the State," an honor that Jefferson deserved as much.[137]

Wythe wove classical references into his judicial decisions in a variety of ways and he drew upon an impressively large array of materials.[138] On occasion, the citations were intended to express a sentiment, as in his intonation of *fiat justitia; ruat coelum* ("let justice be done, even if the heavens fall") in a case where Wythe regarded legislative action as unlawful,[139] one of the first cases to consider the concept of judicial review (courts striking down legislative enactments as unconstitutional) in American jurisprudence.[140] The Latin phrase has found itself today employed as a maxim of judicial independence.[141] Perhaps even more strikingly, Wythe employed classical references as a fitting form of literary simile, drawing comparisons between contemporary and ancient events, and also reaching significant legal conclusions based on this form of analogical reasoning.[142] As for the precedential use of classical sources for judicial decisions, Wythe obviously relied upon Roman law materials (including Justinian's *Digest, Code,* and *Institutes*).[143] Indeed, Wythe was a strong advocate for the adoption of a civil-law style code for Virginia's laws, and the systematization of decisional law.[144]

Although it is more difficult to draw conclusions from the decisions of a collegial judicial body, the U.S. Supreme Court in the early republic period also made selective use of classical citations, although not to the extent that Chancellor Wythe did. (Under the Chief Justiceships of John Jay and Oliver Ellsworth, the Justices rendered seriatem decisions, in sharp contrast to the practice of the Marshall Court where there was usually a single opinion.) This was certainly not because of any lack of training, as James Wilson (1742–1798) was a member of the Court and was among the leading legal classicists of his generation.[145] In an extended passage in *Chisholm v. Georgia,* one of the decisive cases of the early republic period, Wilson employed an extended conceit comparing the democratic spirit of the new country and the Greek city-states.[146] In addition to the sentimental and metaphorical uses of classicism, the U.S. Supreme Court deployed ancient history for its precedential value on issues as varied as sovereign immunity and confiscations of enemy property, with sources cited including Cicero, Demosthenes, Homer, Isocrates, and Plutarch.[147]

4. The Classical Exposures of Particular Framers. It was thus apparent that activists, legislators, lawyers, and judges of the Framing generation were entirely comfortable carrying on a discourse using classical imagery and references. Although a number of individual members of this cohort of American leaders have already been mentioned here, it is worth saying a few extra words about some of these. At the same time, one should not lose sight of the fact that classicism permeated many layers of colonial and early republic society, such that certain kinds of allusions (such as the story in Livy of the Roman king, Tarquin, cutting off the tallest poppyheads – his most prominent opponents[148]) were known to all.[149] Many Americans cultivated classical learning, even if they were not school or college educated. The keeping of "commonplace books," a kind of intellectual scrapbook and diary in which extracts or snippets of verse, poetry, quotations, or the like were recorded, sometimes with reflections by the keeper, was exceedingly prevalent. It is no wonder that Thomas Jefferson could humorously note, "American farmers are the only farmers who can read Homer."[150]

Those who actually gathered in Philadelphia in the summer of 1787 for the Constitutional Convention were exceptional for their political acumen and classical learning, even by American elite standards of the day. Jefferson – with perhaps some levity – called them "demigods."[151] Richard Gummere rightly concluded that "most of the Convention delegates were at home in Latin and in some cases Greek."[152] Even among the noncollegians, the delegates assumed a posture of reflective study. Benjamin Franklin (1706– 1790), by far and away the oldest delegate, was self-taught in Latin, and although he famously grumbled throughout the Convention on the overuse and misuse of ancient allusions (more on which presently), he was not above using a classical *bon mot* when the mood struck him.[153] Earlier in his life as a writer, he published a variant of a Socratic dialogue, and when he assumed the editorship of the Philadelphia *Courant* he promised, "Gentle Readers, we design never to let a paper pass without a Latin motto, which carries in it a charm to the Vulgar, and the Learned admire the pleasure of construing."[154]

Alexander Hamilton (1757–1804) had a lean formal education, having been obliged to leave King's College to join the Continental Army in January 1776. He found time in the army, though, to keep a commonplace book in which he inscribed extracts from Demosthenes, Plutarch's *Lives* of Theseus, Romulus, Lycurgus, and Numa Pompilius, all founders of republics.[155] In the tumultuous political in-fighting of the Washington Administrations, Hamilton devised a secret cypher to refer to political friends and enemies – half of the code names were drawn from Plutarch's *Lives*.[156] Charles Pinckney (1757–1824), one of the delegates from South Carolina, shared the distinction with James Wilson of holding a British University degree. He studied at the Westminister School and went on to Oxford.[157]

John Dickinson (1732–1808), serving as a Delaware delegate but better known for his Pennsylvania connections, was one of the most politically experienced – and controversial – figures of his time.[158] Dickinson was the author of *Letters of a Farmer in Pennsylvania* (a series of 12 installments beginning in 1767), a literary *tour de force* that at once criticized British policies in North America even while counseling reconciliation. *Pennsylvania Farmer* and Dickinson's other prerevolutionary writings drew on an incredible array of classical material, some derived from sources that no other member of the Framing generation employed.[159] Dickinson, of course, was the most vociferous opponent of independence at the Continental Congress in 1776 and refused to sign the Declaration. But being a true patriot he enlisted in the Continental Army as a soldier, and went on to serve as President of Pennsylvania after the revolution. Along with Madison, Dickinson was among the most highly respected classicists at the Constitutional Convention. Then, of course, there was the man who presided over the Convention, America's own classical hero, George Washington (1732–1799). Lacking a classical education, he nonetheless prized ancient learning, requiring that his stepson, Jack Custis, be appropriately trained. Although Washington felt that French and mathematics (for surveying) were more useful subjects than Attic Greek, he nevertheless knew the importance of ancient historical sources from that language.[160]

Of the individuals who actually attended the Constitutional Convention, James Madison (1751–1836) was the first among equals insofar as his classical knowledge was concerned. Madison matriculated at Donald Robertson's boarding school in Dunkirk, and then had an additional two years of study with the Rev. Thomas Martin. Madison's primary education was so strong that upon arrival at the College of New Jersey in 1769, he was able to pass exams in Greek, Latin, New Testament, English, and mathematics with barely two weeks of preparation. He was undoubtedly John Witherspoon's finest student at Princeton, and Madison was assuredly influenced by the Scot's lectures on moral philosophy and rhetoric.[161] Madison religiously kept a commonplace book stocked with classical references.[162] Common themes Madison pursued were the defense of liberty against both monarchs and demagogues, and the proper use of Socratic arguments in pursuit of the commonweal.[163]

What was unique about Madison was his pursuit of classical knowledge as an adult for the instrumental purpose of informing his judgment about forms of American government. Just prior to the meetings at Annapolis and Philadelphia, in late 1785 and mid-1786, Madison retired to his home at Montpelier, and, with the help of two trunks of books sent by

Jefferson from Paris, immersed himself in the ancient and modern histories of confederacies.[164] This research, which Madison organized around
a series of notes for each of the leagues or unions he considered and the
vices and virtues of each,[165] provided the raw material for the interventions
that Madison made at Philadelphia, and were reprinted in altered form in
selected numbers of *The Federalist*.

Outside the Convention precincts many members of the Framing generation awaited the results and would be intimately involved in the subsequent
ratification debates. These individuals were no less classically disposed than
those resident at Philadelphia. George Mason (1725–1792), the author of
the influential Virginia Bill of Rights and one of the leading Antifederalists, was an enthusiastic classicist, although his tastes ran to Virgil and Latin
poetry.[166] John Jay (1745–1829), who would later join Madison and Hamilton
as one of the collaborators for *The Federalist*, received his classical training at
King's College in 1760 and was known to enthusiastically resort to classical
references in his legal pleadings.[167]

That leaves, of course, the two giants of the Framing generation – John
Adams (1735–1826) and Thomas Jefferson (1743–1826) – neither of whom
were in attendance at the Constitutional Convention in Philadelphia, because they were serving, respectively, as American ministers to London and
Paris. Along with Madison and Dickinson, they were also leading classical
scholars among the politicians who dominated American life in the early
republic. As already mentioned, John Adams had a strong classical education
as a schoolboy[168] and at Harvard. He later felt that his college masters had
neglected to have him read other masterpieces of Latin literature,[169] so,
in his mid-20s and in the midst of a struggling law practice he imposed
upon himself a new course of classical study. At twenty-nine, he formed
the Sodalitas Club of like-minded readers in Boston.[170] As James Madison
was doing at nearly the same time, Adams turned to ancient history in the
drafting of a significant piece of research on the nature of constitutional
government, his *Defence of the Constitutions of Government of the United
States of America*,[171] published in London (in installments) beginning in
January 1787. Early chapters, on the nature of ancient governments, arrived
in America in March 1787, just prior to the Constitutional Convention.[172]

In his *Defence*, Adams remarked upon his style of scholarship and also
acknowledged his intellectual debts:

> I wish to assemble together the opinions and reasonings of philosophers,
> politicians, and historians, who have taken the most extensive views of
> men and societies, whose characters are deservedly revered, and whose

writings were in the contemplation of those who framed the American constitutions. It will not be contested that all these characters are united in Polybius, who, in a fragment of his sixth book translated by Edward Spelman, at the end of his translation of the *Roman Antiquities of Dionysius Halicarnassenis*, says – "It is customary with those who professedly treat this subject, to establish three sorts of government – kingly government, aristocracy and democracy. . . . " It is manifest that the best form of government is that which is *compounded of all three*. This is founded not only in reason, but in experience.[173]

Later in life, John Adams, in addition to encouraging the classical scholarship of his son, John Quincy Adams (1767–1848),[174] would defend his use of ancient history. In 1803, after his presidency, Adams turned to writing a commentary on the French Revolution, drawing extensively from classical ideas.[175] In writing to his long-time confidente and correspondent, Dr. Benjamin Rush (1746–1813), he said, "I should as soon think of closing all my window shutters, to enable me to see, as of banishing the Classicks, to improve Republican ideas."[176]

Jefferson's early education has been mentioned already, and his engagement with the classics is reflected in the voluminous commonplace books he kept.[177] Even as a young man, Jefferson cultivated a quiet reputation for classical sophistication. James Duane, a member of the First Continental Congress, called Jefferson "the greatest rubber off of dust that he had ever met with."[178] Other colleagues realized that Jefferson "bore [his] learning lightly and made [his] reading implicit in [his] thought rather than an erudite robing of [his] convictions."[179] Jefferson was an almost compulsive book purchaser, and of the thousands of volumes in his collection, which later formed the core of the Library of Congress, most were on classical subjects.[180] Unlike so many of his contemporaries, Jefferson was even more comfortable working in Attic Greek than in Latin.[181] Even Adams was known to complain in their correspondence that Jefferson's gratuitous use of obscure Greek passages (untranslated, of course) made his meaning hard to follow.[182]

As Jefferson would later comment, "For classical learning I have ever been a zealous advocate . . . I have not, however, [been interested in] a hypercritical knowledge of the Latin and Greek languages. I have believed it sufficient to possess a substantial understanding of their authors."[183] Additionally, Jefferson observed that "the utilities we derive from the remains of the Greek and Latin languages are, first, as models of pure taste in writing. To these we are certainly indebted to the rational and chaste style of modern composition. . . . "[184] Jefferson strived for the clarity and concision of written expression that Sallust and Tacitus used in their histories, while adopting

Demosthenian models for his very rare public speeches. (Jefferson, unlike Adams, was a weak public speaker and assiduously avoided such appearances.) He believed that public oratory, especially on weighty matters, should follow the classical virtues of rationality, simplicity, and brevity, which is why he eschewed politicians who, at great length, pursued Ciceronian flights of fancy.[185]

In his *Notes on the State of Virginia* (1787) – the only book that Jefferson actually published – he remarked on the future of classical education: "The learning of Greek and Latin, I am told, is going into disuse in Europe. I know not what their manners and occupations may call for: but it would be very ill-judged in us to follow their example in this instance.... the [classic] books put into the hands of youth for this purpose may be such as will at the same time impress their minds with useful acts and good principles."[186] As already noted, when founding the University of Virginia at Charlottesville, Jefferson demanded that a classical curriculum be maintained and that entrance requirements be upheld. Knowledge of classical languages, he said, were the "foundation preparatory for all the sciences,... the portico of entry to the university."[187]

As Richard Gummere has written, Jefferson and Adams were the supreme products of classical education in colonial America, and the acme of classical sensibilities: "Adams the Stoic and Jefferson the Epicurean."[188] Even after the tumultuous years of political competition when they refused to correspond with each other, as old men they renewed their friendship that lasted to the day they each died on July 4, 1826 (fifty years to the day of the signing of the Declaration). The classics proved to be a common bond in this correspondence of titans, what has been rightfully called "an American masterpiece."[189] As Adams wrote to Jefferson, the classics were "indispensable,"[190] a sentiment shared widely by members of the Framing generation.

B. CLASSICISM'S VALUES

What virtues did classicism impart to members of the Framing generation? What ideas conveyed through ancient history did the Framers incorporate into their republican constitutionalism? What habits did the study of classics cultivate in the minds of those who drafted, considered, and ratified the Constitution? Although the answers to these questions go to the heart of the intellectual history I am essaying in this volume, a tentative answer at this stage is appropriate before launching into the political philosophy of the Framers and considering the specific, structural elements and features of the American Constitution of 1787.

It is worth considering four broad sets of values that classicism and ancient writers bestowed on the Framers. The first is a sense of historical perspective and insight, conveyed by what was perceived as the rationalism of the ancients. Study of the classics was deemed to be the refinement of useful knowledge, and it is important to realize actually what was regarded as propitious in ancient materials. Second, the classics imparted strong social messages and conventions about virtue, fame, and honor. Personal integrity and trust were essential to the relationships of members of the Framing generation and classical sources dictated a public and political ethic that all respected. In addition, ancient history prescribed a political morality that was drawn upon in making certain crucial assumptions and decisions in the drafting of the Constitution.

Third, classical usages and sources in Latin and Greek formed a virtually complete political vocabulary for the Framing generation, allowing members to effectively communicate ideas to their audience. This was not, however, without its detractors, and there was a strong anticlassicist faction among members of the Framing generation, and their complaints (sometimes quite cogent and relevant) offer a significant counterpoint for the classical worldview of new republic America. Fourth, and finally, the classics offered some styles and modes of thinking that were vitally important for the Framers' understanding of such varied bodies of ideas as natural law and Enlightenment political philosophy. Taken together, these bundles of values were a potent means to condition political life in revolutionary America at the time of the adoption of the Constitution. These values, quite literally, made the minds of the Framing generation.

1. Rationality and Useful Knowledge. A common theme running through the writings of the Framing generation on classical sources was their utility. Three broad ideas were encompassed in this single notion. One was the rational reason of classical writers. Another was the pragmatic utilitarianism of ancient knowledge. The third was the sense of historical perspective gained by classical study.

Reason always figured in the Framing generation's appreciation of the classics. As Jonathan Mayhew preached in his sermon on the repeal of the Stamp Act in 1766, "Having been initiated in youth in the doctrines of civil liberty, as they are taught by such men as Plato, Demosthenes, Cicero, and other persons among the ancients; and such as Sidney and Milton, Locke and Hoadley, among the moderns, I liked them; they seemed rational."[191] What classical rationality meant to members of the Framing generation was some form of right reason derived from universal truths. It was by no means seen as a rejection of Christianity – an idea that would have been abhorrent to the likes of Jonathan Mayhew or John Witherspoon, both ministers of the gospel – but, rather, as a necessary and logical accompaniment of humanist ideals within Christian strictures.

When members of the Framing generation referred to "reason" in their political writings, it was often as a counterpoise to passion. And has been observed by Maynard Smith, the concept of reason in such sources as *The Federalist* is more closely rooted to classical sources, such as Aristotle, than it is to Locke, Spinoza, or more contemporary authors.[192] The passages from Aristotle that Madison and Hamilton quoted in *The Federalist* tended to exalt the quiet contemplation of ideas, a calm, cool, and collected mind which can confront any moral or political crisis.[193] The moral message of the most famous numbers of *The Federalist* is precisely this point that any successful political system must harness and cabin passions, and their organizational manifestations in factions. "In that conviction they associated themselves with the great traditions of classical, and pre-Christian thought."[194]

As has already been discussed, the Framing generation's use of the classics was "eminently practical and purposeful,"[195] verging sometimes on the instrumental. In this pragmatism, Americans came honestly. Commanded by the Puritan and Quaker requirement that knowledge have a utilitarian value, the ideals of Renaissance civic humanism, and a growing emphasis on scientific inquiry (expounded by the likes of Bacon, Locke, and the Royal Society in England), colonial Americans could have hardly been expected to see classical learning in any other way.[196] As Meyer Reinhold has famously observed: classical reading "served effectively as an agent of individual and social progress, directed as it was toward the inculcation of virtue and moral duties, the development of taste, and toward social utility, particularly in the political sphere, for the promotion of freedom and the prosperity of the country."[197] Or, as Americans of the time were wont to quote, Horace's maxim: *omne tulit punctum qui miscuit utile dulci* ("He is the most successful who combines the useful with the pleasurable").[198]

A variety of American institutions fully undertook this challenge to cultivate useful knowledge, including classical studies. Not only were colleges a locus of such activity, but the creation of universities became itself a political object of desire. The Constitutions of Pennsylvania and North Carolina, each adopted in 1776, included the identical provision that: "all useful learning shall be duly encouraged and promoted in one or more universities."[199] In addition, learned societies started to proliferate. In 1769, the American Philosophical Society was formed from the union of two predecessor bodies.[200] Similar organizations, including literary clubs and scientific assemblies, were chartered in other cities.

As one might expect, there was a lively debate whether the study of classics could reasonably be regarded as "useful." An early take on this question came in response to Benjamin Franklin's proposal to establish an English School at the Academy at Philadelphia, and have classical languages and literatures serve as the core of the curriculum. Richard Peters (1704–1776), a provincial official, replied that "there is an abundance of useful knowledge that can be acquired in no other language[s]; it is absolutely incumbent on those who study to capacitate themselves for Professions or who aim at a general education and acquaintance with books, to gain a thorough knowledge of Latin and Greek."[201] And, of course, it is no surprise that Thomas Jefferson would have something to say on this subject, defending his decision to maintain Latin and Greek as the crucial part of the curriculum at the University of Virginia: "But to whom are [the classics regarded as] useful? Certainly not to all men. There are conditions of life to which they must forever be estranged.... [But] it may be truly said that the classical languages are a solid basis for most [fields of endeavor], and an ornament to all the sciences."[202]

As will be seen presently in the context of political discourse, there was a strong intellectual backlash against classicism in education. And the proponents of this anticlassical position sensed that the teaching of ancient languages and literatures was vulnerable precisely on this point of useful knowledge, quite apart from the critique of classicism's relevance to the American political tradition. The leading advocate of anticlassicism, at least in cultural circles, was none other than Dr. Benjamin Rush, the physician and signer of the Declaration, and one of the few individuals in America who could count both John Adams and Thomas Jefferson as good friends. The irony of having this arch opponent of classicism in such amiable proximity to its two greatest exponents sometimes created extraordinarily explosive correspondence.[203] Rush would incessantly pester Adams over his views on classicism, sometimes resorting to outright provocations: "Were every Greek and Latin book (the New Testament excepted) consumed in a bonfire, the world would be a wiser and better place for it," he wrote to Adams in 1810.[204] Adams shot back that Rush harbored a "fanaticism against Greek and Latin."[205] After Rush died in 1813, Adams wrote to Jefferson that "[c]lassics, in spite of our friend Rush, I must think indispensable."[206]

Along with the likes of William Livingston, Francis Hopkinson, Noah Webster, and Thomas Paine,[207] Rush publicly sought to eradicate classicism from school and college curricula. In 1788, in contemplating his "Plan for a Federal University," he sought to develop a course of study "to prepare our youth for civil and public life" and to acquire "those branches of knowledge which increase the conveniences of life, lessen human misery, improve our country, promote population, exalt the human understanding, and establish domestic, social and political happiness."[208] Rush regarded the study of Latin and Greek as elitist, and unworthy of republican ideals.[209] Moreover, he suggested, some subjects of classical study were destructive of public morals, undoubtedly a jibe at the pagan religious values and militarism conveyed in some texts. Finally, the lack of attention given to other subjects could prove to have debilitating effects on the successful development of the country. In 1791, Rush would gloat with James Muir, principal of the Alexandria Academy, that only a few of his boys had elected to study Latin, the remainder pursuing more useful studies in math, the sciences, art, and commerce, or, as Muir said, "who prefer the *useful* to the *ornamental*."[210]

Of course, there was an intellectual middle ground to be achieved on the role of classics in the educational system of the new republic. First of all, the monopoly that classical studies enjoyed over elite society – a "stranglehold" Benjamin Rush would undoubtedly have said – had to be broken, if for no other reason than to accommodate more advanced forms of literary achievement and scientific advancement. This was, after all, the same Framing generation that enshrined in their Constitution, among the powers of Congress, to "promote the Progress of Science and useful Arts, by securing for limited Times to Authors and Inventors the exclusive Rights to their respective Writings and Discoveries."[211] So, it was natural that curricular changes were in the offing. By the same token, a complete backlash against classicism could not be seriously contemplated. Even Benjamin Rush advised his son, in 1792, to continue his Latin studies.[212] Moreover, Rush conceded that although ancient orators and poets "are calculated to impart pleasure only . . . [the historians and philosophers] contain much useful knowledge, capable of being applied to many useful purposes in life."[213]

The Framing generation's sense of history supplied the essential utility of classical studies. This was, of course, manifested in the constant historical references made during the Convention at Philadelphia and the subsequent ratification debates, as will be discussed in substantial detail throughout this book. Forrest McDonald has noted that during the first three weeks of the Convention, "delegates buttressed their arguments with historical examples at least twenty-three times, not counting references drawn from British or colonial or recent American history, inclusion of which would treble the total. John Dickinson, Pierce Butler, Benjamin Franklin, George Mason,

James Madison, James Wilson, Alexander Hamilton, and Charles Pinckney delivered, to their colleagues, lectures that sometimes lasted for several hours on the lessons to be drawn from ancient or modern history."[214] Similar examples of the instrumental and argumentative use of ancient history can be found in the tracts and pamphlets of the period.[215]

The Framers also perceived themselves as part of an historical tradition. Obviously, much of this legacy was derived from British political history and institutions. And although the political theory of liberal English politics was an important influence on the Framing generation, actual historic models of English constitutionalism appeared to matter less to those involved in the actual drafting of the Constitution. Despite repeated suggestions to draw on English institutional forms in structuring the Constitution (particularly application of the notions of parliamentary supremacy, and a subordinate executive), these were rejected as being inapposite examples.[216] Instead, ancient history was seen as being more universal in its lessons. As William Smith, provost of the College of Philadelphia, put it in the early 1750s: history is "a lesson of *Ethics* and *Politics* – an useful Rule of Conduct and Manners thro' life. . . . The Youth are thus sent into the World well acquainted with the History of those Nations they are likely to be most concerned with in Life: and also the History of Greece and Rome, which may justly be called the History of Heroism, Virtue and Patriotism. . . . It is History that, by presenting those bright Patterns to the eyes of Youth, awakes Emulation and calls them forth steady Patriots to fill the Offices of State."[217] And as Meyer Reinhold wrote, "The study of ancient history by the Founding Fathers was thus not a mere antiquarian interest."[218] It served the instrumental purposes of useful knowledge by strengthening the legitimacy of the revolution and the new republic "by linking their private and political lives with a cultural ancestry reaching back to antiquity."[219]

2. Virtue, Fame, and Honor. The Framers also knew that not only were "they living history,"[220] they were *making* it. As early as 1777 John Adams wrote to Richard Henry Lee that "You and I . . . have been sent into life at a time when the greatest lawgivers of antiquity would have wished to live. How few of the human race have ever enjoyed an opportunity of making election of government . . . for themselves or their children."[221] At the Constitutional Convention, Madison remarked that "it was more than probable [that the delegates] were now digesting a plan which in its operations would decide forever the fate of Republican Government."[222] Hamilton concurred, saying that "if we do not give [the republican] form due stability and wisdom, it would be disgraced and lost among ourselves, disgraced and lost to mankind for ever."[223]

In short, the Framers were acutely self-conscious that they were establishing a new political order, and they drew on classical allusions of such previous foundings. George Wythe commented in one of his decisions as Chancellor of the Virginia High Court of Chancery that "National identity is a mystical union of members of successive generations,"[224] and to illustrate his point drew attention to the founding of the Roman republic and the continuity in identity between the citizens who expelled the last Latin king, Tarquin, in 509 BCE and those who defeated the Greek mercenary-King Perseus in Asia Minor in 168 BCE.[225] It was notorious to the Framing generation that, in the words of Tacitus' opening lines in the *Annals*, that Rome was once ruled by kings.[226] And although "the annalists' picture of the founding of the republic is more satisfying as a philosophical object-lesson or a piece of tragic drama than as history,"[227] it was precisely the account in Tacitus, Polybius, and Livy that informed the American sense of that other founding. Although modern historiography has suggested that the Roman republic emerged gradually through a series of modest institutional and legal reforms,[228] the Framing generation would have believed that it came as a result of violent revolution against the tyranny of the last king, Tarquinius Superbus about 500 BCE. After the Roman nobility and people repulsed an Etruscan attempt to reinstitute the monarchy,[229] the republic was on firmer foundations. Indeed, the leading figure of this postrevolutionary period of the Roman republic was the aristocrat Publius Valerius ("Poplicola"), a law-giver as successful as Solon or Lycurgus, immortalized in Plutarch's *Lives*, and the pseudonym selected by Hamilton, Madison, and Jay for their *Federalist Papers*.[230]

It is no surprise that this ancient historical narrative – no matter how flawed as a matter of modern historical sensibilities – would have resonated in American revolutionary society. The Roman republic was virtuous; the later Roman Empire was decadent, aggressive, and evil. Classical history also provided the raw material for this metaphor of abusive empire. Cicero, Tacitus, and Sallust – each writing at the end of the Roman republic and the beginning of the Principate under Augustus and his successors – expressly appealed to their readers as a lament for older virtues and patriotism. The imagery invoked from the writers tended to be of agrarian simplicity. Combined with the writings of the "country party" in England, the target of derision was a new commercial elite, including banks, mercantile firms, stock markets, and the governmental trade apparatus.[231] The planters of Virginia and the Carolinas could certainly agree with their Northern brethren of the 1760s and 1770s that they were all being squeezed by the avarice of London merchants and politicians.

The trope of choice in countering the overweening power of the British Empire was to establish an alternate model of America as, to use Samuel Adams's expression, a "Christian Sparta."[232] Plutarch's *Lycurgus* gave life to an image of Sparta, or Lacadaemon, that was "admired for her stability, maintenance of freedom as a commonwealth for about five hundred years, emphasis on civic virtue, simplicity of life, agricultural base, checks and balances in a mixed constitution, her citizen militia, inner harmony, equilibrium between the extremes of absolute monarchy and extreme democracy, and the dedication of her magistrates and citizens to the republic."[233] Of course, conveniently forgotten in this historic fable is Sparta's militarism and aggression, and the brutality shown towards the slaves (helots) and subjected peoples they conquered, although Alexander Hamilton acknowledged in *Federalist* 6 that "Sparta was little better than a well-regulated camp."[234] In this story of the founding, Americans could take pride in their roughhewn manners, their simple faith, their lack of corruption and financial avarice, and their deep love of freedom. John Dickinson could call the Spartans "as brave and free a people as ever existed," appropriately enough in his *Letters from a Farmer in Pennsylvania*.[235] If ancient Greek mythos did not satisfy, there was always Tacitean imagery, in which Americans were the Teutons heroically resisting Roman imperial assimilation.[236]

The founding imagery of the Constitution was significant in another respect. Those who supported the ratification of the Constitution urged that that would be the only true foundation of the nation. As John Jay observed in *Federalist* 2, at the time of the Declaration, "America was already one connected country . . . one united people, a people descended from the same ancestors, speaking the same language, professing the same religion, attached to the same principles of government, [and] very similar in their manners and customs."[237] Aside from the selective memory of this origination myth (no mention of African slaves or religious dissidents, after all), there was also the small matter of what was not accomplished at the creation: the making of a political state. The timing for true statehood, Jay noted, was not "auspicious" in 1776 and this omission was later "found to be greatly deficient and inadequate."[238] The founding of ancient confederate republics were all, according to Madison, fatally flawed because no stable balance could be struck between the constituencies of the leagues, and each devolved into "anarchy among its members" or "tyranny in the head."[239] Hamilton urged his readers in *Federalist* 15 to mark a departure from these failed experiments and "at last break the fatal charm which has seduced us from paths of felicity and prosperity."[240]

The supporters of the Constitution had to labor under one significant constraint: the proceedings at the Philadelphia Convention were by no means transparent. Antifederalists attacked that "dark conclave," but Publius in *The Federalist* could turn this, to some degree, to advantage. The founding of the American republic was a collegial enterprise, cloaked not with secrecy but with corporate anonymity and rectitude. This was not like the constitution making of ancient days, what with Minos, Theseus, Draco, Solon, Lycurgus, Romulus, and Numa (all featured in Plutarch's *Lives*), handing down the supreme law as they saw fit.[241] The Constitutional Convention was thus a significant "exception" to the "dark and degraded pictures" of other foundings in history.[242] The Framers were above faction, and as Martin Diamond has written, "*The Federalist* contemplates a kind of philosopher-founder the posthumous duration of his rule depends upon 'that veneration which times bestowes upon everything'."[243] Quite clearly, divine providence was at work here, something that Publius – somewhat immodestly given Madison's and Hamilton's role at Philadelphia – is not afraid to invoke: "It is impossible for the man of pious reflection not to perceive in [the work of the Convention], a finger of that Almighty hand which has so frequently and signally extended to our relief in the critical stages of the revolution."[244]

James Madison, of all the Framers, was perhaps most conscious of the foibles of foundings. It was he, after all, who observed in July 1819 that "the infant periods of most nations are buried in silence, or veiled in fable, and perhaps the world may have lost but little which it need regret."[245] A handful of delegates at Philadelphia kept notes of the proceedings, but it was Madison's record that appears to be the most complete, accurate, and faithful. One wonders how he was able to keep such notes even as he was so actively intervening with speeches and statements in the proceedings. In any event, the delegates all agreed to keep their notes and records from the Federal Convention of 1787 for the rest of their respective lifetimes.[246] In this resolve, history and fate would be kind, for in 1836, when he died, Madison was the last living member of the conclave. It is thus his gloss on the Convention, his spin on the proceedings, that have been most influential, and although he certainly did not set out to earn the honor, it is no surprise that he is still called the "Father of the Constitution."[247]

Madison would have likely agreed with Harry Payne's observation that "[a]s a culture hero, the legislator provided the Enlightenment's answer to the Christian saint or the Renaissance prince. Half-mythical, half-historical, the figure of the legislator who shapes and unifies his society dominates the political and historical writings of the philosophers."[248] Indeed, Madison's colleagues and contemporaries positively enthused with praise for ancient law-givers. Noah Webster, writing as a "Citizen of America" in October 1787, declaimed that "Legislators have ever been deemed the greatest benefactors of mankind – respected when living, and often deified after death. Hence the fame of Fohi and Confucius – of Moses, Solon and Lycurgus – of Romulus and Numa. . . . "[249] It was Madison, however, in *Federalist* 38, who offered the most extended consideration of ancient parables of founding, an extract that is worth reprinting at length:

> It is not a little remarkable that in every case reported by ancient history, in which government has been established with deliberation and consent, the task of framing it has not been committed to an assembly of men, but has been performed by some individual citizen of preeminent wisdom and approved integrity. . . .
>
> What degree of agency these reputed lawgivers might have in their respective establishments, or how far they might be clothed with the legitimate authority of the people, cannot in every instance be ascertained. In some, however, the proceeding was strictly regular. Draco appears to have been entrusted by the people of Athens with indefinite powers to reform its government and laws. And Solon, according to Plutarch, was in a manner compelled, by the universal suffrage of his fellow-citizens, to take upon him the sole and absolute power of new-modeling the constitution. The proceedings under Lycurgus were less regular; but as far as the advocates for a regular reform could prevail, they all turned their eyes towards the single efforts of that celebrated patriot and sage, instead of seeking to bring about a revolution by the intervention of a deliberative body of citizens.
>
> Whence could it have proceeded, that a people, jealous as the Greeks were of their liberty, should so far abandon the rules of caution as to place their destiny in the hands of a single citizen? Whence could it have proceeded, that the Athenians, a people who would not suffer an army to be commanded by fewer than ten generals, and who required no other proof of danger to their liberties than the illustrious merit of a fellow-citizen, should consider one illustrious citizen as a more eligible depositary of the fortunes of themselves and their posterity, than a select body of citizens, from whose common deliberations more wisdom, as well as more safety, might have been expected? These questions cannot be fully answered, without supposing that the fears of discord and disunion among a number of counsellors exceeded the apprehension of treachery or incapacity in a single individual. . . . If these lessons teach us, on one hand, to admire the

improvement made by America on the ancient mode of preparing and establishing regular plans of government, they serve not less, on the other, to admonish us of the hazards and difficulties incident to such experiments, and of the great imprudence of unnecessarily multiplying them.[250]

Madison's vision was thus of a founding based on "the intervention of a deliberative body of citizens."[251]

Essential to the Framers' historic sense of their participation in the founding of a new nation was the ideal of honor that went with that. As Gordon Wood has noted, "Probably nothing separates the traditional world of the Founding Fathers from today more than its concern with Honor. Honor was the value genteel society placed on a gentleman and the value a gentleman placed on himself. . . . Honor subsumed self-esteem, pride and dignity, and was akin to glory and fame."[252] Closely connected with the conservation of honor is the accumulation of fame. Douglass Adair has hypothesized that a key motivation for members of the Framing generation was "the lust for the psychic reward of fame, honor [and] glory," with fame being "the action or behavior of a 'great man,' who stands out, who towers above his fellows in some spectacular way. . . . to be widely spoken of by a man's contemporaries and also to act in such a way that posterity remembers his name and his actions."[253] This was quite similar to the ancient Greek mentalité of striving to compete and triumph over one's peers, the phenomenon of *agōnes*.

Indeed, many of the Framers said as much, and quite publicly. Gouverneur Morris at the Constitutional Convention declared that "love of fame is the great spring to noble and illustrious actions."[254] Mild-mannered James Wilson, not one usually given either to rhetorical excess or the search for fame, wrote that "the love of honest and well earned fame is deeply rooted in honest and susceptible minds."[255] The seeking of fame could elicit strong emotions and passions, usually envy and distrust, and the Framers were well aware of these. Alexander Hamilton – who was most often accused of the sin of pride – could, with equal accuracy, write in *The Federalist* that "love of fame is the ruling passion of the noblest minds, which would prompt a man to plan and undertake extensive arduous enterprises for the public benefit,"[256] and, yet, "a man of irregular ambition" could become a tyrant.[257] John Adams was particularly distrustful of fame as the pride of ambition: "the desire of the esteem of others is as real a want of nature as hunger" and "it is a principal end of government to regulate this passion, which in its turn becomes a principal means of government."[258] For the Framing generation, the harnessing of personal ambition became every bit as important as the control of collective factions.[259]

Ancient history and philosophy positively reverberated with examples of leaders who sought – and disavowed – fame.[260] Plutarch's *Lives* were replete with the biographies of founders of republics, who thus acquired great fame and respect.[261] Aristotle declared that "Honor and dishonor are the matters with which the high-minded man is especially concerned."[262] Greek and Latin had many terms to describe this Aristotelian notion: *megalopsychia*, *magnanimitas*, and *magnitudo animi*. In contrast, Cicero reflected that "[i]t is disturbing that it tends to be men of genius and brilliance who are consumed by the desire for endless magistracies and military commands, and by the lust for power and glory."[263] Julius Caesar was held up as being the chief exponent of a man of fame, but, of course, his ambition toppled the institutions of the Roman republic, and the mere mention of his name in the discourse of the Framing generation had problematic consequences. When, over dinner one night in 1791, Hamilton declared to Jefferson that "the greatest man who ever lived was Julius Caesar," Jefferson later reminisced to his friend, Benjamin Rush, that he believed that Hamilton was then plotting a coup, even as he was serving as Secretary of the Treasury under President Washington.[264] Somewhat ironically, just a few months later, Rush received a letter from Adams indicating that he felt Jefferson had succumbed to the temptations of fame.[265]

There were other classical examples of virtue that the Framing generation could draw upon in weighing the pros and cons of ambition. The leading moral example was set by the tale of Cincinnatus, as told in Livy.[266] In the fifth century BCE, Rome was still a small trading village, and its citizens were largely agrarian. Rome was often raided by neighboring city-states or foreign tribes. In 458 BCE, a Roman army was lured into the hills by the Samnians and was trapped. In an act of desperation, the Senate appointed Cincinnatus, a retired general and farmer, as dictator and asked him to save the imperiled legion. He answered his people's call, rescued the expedition, and then, instead of using his virtually total power for personal aggrandizement, promptly resigned his office and returned to his farm. The tale of Cincinnatus assuredly resonated in revolutionary America, and its living embodiment was none other than George Washington.[267] His correspondence, especially while he served as president from 1789 to 1797, was littered with references to Cincinnatus and the ideal of the citizen-soldier-farmer.[268] Although both King George III and Thomas Jefferson had earlier predicted Washington could serve as president-for-life,[269] many were pleasantly surprised when he did not seek a third term, establishing a precedent that was observed by all his successors (save for Franklin D. Roosevelt), and was then enshrined in the Constitution itself.[270] Additionally, the Order of the Cincinnatus – created as a group of former revolutionary war officers – gave additional application to the classical morality tale.

It was thus a common theme of political discourse to derive maxims of virtue from the classics. The Framing generations' penchant for classical pseudonyms has already been noted. Dr. Joseph Warren was reported to have donned a toga before delivering a speech against the British at the Old South Church in Boston in 1775. The subject of his declamation was imperial excess and he denounced the same aspects of antirepublican vices that Cicero itemized for his contemporaries: luxury (*luxuria*) and corruption (*corruptio*). Warren also lauded public virtue (*virtus*).[271] Public virtue and republican ideals were consistently elaborated through classical metaphors and references.[272] As was later observed in *New England Quarterly Magazine*, "The best ages of Rome afford the purest models of virtue that are anywhere to be met with. Mankind are too apt to lose sight of all that is heroic, magnanimous and public spirited.... Left to ourselves, we are apt to sink into effeminacy and apathy."[273]

Especially revealing were the compliments that were bestowed through the use of classical simile.[274] George Mason said of Patrick Henry (1736–1799) that "had he lived about the time of the first Punic War, when the Roman people had arrived at their meridian glory, and their virtue not tarnished, Mr. Henry's talents must have put him at the head of that glorious commonwealth."[275] John Adams likewise called Patrick Henry the "Demosthenes of the American Revolution," and bestowed the sobriquet of "Cicero of America" onto Richard Henry Lee.[276] Benjamin Franklin was compared with Prometheus (the Greek god that brought fire to man), Socrates, Solon, and Cato.[277]

Of course, both the best and worst forms of rhetorical excess were reserved for paeans to George Washington. Parson Weems in his hagiography of Washington managed to cram no less than twelve classical allusions into two sentences: "Washington was as pious as Numa, just as Aristides, temperate as Epictetus, and patriotic as Regulus. In giving public trusts, impartial as Severus; in victory, modest as Scipio – prudent as Fabius, rapid as Marcellus, undaunted as Hannibal, as Cincinnatus disinterested, to liberty firm as Cato, and respectful of the laws as Socrates."[278] The more dignified and genuine funeral eulogies of Washington, made during the period of national mourning from December 1799 to February 1800, likewise praised his virtues in classical terms, almost always drawing from Plutarch's best exemplars of character. Fisher Ames, the great orator and member of Congress, summed it up best when he proclaimed: "Some future Plutarch will search for a parallel to his character. Epaminondas is perhaps the highest name of all antiquity. Our Washington resembled him in the purity and ardor of his patriotism; and like him, he first exalted the glory of his country." But, Ames hastened to add, "there it is to be hoped the parallel ends; for Thebes fell with Epaminondas."[279]

Perhaps, then, more than fame and fortune and honor, the classics taught the Framing generation a unique form and mixture of public and private virtue. The emphasis of education in using the classics to inculcate virtue has already been mentioned here, although one further example might suffice. One of the most popular metaphors on virtue in revolutionary America was the Choice of Hercules. Recounted as part of Xenophon's *Memorabilia*, his intellectual biography of Socrates, the allegory is of the young hero Hercules' decision in choosing between two routes: one of ease and pleasure into the swamp of dissipation, the other, a difficult road leading to the summit of achievement.[280] As Meyer Reinhold has observed it was among the "favorite myth[s of the Founders] because it encapsulated, through the choice faced by the young Hercules between virtue and pleasure, the central theme of American philosophy and education."[281] John Adams could write in 1759, and then repeat again in his published volume, *Defence of the Constitutions*, that "The Choice of Hercules came into my mind, and left an impression which I hope will never be effaced nor long unheeded."[282] It is thus no surprise that visual imagery of the Choice of Hercules was selected by student groups, including the American Whig Society at Princeton, as an expression of their desire for virtue.[283] This theme was even seriously considered for the Great Seal of the United States in 1776.[284]

At no time was the sense of a need for public virtue in America greater than at the drafting and consideration of the Constitution. *New-Jersey Magazine* declaimed in 1787 that "Now it is virtue alone, that qualifies a man for the discharge of ... important offices. ... It is virtue, that gives him a true taste of glory, that inspires him with zeal for his country, and with proper motives to serve it to the utmost of his power. ... The end of all study, therefore, is to make men virtuous."[285] At Virginia's Ratifying Convention, James Madison noted that "[n]o theoretical checks, no form of government can render us secure. To suppose that any form of government will secure liberty or happiness without any virtue in a people, is a chimerical idea."[286] George Washington confirmed this assumption in his *Farewell Address*: "It is substantially true that virtue or morality is a necessary spring of popular government."[287] Clinton Rossiter could thus rightly conclude that "Few people in history have been more given to public moralizing, to proclaiming a catalogue of virtues and exhorting one another to exhibit them, than the American colonists. ... It seems safe to say that no people in history were more dedicated to the notion that free government rests upon public and private morality."[288] What is significant, though, is the extent that virtue was understood by the Framing generation to be consistent with classical models.

3. Polemicism and Anticlassicism. So far, I have portrayed classicism as an unalloyed good in the political discourse of the Framing generation. It would be a mistake, however, to see it strictly in those terms, and, before turning to the contributions of ancient thought to the Framers' constitutional philosophy, it is worth mentioning the abuses of classicism and the strong anticlassical opposition that was apparent among revolutionary politicians.

These countervailing forces were especially apparent in the polemical literature of the period. It is difficult to appreciate – even in this age of robust political writing – that colonial and new republic America was positively ablaze with published sermons, pamphlets, newspapers, broadsides, letters, and other kinds of ephemeral literature that sought to influence the councils of official bodies, to form public opinion, or to attack political or personal enemies.[289] During the revolutionary period, polemical attacks were particularly directed toward loyalist or Tory factions, and often escalated from rhetorical excess into social ostracization, economic and financial boycott, political violence, and (ultimately) exile or murder. Although classical metaphors were never used in America to the same degree as by French revolutionaries to justify the actual liquidation of opposing factions during the Terror,[290] they were still apparent. Even in the calmer days of the Articles of Confederation and the consideration of the Constitution, Federalist and Antifederalist hostilities sometimes degenerated into games of classical namecalling, what with one side declaring the other to be disloyal (in the guise of Brutus), or power-hungry (in the way of Caesar). All of this would be prelude, of course, for the most politically virulent and dangerous time in the young republic's life, the second Washington and first Adams Administrations in which Federalist and Democratic-Republican factions openly split into well-organized and hostile political parties.[291]

Classical allusions could thus become a blunt instrument used to hit adversaries over their collective heads. They also provided a much-needed political template to guide contemporary decision making. The classical yardstick of personal virtue was certainly one of these, but also were certain political truths. Alexander Hamilton could write in *Federalist* 70 that "[e]very man the least conversant in Roman history knows how often that republic was obliged to take refuge in the absolute power of a single man, under the formidable title of dictator, as well against the intrigues of ambitious individuals who aspired to the tyranny – as against the invasions of external enemies who menaced the conquest and destruction of Rome."[292] Hamilton's point was not merely to make the argument for a strong executive branch of the government (more on which in Chapter 3), but also to make a statement about the nature of leadership. The casual way that Hamilton assumes knowledge of ancient history – indeed suggesting that one who is not so "conversant" need hardly have any role in the deliberations – is indicative of the leading place of classicism in conditioning the political debate. Indeed, as Linda Kerber has articulated, the classics "could be used to provide a political vocabulary, a series of heroic examples for patriotic imitation, a sense of proportion."[293]

Some American leaders did, however, rebel against this classical political grammar. The educational views of such as Benjamin Rush and Noah Webster have already been mentioned, and the dismay of some of those in the colonial American intelligentsia about the stranglehold that the classics exerted over young people's studies had some effect. Even at the time of the Revolution, concerns were being raised about the constant use of classical allusions in political discourse. The fiery Thomas Paine, never one to follow the crowd in his rhetorical style or choice of subjects, expressed his scepticism in *The American Crisis* in 1778: "I cannot help being sometimes surprised at the complimentary references which I have seen and heard made to ancient histories and transactions. The wisdom, civil governments, and sense of honor of the states of Greece and Rome, are frequently held up as objects of excellence and imitation. Mankind has lived to very little purpose, if, at this period of the world, they must go back two or three thousand years for lessons and examples."[294] Later, Paine would write about the ambiguous precedential nature of ancient history: "How strangely is antiquity treated! To answer some purposes, it is spoken of as the times of darkness and ignorance, and to answer others, it is put for the light of the world."[295] Other writers would recoil at the ferocity, and lack of humanity, reflected in ancient discussions of political life.[296]

A surprising number of individuals involved either as delegates at the Constitutional Convention at Philadelphia or the subsequent state ratifying conventions expressed substantial doubts about the propriety or relevance of recourse to ancient historical analogies in framing the debate about American constitutionalism. In Philadelphia, Charles Pinckney of South Carolina, despite his prodigious use of classical references, was careful to point out that: "The people of this Country are not only very different from the inhabitants of any State we are acquainted with in the modern world, but I assert that their political situation is distinct from either the people of Greece and Rome or any state we are acquainted with among the Antients. Can the orders introduced by the institution of Solon, can they be found in the United States? Can the military habits and manners of Sparta be resembled to our habits and manners? Are the institutions of Patrician and Plebian known among us? ... Can we copy from Greece and Rome? Can this apply to the yeomanry of America? ... Our situation is unexampled...."[297]

At a crucial moment at Philadelphia in 1787, one of the Convention's most distinguished members decided to make a stand against the use of classical references. On the afternoon of June 28, after a particularly lengthy and tedious lecture by James Madison on ancient confederations and leagues and the structure of the national assembly,[298] Benjamin Franklin had had enough. His proposals for a highly centralized government and unicameral legislature were being eroded daily with constant classical references to the advisability of mixed government and separation of powers. Franklin rose and made this appeal:

> The small progress we have made after 4 or five weeks close attendance and continual reasonings with each other – our different sentiments on almost every question, several of the last producing as many noes as ays, is methinks a melancholy proof of the imperfection of Human Understanding. We indeed seem to feel our own want of political wisdom, since we have been running in search of it. We have gone back to ancient history for models of Government, and examined the different forms of those Republics which have been formed with the seeds of their own dissolution now no longer exist. And we have viewed the Modern States all round Europe, but find none of their Constitutions suitable to our circumstances.[299]

So, old Franklin made a sly proposal. The Convention should institute a daily prayer in order to "humbly appl[y] to the Father of lights to illuminate our understanding," and Franklin fervently beseeched his colleagues to restrain their use of historical examples. Much to the old sage's regret, only three or four of the delegates were willing to give their assent to his motion, and the next day the Convention renewed its deliberations, the infatuation of the members with ancient history undiminished.

At the state ratifying conventions, perhaps the most vigorous anticlassicist sally was made by the Massachusetts delegate, Benjamin Randall, who said: "The quoting of ancient history was no more to the purpose than to tell how our forefathers dig clams at Plymouth...."[300] Henry Abbott at the North Carolina convention half-mockingly suggested that "Some are desirous to know and by whom they are to swear, since no religious tests are required, by Jupiter, Juno, Minerva, Prosperina, or Pluto?"[301] Randall's provocation resulted in a renewed lecture on ancient history by James Bowdoin; Abbot's sarcasm was met with (we may assume, stunned) silence. The simple statement by Mr. Bass, a member of the North Carolina convention, that even though he had "never went to school, and had been born blind," he nonetheless came with "the possession of common sense and reason,"[302] was not calculated to sway the opinions of his colleagues.[303]

Other state conventioneers were more selective in their rejection of ancient precedents. Rufus King at the Massachusetts convention noted that "Much has been said on the instruction to be derived from history on this point [the length of electoral terms]. . . . he presumed to doubt whether this was the case." Likewise, Mr. Upham "expressed the absurdity of conclusions and hypotheses, drawn from ancient governments, which bore no relation to the confederacy proposed; for those governments had no idea of representations as we have."[304] Other delegates could well-appreciate the relevance of ancient history, but were quick to dismiss the aptness of a classical analogy in certain circumstances. James Monroe at the Virginia convention noted "Ancient and modern leagues have been mentioned, to make impressions. Will they admit of any analogy with our situation?"[305] James Wilson at the Pennsylvania convention observed not only that aspects of ancient constitutions may have no suitability for American circumstances, but he also made a significant point about the current state of classical historiography: "But the facts recorded concerning their constitutions [of such institutions as the Achaean league, Lycian confederacy, and Amphictyonic council] are so few and general, and their histories so unmarked and defective, that no satisfactory information can be collected from them concerning many particular circumstances, from an accurate discernment and comparison of which, alone, legitimate and practical inferences can be made from one constitution to another."[306]

In the vigorous public debates that were occurring at the time of the ratification conventions, some writers denounced the use of classicism. In describing John Adams, Silas Deane (1737–1789) complained that "this man, who may have read much, appears to have retained nothing, except law knowledge and the fierce and haughty manners of the Lacedaemonians and first Romans. These he has adopted as a perfect model to form a modern republic by."[307] James Sullivan, writing as Cassius in *Massachusetts Gazette*, ridiculed what he called the aristocratic faction, saying "Some of them pretend to be mighty politicians, – they display a vast knowledge of ancient times – and by their harangues about the conduct of Greece, Rome and Athens, show their acquaintance with the pages of antiquity."[308] William Vans Murray published in 1787 an essay sharply critical of the idealization of antiquity, and argued that references to ancient history for the making of modern republics was only a "fancied analogy," a "phantasm of scientifical superstition."[309]

Those of a proclassical bent expressed some qualms, on occasion. James Wilson returned to his earlier concerns, raised at the Philadelphia convention: "I know that much and pleasing ingenuity has been exerted, in modern times, in drawing entertaining parallels between some of the ancient constitutions and some of the mixed governments that have since existed in Europe. But I suspect that on strict examination, the instances of resemblance will be found to be few and weak . . . and not to be drawn immediately from the ancient constitutions themselves, as they were intended and understood by those who framed them."[310] Alexander Hamilton wrote, around the same time, that "It is as ridiculous to seek models in the simple ages of Greece and Rome, as it would be to go in quest of them among the Hottentots and the Laplanders. . . . Neither the manners nor the genius of Rome are suited to the republic or age we live in. All her maxims and habits were military, her government was constituted for war."[311]

Even Publius writing in *The Federalist* had, on occasion, to rein-in their collective infatuations with ancient history. In *Federalist* 9, Hamilton noted that

> The science of politics . . . like most other sciences, has received great improvement. The efficacy of various principles [of government] is now well understood, which were either not known at all, or imperfectly known to the ancients. The regular distribution of power into distinct departments – the introduction of legislative ballances and checks – the institution of courts composed of judges, holding their offices during good behaviour – the representation of the people in the legislature by deputies of their own election – these are wholly new discoveries, or have made their principal progress towards perfection in modern times. They are means, and powerful means, by which the excellencies of republican government may be retained and its imperfections lessened or avoided.[312]

Madison, in *Federalist* 63, when he wrote on the important subject of the need for a Senate in the new Constitution, and then recited the examples of such aristocratic and elite institutions in antiquity, was quick to make this caveat:

> These examples, though as unfit for the imitation as they are repugnant to the genius of America, are, not withstanding, when compared with the fugitive and turbulent existence of other ancient republics, very instructive proofs of the necessity of some institution that will blend stability

with liberty. I am not unaware of the circumstances which distinguish the American from other popular governments, as well ancient as modern; and which render extreme circumspection necessary, in reasoning from one case to the other. But after allowing due weight to this consideration it may still be maintained that there are many points of similitude which render these examples not unworthy of our attention.[313]

It is important to understand the contours of this anticlassical backlash at the time of the Constitution's consideration. The first point that needs to be made clear is that those who eschewed the use of ancient history as a guide and model in the framing of the American Constitution were in a very distinct minority. As Carl Richard has observed, "The most remarkable aspect of the debates surrounding the drafting of the U.S. Constitution was not the Federalists' narrow victory over the Antifederalists, but the classicists' rout of the anticlassicists. The classical tidal wave carried all before it."[314] For sure, there were sensible limits to the use of classical examples and analogies, and these were best understood by those who knew ancient history best. Hamilton, Madison, Wilson, Pinckney, and Dickinson understood well that it was folly to rely on ancient sources on questions outside the contemplation of classical writers or experience, or to press an historical analogy past its breaking point.

Another significant aspect is that there was no correlation between those who opposed the Constitution as drafted, and those who disliked the use of ancient history in political councils. The Antifederalists were as enthusiastic in their use of the classics as were the partisan supporters of the Constitution. Indeed, as some have observed, this may have been part of their undoing:

> The Antifederalists put themselves at a disadvantage by playing the classical game. They might have noted that all the classical historians and their modern disciples, then practically the sole source of knowledge about ancient history, had been aristocrats, and thus might have dismissed "ancient history" as elitist. Or they may have argued consistently what they only infrequently suggested – that classical analogies were inapplicable to the American context. Instead, because of their own reverence for the classics and because of the lack of any opposing tradition, they played the game, even arguing that their classicists were as good as the opposition's. As a result the deck was stacked against them.[315]

In short, classicism provided the common political vocabulary for participants in the constitutional deliberations of 1787. Even if there was a backlash against the over-use of certain kinds of ancient references, the classics still structured and conditioned the debate.

4. Styles of Classical Thought. Some last words need to be said about the role of classicism in forming the mind and attitudes of the Framing generation. Because of the strong emphasis of classical reading in American education at the time, it is no surprise that certain styles of thought became embedded in public discourse of the time. One element of this was the Aristotelian syllogism, which remained the key mode of logical expression, even with the introduction of Ramist forms in the early eighteenth century.[316]

Because many of the educated class were so superbly trained in Latin, it was inevitable that Latin grammar and syntax would subtly affect their written and spoken expression in English. As Forrest McDonald has observed: "In thinking in eighteenth-century English, . . . a rudimentary knowledge of Latin is highly useful; after all . . . English words were generally closer in meaning to their Latin originals than they are today, and sometimes, as with the use of the subjunctive, it is apparent that an author is accustomed to formulating his thoughts in Latin."[317] Or, as Christian Kopff has pointedly written, "We need to know Latin if we want to think like the Founders."[318] Some of the most evocative words of the American revolution and the Founding period are Latin or Greek in origin: tyranny, republic, citizen, virtue, democracy, and politics, to name just a few. The classics quite literally provided "a vocabulary, a terminology, which [the Framing generation] sometimes used to cope with everyday experience."[319]

Classical learning also profoundly influenced the views of the Framers when it came to certain political truths. "They developed from the classics a suspicious cast of mind. They learned from the Greeks and Romans to fear conspiracies against liberty."[320] Despite the fact that King George III and his ministers in London bore little resemblance to despots of classical times, the American revolutionaries knew that tyranny was an insidious disease. In a somewhat paranoid fashion, the American revolutionaries saw every action from London, including the imposition of light taxes after the successful French and Indian War, as leading to tyranny. In 1767, John Adams, citing to Tacitus, wrote that the Spirit of Liberty depended on the Latin maxim "Obsta Principiis" ("meet the trouble at its start," or, resist the beginnings of tyranny), "knowing that her enemies are swift and cunning, making the earliest advances slowly, silently, and softly."[321] John Dickinson quoted Cicero for the point that "Even though the ruler many not, at the time, be troublesome, it is a sad fact that he can be so, if he takes the fancy."[322]

This same style of argument was used at the time of the ratification of the Constitution. The Antifederalist forces tended to see the federal compact as an elite conspiracy, intended to rob the individual states or people of their hard-fought liberties and to concentrate power in a central government. (Of course, the lack of a Bill of Rights in the Constitution and the absence of anything other than structural checks and balances on the abuse of governmental power gave the Antifederalists a potent argument in this regard.) In contrast, the supporters of the Constitution saw the Antifederalists as conspiring to give government into the hands of mob rule, and thus lead to a dictatorial backlash. These were precisely the classical roads to tyranny: the creeping aristocratic coup or the fomentation of anarchy through the elimination of legitimate governmental power.[323] In these conspiratorial tropes the leading classical models were the insurgencies of Catiline and Caesar. It is no surprise, then, that the ultimate epithet that the members of the Framing generation could hurl against one another was association with these classical conspirators as enemies of liberty.

This also explains why natural law, as expounded through classical sources, was such a popular subject for members of the Framing generation. It was the ultimate antidote to claims of the supremacy of the laws made by the British Parliament and King. This higher or fundamental law – variously denominated as "natural law" or "natural reason" or *ius naturale* – was partially derived from classical sources. These included Aristotle,[324] the Stoics, and most importantly, Cicero's *De Re Publica* and *De Legibus*.[325] Just as significantly, natural law precepts were gleaned from continental jurists such as Grotius, Pufendorf, and Burlamaqui, who heavily relied upon classical history and Roman jurisprudence for their conclusions.[326] The crucial place of universalism and right reason in natural law made it an attractive avenue of discourse for the Framing generation. Because of natural law theory's emphasis on sociability and public virtue it was "recognized by moral philosophers and legal educators as an important support for society and government in a democratic republic."[327] Of course, as already noted, the natural law of antiquity lacked a positively crucial intellectual component: any conception of individual liberty. So, when the Declaration of Independence spoke of "inalienable rights,"[328] this was an argot unknown to classical political theory, and was a unique contribution of the modern, Enlightenment mind.

The slow transition from American revolutionaries to Framers can be seen in their reactions to a *ius naturale*. John Adams could write in 1765: "Let us study the law of nature . . . read the histories of ancient pages; contemplate the great examples of Greece and Rome; set before us the conduct of our British ancestors, who have defended for us the inherent rights of mankind against foreign and domestic tyrants and usurpers."[329] So suffused was a concern for natural law and its intellectual origins at the time of the revolution that the opening lines of the Declaration of Independence makes a direct reference to the "Laws of Nature and of Nature's God" as the initial appeal to mankind for the justness of the American cause.[330] Thomas Jefferson could later write in defining natural law that it is the "appeal to the true fountains of evidence, the head and heart of every rational and honest man, Nature has written her moral laws, and where every man may read them for himself."[331] Even as the Framers came to recognize that their task was to create a positive political and legal order, and not merely (as earlier revolutionaries) to make a break from past traditions, natural law theory continued to exert a powerful influence on their thinking.[332]

That leaves the question of how the classical tradition interacted with other intellectual influences in the making of the Constitution. Without providing a full answer to the historiographic challenge posed above in the Preface – whether (in the contemporary view of intellectual historians) classicism had only a very limited and ornamental influence on the actual framing of the Constitution – it is worth considering how classical sources were seen by the Framing generation as contributing to the insights of common law jurists, protestant Christian theology, and Enlightenment thinking.

First, it is important to realize that the Framing generation was as instrumental in their use of these other sources and evidences of constitutionalism as they were in their appreciation of the classics. Among Enlightenment *philosophes*, particularly Hobbes, Sidney, Harrington, Locke, Nedham, Neville, Trenchard, Hume, Rousseau, and Montesquieu, leaders of the American Revolutionary War scavenged what they could use. This was especially true with Montesquieu's *Spirit of the Laws*, "the most compact and the most complete handbook of the science and history of government at their disposal."[333] To the extent that writers like Montesquieu relied upon ancient history to support their assertions, the Framers were more likely to independently verify those supporting precedents. As Gilbert Chinard noted: "a careful study of the *Records* and *The Federalist* would show that more frequently they went back to the ancient sources from which Montesquieu himself had derived his information, and that they had apparently a first hand acquaintance with ancient historians and ancient history."[334] So it is apparent that insofar as Enlightenment political philosophy was itself premised on a sampling of historical experience,[335] classicism provided the crucial citations.

Then again, there was also the fact that eighteenth century thinkers generally concurred with the conclusions of classical writers. Philosophers in England and France were as smitten with the classical tradition as their American counterparts,[336] and were as intent on extending classical learning to political pursuits. There were obviously differences in emphasis when

Enlightenment political writers expounded on classical writings. For example, English activists of the Whig party, when excoriating the "Court Party," extended the classical distrust of conspiracies of ambition, and the insidious accumulation of power into tyranny, into a fear of all encroachments on individual liberty. Personal freedom was not, itself, a concept readily known to the ancients. The insight of English Enlightenment thinking by such as John Locke and Thomas Gordon was to subtly transform a readily understood classical trope into a useful tool for contemporary political infighting. Whether, as has been argued by some recent intellectual historians,[337] that this principle of Enlightenment liberalism could have been achieved without the classical antecedent, is almost beside the point.[338]

Although less direct, classicism may have exerted some influence on the Framing generation's use of two other sources of thinking: the common law and Protestant theology. As Bernard Bailyn has noted, the corpus of common law decisions was viewed in a way similar to the classical canon, as "a repository of experience in human dealings embodying the principles of justice, equity, and rights; above all, it was a form of history – ancient, indeed immemorial, history; constitutional and national history; and, as history, it helped explain the movement of events and the meaning of the present."[339] The strong historicist inclinations of the Framing generation fully aligned them with a "Whig" interpretation of history, a "study of the past with direct and perpetual reference to the present."[340]

Likewise, along with the Framing generation's understanding, and its belief in covenant theology and Protestant Christianity, there was a strong current of historical desire.[341] "Colonial Americans read Luther, Calvin, and Wesley, sang Isaac Watts's hymns, and studied the King James Bible to gain access to the Roman Empire where primitive Christianity was born and to the earlier world of the Old Testament."[342] The knowledge of Greek that some of the Framers had acquired was used to read Homer and Aristotle and Polybius in the original but also to learn the Greek New Testament so that they could understand the foundational texts of Christianity. As Thomas Jefferson advised his friend, Peter Carr, "[r]ead the Bible . . . as you would read Livy or Tacitus. The facts which are in the ordinary cause of nature, you will believe on the authority of the writer, as you do of the same kind in Livy and Tacitus."[343]

Aside from these direct classical connections with Christian theology, there was also the reinforcement that Calvinism and the Presbyterian Church gave to the concern of concentrating too much power in the hands of particular individuals, offices, or even segments of society.[344] The classical fear of conspiracy and tyranny intermingled with covenant theology's apprehension of power in the hands of sinners. Indeed, whereas Enlightenment philosophy was generally optimistic about the ability of man to be perfected as a political animal (conservative thinkers of Thomas Hobbes's sort excluded, of course), classical sources shared with Protestant Christianity a deep distrust of that notion and fervently believed that, as shown through historical experience, power always corrupted the individuals and institutions it touched.

There is an essential unity to these strands of thought, and despite recent attempts by intellectual historians to disentangle and deconstruct them, this would have been considered odd and unnatural to the members of the Framing generation. John Adams, in his *Letters of Novanglus*, published at the eve of the Revolution in 1774, wrote: "These are what are called revolutionary principles. They are the principles of Aristotle and Plato, of Livy and Cicero, of Sidney, Harrington and Locke; the principles of nature and eternal reason."[345] Thomas Jefferson, writing much later in 1825, made his celebrated valedictory of the reasons and motivations that guided the Sprit of 1776:

> This was the object of the *Declaration of Independence*: Not to find out new principles, or new arguments, never before thought of, not merely to say things which had never been said before; but to place before mankind the common sense of the subject, in terms so plain and firm as to command their assent, and to justify ourselves in the independent stand we are compelled to take. Neither aiming at originality of principle or sentiment, nor yet copied from any particular and previous writing, it was intended to be an expression of the American mind, and to give to that expression the proper tone and spirit called for by the occasion. All its authority rests then on the harmonizing sentiments of the day, whether expressed in conversation, in letters, printed essays, or in the elementary books of public right, as Aristotle, Cicero, Locke, Sidney, etc.[346]

The true intellectual style of the Framing generation was this pragmatic and eclectic mixing and refashioning of intellectual sources in order to make significant advances in political thought. At times, this style produced barely coherent results. This was usually because the instrumental way that the Framers employed sources and evidences of historic practices, with little thought to context. On other occasions – and the framing of the Constitution and its ratification in 1787–1788 is surely one of these – the results were extraordinary and lasting.

TWO

CLASSICAL POLITICAL MODELS
AND THE FOUNDERS

H ANNAH ARENDT OBSERVED IN HER BOOK, *ON REVOLUTION*, THAT
"without the classical example...none of the men of the revolutions on
either side of the Atlantic would have possessed the courage for what then
turned out to be unprecedented action."[1] As has already been narrated in
Chapter 1, the Framing generation regarded the classical tradition as granting useful knowledge and valuable historic precedent on what John Adams
called "the divine science of politics." Classical antiquity also provided the
crucial set of political models (and their dystopian counterparts) from which
the Framers could draw upon in inspiration of their new government. As
Adams observed in 1765, "the knowledge of the principles and construction of free governments...have remained at a full stand for two or three
thousand years," and so he turned his attention to "the ancient seats of
liberty, the Republics of Greece and Rome."[2] Later, in writing to Lafayette
in 1782, he indicated that "I [am]...a republican on principle....Almost
every thing that is estimable in civil life has originated under such governments. Two republican powers, Athens and Rome, have done more honor
to our species than the rest of it. A new country can be planted only by such
a government."[3] Or, as William Livingston referred to in his *Independent
Reflector*, published in 1753, "those free Governments of old, whose History
we so much admire, and whose Example we think it an Honor to imitate."[4]

The Framing generation's use of classicism to form their political theory was thus every bit as instrumental and pragmatic as their other uses
of the classical tradition. For the two crucial structural problems facing
the Framers – balancing powers and functions within the federal government and defining the relationship between the national government and
that of the separate states – the only useful precedents were from antiquity, and so the Framers "were *obliged* to study Greece and Rome, if they
would gain 'experimental' wisdom in the dangers and potentialities of the

republican form."[5] Far from imitating classical models, the Framers were essentially conducting a "political pathology" on earlier forms of government, attempting to understand why they failed or changed in unexpected ways.[6] This intellectual exercise culminated in John Adams's *Defence of the Constitutions of the United States of America* (which he published in early 1787, but had begun drafting much earlier) and James Madison's notes on ancient and modern confederations (prepared in the summer of 1786). At the Constitutional Convention, all of this groundwork bore the fruit that is the subject of this volume. As William Pierce, delegate from Georgia observed, James Madison was the anointed Convention antiquarian (although ably assisted by the likes of John Dickinson, Alexander Hamilton, Luther Martin, and James Wilson) and his lectures, though lengthy, were well-received, as when he "ran through the whole Scheme of the Government, – pointed out the beauties and defects of ancient Republics, compared their situation to ours wherever it appeared to bear any analogy."[7]

Before proceeding, however, to describe the precise ways the Framers used ancient history in formulating the structural Constitution, one must assess the wider implications of the classical tradition's influence on the political philosophy of the Founders. This chapter will unfold by reviewing a handful of discrete themes in the political theory of American constitutionalism. First, and as a matter of historical prelude, it is worth understanding the Framers' attitudes toward great empires and their colonies. Having just emerged from a colonial relationship with Great Britain, classical views on the place of colonies in an imperial system were significant for other purposes in conditioning a political philosophy for the Framing generation.

The second classical strand in the Framers' political theory was the necessity of dividing authority among traditional segments of the populace, what the Framers referred to (based on Polybius' analysis) as "mixed government." Strongly implicit in ideas of mixed government are what the Framers came to realize were principles of separation of powers, and, perhaps even more importantly, the recognition that political power was an unstable and dangerous force that had to be carefully balanced not only among government institutions but also among all sectors of civil society.

Directly related to the concept of mixed government was classical republicanism, the creation of government institutions to rule a society that were neither monarchical (at one extreme) nor purely democratic (at the other). The Framing generation was aware of how the Roman republic was structured in theory and how it operated in practice. They understood as well the workings of some of the Greek city-states and other polities of the ancient Mediterranean. The Framers were troubled, however, by an assumption (advanced by Montesquieu in his *Spirit of the Laws*, but expressed earlier in the writings of Machiavelli) that republics could subsist only in narrow spatial and temporal circumstances. The creation of a durable and robust republic, one that could withstand the challenges of sectionalism, political parties, and faction, as well as class conflict, seemed an insuperable problem for the Framing generation.

The object of this chapter is not to outline the full contours of the Framing generation's engagement with political theory, especially insofar as Enlightenment authors influenced American conceptions of political order. Such is beyond the scope of this volume. That still leaves an appreciation of the sense that the Framers had for various classical models of government. The role of these models and antimodels has already been noted in this book, and certainly elsewhere in the literature. Nevertheless, the influence of Rome, Athens, Sparta, Carthage, and other ancient polities on the thinking of the Framers can hardly be overestimated. At the same time, there was a strong sense among the Framing generation that American political conditions and consciousness would, by virtue of progress and necessity, surpass that of ancient times. This tension – between embracing and rejecting classical models of political organization and constitutionalism – was an enduring theme of intellectual discourse during the Framing period.

A. EMPIRES AND COLONIAL GOVERNANCE

The prevailing (although by no means unanimous) view among colonial Americans was that Greece was a better mother of colonies than Rome, which dominated hers with overbearing might and brutality. This was, to some degree, inconsistent with the Framing generation's schizophrenic view that the Roman republic embodied positive virtues, whereas the Roman Empire was fundamentally dissolute, corrupt, and evil. This cognitive dissonance arose because most of the examples of Roman colonies and colonial policy arose from the earlier republican period. Nevertheless, it is worth considering this underlying example of ancient political practice as it bore on the mind of American colonial politicians, even if it is another example, as Meyer Reinhold put it, of a "model[] of antiquity which Americans perceived ... [as] largely simplistic stereotypes, and these tended to fall into polarised patterns."[8] This is a good topic to begin the process of separating the Framing generation's understanding of ancient history from what we today believe to be the classical reality, based on modern philology and archaeological and inscription evidence.

Most of the American thinking on the subject of ancient colonies occurred as part of the polemical writing that took place after the British adoption of the Townsend duties and Stamp Act taxes, in the immediate wake of the conclusion, in 1763, of the French and Indian War (as the Great War for Empire or Seven Years' War was known in the Americas). James Otis (1724–1783),[9] wrote in 1764 that "Greece was a more generous and a better mother to her colonies than Rome. The conduct of Rome towards her colonies and the corruptions and oppressions tolerated in her provincial officers of all denominations was one great cause of the downfall of that proud republic."[10] The following year, Otis responded to a tract by Martin Howard, a Tory writer favoring for Britain a Roman model of colonization: "'Tis well known the Grecians were kind, humane, just and generous towards their [colonies]. 'Tis as notorious that the Romans were severe, cruel, brutal, and barbarous toward theirs. I have ever pleased myself in thinking that Great Britain since the [Glorious] Revolution might be justly compared to Greece in its care and protection of its colonies. I also imagined that the French and Spaniards followed the Roman example."[11] John Dickinson, in his second *Pennsylvania Farmer* letter, published in 1768, drew this ancient parallel with the newly imposed trade restrictions by the Board of Trade: "When the Carthaginians were possessed of the island of Sardinia, they made a decree that the Sardinians could not raise corn, nor get it in any other way than from the Carthaginians. Then, by imposing any duties they would upon it, they drained any sums they pleased [from the colony]."[12]

In 1771, writing as "Valerius Poplicola," Samuel Adams replied to Governor Thomas Hutchinson's (1711–1780) complimentary attitude toward the Roman model of colonial governance in his *History of Massachusetts Bay*:[13] "Why the conduct of Rome towards her colonies should be recommended as an example to our parent state, rather than that of Greece, is difficult to conjecture, unless it was because, as had been observed, the latter was more generous and a better mother to her colonies than the former. . . . We are willing to render to [Great Britain] respect and certain expressions of honor and reverence, as the Grecian colonies did to the city from whence they deriv'd their origin . . . so long as the colonies were well treated."[14] A few years earlier, Thomas Jefferson copied into his commonplace book an extract from Temple Stanyan's *Greek History* (published in 1751), which concerned Greek colonization of the Mediterranean with the notation that such colonies were politically independent from the metropole from the moment of their establishment.[15]

On the eve of the Revolution, in 1774, Alexander Hamilton wrote this account of Roman colonial policy: "Rome was the nurse of freedom. She was celebrated for her justice and lenity; but in what manner did she govern her dependent provinces? They were made the continual scene of rapine and cruelty. From thence let us learn how little confidence is due to the wisdom and equity of the most exemplary nations."[16] Hamilton was prepared, though, to move beyond historical generalities and to seek some deeper understanding of the evolution of the Roman republic. In a pamphlet published the following year, he recognized that, late in the republic-era, Rome did grant a large measure of self-government to Italian subject cities (as well as citizenship to their inhabitants). Nonetheless, Hamilton observed that "The mistress of the world was often unjust. And the treatment of her dependent provinces is one of the greatest blemishes in her history. Through the want of that civil liberty for which we are now so warmly contending, they groaned under every species of wanton oppression. If we are wise, we shall take a warning from thence; and consider a like state of dependence as more to be dreaded than pestilence and famine."[17]

Obviously, the central passages of the Declaration of Independence are to be construed as an indictment of British colonial policies. Indeed, Jefferson may well have intended it as a bill of particulars, and he summarized the charges in these terms: "the history of the present king of Great Britain is a history of repeated injuries and usurpations, all having in direct object the establishment of an absolute tyranny over these states. To prove this let facts be submitted to a candid world."[18] George Mason defended in 1778 the American colonists' decision to take up arms against Great Britain: "The truth is that we have been forced into it, as the only means of self-preservation, to guard our Country and posterity from the greatest of all Evils, such another infernal Government (if it deserves the Name of Government) as the Provinces groaned under, in the latter Ages of the Roman Commonwealth."[19]

Alone among the Framing generation, John Adams appeared to hold up both Greek and Roman models for his critiques of British colonial policy in North America. In his *Letters to Novanglus* of March 1775 he contended: "there is nothing in the law of nations, which is only the law of right reason applied to the conduct of nations, that requires that emigrants from a state should continue, or be made part of the state. The practice of nations has been different. The Greeks planted colonies, and neither demanded nor pretended any authority over them, but they became distinct, independent commonwealths."[20] Adams also recounted the story, narrated in Livy, of the envoy from the Roman colony of Privernates who threatened rebellion to the Roman Senate, if the colony were not fairly treated. In glowing terms Adams observed that the Senate "had heard the voice of a man and a son of liberty.... The Senate and People of Rome did not interfere in making laws for their colonies, but left them to be ruled by their governors and senates." Adams then challenged a Tory pamphleteer, "Massachusettensis," to "produce from the whole history of Rome, or from the Digest [of Justinian], one example of a *Senatus consultum* or *Plebiscitum* laying taxes on a colony?"[21]

The historic truth of the relative virtues of Greek and Roman colonialism lay, of course, somewhere in the middle of the manichean vision of the Americans. Greek metropoles were not always gracious toward their colonies, nor was the Roman republic always so abusive. We know, for example, from Pliny's *Natural History* that Roman citizenship was extended in the second and first centuries BCE to non-Italians both individually and by communities, and such grants often ameliorated any official discrimination against regions that had earlier been conquered or colonized by the Roman republic.[22] Dionysius of Halicarnassus, in his *Roman Antiquities*, reported that King Tullus Hostilius offered this refutation of Greek colonial policies in Italy: "We look upon it to be neither truth nor justice that mother cities ought of necessity and by the Law of Nature to rule over their colonies."[23]

But the chief classical texts on this point are Thucydides' *History of the Peloponnesian War* and Livy's *History of Rome*, although other works also figure in the discussion. In the opening pages of his *History* (what is known among classicists as "the Archaeology"), Thucydides narrates the establishment of Greek colonies. He observes that over-population of certain areas on the Greek mainland led to colonization of the Aegean islands, the coast of Asia Minor (Ionia), and to southern Italy and Sicily.[24] Cities (*poleis*) also dispatched colonists to win control of strategic areas, or to block incursions or aggressions by adversaries.[25] Most typically, colonies were established to facilitate trade and access to supplies of grain and other foodstuffs, which were in chronically short supply in mainland Greece of antiquity.[26] Colonies affiliated with an originating city, which, in turn were known to be connected with the original tribes or peoples of Greece, those of Ionian, Doric, and Aeolian descent.[27]

Well-known to the Framing generation was the story narrated in Thucydides of the competition between Corinth and Corcyra over the colony at Epidamnus.[28] Because of the complex nature of Greek alliances at the eve of the Peloponnesian War, this incident was noted as one of the precipitating causes of the conflict between Athens and Sparta.[29] Corinth, a city founded by the Dorian tribe and in league with Sparta, had earlier established a colony at Corcyra, on the present-day island of Corfu. Corcyra had declared its independence from Corinth centuries before and they had been naval rivals.[30] Corcyra quickly began to overshadow its mother city in trade and military might, and, indeed, on the eve of the Peloponnesian War Corcyra had the third largest navy in Greece.[31] In any event, Corcyra and Corinth had jointly founded a colony at Epidamnus, which, by virtue of its location far to the north on the Ionian Gulf in Illyria (present-day Albania), was more closely connected with Corcyra.

Events in Epidamnus were about to take an ugly turn, and Thucydides' cautionary tale would have resonance with later readers who had lived through the American Revolution: "As time passed the city of the Epidamnians became great and populous; but civil wars ensued, lasting, it is said, for many years, and in consequence of a war with the neighbouring barbarians they were crippled and stripped of most of their power. Finally, just before the Peloponnesian war, the populace expelled the aristocrats, and they, making cause with the barbarians and attacking Epidamnus, plundered those who were in the city both by land and sea."[32] In 435 BCE, the democratic faction at Epidamnus made an appeal to Corcyra, the "mother-city" of the colony, for aid against the aristocrats and Illyrians, but this was sternly refused.[33] Then, after consulting the oracle at Delphi, the Epidamnians made a diplomatic approach to Corinth, their other cofounder. The Corinthians accepted this plea, for reasons that are quite revealing: "they considered that the colony belonged to them as much as to the Corcyrans, partly also through hatred of the Corcyrans, for the reason that these, though Corinthian colonists, neglected the mother-city. For neither at their common festival gatherings would the [Corcyrans] concede the customary privileges to the Corinthians, nor would they begin with a representative of Corinth the initial rites at sacrifices, as the rest of the colonies did, but they treated them with contempt."[34]

The Corinthians thus used the civil war at Epidamnus as a way to strike back at their ungrateful former colony, Corcyra, which had the hubris to regard themselves as superior to their mother country. Corinth dispatched groups of settlers to Epidamnus, in order to solidify their hold over the colony and to bolster the strength of the popular faction. Corcyra responded to Corinth's interference by throwing their support behind the aristocratic exiles, who "had gone to Corcyra, and pointing to the sepulchres of common ancestors and invoking the tie of kinship had begged the Corcyrans to restore them."[35] The Corcyrans then actually besieged Epidamnus, hoping to restore the oligarchic faction and to expel the Corinthians. The Corinthians responded by assembling a huge expeditionary force to relieve the Corcyran siege at Epidamnus.[36] At this point, the Corcyrans sought to arbitrate the dispute, an offer the Corinthians declined, and then the Corcyrans proceeded to vanquish the Corinthian fleet at Leukimme and the Corcyrans subsequently carried their siege of Epidamnus, establishing their control over the colony.[37] Corinth raised another force, and, at this point, both sides sought allies in the conflict, leading to eventual escalation into the pan-Hellenic conflict that was the Peloponnesian War.

In an appeal made to the Athenians in 433 BCE for a defensive alliance against Corinthian aggression, the Corcyrans made some general remarks about the nature of colonies in ancient Greece: "while every colony honours the mother-country so long as it is well-treated, yet that if wronged it becomes alienated; for colonists are not sent out to be slaves of those who are left behind, but to be their equals."[38] The Corinthians responded to this by renewing their charge of Corcyran arrogance: "although they are colonists of ours, they have constantly stood aloof from us, and now they are at war with us, claiming that they were not sent out to be ill treated. But neither did we colonize them to be insulted by them, but to be their leaders and to receive from them all due reverence. The rest of our colonies, at any rate, honour us, and by our colonists we are beloved more than is any other mother-city."[39]

It is surprising, indeed, that this passage from Thucydides would be regarded by the Framing generation as authority for a view that Greek metropoles were lenient with their colonies. Despite the rhetoric of colonial independence, counterpoised with the obligation of almost filial respect by a colony for its mother-city, the reality of the Corcyran–Corinthian submissions at Athens is that they were competing for control of Epidamnus. At no point after the Epidamnians made their fateful request for Corinthian intervention, did either side appear to give a whit for Epidamnian independence. Whether this reflects Thucydidean realism or pessimism almost does not matter;[40] the point is clearly made that colonies can quickly become pawns in imperial politics. This could not have been lost on an American leadership that lived through the heady times of the British defeat of France in the Great War for Empire, and then was later obliged to seek a French alliance during the American Revolution. In any event, other passages in Thucydides were replete with incidents of colonies being maltreated by their mother-cities, and consequent revolts or changes in alliance.[41]

Roman colonial policies in the middle period of the republic (250–150 BCE) were often progressive, even if self-interested. The republic made a significant legal distinction between Italian, Latin and Roman colonial establishments, and different rules of citizenship applied to each category. This perpetuated the distinction, developed in the early years of the republic as Rome expanded in power and influence through central Italy (acquiring Latin towns) of hierarchies of citizenship. The traditional Roman policy was to make Roman – and thus to extend Roman citizenship – only those colonies that were established as military outposts. Other settlements, which could turn into thriving municipalities, were chartered as Latin or Italian colonies. The Romans were concerned that the free grant of Roman citizenship would encourage depopulation of Latin towns and the movement of people toward vulnerable frontiers.[42] Twice, in 187 and 177 BCE, Latin towns had to request the Roman Senate to return their citizens who had emigrated to Roman colonies and had acquired Roman citizenship under the gracious rule of the *ius migrationis*.[43] In short, Roman policies for colonizing new areas and extending citizenship were sometimes too successful.

It appears that Roman colonies enjoyed a high measure of autonomy and self-government in the crucial periods of the Roman republic. This did not go so far as the experience of certain Greek colonies that attempted to eclipse the power of their mother-cities. It is unlikely that Rome would have long tolerated a rival such as Corcyra was for Corinth, assuming that the upstart was actually presenting a threat to Roman interests. Obviously, as Roman power consolidated in Italy – and later, through conquest, throughout the Mediterranean – Roman colonies came to be regarded as the leading instrument of a Roman *imperium*, which featured the grant of citizenship and general tactics of co-optation to keep subject peoples in order.[44]

It was thus for good reason that the debate over the nature of Greek and Roman colonial policies subsisted until 1787 and 1788 and more than indirectly influenced the Framers' perception of the potential powers to be granted to the national government. At the back of some minds of those at the Philadelphia Convention, was not to expose the planned federal government to the same charge that had earlier been leveled against Roman imperialism and British colonialism. William Grayson at the Virginia ratifying convention was express in his opposition to an increase in federal power, and observed the Roman republic's "remarkable" brutality toward its provinces.[45]

Even proponents of the Constitution, such as John Dickinson, were careful to distinguish the likely relationship between the federal government and states under the Plan of the Convention, as distinct from Roman models: "America is, and will be, divided into several sovereign states, each possessing every power proper for governing within its own limits for its own purposes, and also for acting as a member of the union. They will be civil and military stations, conveniently planted throughout the empire, with lively and regular communications. A stroke, a touch upon any part, will be immediately felt by the whole. Rome, famed for imperial arts, had a glimpse of this great truth; and endeavoured, as well as her hard-hearted policy would permit, to realize it in her *colonies*. They were miniatures of the capital: But wanted the vital principal of sovereignty, and were too small."[46] For

Dickinson the key distinction between a Roman province and an American state (as part of a larger Union), was that the American state had an extra element of sovereignty and autonomy that was unknown to its Roman counterparts.

Above all else, the Framing generation saw the colonial policies of Greece and Rome as counterpoints on the continuum between liberty and tyranny. Drawing the parallel of ancient history with their own recent experiences under British rule, the Framers were very much concerned with creating a government that would not lead to authoritarian rule. Aside from colonial implications, Americans were familiar with Herodotus' narrative of the debate on the Constitutions of the Persians[47] and Aristotle's account in *The Politics* of the first signs of tyranny being heavy taxation and the suppression of citizen militias by the government.[48] Classical antiquity thus provided a cautionary tale of the extreme sorts of government to be avoided (colonial subjugation and tyranny). What remained was to divine the essence of good government.

B. MIXED CONSTITUTIONS AND SEPARATION OF POWERS

If the classical record of colonialism provided only a negative inference to the Framing generation, merely a point of departure, then Polybius' theory of balanced government[49] must be regarded as one of the crucial linchpins of American constitutionalism. Although by no means did the Framing generation rediscover Polybius – his views were filtered through the later writings of Machiavelli and Montesquieu (more on which presently) – they did make a uniquely American gloss on his political philosophy.

There is no substitute for understanding Polybius' views of mixed government than by rendering them in their almost complete form. In volume six of his *Histories*,[50] Polybius digresses from his narration of the Second Punic War, the life-and-death struggle that pitted Rome and Carthage for mastery of the western Mediterranean, and the Macedonian War for control of Illyria and Greece. Polybius observes that "I have always regarded this account as one of the essential parts of my whole design. I have, I am sure, made evident in numerous passages and chiefly in the prefatory remarks dealing with the fundamental principles of this history, where I said that the best and most valuable result I aim at is that readers of my work may gain a knowledge how it was and by virtue of what peculiar political institutions that in less than fifty-three years nearly the whole world was overcome and fell under the single dominion of Rome, a thing the like of which had never happened before."[51]

Having justified his topic, Polybius launched into his theory of mixed government:

Most of those whose object it has been to instruct us methodically concerning such matters, distinguish three kinds of constitutions, which they call kingship, aristocracy, and democracy. Now we should, I think, be quite justified in asking them to enlighten us as to whether they represent these three to be the sole varieties or rather to be the best; for in either case my opinion is that they are wrong. For it is evident that we must regard as the best constitution a combination of all these three varieties, since we have had proof of this not only theoretically but by actual experience, Lycurgus having been the first to draw up a constitution – that of Sparta – on this principle. Nor on the other hand can we admit that these are the only three varieties; for we have witnessed monarchical and tyrannical governments, which while they differ very widely from kingship, yet bear a certain resemblance to it, this being the reason why monarchs in general falsely assume and use, as far as they can, the regal title. There have also been several oligarchical constitutions which seem to bear some likeness to aristocratic ones, though the divergence is, generally, as wide as possible. The same holds good about democracies. The truth of what I say is evident from the following considerations. It is by no means every monarchy which we can call straight off a kingship, but only that which is voluntarily accepted by the subjects and where they are governed rather by an appeal to their reason than by fear and force. Nor again can we style every oligarchy an aristocracy, but only that where the government is in the hands of a selected body of the justest and wisest men. Similarly that is no true democracy in which the whole crowd of citizens is free to do whatever they wish or purpose, but when, in a community where it is traditional and customary to reverence the gods, to honour our parents, to respect our elders, and to obey the laws, the will of the greater number prevails, this is to be called a democracy. We should therefore assert that there are six kinds of governments, the three above mentioned which are in everyone's mouth and the three which are naturally allied to them, I mean monarchy, oligarchy, and mob-rule. Now the first of these to come into being is monarchy, its growth being natural and unaided; and next arises kingship derived from monarchy by the aid of art and by the correction of defects. Monarchy first changes into its vicious allied form, tyranny; and next, the abolishment of both gives birth to aristocracy. Aristocracy by its very nature degenerates into oligarchy; and when the commons inflamed by anger take vengeance on this government for its unjust rule, democracy comes into being; and in due course the licence and lawlessness of this form of government produces mob-rule to complete the series. The truth of what I have just said will be quite clear to anyone who pays due attention to such beginnings, origins, and changes as are in each case natural. For he alone who has seen how each form naturally arises and develops, will be able to see when, how, and where the growth, perfection, change, and end of each are likely to occur again.[52]

In this dense passage we have a number of independent thoughts being woven by Polybius. One is a typology of government, a categorization scheme which attempts to articulate the broadest patterns of government by individuals (kingship), elites (aristocracy), and the people (democracy). Polybius acknowledges his debt to Plato,[53] but as much as said that Plato's arguments "are subtle and stated at great length, they are beyond the reach of all but a few."[54] In any event, Polybius is actually attempting a new formulation of this age-old conundrum of human government.[55]

The second theme is a related idea of dynamic cyclical change and decline through political revolutions (anacyclōsis, or ἀνακύκλωσις).[56] He later observed that constitutions, like people, pass through three phases (πολιτεία) of growth (αὔξησις), prime (ἀκμή) and decline (φθίσις).[57] Polybius makes clear that these various "pure" forms of government inevitably and inexorably must degenerate into their evil triplets – tyranny, oligarchy and ochlocracy (mob rule) – and then into the inevitable backlash of an opposing faction. Indeed, Polybius later in this section elaborates a lengthy narrative of the generational succession of various kinds of government,[58] and concludes "Such is the cycle of political revolution, the course appointed by nature in which constitutions change, disappear, and finally return to the point from which they started."[59]

Polybius' last – and most influential – point was his prescriptive notion that the best government was one that mixed the various attributes of monarchical, aristocratic, and democratic modes of governance. Speaking in relation to the constitution established (probably apocryphally) by Lycurgus at Sparta, Polybius noted the beneficial effects of mixed government and also offered this extended metaphor of the "ship of state":

Lycurgus had perfectly well understood that all the above changes take place necessarily and naturally, and had taken into consideration that every variety of constitution which is simple and formed on principle is precarious, as it is soon perverted into the corrupt form which is proper to it and naturally follows on it. For just as rust in the case of iron and wood-worms and ship-worms in the case of timber are inbred pests, and these substances, even though they escape all external injury, fall a prey to the evils engendered in them, so each constitution has a vice engendered in it and inseparable from it. In kingship it is despotism, in aristocracy oligarchy, and in democracy the savage rule of violence; and it is impossible, as I said above, that each of these should not in course of time change into this vicious form. Lycurgus, then, foreseeing this, did not make his constitution simple and uniform, but united in it all the good and distinctive features of the best governments, so that none of the principles should grow unduly and be perverted into its allied evil, but that, the force of each being neutralized by that of the others, neither of them should prevail and outbalance another, but that the constitution should remain for long in a state of equilibrium like a well-trimmed boat, kingship being guarded from arrogance by the fear of the commons, who were given a sufficient share in the government, and the commons on the other hand not venturing to treat the kings with contempt from fear of the elders, who being selected from the best citizens would be sure all of them to be always on the side of justice; so that that part of the state which was weakest owing to its subservience to traditional custom, acquired power and weight by the support and influence of the elders. The consequence was that by drawing up his constitution thus he preserved liberty at Sparta for a longer period than is recorded elsewhere.[60]

Before considering the impact of Polybius' theory of mixed government (along with its analogous principle of separation of powers) on later political thinkers and the Framing generation, it is worth considering whether the theory actually corresponds with classical reality. Excluding for the moment the constitution of the Roman republic (which Polybius discusses at length and which will be considered presently), his description of the Spartan, Cretan, and Punic constitutions were highly fictionalized and idealized, intending to score points more through moralizing than by accurate historical analysis.[61]

For starters, the Lycurgan Constitution of Sparta was apocryphally dictated by a law-giver and, at least as rendered by Polybius, was not the product of social experience.[62] Polybius did raise concerns over Spartan militarism and expansion, and observed that the Lycurgan Constitution was not so well-suited to finance and supply such military adventures.[63] Likewise, Polybius concluded that the Carthaginian constitution was already in decline by the time of the climactic Second Punic War, and that too much power had devolved into the hands of the people and, consequently, this affected the quality of the councils and decision making during the conflict.[64] Throughout his discussion, Polybius emphasizes societal and constitutional restrictions on the accumulation of wealth by different classes of society. He concludes that the Spartan model of prohibiting commerce by the ruling class rendered it impossible to mobilize capital on behalf of the state, whereas, at the other extreme, Cretan and Carthaginian society too readily lauded wealth over honor and virtue.[65]

One problem with Polybius' discussion of non-Roman constitutions of antiquity was his lack of a coherent chronology. For example, the governments of certain Cretan cities in the seventh and sixth centuries BCE did approximate later Spartan models, but they did not last long. Rather, it appears that Polybius was settling a more contemporaneous score by criticizing the use of Cretan mercenaries in the Hellenic world of the second century BCE and denouncing the lack of respect that Cretan cities had for Greek unity.[66] As for the Spartan constitution, as an historic matter it *was* the product of evolution over the course of five centuries, and hardly sprang (as from the head of Zeus) from one lawgiver. The accepted historical explanation is that political power in Sparta in the eighth and seventh centuries BCE resided in a landed aristocracy, and it was only with the challenges of the First Messenian War that the model of the Lycurgan Constitution began to form with power acquired by the five *ephors* or supreme magistrates, who, along with the two hereditary kings (*basileîs*), the thirty-strong *gerousia* (or senate), and an annual general assembly of the entire citizenry, were the leading institutions of the Spartan state.[67]

Despite Cicero's later suggestion,[68] the Spartan ephors were not representatives of the common people, in the same way as the tribunes of the plebs were in the Roman constitutional scheme. Instead of exercising a political counterbalance to the aristocracy, the Spartan ephors were simply another branch of government, drawn from the entire citizenry.[69] The Spartan kings were the ceremonial leaders of the state and led the Spartan armies in battle, and were assigned sacerdotal and quasijudicial functions at home.[70] The kings could actually be removed by impeachment by the ephors (and a vote in the gerousia),[71] and, besides, tended to counter-balance each other's authority because of the rivalry between the Agiad and Eurypontid branches.[72] Although the ephors (through their authority over the popular assembly and oversight of state institutions) possessed awesome authority – Xenophon noted that it verged on the despotic[73] – the ephors were essentially selected by lot, served only one-year terms, individuals could stand only once, and were subject to public audit at the end of their terms.[74] By contrast, the gerousia was a permanent body consisting of members of the aristocracy who were over the age of sixty, and elected for life by direct acclamation of the citizenry.[75] The gerousia was the repository of wisdom and caution in the Spartan state, and tended to provide stability when the kings were young or weak, and when elections produced an uninspired group of ephors or one or more that were too ambitious for their own good.

In his discussion of the Spartan constitution, Polybius is ultimately hoist on the same chronological petard as his consideration of Cretan models. He nowhere indicated that the Spartan government, despite being a mixed constitution, degraded even before their defeat at the hands of Thebes, the Macedonian invasion under Philip and Alexander, and the Roman conquest of the second century BCE. Despite Lycurgus' best intentions, substantial income inequalities did insinuate themselves into Spartan society. At the same time, it became increasingly difficult to repress the helots and conquered peoples, while also pursuing a policy of expansion and conquest against Athens and her allies in the Peloponnesian War. The rigid form of government, despite its adherence to the precepts of a mixed constitution, was nearly totalitarian in scope, and was simply unsustainable.[76]

Even before Polybius' discussion, similarities between the constitutions of Sparta and Carthage, the Phoenician city-state on the North African coast, had already been drawn in the classical canon. Isocrates in his *Nicoles* observed that both Sparta and Carthage were oligarchic "at home" and monarchical in war abroad.[77] Aristotle's *Politics* contains a long extract on the Carthaginian constitution.[78] He reiterated that both Spartan and Punic governments were mixed, and were models of internal order and stability (*eunomia*, in Greek) insofar as neither had been the subject of a violent overthrow within centuries (Aristotle was writing in the fourth century BCE). Carthage had elected kings (known as *suffetes*), not necessarily drawn from the same royal lineages. Moreover the suffetes and the self-sustaining group of elders (*pentarchies*), who were the judges of the supreme criminal tribunal, could exercise governmental power without recourse to the people, but, if the kings (on the one hand) and pentarchies and Council were at an impasse the matter was submitted to the people for determination. Aristotle nevertheless criticized the Carthaginian polity as lacking the high civil, moral, and intellectual virtues of its Greek counterparts. This account is at slight variance with Polybius who noted that "the people were supreme in matters proper to them."[79] Even more confusingly, Polybius refers both to a Carthaginian Senate and a Council of One Hundred and Four,[80] and the best guess is that the Council was elected from among the members of the larger Senate.

What is clear from this murky picture is that Carthage was virtually a complete oligarchy. The process of democratization that Polybius noted as the undermining of the Punic constitution must have occurred later in the period of Carthage's wars against Rome. One view, confirmed by Livy,[81] was the significance of Hannibal's attempted reform of the Council of One Hundred and Four, sitting as a High Court. Hannibal proposed to make that body annually elected, as opposed to being elected for a life term, and to prohibit a member from being elected more than twice in succession. This was seen as an attempt to break the monopoly of the leading Punic families over the Carthaginian government, to give more power to the people, and (probably) to increase the authority of the Barca family over the conduct of the war against Rome.[82]

We now must turn to Polybius' lengthy narrative of the mixed Roman constitution. Without anticipating the broad outlines of Roman republicanism (to be surveyed next), it is worth extracting Polybius' commentary on the salient features of Roman political organization:

> The three kinds of government that I spoke of above all shared in the control of the Roman state. And such fairness and propriety in all respects was shown in the use of these three elements for drawing up the constitution and in its subsequent administration that it was impossible even for a native to pronounce with certainty whether the whole system was aristocratic, democratic, or monarchical. This was indeed only natural. For if one fixed one's eyes on the power of the consuls, the constitution seemed completely monarchical and royal; if on that of the senate it seemed again to be aristocratic; and when one looked at the power of the masses, it seemed clearly to be a democracy. The parts of the state falling under the control of each element were and with a few modifications still are as follows.[83]

Polybius then concentrated on the three great branches of the Roman constitution: the high magistracies, in the form of the two consuls elected annually; the Senate; and the people, acting either through popular assemblies or through their tribunes.

> The consuls, previous to leading out their legions, exercise authority in Rome over all public affairs, since all the other magistrates except the tribunes [of the people] are under them and bound to obey them, and it is they who introduce embassies to the senate. Besides this it is they who consult the senate on matters of urgency, they who carry out in detail the provisions of its decrees. Again as concerns all affairs of state administered by the people it is their duty to take these under their charge, to summon assemblies, to introduce measures, and to preside over the execution of the popular decrees. As for preparation for war and the general conduct of operations in the field, here their power is almost uncontrolled; for they are empowered to make what demands they choose on the allies, to appoint military tribunes, to levy soldiers and select those who are fittest for service. They also have the right of inflicting, when on active service, punishment on anyone under their command; and they are authorized to spend any

sum they decide upon from the public funds, being accompanied by a quaestor who faithfully executes their instructions. So that if one looks at this part of the administration alone, one may reasonably pronounce the constitution to be a pure monarchy or kingship. . . .

To pass to the senate. In the first place it has the control of the treasury, all revenue and expenditure being regulated by it. For with the exception of payments made to the consuls, the quaestors are not allowed to disburse for any particular object without a decree of the senate. And even the item of expenditure which is far heavier and more important than any other – the outlay every five years by the censors on public works, whether constructions or repairs – is under the control of the senate, which makes a grant to the censors for the purpose. Similarly crimes committed in Italy which require a public investigation, such as treason, conspiracy, poisoning, and assassination, are under the jurisdiction of the senate. Also if any private person or community in Italy is in need of arbitration or indeed claims damages or requires succour or protection, the senate attends to all such matters. It also occupies itself with the dispatch of all embassies sent to countries outside of Italy for the purpose either of settling differences, or of offering friendly advice, or indeed of imposing demands, or of receiving submission, or of declaring war; and in like manner with respect to embassies arriving in Rome it decides what reception and what answer should be given to them. All these matters are in the hands of the senate, nor have the people anything whatever to do with them. So that again to one residing in Rome during the absence of the consuls the constitution appears to be entirely aristocratic; and this is the conviction of many Greek states and many of the kings, as the senate manages all business connected with them.

After this we are naturally inclined to ask what part in the constitution is left for the people, considering that the senate controls all the particular matters I mentioned, and, what is most important, manages all matters of revenue and expenditure, and considering that the consuls again have uncontrolled authority as regards armaments and operations in the field. But nevertheless there is a part and a very important part left for the people. For it is the people which alone has the right to confer honours and inflict punishment, the only bonds by which kingdoms and states and in a word human society in general are held together. For where the distinction between these is overlooked or is observed but ill applied, no affairs can be properly administered. How indeed is this possible when good and evil men are held in equal estimation? It is by the people, then, in many cases the offences punishable by a fine are tried when the accused have held the highest office; and they are the only court which may try on capital charges. . . . Again it is the people who bestow office on the deserving, the noblest regard of virtue in a state; the people have the power of approving or rejecting laws, and what is most important of all, they deliberate on the question of war and peace. Further in the case of alliances, terms of peace, and treaties, it is the people who ratify all these or the reverse. Thus here again one might plausibly say that the people's share in the government is the greatest, and that the constitution is a democratic one.[84]

Polybius recognized that this broad conspectus of the mixed Roman constitution was "imperfect owing to the omission of certain details,"[85] but he nonetheless vigorously defended his broad generalizations.[86] Polybius was particularly interested in the way that "political power is distributed among the different parts of the state, [and] how each of the three parts is enabled, if they wish, to counteract or co-operate with the others."[87] What ensues in Polybius' narrative is the now famous passage on the checks and balances of Roman constitutional institutions, what with the consuls, Senate, and people able to block extreme action by any of the other agencies of the state. "For when one part having grown out of proportion to the others aims at supremacy and tends to become too predominant, it is evident that, as for the reasons above given none of the three is absolute, but the purpose of the one can be counterworked and thwarted by the others, none of them will excessively outgrow the others or treat them with contempt. All in fact remains *in statu quo*, on the one hand, because any aggressive impulse is sure to be checked and from the outset each estate stands in dread of being interfered with by the others. . . ."[88] Polybius concluded that "[s]uch being the power that each part has of hampering the others or co-operating with them, their union is adequate to all emergencies, so that it is impossible to find a better political system than this."[89]

Polybius provided one of the clearest descriptions of the condition of the Roman republic at the time of their catastrophic defeat at the battle of Cannae (216 BCE), the lowpoint of Roman fortunes during the Second Punic War.[90] He was writing much later, of course (he died around the year 118 BCE), and so he had personally observed that many of the constitutional institutions of the Roman republic that he had so favorably noted were already in decline.[91] Indeed, he made clear that the Roman republic, even founded on the sound principles of a mixed constitution, was not immune from the inevitable process of political revolution or anacyclōsis:

That all existing things are subject to decay and change is a truth that scarcely needs proof; for the course of nature is sufficient to force this conviction on us. There being two agencies by which every kind of state is liable to decay, the one external and the other a growth of the state itself, we can lay down no fixed rule about the former, but the latter is a regular process. I have already stated what kind of state is the first to come into being, and what the next, and how the one is transformed into the other; so that those who are capable of connecting the opening propositions of this inquiry with its conclusion will now be able to foretell the future unaided. And what will happen is, I think, evident. When a state has weathered many great perils and subsequently attains to supremacy and uncontested sovereignty, it is evident that under the influence of long established prosperity, life will become more extravagant and the citizens more fierce in their rivalry regarding office and other objects than they ought to be. As these defects go on increasing, the beginning of the change for the worse will be due to love of office and the disgrace entailed by obscurity, as well as to extravagance and purse-proud display; and for this change the populace will be responsible when on the one hand they think they have a grievance against certain people who have shown themselves grasping, and when, on the other hand, they are puffed up by the flattery of others who aspire to office. For now, stirred to fury and swayed by passion in all their counsels, they will no longer consent to obey or even to be the equals of the ruling caste, but will demand the lion's share for themselves. When this happens, the state will change its name to the finest sounding of all, freedom and democracy, but will change its nature to the worst thing of all, mob-rule.

Having dealt with the origin and growth of the Roman republic, and with its prime and its present condition, and also with the differences for better or worse between it and others, I may now close this discourse more or less so.[92]

But despite the clarity of Polybius' narrative and the strong correlation with his theory of mixed government and the ruinous effects of anacyclōsis, the modern historiography of the Roman republic reveals clear faults in Polybius' discussion, and some of these cannot be forgiven (as Polybius attempts) in his quest for simplification. For example, he implies that the Roman magistracy (the set of officers that included the consuls, praetors, tribunes, censors, and aediles) were organized in a strict hierarchy, with the two annually elected consuls at the top of the pyramid. The reality (as Polybius partially admits in relation to the quaestors) was that these officers had different jurisdictions and prerogatives, and did not act entirely in lockstep.[93] To have dwelt on this point would have obviously diminished Polybius conclusion that the Roman republic featured a unified executive that had monarchical attributes. Polybius' account of senatorial prerogatives in the republic was quite complete, although senatorial discretion diminished over time as legislation was adopted and was followed.[94] Indeed, the whole tenor of Polybius' account is of a rigid and unyielding constitutional allocation of authority between different segments of civil society, with little flexibility.[95] He does acknowledge that when the three cohorts of political power – the leaders (consuls), aristocracy (Senate), and people – cooperated with each other, the republic was able to respond to any crisis, even Hannibal at the gates of the city.

In short, the idealized Roman constitution that Polybius presents may have been a good bit more complex and supple than would have been truly consistent with his vision of a mixed government with hermetically sealed spheres of authority between different cohorts of society.[96] Indeed, this was belied by the official style of the Roman republic, the phrase *senatus populusque Romanus* (the Senate and People of Rome), invariably rendered in the form, "SPQR." There was no unified executive that exercised monarchical powers, save during times of true crisis and the later decay of the republic. The senate as an aristocratic institution was not a real legislature. Membership in the senate was based chiefly on family ties, and only occasionally on extraordinary merit. As Andrew Lintott has observed, "The aristocratic element in the Roman republic appears in the senate's range of administrative powers in finance and foreign affairs, and its capacity to obstruct magistrates, as Polybius saw."[97]

Lastly, it has been observed that Polybius may have deliberately underplayed the role of the democratic institutions in the Roman Constitution. These had evolved from the reaction of the people to the establishment of an autocracy under the *decemviri* in around 450 BCE.[98] The college of the ten tribunes of the plebs is barely mentioned, and the role of the popular assemblies is minimized, in order for Polybius to make his later point that the republic was degenerating into a democracy and its adverse counterpoint of mob rule. The reality, of course, was that the popular assemblies in which the will of the Roman people was manifested were by no means democratic institutions in the same way as assemblies at Athens were. Such assemblies as the *comitia centuriata* and *comitia tributa* could only be summoned by a magistrate, who directed the proceedings by framing the agenda and the matters to be voted. In short, these bodies lacked any real legislative initiative.[99] By tradition and statute, the decrees of the *concilium plebis* (*plebis scita*), were binding.[100] There were also substantial limits on those who could participate in these councils, citizenship being just one requirement in some instances.[101] Despite this, the assemblies were influential and, notwithstanding Polybius' suggestion, the people were not always beholden to aristocratic interests (whether by cooptation or bribery).[102] There were, nevertheless, striking fluctuations in the powers of the popular tribunes who, on occasion, were able to exercise authority that rivaled the senate's and the leading magistrates, whereas at other times, they acquiesced to aristocratic prerogatives.[103]

Polybius, for all his historiographic faults, remained the leading narrator of the Roman republic's constitution. Cicero's writings were certainly incomplete on this subject, and it is by no means clear when Cicero was referring to the actual operation of governmental institutions and when he was substituting his preferences for an ideal constitution.[104] Cicero also may not have acknowledged his intellectual debt to Polybius, and his writings may be faulted for only being derivative of the earlier Greek historians.[105] Cicero's *De re Publica* (first circulated in 52 BCE) – a text which was only fully reconstructed in the early nineteenth century and thus would have been known to the Framing generation in fragments – briefly took issue with Polybius' theory of anacyclōsis and concluded that there was no single, one-way dynamic of political revolutions, and that oligarchy could as easily devolve into tyranny as it could mob rule.[106] In *De Legibus* (c. 52 BCE), Cicero, like Polybius, expressed wariness of the democratic elements of the Roman constitution and sought to minimize them in his narrative, or to paint a picture of their subordinate place in his idealized vision of the republic.[107] He made an explicit attack against the office of the plebian tribunes, which he called "a mischievous thing, born in civil strife and tending to civil strife."[108] Indeed, Cicero emphasizes the monarchical aspects of the constitution, what he termed the *imperium*, and the necessity of a strong executive.[109] In short, Cicero's constitutional narrative is as much blinded by his political grudges and predilections[110] as Polybius' was by his theoretical adherence to the inevitability of anacyclōsis.

It is worth briefly sketching how the theory of mixed government was transmitted to the modern political tradition.[111] As already discussed in Chapter One, Enlightenment thinkers certainly had access to Polybius, Aristotle, Xenophon, Livy, and Cicero in their original texts. Also, members of the Framing generation had the advantage of seeing glosses on mixed constitutional theory through a number of sources, chiefly, Machiavelli, Hobbes, Harrington, Montesquieu, and Blackstone.[112] Niccolò Machiavelli's *Discourses on Livy* (1531) was no less influential than his *Prince*, and both were testaments to fifteenth-century political thought. The *Discourses* contain, in book one, chapter 1, a precis of Polybius' theory of anacyclōsis.[113] Indeed, Machiavelli observed that "wiser men hold the opinion that there are six kinds of governments: three of these are very bad; three others are good in themselves but so easily corruptible that they also come to be pernicious. . . . [s]ince those men who were prudent in establishing laws recognized this defect, they avoided each of the forms by itself alone and chose a form of government that combined them all, judging such a government to be steadier and more stable, for when in the same city there is a principality, an aristocracy, and a democracy, one keeps watch over the other."[114]

Machiavelli held up Rome as the best example of a mixed constitution in antiquity, giving relatively shorter shrift to Lycurgus' constitution at Sparta.[115] But, unlike Cicero, Machiavelli had more praise for the popular institutions of the Roman republic – including the tribunes of the plebians[116] – perhaps a surprising observation in view of Machiavelli's notorious realpolitik.[117] Nonetheless, Machiavelli was careful to say that, if left unchecked, popular institutions will overwhelm other cohorts of government (particularly aristocratic organs and bodies), and this could easily lead to the overthrow of the commonwealth,[118] as occurred at Rome in the first century BCE. Finally, Machiavelli observed that a system of the grant of extraordinary but temporary powers upon an individual – a dictator (in the classical,[119] not the modern and pejorative sense) – was essential in order for republics to respond to true crises.[120] Machiavelli dwelled on the election of the decemvirate in the fifth century BCE, which was charged with making the laws (that included the famous Twelve Tables), but quickly degenerated into a tyranny, and was overthrown with the institution of a more balanced constitution.[121]

Machiavelli was thus tacitly telling the rest of the story, left uncompleted by Polybius, of the Roman republic's decline and ultimate overthrow. Machiavelli also added another element to the equation of mixed constitutionalism when he noted: "either you discuss a republic that wishes to create an empire, like Rome, or you discuss one that is satisfied to maintain itself."[122] Machiavelli suggested that a republic bent on expansion will tend to accelerate the process of conversion from aristocracy to democracy, and thence to mob rule, anarchy, and back to monarchy. A commonwealth content to remain within its own boundaries – and here he cites Sparta and Venice as examples – will be able to subsist longer, but once such polities succumb to the allure of imperialism, they will be doomed as republics.[123]

Montesquieu's *Spirit of the Laws* added yet other nuances to the Polybian canon of mixed government, discussing, in detail, Sparta's military state, Athens' commercial and popular democracy, and Rome's republic.[124] His typology of government was the division between republican, monarchical, and despotic forms.[125] Montesquieu clearly recognized the Polybian archetypes of monarchy, aristocracy, and democracy, and he was much concerned with the relative virtues exhibited by participants in each constitution.[126] For Montesquieu, the primary value of mixed government was the moderation it imposed on all segments of society. Ambition, avarice, and aggrandizement are channeled into forms that are socially useful for the commonwealth.[127] At the same time, Montesquieu restated the Machiavellian critique (first mooted by Polybius) that Athenian demagoguery, Spartan militarism, and Roman imperialism were the chief causes of the failing of republican virtues.[128] Indeed, this view was shared by the Framing generation. Hamilton observed in *Federalist* 6 that "Sparta was little better than a well-regulated camp; and Rome was never sated of carnage and conquest;"[129] Madison concluded that "the liberties of Rome proved the final victim to her military triumphs."[130] When the state lacks restraint and moderation in its objectives, it is hardly surprising that its social constituents would have a paucity of virtue.

Montesquieu also recognized the operation of this dynamic in republican Rome, and added a twist to Polybius' theory of anacyclōsis: "The government of Rome, after the expulsion of the kings, should naturally have been a democracy....and yet this did not happen....The prosperity of states is frequently greater in the insensible transition from one constitution to another than in either of those constitutions. Then it is that all the springs of government are upon the stretch, that the citizens assert their claims, that friendships or enmities are formed among the jarring parties, and that there is a noble emulation between those who defend the ancient and those who are strenuous in promoting the new constitution."[131] Rome was no protodemocracy, and certainly no liberal government in the sense used by Enlightenment philosophes: "It is necessary to observe," Montesquieu wrote, "that the three powers [monarchical, aristocratic and democratic] may be very well distributed [at Rome] in regard to the liberty of the constitution, though not so well in respect to the liberty of the subject."[132] This was crucial for Montesquieu's distinction that "[d]emocratic and aristocratic states are not in their own nature free. Political liberty is to be found only in moderate governments; and even in these it is not always found."[133]

Machiavelli's and Montesquieu's notions of mixed government were amplified and transmitted to the Framing Generation by English Enlightenment political and legal writers. English constitutionalists of the 1640s and 1650s such as John Milton, Marchamont Nedham, and Charles Dallison – who were allied with both the monarchical and parliamentary forces in the English Civil War – expounded a theory of separating legislative from executive power, and giving primacy to the former.[134] Of course, it was Thomas Hobbes, drawing extensively from Jean Bodin's *Six Books of the*

Republic (1576),[135] who articulated the most coherent theory of a single, unitary sovereignty. Hobbes's *Elements of Law* (1640) and *The Leviathan* (1651) were well known to the Framers, and although Hobbes generally disclaimed the use of ancient history and classical allegory in his writing (unlike Machiavelli and Montesquieu), there were certainly some examples of such material in his works.[136]

It was ultimately left to John Locke, writing in *Two Treatises of Government* (1690), and to James Harrington's *The Commonwealth of Oceana* (1656), to articulate a modern vision of separation of powers that would most influence the Framers.[137] Harrington, writing in response to Hobbes's *Leviathan*, noted that "[a]n equal commonwealth . . . is a government . . . arising into the superstructures or three orders, the senate debating and proposing, the people resolving, and the magistracy executing by an equal rotation through the suffrage of the people given by the ballot."[138] It was essential, according to Harrington, that an aristocratic senate be counterposed with a popular assembly. Harrington relied upon an extensive vetting of ancient history (what he called "ancient prudence") to describe the role of senates in ancient republics (more on which in Chapter 3), but he cited Thucydides' discussion of the Athenian polity for the principle of a balance between institutions of government.[139] Likewise, in Harrington's *Commonwealth*, popular assemblies had only limited power. He was sharply critical of Athenian popular democracy, while endorsing the limited constitution of popular assemblies at Sparta and Rome.[140] In this way, idioms of mixed government came to be subtly transformed into the idea of separation of powers. In any event, for writers such as Harrington, the inspiration was classical antiquity.

Metaphors of mixed government made a return in English constitutional thought with the 1734 publication of Henry St. John Viscount Bolingbroke's *A Dissertation Upon Parties*.[141] He endorsed a "mixture of monarchical, aristocratical and democratical power, blended together in one system, and by these three estates balancing one another. . . ."[142] Quoting Tacitus, Bolingbroke observed that the enduring problem of mixed government was "how to fix that just proportion of each [social cohort], how to hit that happy temperament of them all in one system. . . ."[143] Bolingbroke's critique of the constitution of the Roman republic (as distinct from the later empire) was that it lacked an effective monarchical element.[144] Roman political life during the republic, as described by Bolingbroke, was always characterized by the social conflict between the patrician and plebian orders, especially over agrarian reform.[145] "When the [Roman] senate was inflexible," Bolingbroke wrote, "the people had immediate recourse to sedition. When the people was refractory, the senate had recourse to a dictator."[146]

William Blackstone, in his *Commentaries on the Laws of England*, gave a tip of the hat to Polybius' tripartite schematic of government, although without mentioning him by name. But "the antients," he wrote, "had in general no idea of another permanent form of government" other than monarchy, aristocracy, and democracy.[147] Indeed, Blackstone attributed to Tacitus the quite pessimistic idea that "mixed government, formed out of them all, and partaking of the advantages of each, as a visionary whim, and one that, if effected, could never be lasting or secure."[148] From these premises, Blackstone proceeded to laud the unwritten English constitution that balanced the interests of the monarchy (Crown), aristocracy (reflected in the House of Lords), and democracy (the House of Commons).[149] This, he declared, was a "singular constitution, selected and compounded from the . . . three usual species of government."[150] David Hume had much the same views, emphasizing the power and fractiousness of the Roman popular assemblies.[151]

With this classical and Enlightenment pedigree it should come as no surprise that the concept of mixed government was profoundly influential for the Framing generation, especially as transmitted through the works of Montesquieu and Blackstone. The leading Polybian exponent among the American political leadership of the time certainly had to be John Adams.[152] Writing in his *Defence of the Constitutions of the United States*, which was avidly read by the delegates at the Philadelphia Convention,[153] Adams indicates that among the "opinions and reasonings of philosophers, politicians and historians, who have taken the most extensive views of men and societies, whose characters are deservedly revered, and whose writings were in the contemplation of those framed the American constitutions[,] [i]t will not be contested that all these characters are united in Polybius. . . . "[154] Likewise, Thomas Jefferson was an enthusiastic reader of Polybius and a cautious supporter of mixed government, although he criticized the Roman republic with its "heavy-handed unfeeling aristocracy, over a people ferocious, and rendered desperate by poverty and wretchedness."[155] The "testimony of Polybius" figures prominently also in Madison's *Federalist* 63,[156] and (as shall be seen presently) in the separation of powers discussion in *Federalist* 47. Invocations of the precept of mixed government were made at the Philadelphia Convention,[157] and at some of the state ratifying conventions.[158]

Nonetheless, Adams felt himself at liberty to disagree with some of Polybius' premises and conclusions.[159] He appeared, for example, to take issue with Polybius' view of the inevitability of political change. Adams recognized that Polybius at least was "more charitable in his representation of human nature than Hobbes, Mandeville, Rochefoucauld, Machiavel,

Beccaria, Rousseau, [and] de Lolme."[160] Adams noted that "[t]he generation and corruption of governments, which may, in other words, be called the progress and course of human passions in society ... are very much to our purpose, to show the utility and necessity of different *orders* of men, and an *equilibrium* of powers and privileges. They demonstrate the corruptibility of every species of simple government, by which I mean a power without a check, whether in one, a few, or many."[161]

Despite this, Adams believed in the perfectability of government and believed that Polybius' model of a mixed constitution could be further refined: "The constitutions of several of the United States, it is hoped, will prove themselves improvements both upon the Roman, the Spartan, and the English commonwealths."[162] He expressed the sincere hope that "the institutions now made in America will not wholly wear out for thousands of years."[163] Adams was cognizant of the mortality of ancient constitutions, notwithstanding their adherence to mixed precepts.[164] That is why, undoubtedly, he sought to find errors and omissions in the operation of Roman, Spartan, and Carthaginian government. Adams regarded the Carthaginian charter, though similar to some of the new constitutions of the American states, as flawed because it lacked a strong executive that could mediate between the popular assemblies and the senate. The Spartan constitution of Lycurgus – although the longest-lived of antiquity – Adams viewed as being premised on unsustainable values of martial glory, competition, austerity, and unquestioned allegiance to the state. He barely even credits the Athenian constitution of Solon as being worthy of consideration.[165] Yet Adams later argued in his *Discourses on Davila* (published in 1790), that "a Balance, with all its difficulty, must be preserved, or liberty is lost forever. Perhaps a perfect balance, if it ever existed, has not been long maintained in its perfection; yet, such a balance as has been sufficient to liberty, has been supported in some nations for many centuries together."[166]

There were members of the Framing generation who were skeptical of the application of mixed government precepts to American constitutionalism. After all, no one was seriously suggesting a reinstitution of monarchy or the constitutional recognition of an aristocratic class of people. James Wilson kept his doubts on this point quiet at the Philadelphia Convention, but when the proposed Constitution later came under attack, at the Pennsylvania Ratifying Convention, as being antidemocratic, he was compelled to agree that a mixed constitution would be an "improper government for the United States ... because it is suited to an establishment of different orders of men." In order to reconcile political theory with the impelling need to ratify the Constitution, Wilson observed: "What is the nature and kind of government which has been proposed for the United States by the late Convention? In principle, it is purely democratical. But the principle is applied in different forms, in order to obtain the advantages, and exclude the inconveniences, of the simple modes of government."[167] Wilson was well aware that the Antifederalist forces would ruthlessly exploit the classical rhetoric and exemplars of mixed government as a way to portray the Constitution as a vehicle for imposing an oligarchy on the country.[168] Because of his scholarly use of arguments based on mixed government principles in his *Defence* and *Discourses*, John Adams was always dogged by the charge that he was a secret advocate of hereditary monarchy and a landed aristocracy.[169]

It is thus one of the great ironies of the Framing period that those who most enthusiastically supported mixed government as a crucial theoretical insight in the drafting of the Constitution would later denounce it as fundamentally antidemocratic. This later became one of the intellectual battle fronts in the political conflict between the newly formed Federalist and Democratic-Republican parties. Jefferson quickly saw the political liabilities of uttering any theory that even had the whiff of aristocratic favor, and he was quick to repudiate Montesquieu's version of the mixed constitution and could, by 1816, write that the Roman republic never knew "one single day of free and rational government" and that "the introduction of [the] new principle of representative democracy has rendered useless almost anything written before on the structure of government."[170] James Madison would also disavow his position at Philadelphia, and by 1791 – when he was serving as Jefferson's political lieutenant – sharply criticized Adams and the Federalists.[171] When, in 1821, he began organizing his notes of the Philadelphia Convention for posthumous publication, Madison made sure to include a *mea culpa* for his advocacy of mixed government as a reason to support property qualifications for electors of members of the House of Representatives.[172] The intellectual rout against the influence of mixed government principles in American politics was complete by the time John Taylor's volume, *An Inquiry into the Principles of the Government of the United States* was published in 1814.[173] Any suggestion of balancing government between monarchical, aristocratic, and popular interests would have been regarded as reactionary, if not outright laughable, by the Jacksonian revolution of the 1830s.

The enduring legacy of the ancient theory of mixed constitutions thus came to be manifested in the notion of separation of powers. If mixed government speaks to maintaining the equilibrium between divergent social cohorts, separation of powers is concerned both with the checks and balances between the actual institutions of constitutional government (what we might call distribution of powers), and the fundamental differentiation of governmental functions (legislative, executive, and judicial) that is essential for promoting good government and safeguarding individual liberties. As already indicated in this chapter, it was certainly possible for the Framers to pull these distinct strands of thought out of the writings of classical authors. Aristotle, in his *Politics*, made this formulation of good government:

> All forms of constitution then have three factors in reference to which the good lawgiver has to consider what is expedient for each constitution; and of these factors are well-ordered the constitution must of necessity be well-ordered, and the superiority of one constitution over another necessarily consists in the superiority of each of these factors. Of these three factors one is, what is to be the body that deliberates about common interests, second the one connected with the magistracies, that is, what they are to be and what matters they are to control, and what is to be the method of their election, and a third is, what is to be the judiciary.[174]

From Aristotle's *Athenian Constitution*, it was later known that the Council was barred from passing sentences of death (such being reserved to differently constituted juries), and that the appointment of courts was a function of separate institutions.[175] So even in the heavily unicameral and unitary model of the Athenian extreme democracy, there were some notional limits on the exercise of authority by particular institutions, designed as a check on popular excesses or the abuse of power by individuals or cabals. Certainly in the classical literature on the Spartan government, there was evidence of an implied system of distribution of powers between the hereditary dual monarchy, the ephors selected for 1-year terms, and the permanent body of elders (elected for life) in the georusia.[176]

From Polybius and Livy, it was possible to piece together details of the prerogatives and functions of different Roman political bodies and magistrates (the senate, popular assemblies, consuls, and other officers).[177] The senate had a privileged place in the constitutional scheme of Roman government during the republic because it was the only true deliberative body, delivering advice to magistrates (*consilium*) as well as formal resolutions (*senatus consulta*).[178] The popular assemblies (the comitia centuriata, comitia tributa, and comitia curiata[179]) were primarily convened to discuss a set agenda or to ratify or reject an already agreed-upon course of action. The senate was also the corporate body that could purport to claim additional responsibilities and functions over time, but, interestingly, the power to create legislation of general application was never one of these. With certain narrow exceptions, such general legislation (in the fields of criminal law or private law) was the province of the popular assemblies, although one must imagine that the drafting of these was left to smaller committees, probably controlled by the same aristocratic factions that dominated the senate. Interestingly, though, the senate in 98 BCE, through the *lex Caecilia Didia*, sought to exercise a veto over legislation enacted by other bodies.[180]

The analytically distinct concept of separation of powers obviously must flow from an antecedent idea: that the councils and officers of state have clearly defined authority. In the Roman republic the notion of *potestas* was clearly seen as the proper limit of the jurisdiction and capacity of an official, as legitimized by law (*lex*) or custom (*consuetudo* and *mos*).[181] Combined with potestas was the ceremonial right of coercion (*coercitio*), which involved the display of the *fasces* (the symbol of authority of the republic) and the use of the lictors to command obedience to the officer's orders and decrees.[182] The highest form of potestas was *imperium*, which referred to the holding of a military command, but which could also confer upon the holder certain judicial authority as well.[183] In truth, judicial power in the Roman republic was split among a bewildering array of officials, exercising a variety of jurisdictions, but generally speaking, the praetors held much of the competence over civil disputes, whereas they shared that power with the consuls and popular bodies over the hearing of criminal charges.

For the high magistrates of the republic, another structural limit on power was the institutional check of colleagueship (*collegio*): there were always two consuls, two censors, and (after 242 BCE) at least two or more praetors.[184] With the exception of certain acts that required the concurrence of both sets of magistrates (such as the censors stripping an individual of his citizenship[185]), potestas resided in the individual officeholder. Among the consuls, some additional priority was given to the *consul prior* (the one who held the first monthly office because of seniority by virtue of age, previous service as consul, or the first to achieve the requisite votes for election).[186] Essentially, those (such as consuls) who shared the same potestas alternated in authority, typically on an every-other-month arrangement. (There was an exception to this during military campaigns, and, besides, it was rare for two consuls to take the field in the same campaign; they were usually assigned different theaters of war (*provincia*).[187]) One magistrate could, depending on the situation, obstruct the exercise of the authority of his colleague, simply by countermanding an order in the following month. Disputes were resolved by agreement among the consuls, the performance of auspices, or (more practically) the drawing of lots. Although the multiplicity of office was originally intended as a pragmatic solution to finding enough leadership to make decisions, it did evolve into a self-consciously designed system of checks and balances.[188]

The Roman consuls clearly exercised a bundle of authority that approximated executive power. They were the senior magistrates of the republic and could, within grounds provided for by law, obstruct the decisions of junior officers (provided that such were within the potestas of the consulship). Although they were primarily selected for their military prowess in the field, they were burdened with duties of local administration at Rome and in the Latin homeland.[189] Among these was consultation on foreign affairs and budgetary questions with the senate, and also the supervision of the apparatus of justice (which was primarily the responsibility of those praetors based in Rome). There was no real structural concept of judicial independence in ancient Rome. The crucial judicial office of the republic – the praetor – was an executive function. It was the praetor who allowed for the maintenance of a civil action, and he could also influence the bringing of a criminal indictment. Nonetheless, the judges (*iudex*) and jury bodies (the *recuperatores, consillium*, and assembly bodies) for these legal proceedings were drawn from the ranks of the aristocratic class of legal experts (*iurisprudentes*) or the wider citizen rolls.[190]

Another structural check was the method of election or selection of the key officers of the Roman republic. Although the distinction between patricians and plebians (nonnoble families) was crucial to the principle of the Roman mixed constitution, after the fourth century BCE virtually every office was available to member of the *equites* and common classes.[191] In 367 BCE the first plebian was elected to the consulship, and after 342 BCE the custom was that at least one consul had to be from among the people (in 172 BCE, and after, there were some years where two plebians were elected).[192] Generally, the primary impediment to plebian dominance of the magistracies of the republic was the well-respected custom – codified by the dictator Sulla's reforms of 81 BCE – that individuals had to achieve a certain age to qualify for particular offices (the quaestorship was 30, for the praetorship 39, and the consulship 42),[193] and to have served in more junior posts before being considered for higher offices. This progression in officeholding was known as the *cursus honorum* (literally, "the race for offices").[194] The highest offices (the consuls and praetors) were elected by the *comitia centuriata*, in which (it is speculated) a weighted voting system was used that favored the propertied classes, as well as older (and, presumably, wiser) voters.[195] Last, there was a clear social stratification in force for elections to high offices. In the approximately 400 years of the Roman republic, only on fifteen occasions was a man elected as consul who had no senatorial forebears.[196]

The members of the senate were qualified and appointed by a process (*lectio*) overseen by the censors, and the number in that body approximated three hundred, at least in the later republic period. Full membership in the senate (*senior*) was only possible by having served in a high magistracy, and otherwise received the censor's approbation of "those permitted to deliver their opinion in the senate."[197] Interestingly, no explicit property qualification for senators was imposed until the time of Augustus and the Principate. It was thus possible, from an early time, for plebians to be selected for senate membership.[198] The criterion for membership in the senate during the republic was age, officerial experience, and good moral character (as adjudged by the censors).[199] In order to ensure a supply of individuals who could sit in the senate and to lend assistance with the discharge of its duties (such as delegations abroad and investigations), the body co-opted younger men (*iuniores*), usually those who would qualify for senatorial rank, but for not having attained the requisite age.[200] When conditions required – as with the literal decimation of the Roman aristocratic ranks after the battle of Cannae – membership in the senate could be replenished by adjusting the office qualifications (to permit those who had held only more junior posts) and drawing from the equestrian class of society. The Senate was organized into classes according to rank, based usually on the highest offices previously held by the member (such that retired consuls had precedence over ex-aediles). Speaking in the senate was by seniority. For much of the history of the republic, the senate was presided over by one chosen as among the oldest and most respected members (the *princeps senatus*), or by a selected chair, although technically the senate could only be summoned and transact formal business by a sitting magistrate invested with imperium – usually a consul or the *praetor urbanus*.[201] Voting, although rare in the senate (because of the search for consensus), was by division.

The last element in the Roman conception of separation of powers involves the prerogatives of the college of ten tribunes of the people (*tribunus plebis*). This office was the product of the Conflict of the Orders in the early republic,[202] and was a fixture of the constitution after 457 BCE. Qualified and elected from the plebian class (although patrician-born men could serve if they had been legally adopted into plebian families), the tribunes exercised a variety of functions.[203] They chaired assemblies of the plebians, which had a limited initiative in framing popular legislation, *plebescita*, which could be given general application (in most periods of the republic) even without ratification by the senate. The tribunes also had prosecutorial responsibility in trials of treason (*perduellio*).[204] Tribunes had the right to appear ex officio in the senate and initiate matters.[205]

Actually, the tribunes' most famous attribute was their power of obstruction in the senate and popular assemblies, and over the decisions of the high magistrates of the republic. This was referred to generally as *intercessio*, but in the specific context of the negativing of legislation or decrees, it was known, of course, as the veto. Polybius famously observed that "if a single one of the tribunes interposes, the senate is unable to decide finally about any matter, and cannot even meet to hold sittings."[206] The tribunes could forestall the enactment of legislation from the popular assemblies,[207] although a tribune could not really block the election of a magistrate or official.[208] Finally, the tribunes (sometimes, only after consulting as a group) could intercede on behalf of a plebian by way of an appeal or avoidance of a criminal punishment, what was called *auxilium* (or sometimes, *provocatio*), a right exercisable within Rome (marked by the first milestone outside the city walls, the *pomerium*).[209] Intercessio in all of these forms depended on the tribune's legal and religious sacrosanctity – he, along with his junior associate, the plebian aedile, was quite literally immune from interference, on pain of death.[210] Under such leaders as the Gracchi brothers, the tribunate could exercise substantial power; under such opportunists as Sulpicius (Marius's crony) it could verge on the tyrannical. For much of the republic's history, plebian tribunes could aspire to the higher offices of praetor and consul, although during the period of Sulla's reforms (81–70 BCE), the powers of the tribunate were decreased and holders could not seek higher office.[211]

From this description of the Roman Constitution in the middle and late republic periods (the third and second centuries BCE), it is apparent that although there may have been a classical understanding of a division of authority between various institutions of government, and also of a sense of the need for checks and balances between those offices and bodies (and the social cohorts they represented), there was no true separation of powers in the sense we understand today. Legislative authority (meaning the power to initiate binding laws) was dispersed among a variety of assemblies, the senate, and some magistracies.[212] Executive power was more concentrated, but there was hardly a unified executive. Judicial authority was exercised both by the magistrates (the praetors), and the assemblies, with no provision for a truly distinct and independent judiciary. Powers in the idealized Roman Constitution may have been allocated to different offices and councils, but there was no separation of executive, legislative, and judicial functions and certainly no prohibition on the same magistrate or body exercising more than one of those prerogatives.

The Framing generation was well aware of the limitations of the classical canon in this regard. Roman, Spartan, Athenian, and Carthaginian institutions might have provided guidance on the allocation of authority among government institutions as a system of checks and balances (more on which later in this Chapter), but not as a true separation of power. John Adams could observe in his *Defence* that there were only three major discoveries about the "constitution of a free government" made after the time of Polybius, but they are awesomely significant: "[r]epresentations, instead of collections, of the people; a total separation of the executive and legislative power, and of the judicial from both; and a balance in the legislature, by three independent, equal branches. . . . "[213] Moreover, Adams wrote that the Roman republic – at least as related by Polybius – was flawed in precisely this respect: "The distribution of power was . . . never accurately or judiciously made in that constitution. The executive was never sufficiently separated from the legislative, nor had these powers a control upon each other defined with sufficient accuracy. The executive had not the power to interpose and decide between the people and the senate."[214]

Even more specifically, Adams saw the defect in the Roman Constitution's assumption that a mixed government (representing different social segments) was the same thing as a constitution that imposed effective checks and balances on the abuse of power. In referring to Manlius Valerius' speech in the senate (advocating greater power to the plebians), as reported in Dionysisus of Halicarnassus' *Roman Antiquities*,[215] Adams observed:

> It is surprising that Valerius should talk of an equal mixture of monarchical, aristocratical, and democratical powers, in a commonwealth where they were so unevenly mixed as they were in Rome. There can be no equal mixture without a negative in each branch of the legislature. . . . The consuls in Rome had no negative; the people had a negative, but a very unequal one, because [they did not have] the same time and opportunity for cool deliberation. The appointment of tribunes was a very inadequate remedy. What match for a Roman senate was a single magistrate seated among them? . . . . It is really astonishing that such people as Greeks and Romans should have ever thought that four or five ephori [in Sparta], or a single tribune, or a college of ten tribunes [in Rome], an adequate representation of themselves. . . . [216]

The Framing generation thus quickly moved from the political abstraction and irrelevancy of the idea that governmental institutions somehow authentically "represented" social groups (such as the senate embodying an aristocracy). To this end, they hardly needed the insights of Whig constitutionalists or Enlightenment *philosophes*.[217] When Montesquieu observed that "[w]hen the legislative and executive powers are united in the same person, or in the same body of magistrates, there can then be no liberty.... [and] there is no liberty, if the power of judging be not separated from the legislative and executive,"[218] the Founders were already well aware of this lesson based on their colonial experiences with conflicts between provincial governors, councils, and assemblies.[219] The problem for the Framers was to design a national government where functions and powers were distinct and separate, but under the revolutionary precept of popular sovereignty.[220] In any event, the articulation of the broad principle of separation of powers had already been accomplished in the state constitutions adopted after 1776.[221] Perhaps the most articulate expression of this was in the Bill of Rights to the 1784 New Hampshire Constitution (still in force to this day): "In the government of this state, the three essential powers thereof, to wit, the legislative, executive and judicial, ought to be kept as separate from and independence of each other, as the nature of free government will admit, or as is consistent with that chain of connection that binds the whole fabric of the constitution in one indissoluble bond of union and amity."[222]

Although other aspects of the federal Constitution's separation of powers will be considered in the next chapter, it suffices to mention here that the final version of the Constitutional text at least rhetorically adheres to the principle. Each branch of the government is the subject of its own Article in the Constitution, and each begins with a clause that allocates or "vests" the respective legislative, executive, and judicial powers.[223] Even though there is a substantial interplay between the branches – especially with the appointment of personnel to staff the various branches (senatorial confirmation of executive branch appointees and presidential appointment of judges, with the advice and consent of the senate, are just two examples) – the functions of the branches are not often conflated. Indeed, an early proposal made at Philadelphia to introduce into the constitutional structure a "Council of Revision," consisting of members of the executive and judiciary and which would have reviewed acts of Congress, was rejected precisely because it would have, in James Wilson's view, improperly "mixed" judicial and executive functions.[224] Interestingly, James Madison supported this innovation because "[a]n association of Judges in this revisionary function would both double the advantage and diminish the danger. It would also enable the Judiciary Department to better defend itself against Legislative encroachments."[225] Despite Madison's plea, a proposal for a Council of Revision – a fourth branch of government – was defeated, to be replaced with the Presidential prerogative to veto congressional legislation (subject to an override). And, as is well known, no provision in the Constitution expressly granted a judicial power to review legislation, aside from the general vesting of "judicial Power" in the courts. That was developed later in American jurisprudence, finally culminating in Chief Justice John Marshall's opinion in *Marbury v. Madison*.[226]

James Madison would have cause to vigorously defend the draft Constitution's adherence to separations of powers principles. In *Federalist 47* he lauded this "invaluable precept in the science of politics," and gave credit to Montesquieu "who is always consulted and cited on this subject. . . . [even] if he be not the author" of the theory.[227] Madison was obliged to respond to "[o]ne of the principal objections inculcated by the more respectable adversaries to the Constitution, is its supposed violation of the political maxim, that the legislative, executive, and judiciary departments ought to be separate and distinct. In the structure of the federal government, no regard, it is said, seems to have been paid to this essential precaution in favor of liberty. The several departments of power are distributed and blended in such a manner as at once to destroy all symmetry and beauty of form, and to expose some of the essential parts of the edifice to the danger of being crushed by the disproportionate weight of other parts."[228]

Madison was compelled to attack this critique at its theoretical roots. After canvassing the provisions of the state constitutions then in force, he noted that "notwithstanding the emphatical and, in some instances, the unqualified terms in which this axiom has been laid down, there is not a single instance in which the several departments of power have been kept absolutely separate and distinct."[229] Madison could nevertheless conclude that the federal Constitution avoided the key failings of the earlier state constitutions, and was closer in execution to the true meaning of the separation of powers principle enunciated by Montesquieu, and, presumably, by earlier classical writers.[230] For Madison, the separation of powers principle was vindicated where "the powers properly belonging to one of the departments ought not to be directly and completely administered by either of the other departments. It is equally evident, that none of them ought to possess, directly or indirectly, an overruling influence over the others, in the administration of their respective powers."[231] Indeed, Madison concluded, "unless these departments be so far connected and blended as to give to each a constitutional control over the others, the degree of separation which the maxim requires, as essential to a free government, can never in practice be duly maintained."[232]

The Framing generation viewed separation of powers principles as the practical application of the concept of mixed government. This amalgamating of constitutional metaphors clearly posed uncomfortable problems for the Framers, as Gary Wills has observed.[233] The important point is that they viewed this problem as admitting a solution from experience only; theory was but of limited help. In the constitutional debates in 1787 and 1788 the primary sources for evidence of balanced and stable government was that under the British system of the eighteenth century, the state constitutions ordained after 1776, and the experience of ancient republics. It is now worth turning to the Framers' perception of classical republicanism, at least insofar as that concept was distinct from mixed government and separation of powers.

C. CIVIC REPUBLICANISM

One fundamental dilemma facing the Framing generation was whether the classical model of a republic was even achievable for America.[234] On this point, Montesquieu's extended discussion was regarded as accurate – and immensely problematic:

> It is natural for a republic to have only a small territory; otherwise it cannot long subsist. In an extensive republic there are men of large fortunes, and consequently of less moderation; there are trusts too considerable to be placed in any single subject ....
>
>   In an extensive republic the public good is sacrificed to a thousand private views; it is subordinate to exceptions, and depends on accidents. In a small one, the interest of the public is more obvious, better understood, and more within reach of every citizen; abuses have less extent, and of course are less protected.
>
>   ....
>   If a republic be small, it is destroyed by a foreign force; if it be large, it is ruined by internal imperfection.[235]

These remarks were Montesquieu's reaction to Machiavelli's maxim that "either you discuss a republic that wishes to create an empire, like Rome, or you discuss one that is satisfied to maintain itself."[236]

   In view of this gloss on the classical republican tradition, the Framers were on the horns of an awful dilemma. A union of the American states would seem to dictate either the situation that Montesquieu feared (having the commonwealth rent apart by internal class divisions), or set the United States on the ill-fated course for empire. Retaining localized sovereignties in the fourteen states of 1787 would have made them ripe for the picking by avaricious colonial powers, not the least of which would be a vengeful Great Britain. Worst of all, James Madison noted in *Federalist* 9, "we shall be driven to the alternative either of seeking refuge at once in the arms of monarchy, or of splitting ourselves into an infinity of little, jealous, clashing, tumultuous commonwealths, the wretched nurseries of unceasing discord and the miserable objects of universal pity or contempt."[237]

This argument indeed proved to be a cudgel in the hands of the Antifederalists. George Clinton of New York, writing as Cato, certainly echoed this fear in an essay published in October 1787.[238] Among the Antifederalist forces, the ever-anonymous Brutus, also writing in New York, was deeply pessimistic: "History furnishes no example of a free republic, anything like the extent of the United States. The Grecian republics were of small extent, so also was that of the Romans. Both of these, it is true, on process of time, extended their conquests over large territories of country; and the consequence was, that their governments were changed from that of free governments to those of the most tyrannical that ever existed in the world."[239] Samuel Bryan, writing as "Centinel" in February 1788, echoed the same point: "the testimony of experience, the opinions of the most celebrated writers, and the nature of the case demonstrated in the clearest manner that so extensive a territory as the United States could not be governed by any other mode than a confederacy of republics...."[240] It was the academic eccentric, James Winthrop (1752–1821), writing as "Agrippa," who put the sharpest point on this riposte: "the ideal of an uncompounded republic, on an average one thousand miles in length and eight hundred in breadth, and containing six millions of white inhabitants all reduced to the same standard of morals, of habits, and laws, is in itself an absurdity, and contrary to the whole experience of mankind."[241]

John Stevens, Jr. (1749–1838), writing as "Americanus," attempted to defuse this Antifederalist screed based on Montesquieu's maxim. "Wretched indeed," he wrote,

> would be our political institution, had we been governed by the 'axioms' of European writers on politics.... Montesquieu tells us that *a Republic must have only a small territory*. But how, I would ask, would he, or Locke, or any other political writer in Europe, be warranted in insisting on this assertion as *an irrefragable axiom?* ... Montesquieu's maxim may be just, for aught I know, when applied to such republican Governments as Sparta. This commonwealth affords us a striking instance of the absurdities mankind is capable of when they blindly submit themselves to the guidance of passion and prejudice. Had we not the undoubted evidence of history, it could never be believed, at this time of day, that such a monstrous political prodigy could really have existed. This institution was founded upon Montesquieu's principle of Republican Government, viz. virtue: by virtue, here, is not meant morality; but an enthusiastic attachment to the political system of the country we inhabit. By the force of this mistaken

principle, however, the Government, which Lycurgus established in Sparta, was supported for ages. It is unnecessary for me to attempt a delineation of this wonderful institution, against which the feelings of humanity, every generous sentiment of the human heart, revolt with horror.[242]

Indeed, Americanus sought to turn Machiavelli and Montesquieu on their respective heads:

'A Republic must have only a small territory, otherwise it cannot long subsist.' But I utterly deny the truth of this 'axiom' of the celebrated civilian. . . . A collection of smaller States, united under one federal head, by a Constitution of Government similar to the one at present under consideration, is capable of a greater degree of real permanent liberty, than any combination of power I can form an idea of. . . . The gusts of passion, which faction is ever blowing up in 'a small territory,' lose their force before they reach the seat of Federal Government. Republics, limited to a small territory, ever have been, and, from the nature of man, ever will be, liable to be torn to pieces by faction. When the citizens are confined within a narrow compass, as was the case of Sparta, Rome, etc., it is within the power of a factious demagogue to scatter sedition and discontent, instantaneously, through every part of the State.[243]

Ultimately, Stevens sought a reconciliation of his views with those of Montesquieu for a thoroughly instrumental end: "to deprive [his Antifederalist foes] of the assistance of this powerful auxiliary, on this occasion at least."[244] The trick was to distinguish the classical precedents that Montesquieu was using: "Should I be able to prove that the Governments of these [ancient] States were founded on principles totally different from those which Montesquieu here had in view, it will then be manifest that Cato has lugged him into a controversy in which he is in no ways concerned."[245] Americanus referred again to the near-totalitarian aspects of the Spartan regime: "The life of a citizen was one continued effort of self-denial and restraint."[246] Although the Romans did not go so far, that republic's constitution seemed to allow magistrates "inspecting into the lives and conduct of every citizen – the public good superceded every consideration of a private nature. . . ."[247] Americanus concludes in distinguishing the fundamentally illiberal nature of ancient republics: "As from the very nature of this sort of Government there can be no regular checks established for preventing the abuse of power, the people are in great measure constrained to rely on the patriotism and virtue of those citizens who compose the Government . . . Without a due attention to these distinctive properties of Republics of antiquity, we cannot form an adequate idea of the immense advantages of a representative legislature. The people of Rome, of Sparta, etc., were obliged to keep a constant eye on the conduct of their rulers for this reason, and that they might be enabled to exercise their right of a personal vote on public affairs, it was absolutely necessary that the citizens be confined within a small compass."[248]

John Stevens's "Americanus" is a significant figure in the intellectual landscape – he is among the very few ardent Federalists who was (publicly, at least) an anticlassicist. His writings offer perhaps the most cogent view expressed on the relative merits of ancient republics. Without some organ of governmental representation of the People, a republic could not grow large without tyranny. Neither the Spartan gerousia or citizen meetings, nor the Roman senate or popular assemblies, qualified in this respect. Perhaps even more subversively, Americanus was critical of classical republican virtues, traits that other members of the Framing generation regularly lauded. Stevens saw ancient republican virtue as potentially exclusionary, atavistic, aggressive, and authoritarian.[249] In this way, he echoed the thoughts of Noah Webster, who wrote under the pen name "Citizen of America":

> Montesquieu supposed virtue to be the principle of a republic. He derived his notions of this form of government, from the astonishing firmness, courage and patriotism which distinguished the republics of Greece and Rome. This virtue consisted in pride, contempt of strangers and martial enthusiasm which sometimes displayed itself in defence of their country. These principles are never permanent – they decay with refinement, intercourse with other nations, and increase of wealth. No wonder then that these republics declined, for they were not founded on fixed principles; and hence authors imagine that republics cannot be durable.[250]

Instead, Webster would have stressed, as essential to republican virtue, the widespread "possession of real property in fee-simple."[251] Property ownership would thus replace stern virtue as the cornerstone of the American republic.

The last aspect of Stevens's writing as Americanus is its eery resonance[252] with James Madison's celebrated[253] discourse, in *Federalist* 10, on the dangers of faction in the commonwealth and the republican cure:

> the greater number of citizens and extent of territory which may be brought within the compass of republican than of democratic government; and it is this circumstance principally which renders factious combinations less to be dreaded in the former than in the latter. The smaller the society, the fewer probably will be the distinct parties and interests composing it; the fewer the distinct parties and interests, the more frequently will a majority be found of the same party; and the smaller the number of individuals

composing a majority, and the smaller the compass within which they are placed, the more easily will they concert and execute their plans of oppression. Extend the sphere, and you take in a greater variety of parties and interests; you make it less probable that a majority of the whole will have a common motive to invade the rights of other citizens; or if such a common motive exists, it will be more difficult for all who feel it to discover their own strength, and to act in unison with each other. Besides other impediments, it may be remarked that, where there is a consciousness of unjust or dishonorable purposes, communication is always checked by distrust in proportion to the number whose concurrence is necessary.

Hence, it clearly appears, that the same advantage which a republic has over a democracy, in controlling the effects of faction, is enjoyed by a large over a small republic, – is enjoyed by the Union over the States composing it.[254]

This was the ultimate reproof of Montesquieu's small republic axiom.[255] And although *Federalist* 10 does not contain any discussion of ancient history, other essays by Publius do.[256] Indeed, Madison in *Federalist* 14 went so far as to slyly attack Montesquieu's competence as an historian:

> A democracy, consequently, will be confined to a small spot. A republic may be extended over a large region.
>
> [In opposition to this thesis] may be added the artifice of some celebrated authors, whose writings have had a great share in forming the modern standard of political opinions. Being subjects either of an absolute or limited monarchy, they have endeavored to heighten the advantages, or palliate the evils of those forms, by placing in comparison the vices and defects of the republican, and by citing as specimens of the latter the turbulent democracies of ancient Greece and modern Italy. Under the confusion of names, it has been an easy task to transfer to a republic observations applicable to a democracy only; and among others, the observation that it can never be established but among a small number of people, living within a small compass of territory.[257]

In short, Madison is suggesting here that any reliance on the experiences of ancient Greek *poleis* for the "small republic" thesis is bound to be in error because these polities were actually democracies, and not republics. But Madison was guilty of his own form of generalization because, assuredly, very few of the Greek poleis were true democracies or even had substantial democratic features. The Spartan constitution under the Lycurgan model, which Madison would have been undoubtedly familiar from his classical reading, was by no stretch of the imagination a democracy. So while Madison's rebuttal of Montesquieu was novel and effective, it can hardly be complimented for its historic accuracy.[258] Nevertheless, Madison's point found a second in the writing of James Winthrop as Agrippa, who commented that "Republicanism appears [in Greece and Rome] in its most disadvantageous form. Arts and domestic employments were generally committed to slaves, while war was almost the only business worthy of a citizen. Hence arose their internal dissensions."[259]

Madison seems also to have been equating a "true" republic with the use of representative bodies. Here, he was aware of a key historic trend: "The scheme of representation as a substitute for a meeting of the citizens in person being at most but very imperfectly known to ancient polity, it is more modern times only that we are to expect instructive examples."[260] Indeed, at least within the context of individual *poleis*, the ancient Greeks had no word for such a representative body.[261] Although Madison later acknowledged that "the position regarding the ignorance of the ancient governments on the subject of representation is by no means precisely true in the latitude commonly given it,"[262] for Madison, representation was the crucial ingredient that allowed republics to break from the spatial limitations of Montesquieu's axiom. Greater size for the American republic – as organized under a federal, not a national, scheme[263] – could not only be more stable, but also better preserve liberty and security, than any other form of political arrangement.[264]

The Framing generation was thus obliged to adopt some crucial ideas from classical republicanism, while also rejecting others. As Meyer Reinhold has observed, the Framers were right to regard "the definitive modalities and values" of ancient republics: "commonwealths of small territorial size with socially and culturally homogenous populations; . . . enjoy[ing] a good measure of self-sufficiency through basic agricultural economies; they inculcate and manage a frugal lifestyle; they are adverse to an economy based on commerce; and strive for maximum stability, being distrustful of dynamic change. Above all, they were deemed moral communities with a strong sense of the primacy of community and subordination of personal interest to the good of the whole."[265]

By contrast, the American commonwealth had to accommodate a large territory, a diverse and growing populace, an aggressively commercial class, and citizens that would likely be fractious, self-seeking, and expect a high degree of personal comfort and private autonomy.[266] John Adams could thus write in 1785 that "[o]ur countrymen may be the nearest [to republican citizens], but there is so much wealth among them, and such a universal rage of avarice, that I often fear they . . . will become like the rest of the world."[267] Alexander Hamilton observed at the Philadelphia Convention that "[h]e acknowledged himself not to think favorably of Republican Government. . . . It was certainly true that nothing like an equality of property existed: than an inequality would exist as long as liberty existed, and that it would unavoidably result from that very liberty itself. This inequality of property constituted the great and fundamental distinction in Society."[268] Lastly, and most importantly, because of their colonial and revolutionary experiences, Americans had a high degree of distrust, fear, and (even) contempt for the exercise of governmental power.[269]

This may partially explain the attraction of the mercantile republic model for the Framing generation. If Rome was too particularistic and martial, and the Spartans were too brutal and austere, that left such ancient polities as Carthage worthy of consideration. John Adams praised Carthage as a commercial republic that managed, until its final days, to remain "untainted with luxury and venality" and "their frugality of manners and integrity in elections."[270] As James Winthrop's Agrippa observed: "we find Carthage cultivating commerce, and extending her dominions for the long space of seven centuries, during which time the internal tranquility was never disturbed by her citizens. Her national power was so respected, that for a long time it was doubtful whether Carthage or Rome should rule."[271] Likewise, Pelatiah Webster, "A Citizen of Philadelphia," wrote in 1787 that "[t]he Carthaginians acquired an amazing degree of strength, wealth, and extent of dominion, under a republican form of government."[272] Alexander Hamilton was quick to observe that commercial republics were just as likely to become aggressors in futile conflicts: "Carthage, though a commercial republic, was the aggressor in the very war that ended in her destruction."[273] Likewise, he could have mentioned Athens' ill-fated slide into conflict against Sparta in the Peloponnesian War. Indeed, in more modern times, the Venetian republic suffered from the same fate.[274] And, besides, commercial power could aggregate into the hands of a permanent mercantile aristocracy, which was no better than power in the hands feudal lords or a landed gentry.[275]

The Framers had no desire to hitch their fortunes to a model of Punic commercialism. After all, Polybius had observed:

> The constitution of Carthage seems to me to have been originally well contrived as regards its most distinctive points. For there were kings, and the house of Elders was an aristocratical force, and the people were supreme in matters proper to them, the entire frame of the state much resembling that of Rome and Sparta. But at the time when they entered on the Hannibalic War, the Carthaginian constitution had degenerated, and that of Rome was better. . . . [t]he multitude at Carthage had already acquired the chief voice in deliberations; while at Rome the senate still retained this; and hence,

as in one case the masses deliberated and in the other the most eminent men, the Roman decisions on public affairs were superior, so that although they met with complete disaster, they were finally by the wisdom of their counsels victorious over the Carthaginians in the war.[276]

Polybius was clearly critical of the democratizing influences at Carthage and the official corruption it engendered. He was especially harsh in his condemnation of the Punic practice of candidates for office bribing the citizens for their votes.[277] This lapse in the Punic republic's moral character obviously extended to its conduct of military matters, and Carthaginian reliance on sea power and on mercenaries – instead of Rome's use of citizen legions – was certainly one crucial cause in their defeat in the Second Punic War.[278] The Carthaginian republic – oligarchic, mercantile, naval, and decadent – looked too much to the Framing generation like the British Empire that they had just rebelled from.

There was, of course, one other ancient model of government that the Framers could draw upon, but for them the Athenian constitution was the ultimate dystopia that had to be avoided at all costs in the formulation of the American republic.[279] "It is impossible," Hamilton wrote in *Federalist* 9,

> to read the history of the petty republics of Greece and Italy without feeling sensations of horror and disgust at the distractions with which they were continually agitated, and at the rapid succession of revolutions by which they were kept in a state of perpetual vibration between the extremes of tyranny and anarchy. If they exhibit occasional calms, these only serve as short-lived contrast to the furious storms that are to succeed. If now and then intervals of felicity open to view, we behold them with a mixture of regret, arising from the reflection that the pleasing scenes before us are soon to be overwhelmed by the tempestuous waves of sedition and party rage.[280]

Fisher Ames, speaking before the Massachusetts Convention, railed against the "volcano of democracy" and "the paltry democracies of Greece and Asia Minor, so much extolled, and so often proposed as a model for our imitation."[281] Or, as James Madison put it so pungently in *Federalist* 55: "Had every Athenian citizen been a Socrates; every Athenian assembly would still have been a mob."[282]

The Polybian canon certainly supported this conclusion: "the Athenian populace always more or less resembles a ship without a commander. . . . After having averted the greatest and most terrible dangers owing to the high qualities of the people and their leaders, it has come to grief at times by sheer heedlessness and unreasonableness in seasons of unclouded tranquillity."[283] Putting aside Polybius' notorious prejudice against Athenian institutions,[284] there was substantial truth in his condemnation of Athenian inconstancy.[285] Speaking more generally, Madison observed that "Hence it is that such democracies have ever been spectacles of turbulence and contention; have ever been found incompatible with personal security or the rights of property; and have in general been as short in their lives as they have been violent in their deaths."[286] Nevertheless, even Madison realized that Athenian democracy relied upon representative institutions:

> In the most pure democracies of Greece, many of the executive functions were performed, not by the people themselves, but by officers elected by the people, and REPRESENTING the people in their EXECUTIVE capacity. Prior to the reform of Solon, Athens was governed by nine Archons, annually ELECTED BY THE PEOPLE AT LARGE. The degree of power delegated to them seems to be left in great obscurity. Subsequent to that period, we find an assembly, first of four, and afterwards of six hundred members, annually ELECTED BY THE PEOPLE; and PARTIALLY representing them in their LEGISLATIVE capacity, since they were not only associated with the people in the function of making laws, but had the exclusive right of originating legislative propositions to the people.[287]

John Adams concurred in this judgment, noting that "The republic of Athens ... was, for a short period of her duration, the most democratical commonwealth of Greece. ... During this period, the people seem to have endeavoured to collect all authority into one centre, and to have avoided a composition of orders and balances. ... Their government consisted in a single assembly of nine archons chosen annually by the people. ... But this form of government had its usual effects, in introducing anarchy, and such a general profligacy of manners. ... "[288]

Indeed, the Framers knew from their reading of Aristotle that Athens could not have been regarded as a true democracy, but rather had aristocratic tendencies, which manifested themselves in limitations on citizenship (extended only to a portion of actual residents), suffrage, and office holding, as well as the toleration of the institution of slavery.[289] But it was the selection of leaders by the drawing of lots among eligible citizens and the short terms of the officers that was regarded as being the antithesis of a representative republic.[290] The Council of Five Hundred (*areopagos* or *boule*) was selected in this fashion, and the Council, in turn, convened the Assembly (*ekklesia*) of citizens. The magistrates (*arkhe*) of the Athenian polity – the arkhon, basileus, polemarch, and six thesmothetai (collectively known as the arkhons) – may have held longer terms.[291] Nonetheless, the Framing generation properly understood that governance of the Athenian polity was fickle, that fine leaders could be turned out for minor infractions and demagogues could be installed in their place. As political elites having previously sown the whirlwind of the American Revolution, it is hardly surprising that the Athenian model would have been distasteful, if not positively repellent.

For all these reasons, the Framing generation was obliged to fashion an amalgam of ancient republics in order to produce a working model for the new American state. Although, as Montesquieu mused, "[i]t is impossible to be tired of so agreeable a subject as ancient Rome,"[292] the Framers well-understood the dangers and defects of Roman republicanism-turned-tyranny perhaps as much as Spartan militarism, Punic greed, and the Athenian mobocracy. Together with the lessons learned from the colonial policies of ancient empires, as well as Polybius' theory of mixed government and its practical application in separation of powers among classical governmental institutions, the Framers were armed with an impressive array of political experiences and values to guide them in drafting the Constitution.

THREE

CONSTITUTION-MAKING AND ANCIENT HISTORY

As is abundantly clear from their voices quoted in chapter 2, the Founders were preoccupied with endowing substantial competence to the new general government of the United States. At the same time, the Framers of the structural Constitution were positively obsessed with cabining and controlling the exercise of governmental authority. This meant preventing the accumulation of power in any one branch of the federal government, protecting the prerogatives of the individual states, and (most difficult of all) ensuring that no particular social segment or cohort gained at the expense of the common weal. Government, as Alexander Hamilton observed, had to be poised on a knife-edge by having "[p]ower [be made] always the rival of power."[1]

The control of power was thus regarded by the Framing generation as being intimately related to the preservation of individual liberty. At this level of inquiry, there was a fundamental unity between the "structural Constitution" of the first seven articles of the national Charter and the "rights Constitution" of the Bill of Rights' ten amendments. Indeed, the distinction between these two aspects of American constitutionalism may be an utter fiction. After all, the Tenth Amendment provides a central tenet of federalism in its reservation of state powers.[2] Moreover, the main body of the Constitution not only explicitly provides the affirmative legislative powers of Congress (and, by implication, of the national government), but specifically prohibits the general government from legislating against the "Privilege of the Writ of Habeas Corpus,"[3] commands that "No Bill of Attainder or ex post facto Law shall be passed,"[4] and ensures that no "religious Test shall ever be required as a Qualification for any Office or public Trust under the United States."[5] In a parallel set of provisions, the states are barred from adopting ex post facto legislation, or any "Law impairing the Obligation of Contract."[6] Finally, the Constitution of 1787 provided for a right to a jury trial and favorable venue for criminal defendants,[7] and limited the power of the national government to prosecute and punish individuals for the crime of treason.[8] Many of these liberties were further amplified in the Bill of Rights.

Nevertheless, when we speak of the structural Constitution, the important distinction we are making has to do with the allocation of power among government institutions. Whether expressed in the idioms of federalism, separation of powers, the limited and enumerated authority of the national government, judicial restraint and rectitude, or of plenary and foreign relations powers of the United States, the crucial idea at work is that the Framers desired an energetic and effective government, while ensuring against tyranny. The lessons the Framing generation derived from ancient political discourse and experience amply proved to them the necessity of guarding against the rapid and dangerous accumulation of power within certain government offices and branches. At the same time, the federal government had to be endowed with robust authority "in Order to form a more perfect Union, establish Justice, insure domestic Tranquility, provide for the common defence, promote the general Welfare, and secure the Blessings of Liberty...."[9]

Five clusters of issues fundamentally defined the structural Constitution crafted in Philadelphia in 1787 and ratified by the state conventions in the years following. Each of these was broadly divisive and controversial for the delegates at the Constitutional Convention and in the subsequent ratification debates. As I will discuss at length in this chapter, for each of these issues classical precedents and experience proved crucial in providing the Framers with a workable solution to the fundamental problems of ordered liberty and divided power. First, and perhaps most significant, of the challenges was the creation of an effective federal government, which improved on the lackluster record of the Articles of Confederation, but which did not go so far as to unduly limit (or even extinguish) state sovereignty. Second, there was the difficulty of balancing democratic and elite influences in the national legislature, and here the acceptance of bicameralism as a working principle and the establishment of a Senate was decisive. Third, the next difficulty for the Framers was the conception of a unitary executive branch, with broad authority to influence the legislative process (through use of a veto), and to carry out the laws, while, at the same time, being constrained by other checks. Fourth, there was the problem of ordaining an independent judiciary as a separate branch of government, and, just as difficult, conceiving of the proper role of judges in a democratic society, interacting with congressional enactments, American common law traditions, and the institution of citizen juries. Fifth, for a nation born of conflict and dependent on the kindness of strangers, there was the matter of delimiting the war- and treaty-making powers of the federal government, and to reach a critical understanding of the role of standing armies and the law of nations in making the new country. These elements – federalism, bicamerlism, a unified Executive, an independent Judiciary, and the foreign relations power – are the five pillars of the structural Constitution. Deep within the intellectual roots and resolutions of these foundational traditions lies the classical legacy for the American republic.

Before I can coherently discuss these five aspects of structural constitutionalism and their ancient analogues, I am obliged to confront two uncomfortable issues, which provided a silent subtext to much of the deliberations in Philadelphia. These were the ascertainment of qualifications of electors for federal offices, and the constitutional recognition of slavery. Indeed, the resolution of both of these issues was decisive for the future of the republic. Voting qualifications of citizens, restrictively construed in the late eighteenth century, were gradually liberalized, giving real impetus to the democratic revolutions of Jefferson's presidential victory in 1800 and Andrew Jackson's in 1828. As for the institution of slavery, that quite literally brought the American republican experiment to its near-death experience of the Civil War. Both voting qualifications and slavery were considered by the Framing generation as part of the Constitutional compact, but only by indirection; very few provisions of the national charter are actually devoted to those subjects.[10] As with the other pillars of American constitutionalism, classical authorities were cited with some particularity by the Framers, but with very mixed and indifferent results.

The qualifications of electors for federal offices were primarily an issue for the composition of the members of the House of Representatives, the popularly elected lower house of Congress. After all, members of the Senate were, under the original constitutional scheme,[11] chosen by the respective state legislatures, a situation that was only changed by the adoption of the Seventeenth Amendment in 1913, which provided for the direct election of senators by the people.[12] Moreover, as I will discuss in Chapter 4, the executive office of the president was selected by the indirect institution of an electoral college.[13] Representation in the House of Representatives was intended by the Framers to ensure a popular basis of legitimacy for the national government, a nod to a democratic institution in a mixed constitution (counterpoised with an aristocratic Senate and an energetic, unitary Executive). The House was to be a mirror of the nation, to encompass the "reception of all the different classes of citizens in order to combine their interests and feelings of every part of the community, and to produce a true sympathy between the representative body and its constituents."[14]

The crucial question for the Framers was whether to directly embody a property qualification for voters into the Constitution. In this respect, the classical tradition offered only ambiguous lessons. The Athenian legislative assembles, or *ekklēsia*, certainly demanded that citizen members had properly discharged their civic duties, including military service.[15] In Rome, adult male citizens were qualified to participate in the popular assemblies, although voting restrictions were imposed against manumitted slaves and the descendants of freedmen.[16] There was an essential form of property qualification observed in the composition of the *comitia centuriata*, although it was not observed in the right to vote. This body had been originally formed as the citizen militia of Rome, and it mustered on the Campus Martius, or parade ground outside the city. That is why it was sometimes called the *exercitus*. Citizens were not assigned to centurias based on tribal or clan affiliation (as with the *comitia tributa*), but, rather, by virtue of the extent of military equipage and service they could render to the republic.[17] As organized by King Servius Tullius in the sixth century BCE, the comitia centuriata gave an effective majority to those cohorts organized into cavalry and heavy infantry *classis*, membership in which was reserved for those citizens of sufficient property holdings to maintain those units. The lowest orders of society, those who paid merely a capitation tax (and were thus known as *capite censi*) were relegated to the sixth class. As Servius Tullius was later quoted by both Cicero and Dionysius of Halicarnassus, the intention was that "the greatest number of people should not have the greatest influence."[18] Also, in the comitia tributa, the voting was more heavily weighted toward the more numerous, but less populated, rustic tribes, thus disadvantaging the urban, and mostly landless, citizenry.[19]

The right of franchise in popular assemblies at both Rome and Athens was also limited by conceptions of citizenship. The Social Wars of the second century BCE pitted the relatively small cadre of the citizen-residents of Rome, itself (the *Quirites*), along with Rome's Latin neighbors, against the Italian subject cities – which constituted the vast majority of the Roman legions, and which, yet, were denied the vote in the popular assemblies. After that conflict, citizenship in the republic was extended to wider groups. During this period, when the assemblies met in July as electoral colleges to designate the republic's top officers (such as the consuls), nearly a quarter of the roughly 900,000 registered citizens recorded in the census of the period, attended the assemblies.[20] When special legislation was being deliberated – especially land redistribution and other agrarian issues – the numbers of citizens attending from the provinces and rural areas swelled the numbers in the assemblies.[21]

The Framing generation was well aware of these classical precedents for voting qualifications for electors. Noah Webster, writing as a "Citizen of America" in a pamphlet titled, *An Examination into the Leading Principles of the Federal Constitution*, published in Philadelphia in October 1787, dwelt at length on property qualifications for the franchise and drew extensively from ancient examples. In a somewhat tendentious tone, Webster took the position that the Roman republic had cause to regret its quick extension of voting rights to its Italian subjects after the Social War: "for however reasonable it might appear to admit the allies to a participation of the rights of citizens, yet the concession destroyed all freedom of election. It enabled an ambitious demagogue to engage and bring into the assemblies, whole towns of people, slaves and foreigners; – and every thing was decided by faction and violence."[22] And yet, in a later passage in Webster's essay, he extolled the political power of the plebian classes in the Roman republic, especially the extent to which those groups were able to assert control over the governing institutions of the state. "The Roman proceeded thus step by step," Webster concluded, "to triumph over aristocracy.... [T]he people, by reducing the interest of money, abolishing debts, or by forcing other advantages from the patricians, generally held the power of governing in their own hands."[23]

What was notable about Webster's observations was that he vigorously sought to document his classical authority. His source for the insight on the dilution of the franchise was Montesquieu, but not the volume, *The Spirit of the Laws*. Rather, Webster consulted a lesser-known work, *Considerations on the Causes of the Greatness of the Romans and their Decline*, first published in 1734 and then in a revised edition in 1748.[24] Montesquieu was, if anything, even more critical of the mob influence over Roman popular assemblies: "The ambitious brought entire cities and nations to Rome to disturb the voting to get themselves elected. The assemblies were virtual conspiracies; a band of seditious men was called a *comitia*. The people's authority, their law and even the people themselves became chimerical things, and the anarchy was such that it was no longer possible to know whether the people had or had not adopted an ordinance."[25] Webster likewise drew on Walter Moyle's early eighteenth-century *Essay upon the Constitution of the Roman Government*,[26] along with its gloss on Livy's annalist text, for his supposition of the expanding franchise of the plebian classes and the gradual elimination of property qualifications for electors. The unstated assumption of these historic musings was, of course, a causal explanation of the progressive corruption of the Roman republic and its ultimate downfall.

Unlike Webster, James Wilson in his positions taken on the floor of the Constitutional Convention and in his contemporaneous writings was a forceful advocate for direct popular election of both the House and Senate. Indeed, he supported the notion that the proposed Constitution be ratified by popularly elected conventions in each state, a policy that has been characterized as "the most audacious and altogether unqualified appeal to the notion of popular sovereignty and majority rule that had ever been made, even in America."[27] He took issue with James Madison, who supported the idea of imposing a freehold qualification for voting.[28] In his *Lectures on Law*, first delivered in 1790, Wilson observed that "The pyramid of government – and a republican government may well receive that beautiful and solid form – should be raised to a dignified attitude: but its foundations must, of consequence, be broad, and strong, and deep."[29] He went on to praise "the small republicks of Greece, and in the first ages of the commonwealth of Rome, [where] the people voted in their aggregate capacity."[30] Even while recognizing that direct democracy of this sort was impracticable in a large republic, and could degenerate into a mobocracy, Wilson tended to the view that ancient models of more participatory voting were to be favored.

Wilson's fellow delegates at Philadelphia heeded the warnings expressed by Noah Webster's "Citizen of America." The constitutional text provided that "the Electors in each State [for members of the House of Representatives] shall have the Qualifications requisite for Electors of the most numerous Branch of the State Legislature."[31] In short, federal elections for Representatives would adopt any property qualifications for voters imposed by state constitutions for the election of state representatives. As Wilson surveyed in his *Lectures*, the majority of states did impose a freehold or property-owning requirement for voting.[32] Madison could thus write in *Federalist* 45 that "Even the House of Representatives, though drawn immediately from the people, will be chosen very much under the influence of that class of men whose influence over the people obtains for themselves an election into the State legislatures."[33] Madison further defended the constitutional compromise on voter qualifications in these terms:

> The definition of the right of suffrage is very justly regarded as a fundamental article of republican government. It was incumbent on the convention, therefore, to define and establish this right in the Constitution. To have left it open for the occasional regulation of the Congress, would have been improper for the reason just mentioned. To have submitted it to the legislative discretion of the States, would have been improper for the same reason; and for the additional reason that it would have rendered too dependent on the State governments that branch of the federal government which

ought to be dependent on the people alone. To have reduced the different qualifications in the different States to one uniform rule, would probably have been as dissatisfactory to some of the States as it would have been difficult to the convention. The provision made by the convention appears, therefore, to be the best that lay within their option. It must be satisfactory to every State, because it is conformable to the standard already established, or which may be established, by the State itself. It will be safe to the United States, because, being fixed by the State constitutions, it is not alterable by the State governments, and it cannot be feared that the people of the States will alter this part of their constitutions in such a manner as to abridge the rights secured to them by the federal Constitution.[34]

The Constitution thus enshrined some classical notions of property ownership as being a surrogate for the political worth of individuals. It is, as Madison noted in a somewhat unrelated context in *Federalist* 10 that inequality manifests itself in the "different and unequal faculties of acquiring property," the protection of which is the "first object of government."[35] While no attempt need be made here to resurrect a purely economic reading of the Constitution as vindicating the interests of the propertied classes in America,[36] there was a manifest understanding among the Framing generation that the maintenance of some forms of property qualifications for voting was a necessary bulwark against the degradation of republican virtues. Indeed, the experience of ancient Athenian democracy and the decline of Roman republican institutions were a prime exhibit in this political proof.

If the qualifications of electors were a subject worthy of classical exemplars, the ancient institution of slavery was not. And, as with most things associated with slavery and the framing of the Constitution, the public discourse on the subject was convoluted and muted. At the Philadelphia Convention, historic references to slavery in antiquity were made. In the climactic debate on a constitutional provision to restrict the slave trade, South Carolina's Charles Pinckney told the delegates, "if slavery be wrong, it is justified by the example of all the world." He cited the example of Greece, Rome, and other ancient States. . . . [and] in all ages one half of mankind have been slaves."[37] Counterpoised with this observation was Colonel Mason's savage critique of the institution: "Slavery discourages arts and manufactures. The poor despise labor when performed by slaves. . . . They produce the most pernicious effect on manners. Every master of slaves is born a petty tyrant. They bring the judgment of heaven on a Country. As nations can not be rewarded or punished in the next world they must be in this. By an inevitable chain of causes and effects providence punishes national sins, by national calamities. . . . He mentioned "the dangerous insurrections of the slaves in [ancient] Greece and Sicily."[38] And John Dickinson noted that "Greece and Rome were made unhappy by their slaves."[39] Or, finally, in Thomas Jefferson's aphorism (cribbed from Suetonius), the institution of slavery was like having "the wolf by the ears: it is unjust to hold it, but it is unsafe to let it go."[40]

The Framing generation was thus beset with two competing historical allegories of slavery. The first was the moral inevitability of slavery, of the inherent strength of the institution through time.[41] This was Pinckney's view, but its counterpoint would later be revealed by John Marshall, the great Chief Justice, who had earlier been a student of George Wythe. Writing for the Supreme Court in *The Antelope*,[42] Marshall – and indeed what remained of the American revolutionary leadership – confronted the moral and historic premises of the institution of slavery. Despite the tradition of natural law scholarship that arose from Romanist and civil law interest from the classically trained Framing generation, and embodied in scholars and judges like Justice Joseph Story (1779–1845),[43] Marshall took a positivist turn on the legal suppression of slavery and reached this conclusion: "It is matter of notorious history, that both in ancient and modern Europe, the condition of slavery, and the commerce in slaves, were sanctioned by the universal practice, and law of nations. The very definition of slavery in the civil law, which has been copied by writers on public law, shows that it was an institution established by positive law, against the law of nature: *Servitus est constitutio juris gentium, qua quis dominio alieno contra naturam subjicitur.*"[44]

In this regard, the conditions of slavery during Roman times were manifestly misunderstood by the Framing generation. In making a peculiar defense of American slavery, Thomas Jefferson asserted in his *Notes on the State of Virginia* that Roman slaves were treated more harshly than their American counterparts, but, "[y]et, notwithstanding these and other discouraging circumstances among the Romans, their slaves were often the rarest artists. They excelled too in science, insomuch as to be usefully employed as tutors to their masters' children. . . . But they were of the race of whites. It is not their [African slaves'] condition, then, but nature, which has produced the distinction."[45] And while Jefferson acknowledged that many Roman slaves were later manumitted, and entered Roman society with certain rights (although as freedmen, rarely equaling those of citizens), he disclaimed any such future for African-Americans.[46]

The realities of the classical institutions of chattel slavery were very different from what Jefferson and his contemporaries supposed. In Athens, virtually all slaves were foreign captives taken in battle, or their descendants.

Although there was a hereditary class of *helots*, or agrarian subjugated peoples in near serf-like conditions at Sparta, this was exceptional in ancient Greece. Slavery could be imposed as a punishment for a criminal offense or for the failure to pay debts, but this was quite rare.[47] Although classical literature tended to emphasize the role of slaves as domestic servants and city workers, their primary function in Athens, as in the early Roman republic, was to replace the labor of citizen-farmers drawn away for military service and to supply the chronically undercapitalized agrarian sectors.[48]

Although this has been hotly disputed in the case of ancient Athens,[49] it seems undoubted that the Roman institution of slavery, like that in the Americas, was primarily intended to support agrarian economies and the livelihood of the landed gentry.[50] It was supposed that Roman slavery vastly accelerated in scope in the late republic period, particularly after Rome's victory in the Second Punic War and its transmarine expansion through the Mediterranean. This thesis posited that imperial expansion dictated greater demand for food, which, in turn, required more slaves, and which (of course) dictated further wars of conquest and subjugation.[51] Although this simplistic dynamic was disproved during the long periods of (either) peace on Rome's frontiers or civil conflicts (where Roman citizens were not subject to enslavement), this was the historiographic lesson advanced by both Montesquieu in his *Considerations on the Causes of the Greatness of the Romans and their Decline* and Edward Gibbons's towering work, *History of the Decline and Fall of the Roman Empire*, the first installment of which was published in 1776. Indeed, it is surprising that to the extent Jefferson greatly admired Gibbons's work,[52] he appeared to ignore its conclusion that the Roman institution of slavery, while not as harsh and exploitative as its modern analogues, contributed to the fall of Roman institutions.[53]

Of course, this was the other classical trope of slavery understood by the Framing generation – that as inevitable and necessary as slavery appeared to be, the institution contained the seeds of destruction for any polity that countenanced it. It was not only the risk of slave revolts and other forms of civil disorders that were well known from classical times, but it was also the brooding sense of unease and doom that infected many legislative initiatives. The Framers would have undoubtedly been familiar with Seneca's story of how the Roman senate rejected a proposal that all slaves in the city wear distinctive clothing to indicate their servile status, for fear that the heightened awareness of their own numbers would encourage the slaves to rebel.[54] Aside from attacking the health of the commonwealth, slavery also subverted and undermined the moral well-being of all slaveholders. In this more intimate context, there was Pliny's lament that even gentle and kind masters were routinely subject to physical threats by their slaves,[55] counterpoised with the harsh prescriptions of Xenophon, in his *Oeconomicus*, on the proper management of estates and the use of slave labor.[56]

However one regards the mixed classical legacy of slavery and the cognitive dissonance it imposed on the Framing generation, the Constitution's treatment of slavery was assuredly its greatest moral and political failure. Make no mistake, although the text quite self-consciously never refers to slaves (or slavery) by name, so as not to give the institution constitutional legitimation, such provisions as the Fugitives Clause of Article IV,[57] the protection given to the slave trade until 1808,[58] the authority of the federal government to "suppress Insurrection" and "domestic violence"[59] (presumably including slave revolts), and the notorious Three-Fifths compromise for the counting of (otherwise nonvoting) slaves in elections to the House of Representatives and Presidential Electoral College,[60] the institution was ingrained into the governmental form adopted in 1787.[61]

The slavery provisions, along side those concerned with the qualifications of electors for federal office, would have profound effects on other aspects of the structural Constitution. Indeed, these two issues show the substantial overlap between our national charter as a rights-conferring document and a neutral arbiter of governance institutions. My task for this chapter is to illustrate the classical legacy for the remaining pillars of the structural Constitution, and the best place to begin is the fundamental question of the balance between state and national governments in a federal context.

A. CONFEDERATIONS AND LEAGUES

1. **The Articles of Confederation as Precursor.** The delegates who gathered at Philadelphia in the summer of 1787 were not writing on a blank slate when it came to their thinking about the nature of sovereignty for a national government of the United States. This problem was, of course, confronted by the Framers at the time of the Declaration of Independence in 1776. Indeed, just after the Declaration's proclamation, the Signers proceeded to consider drafts of the Articles of Confederation and Perpetual Union. As Robert Clinton has observed:

> The locus of sovereignty after independence was and is a subject of serious dispute. Some argue that the First Continental Congress contemplated the establishment of an independent sovereign nation and that the states were merely invited by that national government to continue to function as administrative units. Others argue that state legislatures, as successors to the recipients of the royal charters, in theory succeeded to the sovereignty

that rested with the Crown prior to the Declaration of Independence. Obviously, the royal governor and his council were remnants of the monarchical system that the colonists successfully overthrew. Therefore, the newly independent states did not favor centralized executive authority. The government ultimately created by the Articles of Confederation amounted to a loose confederation of states that derived its authority from acceptance of the principles of the confederation by the state legislatures through ratification.[62]

These concerns were certainly manifest in the debates before the Continental Congress over the text of the Articles. The crucial provisions were those that articulated the scope and nature of the confederal government. One group of these set a hopeful tone for the document. According to their title, the Articles created a "perpetual Union," and Article XIII propounded a form of supremacy clause:

> Every state shall abide by the determinations of the united states in congress assembled, on all questions which by this confederation are submitted to them. And the Articles of this confederation shall be inviolably observed by every state, and the union shall be perpetual; nor shall any alteration at any time hereafter be made in any of them; unless such alteration be agreed to in a congress of the united states, and be afterwards confirmed by the legislatures of every state.[63]

Moreover, Article III proclaimed: "The said states hereby severally enter into a firm league of friendship with each other, for their common defence, the security of their Liberties, and their mutual and general welfare, binding themselves to assist each other, against all force offered to, or attacks made upon them, or any of them, on account of religion, sovereignty, trade, or any other pretence whatever."[64]

In sharp contrast to these clauses, Article II announced that "Each state retains its sovereignty, freedom and independence, and every Power, Jurisdiction, and right, which is not by this confederation expressly delegated to the United States, in Congress assembled."[65] By this provision it was made clear that the confederation had only limited powers – and these were specifically enumerated in the following Articles.[66] Certain powers were deliberately *not* allocated to the Confederation government: most notably, the authority to levy direct taxes and competence over regulation of interstate and international commerce.[67]

A further limitation on the nature of the Confederation was purely structural: all power of the confederal government was vested in a single-branch entity known simply as "Congress." The Articles did not create any true executive authority, and thus only authorized Congress "to appoint a committee, to sit in the recess of congress, to be denominated 'A Committee of the States,' and to consist of one delegate from each state; and to appoint such other committees and civil officers as may be necessary for managing the general affairs of the united states under their direction.... "[68] Aside from a specialized tribunal established to hear cases of appeals of maritime captures,[69] the Articles created no separate judiciary to handle disputes between citizens of the Confederacy. Highly contentious land disputes between states were to be adjudicated and settled by Congress, itself, sitting as a "court of last resort on appeal."[70]

The last – and ultimate – constraint on the power of Congress was its membership and voting procedures. Delegations were appointed in a manner directed by state assemblies and served at the sufferance of state authorities.[71] Delegates received their compensation solely from the states,[72] and this restriction was later justified out of fear of the official corruption which "prostrat[ed] those ancient republics, which are seen no more but in the pages of history."[73] Moreover, Article V declared that "[i]n determining questions in the united states, in Congress assembled, each state shall have one vote."[74] When Congress was fully assembled, a majority vote was needed for action, but when the Committee of the States was convened, it could transact business on the votes of nine states.[75] In short, the Congress established under the Articles of Confederation was purely a creature of the states, a forum for the representation of state interests.[76] The Articles of Confederation were essentially conceived as a treaty or compact of union between the states, instead of an organic body representing the interests of the people directly.[77]

Without question, this was recognized at the time of the drafting of the Articles. When the one state—one vote language of Article XVII (what would later become Article V, clause 4) was proposed, Mr. Chase of Maryland noted that "this article was the most likely to divide us of any one proposed in the" draft.[78] Some delegates, including Benjamin Franklin and John Adams, advocated for proportional representation based on the population of the colonies, for otherwise smaller States would gain too much power.[79] Of course, they represented Pennsylvania and Massachusetts respectively, two of the four most populous colonies. The Rev. John Witherspoon, representing New Jersey, a midsized colony, made the argument for equal State representation: "if an equal vote be refused, the smaller states will become the vassals of the larger; and all experience has shown that the vassals and subjects of free states are the most enslaved. He instanced the Helots of Sparta, and the provinces of Rome."[80] And while Stephen Hopkins of Rhode Island observed that "too little is known of the ancient confederations to say what was their practice,"[81] he did draw on the experience of German, Dutch, and Belgian confederations, in which each constituent province received one vote in league councils. Other delegates observed that equal voting had brought about the "decay of the liberties of the Dutch Republic" and the actual ruination of the Belgic confederacy.[82]

Later proposals were made (when the Articles were discussed in October 1777) for proportional representation of one Congressional delegate for every 50,000 or 30,000 inhabitants in a state. These were only supported by the Virginia and Pennsylvania delegations, and were soundly defeated.[83] A different tack – having "the quantum of representation for each State ... computed by numbers proportioned according to its contribution of money or tax levied" for the union – received only Virginia's concurrence.[84] With these initiatives rejected, the one state-one vote plan was incorporated into the Articles.[85] Despite the text of the Articles being effectively finalized in July 1778, it took an additional three years for them to receive the ratifications of all the states. The Articles were thus in force from March 1781 to the final ratification of the Constitution in 1788.

The consequences of this confederal scheme were mixed. It should not be forgotten that the Articles provided at least an inchoate governmental structure that made it possible to prosecute to a successful completion the rebellion and separation from Great Britain, albeit with substantial difficulties. But, as has been observed by Robert Clinton,

> Experience with the Articles of Confederation indicated many of its defects. These included lack of effective executive and judicial authority and the resulting Congressional inability to directly enforce or implement national law; state recalcitrance to or rejection of decisions of the Congress ... ; ponderous machinery for the resolution of interstate disputes; disputes between the states and Congress over the appropriate allocation of authority under the Articles and the lack of any effective mechanism to secure a final resolution of such conflicts; and chronic financial crisis as states failed to honor congressional requisitions. ... The breakdown of the colonial system spawned by the Revolution, the economic dislocations caused by the conflict, and economic problems that emerged in the aftermath of the Revolution indicated a need [also] to revise the economic arrangements that had governed colonial trade.[86]

As if all of this was not enough, the worsening economic conditions produced actual unrest in the form of Shay's Rebellion in western Massachusetts in 1786. All of this motivated the Continental Congress to propose a convention at Annapolis to amend the Articles of Confederation. Although this rump meeting in September 1786 (delegations from only six states appeared) produced no substantive results, the conference called for a convention to meet in Philadelphia on the second Monday in May 1787 to consider whatever "further provisions" might be necessary to render "the constitution of the Federal Government adequate to the exigencies of the Union."[87]

The standard view of the Framing generation is that it regarded the Articles of Confederation as a manifest failure.[88] It is notable that among both advocates and opponents of the Constitution drafted at Philadelphia in 1787, there was a surprising degree of unanimity that the Articles were fatally flawed. Alexander Hamilton, in *Federalist* 15, acknowledged this: "opponents as well as . . . friends of the new Constitution . . . in general appear to harmonize in this sentiment, at least, that there are material imperfections in our national system, and that something is necessary to be done to rescue us from impending anarchy."[89] Melancthon Smith (1744–1798), writing as "A Plebian," proclaimed in a New York pamphlet in 1787 that "The importance of preserving an union, and of establishing a government equal to the purpose of maintaining that union, is a sentiment deeply impressed on the mind of every citizen of America. It is now no longer doubted, that the confederation, in its present form, is inadequate to that end: Some reform in our government must take place: In this, all parties agree. . . . "[90]

A significant point that is often lost in this conventional historiography was that there was a substantial intellectual debt that the drafters of the Constitution owed to the signers of the Articles. Of course, it *was* virtually the same group of people, and, as James Madison candidly noted "The truth is, that the great principles of the Constitution proposed by the convention may be considered less as absolutely new, than as the expansion of principles which are found in the articles of Confederation. The misfortune under the latter system has been, that these principles are so feeble and confined as to justify all the charges of inefficiency which have been urged against it, and to require a degree of enlargement which gives to the new system the aspect of an entire transformation of the old."[91] Even the most ardent detractors of the Articles had to admit that, as Gordon Wood has recently observed, "What is truly remarkable about the Confederation is the degree of union that was achieved. The equality of the citizens of all states in privileges and immunities, the reciprocity of extradition and judicial proceedings among the states . . . , the elimination of travel and discriminatory trade restrictions between states, and the substantial grant of powers to the Congress . . . made the league of states as cohesive and strong as any similar sort of republican confederation in history – stronger in fact than some Americans had expected."[92]

2. The Political Theory of Confederation. And it was precisely that sense of historical perspective that absorbed the Framers as they began to contemplate a new form of government to replace the Articles of Confederation. For the Framing generation, recourse to earlier writers on political theory offered little guidance, or solace. For example, Machiavelli's musings on whether republics or princes were more likely to keep their words in confederations were bolstered by substantial evidence from ancient history. He concluded that both were likely to defect from alliances and leagues whenever circumstances suited.[93]

The Framers would have also been familiar with Samuel Pufendorf's description, in his 1688 volume, *On the Law of Nature and Nations*,[94] of a "perpetual treaty" concluded between autonomous states in order to provide for common defense and establish a "system" of governance.[95] Pufendorf distinguished such league systems from "simple" defensive treaties.[96] Moreover, he observed that such leagues should provide for certain powers granted to the "system," while others would remain vested in the constituent polities:

> We have said that in treaties of this kind [perpetual treaties] the exercise of only certain parts of the supreme sovereignty is made to depend upon the consent of the associated states. For it hardly seems likely that the affairs of several states could be so closely interwoven that it would be to the advantage of one and all of them that no part of the supreme sovereignty be exercised without the consent of all. Or if there were any such, it would have been more to their advantage to unite in one state than to be joined only by a treaty. Therefore, it is convenient that the individual states reserve for themselves liberty in the exercise of those parts of supreme sovereignty, the manner of conducting which is of little or no interest, at least directly, to the rest. The same is true as well of such business as is of daily occurrence, or will not suffer the delay consequent upon a discussion of it with others. But matters upon which the safety of the entire league depends may with entire fairness be considered in common council.[97]

Pufendorf went on to distinguish the prerogatives of the league (over war, foreign relations, and even "joined taxes") from those of the constituent entitles (including "commercial treaties, taxes which are required for the needs of the individual states, the appointment of magistrates, laws, the right over citizens of life and death, matters of religion").[98]

Emmerich de Vattel's 1758 *The Law of Nations*[99] – assuredly the single most influential international law treatise for the Framing generation[100] – articulated a notion of defensive alliances and political leagues, especially for groupings of weaker nations,[101] even as he announced a new notion of the European powers regulating their affairs through a balance-of-power mechanism. In a political union, Vattel noted that the constituent states "have also the right mutually to favor one another, to the exclusion of the sovereign whom they fear; and by the privileges of every sort, and especially by the commercial privileges which they will mutually grant to one another's subjects, and which they will refuse to the subjects of that dangerous sovereign, they will add to their strength. . . . "[102]

Vattel's conception of a defensive union of weaker states was unquestionably a more modest idea than Pufendorf's "perpetual treaty" between entities creating a "system" of delegated and enumerated powers, but both were clearly weighed by the drafters of the Articles of Confederation. We know that Vattel's text was actually used and consulted by the Continental Congress.[103] In one respect, Vattel's idea proved to be quite durable when he wrote that "a number of sovereign and independent States may unite to form a perpetual confederation, without individually ceasing to be perfect States. Together they will form a confederate republic. Their joint resolutions will not impair the sovereignty of the individual members, although its exercise may be somewhat restrained by reason of voluntary agreements."[104] In using this language, Vattel appeared to borrow from Montesquieu, who likewise discussed confederative republics and observed: "This form of government is a convention by which several petty states agree to become members of a larger one, which they intend to establish. It is a kind of assemblage of societies that constitute a new one, capable of increasing by means of further associations, till they arrive to such a degree of power as to be able to provide for the security of the whole body. It was these associations that so long contributed to the prosperity of Greece. By these the Romans attacked the whole globe, and by those alone the whole globe withstood them."[105] Although he would later, in his *Spirit of the Laws*, call into question some of the laws adopted by these confederative republics,[106] the Framing generation clearly adopted Montesquieu as the intellectual progenitor of the Constitution's federalism provisions.

For example, Alexander Hamilton, in *Federalist* 9, directly quoted Montesquieu's language,[107] and went on to note that the Constitution attempted to achieve just such an "assemblage of societies," and

[s]o long as the separate organization of the members be not abolished; so long as it exists, by a constitutional necessity, for local purposes; though it should be in perfect subordination to the general authority of the union, it would still be, in fact and in theory, an association of states, or a confederacy. The proposed Constitution, so far from implying an abolition

of the State governments, makes them constituent parts of the national sovereignty, by allowing them a direct representation in the Senate, and leaves in their possession certain exclusive and very important portions of sovereign power. This fully corresponds, in every rational import of the terms, with the idea of a federal government.[108]

James Madison likewise offered a distinction between "simple" and "compound" republics when he noted that "[i]n the compound republic of America, the power surrendered by the people is first divided between two distinct governments, and then the portion allotted to each subdivided among distinct and separate departments."[109] At the Philadelphia Convention, Madison elaborated this distinction:

[I]t would be a novel & dangerous doctrine that a Legislature could change the constitution under which it held its existence. . . . He considered the difference between a system founded on the Legislatures only, and one founded on the people, to be the true difference between a league or treaty, and a Constitution. The former in point of moral obligation might be as inviolable as the latter. In point of political operation, there were two important distinctions in favor of the latter. 1. A law violating a treaty ratified by a preexisting law, might be respected by the Judges as a law, though an unwise or perfidious one. A law violating a constitution established by the people themselves, would be considered by the Judges as null & void. 2. The doctrine laid down by the law of Nations in the case of treaties is that a breach of any one article by any of the parties frees the other parties from their engagements. In the case of a union of people under one Constitution, the nature of the pact has always been understood to exclude such an interpretation.[110]

James Wilson, writing later in his law *Lectures*, appeared to agree: "[T]he United States have been formed into one confederate republick; first, under the articles of confederation; afterwards, under our present national government."[111] Even the opponents of the Constitution appeared to agree that its ostensible purpose was to establish a "confederal republic" of divided sovereignty between a national and the state governments.[112] Their only qualm was whether this was, in fact, possible.

3. The Framers' Classical Exegesis. To answer that decisive question, the Framers knew they had to rely on historical experience, particularly that offered by classical times. It is as Carl Richard has pungently suggested that "[u]ncovering the cancers which had killed the [ancient] republics was the principal obsession of the founders' leading coroners."[113] James

Madison was among the first to assemble and mobilize this information about ancient leagues and confederations.[114] As early as 1784, Madison had set about obtaining every treatise he could find about ancient and modern confederations. He instructed Jefferson, then the American minister in Paris, to acquire the appropriate volumes, explaining to him that his research was necessitated insofar as "the operations of our own [confederation] must render all such lights of consequence."[115] Every spring and summer in the years 1784, 1785, and 1786, Madison retired to his estate at Montpelier and perused the consignments of volumes that Jefferson had shipped him.[116] Among the books that were particularly useful to Madison was Fortuné Barthélemy Félice's three-volume *Code de l'humanité*. In any event, by June 1786,[117] Madison had completed his *Notes on Ancient and Modern Confederacies* and these schematic outlines enabled him to speak with confidence on the subject on the floor of the Philadelphia Convention in 1787, and at the Virginia Ratifying Convention in 1788, as well as being the basis of expanded treatment in *Federalist* numbers 18, 19, and 20.[118]

In the relevant portion of his *Notes*, Madison identified three separate ancient leagues – the Lycian Confederation, Amphictyonic League, and Achaean Confederacy – and proceeded to make some particular observations (with citations), as well as record the evidences of what Madison termed "federal authority" for the league, as well as the "vices," or defects, of the confederation. Of the Lycian Confederation – a group of Greek city-states situated in Asia Minor (today's Turkey on the Aegean Sea), which confederated from 200 to 43 BCE – Madison said relatively little, except for noting that the votes of each of the Greek cities in this league was based on the pecuniary contributions of its members, a model that Madison noted that Montesquieu endorsed.[119] Madison also quoted a long passage from the work of Ubbo Emmius (1547–1625), particularly his posthumously published 1632 treatise on *Repraesentans Graecorum Respublicae* (Greek Representative Republics), probably the first scholarly work published on the subject.[120] According to Emmius' passage (glossing a fragment from Strabo's *Geography*), the Lycian League divided its city-members into three classes. The largest class got three votes in the league assembly; those of the second rank got two votes; cities of the smallest size received just one. "In the same proportion they also made contributions and performed other duties. This was reasonable and equitable, for those who possess more should contribute more to the common use. ... "[121]

The Achaean Confederacy, like the Lycian Confederation, persisted until the consolidation of the Roman conquests of the eastern Mediterranean in the first century BCE. This confederacy, which flourished from 280 to 146 BCE in the south of Hellas, was intended specifically to resist outside aggressors who would dominate Greece after the Peloponnesian War, particularly Macedon to the north.[122] Citing to Polybius (who was the confederacy's cavalry commander before allying with the Romans) and Félice, Madison noted that the territorial extent of that league was quite large, and the member cities "enjoyed a perfect equality, each of them sending the [same] number of deputies to the [Confederacy] Senate."[123] Among the advantages of federal authority of the Achaean entity was the power to make war and peace, send and receive ambassadors, annually appoint a *strategos* (what Madison termed a "Captain General"), and adopt uniform laws and weights and measures.[124] The officers of the Confederacy appeared to include two "pretors" (as Madison – borrowing from Livy – called them) and ten magistrates, which, according to Emmius, "were elected by the community every spring and their advice was usually followed by the praetor. Their powers were only a rank below the praetor's, and no business went before the assembly without their approval."[125] Despite the relatively sophisticated structure of the Achaean Confederacy, what with such institutional machinery as an assembly and officers, Madison still listed among its vices the failure to maintain unity among its members, especially in the face of hostile aggressors.[126] In this he agreed with John Adams's views, published in Adams's *Defence of the Constitutions*, skeptical of Polybius' reporting of events,[127] and preferring, instead, Plutarch's account of the confederacy's leader, Aratus, who declared that "small cities could be preserved by nothing else but a continual and combined force, united by the bond of common interest."[128]

That left for Madison's discussion in his *Notes* the Amphictyonic League. Although he was somewhat uncertain about the origins of this confederation, Madison did seem to realize that it had some connection with the religious functions of the famous Temple of Apollo at Delphi. Quoting a passage from an Aeschines oration, Madison noted that "[t]he Amphyctions took an oath mutually to defend and protect the United Cities – to inflict vengeance on those who should sacrilegiously despoil the temple at Delphos – to punish the violators of this oath – and never to divert the water courses of any of the Amphyctionic Cities either in peace or in war."[129] Madison understood that each member of the League sent two deputies to the Amphictyonic Council, and this body had the power to declare and conduct war against transgressors, to finally resolve disputes among the members, to manage the affairs of the Temple (including the conduct of the Olympic games), and the right to admit new members.[130]

Among its vices, Madison noted that when the Amphictyonic Council was exercising its judicial functions, "[i]t happened but too often that the Deputies of the stronger Cities awed and corrupted those of the weaker, and that Judgment went in favor of the most powerful party."[131] Even more seriously, the League was unable to avoid or manage conflict amongst its members, and so "The Execution of the Amphyctionic powers was very different from the Theory."[132] In an interesting aside to himself, Madison scribbled, "Quer. whether Thucidides or Xenophon in their Histories ever allude to the Amphyctionic authority which ought to have kept the peace?"[133] Lastly, Madison observed that the spectacular collapse of the League in the face of Philip II of Macedon's intervention in Greek affairs was a notable failure.[134]

Madison's *Notes* went on, of course, to consider more modern confederations, including those subsisting in Switzerland and The Netherlands, but his conclusions on ancient leagues were largely replicated throughout his intellectual project. The most common vice of political leagues, the one that "seems to have been mortal to the ancient Confederacies, and to be the disease of the modern," was the absence of a controlling central authority.[135] Jack Rakove has rightly called Madison's *Notes on Ancient and Modern Confederacies* "a powerful and comprehensive analysis of the problems of federalism and republicanism. . . . [H]is reassessment of these issues was neither merely intellectual nor merely synthetic. Its originality lay in part in its self-conscious willingness to challenge received wisdom, even if that wisdom took the form of clichés about small republics and separation of powers."[136]

Madison knew that he would have to be well-prepared with his ancient history. Given the classical predilections of his colleagues at Philadelphia, he understood that historical knowledge informed the kind of analogical and deductive reasoning his supporters and opponents, alike, would respect.[137] As we know of the proceedings of the Constitutional Convention, Madison's researches did not go wasted. Interestingly, though, the first to raise the subject of ancient leagues was Alexander Hamilton, in his maiden speech before the Convention on June 18, 1787.[138] The context was debate over the rival propositions of Edmund Randolph's (1753–1813) ambitious Virginia Plan for a fully constituted national government and William Paterson's (1745–1806) much more narrowly tailored and state-centered New Jersey Plan for a limited federative government.[139] Hamilton rose and gave a speech, the outline of which still survives, along with the contemporaneous reports of those (including Madison) who were recording the proceedings. Hamilton introduced five essential considerations for a national government, the last of which he characterized as "influence," by which "did not [mean] corruption, but a dispensation of those regular honors & emoluments, which produce an attachment to the Government."[140] Hamilton expressed a particular worry, and drew on the experience of ancient leagues to confirm it:

> All the passions then we see, of avarice, ambition, interest, which govern most individuals, and all public bodies, fall into the current of the States, and do not flow in the stream of the Genl. Govt. The former therefore will generally be an overmatch for the Genl. Govt. and render any confederacy, in its very nature precarious. Theory is in this case fully confirmed by experience. The Amphyctionic Council had it would seem ample powers for general purposes. It had in particular the power of fining and using force agst. delinquent members. What was the consequence. Their decrees were mere signals of war. The Phocian war is a striking example of it. Philip at length taking advantage of their disunion, and insinuating himself into their Councils, made himself master of their fortunes.[141]

Or, as reported by Robert Yates (a fellow New York delegate), Hamilton observed that "[h]istory shows that the decrees [of the Amphyctionic Council] were disregarded, and that the stronger states, regardless of their power, gave law to the lesser."[142]

Hamilton and Madison were combined in their opposition to Paterson's proposal, which, they believed, was simply a rehash of the now-discredited Articles of Confederation. The following day, June 19, 1787, Madison rose on the Convention floor and delivered a devastating critique of the New Jersey Plan. Among his criticisms of the very limited form of national government granted under Paterson's scheme were these points:

> Will it secure the Union against the influence of foreign powers over its members[?] [Madison] pretended not to say that any such influence had yet been tried: but it was naturally to be expected that occasions would produce it. As lessons which claimed particular attention, he cited the intrigues practised among the Amphyctionic Confederates first by the Kings of Persia, and afterwards fatally by Philip of Macedon: among the Achaeans, first by Macedon & afterwards no less fatally by Rome. ... The plan of Mr. Paterson, not giving to the general Councils any negative on the will of the particular States, left the door open for the like pernicious machinations among ourselves ...
>
> He begged the smaller States which were most attached to Mr. Paterson's plan to consider the situation in which it would leave them. ... The coercion, on which the efficacy of the plan depends, can never be exerted but on themselves. The larger States will be impregnable, the smaller only can feel the vengeance of it. He illustrated the position by the history of the Amphyctionic Confederates. ... It was the cobweb which could entangle the weak, but would be the sport of the strong.[143]

Again, Yates's version of the debates puts an even sharper point on the tenor of Madison's remarks: "It is evident, if we do not radically depart from a federal plan, we will share the fate of ancient and modern confederacies. The Amphyctionic council, like the American congress, had the power of judging in the last resort in war and peace – call out forces – send out ambassadors. What was its fate or continuance? Philip of Macedon, with little difficulty, destroyed every appearance of it. The Athenian [League] had nearly the same fate."[144]

At the end of that day's debate, Madison and Hamilton had acquired an important ally in the form of James Wilson of Pennsylvania, who declared that "I am for a national government, though the idea of federal is, in my view, the same. . . . In all extensive empires a subdivision of power is necessary. Persia, Turkey, and Rome, under its emperors, found it necessary."[145] To this, Hamilton heartily concurred: "Establish a weak government and you must at times over-leap the bounds. Rome was obliged to create dictators."[146] Wilson, however, remained unconvinced (as he would later make clear) about the relevance of much of the ancient history being bandied about: he "urged the necessity of two branches [national and state governments]; observed that if a proper model were not to be found in other Confederacies it was not to be wondered at. The number of them was small & the duration of some at least short. The Amphyctionic & Achaean were formed in the infancy of political Science; and appear by their History & fate, to have contained radical defects. . . ."[147]

The opponents of a robust national government under the Virginia Plan were by no means cowed. When the Convention renewed debate on this point on June 27, Luther Martin (1748–1826), attorney general and delegate of Maryland – a leading small state – delivered what even the normally generous Robert Yates called a "diffuse, and in many instances desultory" argument.[148] In the midst of his three-hour oration he did mention that the "Lacedemonians insisted, in the Amphictionic council to exclude some of the smaller states from a right to vote, in order that they might tyrannize over them. If the [Virginia] plan now on the table be adopted three states in the union [presumably referring to New York, Pennsylvania, and Virginia] have the controul, and they may make use of their power when they please."[149] Moreover, Martin noted that "[i]t was the ambition and power of the great Grecian states which at last ruined th[e] respectable [Amphictyonic] council."[150]

Madison could not let such a challenge go unanswered, and on June 28, he gave the lengthy speech that drew Benjamin Franklin's pointed jibe for an end to classical allusions and historical analogy.[151] Madison's point was that a strong national government was needed to control the impulses of state rivalries. An unintended consequence of the New Jersey Plan would be to set small states at the mercy of their larger neighbors, and Madison's argument made an elaborate historical proof, which is worth setting out at length:

> Was a combination to be apprehended from the mere circumstance of equality of size? Experience suggested no such danger.... It had never been seen that different Counties in the same State, conformable in extent, but disagreeing in other circumstances, betrayed a propensity to such combinations. Experience rather taught a contrary lesson. Among individuals of superior eminence & weight in Society, rivalships were much more frequent than coalitions. Among independent nations, pre-eminent over their neighbours, the same remark was verified. Carthage & Rome tore one another to pieces instead of uniting their forces to devour the weaker nations of the Earth.... England & France have succeeded to the pre-eminence & to the enmity. To this principle we owe perhaps our liberty. A coalition between those powers would have been fatal to us. Among the principal members of ancient & Modern confederacies, we find the same effect from the same cause. The contentions, not the Coalitions of Sparta, Athens & Thebes, proved fatal to the smaller members of the Amphyctionic Confederacy.... Were the large States formidable singly to their smaller neighbours? On this supposition the latter ought to wish for such a general Govt. as will operate with equal energy on the former as on themselves. The more lax the band, the more liberty the larger will have to avail themselves of their superior force. Here again Experience was an instructive monitor. What is ye situation of the weak compared with the strong in those stages of civilization in which the violence of individuals is least controuled by an efficient Government? The Heroic period of Ancient Greece ... answer this question. What is the situation of the minor sovereigns in the great society of independent nations, in which the more powerful are under no control but the nominal authority of the law of Nations? Is not the danger to the former exactly in proportion to their weakness. But there are cases still more in point. What was the condition of the weaker members of the Amphyctionic Confederacy. Plutarch [life of Themistocles] will inform us that it happened but too often that the strongest cities corrupted & awed the weaker, and that Judgment went in favor of the more powerful party.[152]

Despite the erudition of his arguments, Madison knew by the end of June 1787 that he would have to compromise on some elements of his strong national government and that the Virginia Plan would have to be diluted with some elements of Paterson's proposal. Oliver Ellsworth (1745–1807), one of Connecticut's delegates, made on June 30 a careful argument for some sort of institutional protection for the prerogatives of smaller states in the national government. Madison was forced to admit that he had to do "justice to the able & close reasoning of Mr. E[llsworth] but must observe that it did not always accord with itself. . . . Mr. E[llsworth] had also erred in saying that no instance had existed in which confederated States had not retained to themselves a perfect equality of suffrage. . . . [H]e reminded Mr. E. of the Lycian confederacy, in which the component members had votes proportioned to their importance, and which Montesquieu recommends as the fittest model for that form of Government. . . . [T]he History & fate of the several confederacies modern as well as Ancient, demonstrating some radical vice in their structure. . . ."[153]

At this pivotal moment at Philadelphia, a fateful adjustment – brokered by Oliver Ellsworth, and thus known as the "Connecticut compromise," even though Madison's plan was roundly defeated – was made which directed the rest of the proceedings. The more radical elements of Madison's and Randolph's plan – including the ability of the national legislature to directly "negative" (as Madison put it), or veto, state statutory enactments – were set aside.[154] Even more important was the agreement to establish Congress as a two-chambered legislature, with the lower house being composed by proportional representation and the upper body constituted on the basis of state equality, but with individual members voting (and not by states as with the Articles of Confederation Congress).[155] More on the impact of these significant developments on the structural Constitution's bicameralism will be considered later in this chapter, but it is important to take stock of the effect of the Connecticut compromise here.

Madison, for one, had the feeling of history repeating itself. In a letter to Jefferson in Paris, dated from October 1787, Madison expressed the fear that the Constitution would be a short-lived political experiment, doomed to repeat the failure of the ancient leagues he had studied over the previous years.[156] Madison's conclusion – drawn from his historic research – was that the primary failing of previous confederation systems was to effectively integrate the constituent polities into a federal system. One such way was to make the decision-making processes of the confederal governments be completely based on the relative strength and population of the component polities, and thus to avoid the fatal attraction of one state—one vote mechanisms. The other was to devolve so much authority on the league so as to necessarily concentrate power at the center. Madison felt that the Constitution of 1787, despite its notable improvements on the language of the Articles of Confederation and its more extensive grant of powers to the national government, still failed to fully avoid the pitfalls of past confederations.

4. *The Federalist Papers* and the Ratification Debates. If Madison, in the fall and winter of 1787, harbored doubts about his handiwork in fashioning the Constitution, he kept them well-hidden from public view. Indeed, in *The Federalist Papers* he had the opportunity, again and again, to return to the historical analogs of ancient confederacies and to draw favorable conclusions about the form and structure of the Constitution. Interestingly, it was Alexander Hamilton who first broached the subject. In *Federalist* 9, Hamilton amplified Montesquieu's concept of leagues as an "assemblage of societies" and seconded his endorsement of the Lycian Confederacy's weighted voting scheme for large, middling, and small cities, while also noting that "The COMMON COUNCIL had the appointment of all the judges and magistrates of the respective CITIES. This was certainly the most delicate species of interference in their internal administration; for if there be any thing that seems exclusively appropriated to the local jurisdictions, it is the appointment of their own officers."[157] In case any of Publius' readers had missed the point, Hamilton sharpened it later in *Federalist* 16:

> THE tendency of the principle of legislation for States, or communities, in their political capacities, as it has been exemplified by the experiment we have made of it, is equally attested by the events which have befallen all other governments of the confederate kind, of which we have any account, in exact proportion to its prevalence in those systems. The confirmations of this fact will be worthy of a distinct and particular examination. I shall content myself with barely observing here, that of all the confederacies of antiquity, which history has handed down to us, the Lycian and Achaean leagues, as far as there remain vestiges of them, appear to have been most free from the fetters of that mistaken principle, and were accordingly those which have best deserved, and have most liberally received, the applauding suffrages of political writers.[158]

It was in *Federalist* numbers 18, 19, and 20, that Madison (later acknowledging Hamilton's collaboration) was able to fully elaborate the historical project first undertaken in his *Notes on Ancient and Modern Confederacies*. *Federalist* 18 is indisputably a remarkable synthesis of Madison's classical historiography. In order to explain the project to the readers, it was announced that Publius would embark on a "concise review of the events that have attended confederate governments."[159] The discussion of the Amphictyonic

and Achaean leagues were intended to provide "a very instructive analogy to the present Confederation of the American States,"[160] and were to
"suppl[y] . . . valuable instruction."[161] By comparing and contrasting these
two Greek institutions, Publius sought to drive home his earlier point that
a confederacy without ample centralized powers was doomed.

Consider first Publius' account of the Amphictyonic League:

> The members retained the character of independent and sovereign states,
> and had equal votes in the federal council. This council had a general
> authority to propose and resolve whatever it judged necessary for the
> common welfare of Greece; to declare and carry on war; to decide, in the
> last resort, all controversies between the members; to fine the aggressing
> party; to employ the whole force of the confederacy against the disobedient;
> to admit new members. The Amphictyons were the guardians of religion,
> and of the immense riches belonging to the temple of Delphos, where they
> had the right of jurisdiction in controversies between the inhabitants and
> those who came to consult the oracle. As a further provision for the efficacy
> of the federal powers, they took an oath mutually to defend and protect the
> united cities, to punish the violators of this oath, and to inflict vengeance
> on sacrilegious despoilers of the temple.
>
> In theory, and upon paper, this apparatus of powers seems amply suf-
> ficient for all general purposes. In several material instances, they exceed
> the powers enumerated in the articles of confederation.[162]

Sadly, however, as Publius concluded, "[v]ery different, nevertheless, was the
experiment from the theory. The powers, like those of the present Congress,
were administered by deputies appointed wholly by the cities in their political capacities; and exercised over them in the same capacities. Hence the
weakness, the disorders, and finally the destruction of the confederacy."[163]
Madison was compelled to conclude, along with many of his colleagues,
that the Amphictyonic League lacked real coercive power over its members.
Indeed, at the Virginia Ratifying Convention this was a rallying-point for
Antifederalist forces, who suggested that no confederation in history had
ever been able to effectively compel obedience, and thus would be inevitably
beset by unrest and dissension.[164] Indeed, the singular triumph of the Amphictyonic League in repulsing Xerxes' invasions of Greece (499–479 BCE) was
nearly prevented by Greek disunity, resolved only at the last moment.[165]

Publius proceeded to recount (with the help of Plutarch and the Abbé de
Mably) the progressive subversions of the Amphictyonic League, and the
rivalries of the hegemonic cities in Greece (Athens, Sparta, and Thebes). All
of this culminated in the intrigues of Philip II of Macedon, a fable which

Publius told with evident relish for its (obvious) parallels with colonial and revolutionary history:

> As a weak government, when not at war, is ever agitated by internal dissentions, so these never fail to bring on fresh calamities from abroad. The Phocians having ploughed up some consecrated ground belonging to the temple of Apollo, the Amphictyonic council, according to the superstition of the age, imposed a fine on the sacrilegious offenders. The Phocians, being abetted by Athens and Sparta, refused to submit to the decree. The Thebans, with others of the cities, undertook to maintain the authority of the Amphictyons, and to avenge the violated god. The latter, being the weaker party, invited the assistance of Philip of Macedon, who had secretly fostered the contest. Philip gladly seized the opportunity of executing the designs he had long planned against the liberties of Greece. By his intrigues and bribes he won over to his interests the popular leaders of several cities; by their influence and votes, gained admission into the Amphictyonic council; and by his arts and his arms, made himself master of the confederacy.
>
> Such were the consequences of the fallacious principle on which this interesting establishment was founded. Had Greece, says a judicious observer on her fate, been united by a stricter confederation, and persevered in her union, she would never have worn the chains of Macedon; and might have proved a barrier to the vast projects of Rome.[166]

By way of contrast, Publius observed that the Achaean League was "far more intimate, and its organization much wiser, than in the preceding instance. It will accordingly appear, that though not exempt from a similar catastrophe, it by no means equally deserved it."[167]

Madison must have had an opportunity to develop further research on the Achaean Confederacy, because his description in *Federalist* 18 was much more fully realized than his earlier *Notes*:

> The cities composing this league retained their municipal jurisdiction, appointed their own officers, and enjoyed a perfect equality. The senate, in which they were represented, had the sole and exclusive right of peace and war; of sending and receiving ambassadors; of entering into treaties and alliances; of appointing a chief magistrate or praetor, as he was called, who commanded their armies, and who, with the advice and consent of ten of the senators, not only administered the government in the recess of the senate, but had a great share in its deliberations, when assembled. According to the primitive constitution, there were two praetors associated in the administration; but on trial a single one was preferred.

> It appears that the cities had all the same laws and customs, the same weights and measures, and the same money. But how far this effect proceeded from the authority of the federal council is left in uncertainty. It is said only that the cities were in a manner compelled to receive the same laws and usages.
>
> ... [T]here was infinitely more of moderation and justice in the administration of its government, and less of violence and sedition in the people, than were to be found in any of the cities exercising SINGLY all the prerogatives of sovereignty. The Abbe Mably, in his observations on Greece, says that the popular government, which was so tempestuous elsewhere, caused no disorders in the members of the Achaean republic, BECAUSE IT WAS THERE TEMPERED BY THE GENERAL AUTHORITY AND LAWS OF THE CONFEDERACY.[168]

Publius was clearly endorsing the superior structure and institutional machinery of the more geographically limited Achaean League, as opposed to the pan-Hellenic aspirations (as Madison regarded them) of the Amphictyonic Council. Although the Achaean Confederacy was able to survive the Macedonian absorption of the fourth century BCE, it was only because the league's members played the dangerous game of requesting aid from outside hegemons in order to fend off Greek rivals, or to settle internal disputes. Ultimately, the Achaean Confederacy fell to the intrigues of the Romans, and "[b]y these arts this union, the last hope of Greece, the last hope of ancient liberty, was torn into pieces; and such imbecility and distraction introduced, that the arms of Rome found little difficulty in completing the ruin which their arts had commenced."[169]

The clear message of these two morality tales was that the chief concern for confederal republics was "the tendency of federal bodies rather to anarchy among the members, than to tyranny in the head."[170] But Publius was by no means consistent in this point, since in the same paper, he was obliged to observe that, at least for the Amphictyonic League, "[t]he more powerful members, instead of being kept in awe and subordination, tyrannized successively over all the rest."[171] Indeed, they were joined in these views by John Dickinson, writing his *Letters of Fabius* in early 1788.[172] Fabius warned that the Amphictyonic council came to grief because of the "ambitious, avaricious and selfish projects of some of" its members.[173] "Their affairs were shattered by dissensions, emulations, and civil wars, artfully and diligently fomented by princes who thought it their interest.... "[174] Hamilton, Madison, and Dickinson all knew that the chief source of criticism of the Constitution was the renewed concern of smaller states that they would be dominated in the new Union, and that the national government's powers would progressively aggregate and dismantle the authority and prerogatives of the state governments.

It was incumbent on Publius to raise the specter of insidious outside forces that would work to subvert the republic, and ancient history provided plenty of examples of the successful use of this divide-and-conquer tactic. So it was that Philip II's undermining of the Amphictyonic League and Rome's subjugation of the Achaean Confederacy became virtual code phrases for possible French, Spanish, or British imperial designs on the young republic, potentially riven by regional divides. Madison spoke directly to this in *Federalist* 43 when, quoting Montesquieu, he observed: "Governments of dissimilar principles and forms have been found less adapted to a federal coalition of any sort, than those of a kindred nature.... 'Greece was undone,' he adds, 'as soon as the king of Macedon obtained a seat among the Amphictyons.' In th[at] latter case, no doubt, the disproportionate force, as well as the monarchical form, of the new confederate, had its share of influence on the events."[175]

The other objective for Publius' use of classicism in *The Federalist* was to provide some historical comfort for those who worried that the new national government under the Constitution would prove to be a juggernaut.

> We have seen, in all the examples of ancient and modern confederacies, the strongest tendency continually betraying itself in the members, to despoil the general government of its authorities, with a very ineffectual capacity in the latter to defend itself against the encroachments. Although, in most of these examples, the system has been so dissimilar from that under consideration as greatly to weaken any inference concerning the latter from the fate of the former, yet, as the States will retain, under the proposed Constitution, a very extensive portion of active sovereignty, the inference ought not to be wholly disregarded. In the Achaean league it is probable that the federal head had a degree and species of power, which gave it a considerable likeness to the government framed by the convention. The Lycian Confederacy, as far as its principles and form are transmitted, must have borne a still greater analogy to it. Yet history does not inform us that either of them ever degenerated, or tended to degenerate, into one consolidated government. On the contrary, we know that the ruin of one of them proceeded from the incapacity of the federal authority to prevent the dissensions, and finally the disunion, of the subordinate authorities. These cases are the more worthy of our attention, as the external causes by which the component parts were pressed together were much more numerous and powerful than in our case; and consequently less powerful ligaments within would be sufficient to bind the members to the head, and to each other.[176]

In short, if Greek confederations were able to divine the proper mixture of central and local authority in a league system, and survive (albeit briefly) in far more adverse historical and political circumstances, it would be possible for the American republic under the Constitution to flourish.

It was by no means clear for those who debated and ratified the Constitution in late 1787 and early 1788, what the limits of national authority would be under the new charter. It was, of course, not publicly revealed that the Philadelphia Convention had considered even more extraordinary powers being given to the central government, including (in the Virginia Plan) the ability to actually negative contrary state enactments. Instead, what the public perceived was a scheme in which federal law *was*, in fact, supreme. That was the clear import of a provision in Article VI, which ordained that "This Constitution, and the Laws of the United States which shall be made in Pursuance thereof; and all Treaties made, or which shall be made, under the Authority of the United States, shall be the Supreme Law of the Land; and the Judges in every State shall be bound thereby, any Thing in the Constitution or Laws of any State to the Contrary notwithstanding."[177]

Hamilton did attempt to downplay the significance of what came to be known as the Supremacy Clause.[178] It, combined with an extraordinary long list of the legislative authority of Congress, appeared to belie protestations that the national government was merely one of limited and enumerated powers. This was especially the case because Article I, section 8 culminated in the sweeping power "To make all Laws which shall be necessary and proper for carrying into Execution the foregoing Powers, and all other Powers vested by this Constitution in the Government of the United States, or in any Department or Officer thereof."[179] Madison, in *Federalist* 44 answered critics who suggested that this was a virtual blank-check of powers to the national government, one that would fatally undermine the system of federalism in the Constitution.[180] Indeed, Madison observed that the Sweeping Clause was properly construed as a constraint on the federal government's implied powers, for "[h]ad the Constitution been silent on this head, there can be no doubt that all the particular powers requisite as means of executing the general powers would have resulted to the government, by unavoidable implication. No axiom is more clearly established in law, or in reason, than that wherever the end is required, the means are authorized; whenever a general power to do a thing is given, every particular power necessary for doing it is included."[181] Madison's position was thus more modest compared to that of James Wilson, who was among the first to argue, in his 1785 pamphlet, *Considerations on the Bank of North America*, that even under the Articles of Confederation, the national government enjoyed, in addition to the powers specifically delegated, "general powers . . . resulting from the union of the whole."[182] This notion of inherent law-making powers of a central government was a central tenet of Wilson's strong brand of nationalism, and tended to place him more in alignment with Hamilton's views.

As a reflection of this, in Wilson's *Lectures on Law*, first formally delivered in 1790 (but the sentiments announced in which had been notorious prior to that date[183]), he offered a far more sanguine vision of ancient Greek confederations than Madison had done in *Federalist* 18. Devoting a whole chapter to "Man, in Confederation," Wilson was able to derive four key ingredients for successful confederations. The first was a common purpose, best reflected in the Amphictyonic League's mission to protect Greece from barbarian rule and religious defilement. The "Amphyctionic Council," as Wilson called it, was as "Congress of the United States of Greece. The delegates who composed that august assembly, represented the body of the nation, and were invested in the full power to deliberate and resolve upon whatever appeared to them to be most conducive to the public prosperity.... From the moment of its establishment, the interests of their country became the common concern of all the people of Greece. The different states, of which the union was composed, formed only one and the same republic."[184] Wilson's praise (shared by some of his contemporaries[185]) for the structure of the Amphictyonic League was unbounded – it "performed wonderful actions, and supported, for so long a time, the character of the pride of nations," and its establishment "should be admired, as a great master-piece in human politics."[186] Of course, that led to difficulties insofar as Wilson had to explain to his students and readers why the Amphictyonic League failed so spectacularly in the face of Macedonian aggression. This, Wilson asserted, was the result of "when Greece herself began to degenerate, her representative body was contaminated with the general corruption."[187]

From the experience of the Lycian Confederacy, Wilson derived his second virtue, and he echoed Montesquieu's endorsement of the Lycians weighted voting mechanism, and observed that "[t]his republic was celebrated for its moderation and justice."[188] In large measure this was attributable to the fact that the Lycian cities shared a common form of government – a problem that would plague the Amphictyonic League once it admitted the Macedonian kingdom to its membership.[189] Moreover, Wilson observed that "[i]n a confederated republic, consisting of states of unequal numbers, extent, and power, the influence of each ought to bear a corresponding proportion."[190]

The third element for successful confederal government Wilson derived from the historical record of the Achaean League, which (unlike the Amphictyonic Council) required a commonality of laws among its members. Wilson noted, as had Madison, that in "Achaia, all the cities had the same money, the same weights and measures, the same customs and laws. The popular government, we are told, was not so tempestuous in the cities of Achaia, as in some of the other cities of Greece; because, in Achaia, it was tempered by the authority and laws of the confederacy. Indeed it is unquestionable, that, in this confederacy, there was much more moderation and justice, than was to be found in any of the cities exercising singly all the prerogatives of sovereignty."[191] Or, as John Dickinson's Fabius put it, "So uniform were they, that all seemed to be but one state."[192] This sentiment was echoed by James Monroe, on the floor of the Virginia Ratifying Convention. "The Achaean league," he observed, "had more analogy to ours, and gives me great hopes that the apprehensions of gentlemen with respect to our confederacy are groundless."[193] Quoting at length from Polybius, Monroe concluded that "[t]his league was founded on democratical principles, and, from the wisdom of its structure, continued a far greater length of time than any other. Its members, like our states, by their confederation, retained their individual sovereignty, and enjoyed a perfect equality."[194]

The fourth, and final, ingredient for enduring league systems Wilson drew from a surprising source not mentioned at all by Madison: Tacitus' description of the ancient Germanic leagues of the Suevi, formed as a response to Roman imperial incursions into Germany in the first century BCE and first century CE. Of interest to Wilson was the war leadership conferred on one elected tribal official, a *princeps pagorum*.[195] Wilson clearly believed that strong and unified leadership, particularly in the context of war powers, was a necessity for any confederal republic, even one as inchoate as the ancient Germanic tribes.

5. The Historic Reality of Ancient Greek Leagues. Together, Madison and Wilson sought to create a historiographic synthesis of the strengths and weaknesses of ancient leagues and to distill the essence of successful confederative governments. A number of scholars have rightly observed,[196] however, that the Framing generation's comprehension of ancient Greek leagues was superficial and largely dependent on selective readings of canonical texts and the secondary literature of such histories as that of the Abbé de Mably, who articulated the view that the Amphictyonic Council was "une république fédérative"and "les états généraux de la Grèce."[197] Periodically Wilson and Publius and others remarked on the very "imperfect monuments"[198] history had left of the Greek confederations, such that they "could have supplied but a very small fund of applicable remarks."[199] Melancthon Smith in speaking before the New York Ratifying Convention made the rather salient point that "It had been observed that no example of federal republics had succeeded. It was true that the ancient confederated republics were all destroyed; so were those which were not confederated; and all ancient governments, of every form, had shared the same fate."[200]

So before leaving this topic, it is worth considering what the historic reality of ancient Greek confederations was, and whether the Framing generation was correct in putting so much emphasis on the political experience of those polities. For starters, it needs to be borne in mind that aside from sparse Biblical evidence of political leagues among the ancient Israelites,[201] and Tacitus' and Ceasar's reporting of ancient Gallic and Germanic tribes,[202] all the historic evidence does arise from the period of Greek political life in the years 500 BCE (the beginning of the Persian, or Medic, Wars) to about 50 BCE (the final acts of Roman absorption). In the Greek world there was a bewildering array of military alliances (both defensive and offensive), and political grants of rights to the citizens of other polities.[203]

Before turning to the status of ancient Greek political unions, it is important to first lay to rest doubts about the Amphictyonic Council. *Amphictyones* were local religious leagues based on a common cult. As Adcock and Mosley have pointed out, "they were local or regional associations with a communal religious center."[204] The center might be a common altar, such as the one where the sea god Poseidon was worshipped at Panionium in Priene. It also might be the site of a religious festival or games.[205] The maintenance of religious institutions led to the development of political and economic ties between the members of these religious leagues. Such ties might have meant the conclusion of generic treaties in which members swore perpetual peace and protection of the common sites of the league.[206] A variety of sites were variously associated with the gods Apollo, Demeter, Poseidon, and Athena.[207]

Of these institutions, the *amphictyony* established to maintain the Oracle at Delphi was the most prominent. The twelve tribes of the Delphic Amphictyony appointed officials to take charge of the care and maintenance of the center, but twice a year a formal meeting of the representatives (*hieromnemones* and *pylagoroi*) was summoned.[208] These meetings observed a rule of strict sovereign equality: each tribe had equal voting power. Athens and Sparta were thus placed on par with tribes represented by the Dorians and Ionians.[209] On occasion these meetings had a decidedly political overtone, so the delegates were formally accredited by the city-state members of the amphictyony.[210] This was especially so when the Amphictyonic council was called to vote sanctions (usually in the form of a punitive military expedition) against a transgressing member.[211]

A number of instances have been recorded of hostilities being launched under the authority of the Delphic Amphictyony. In the First Sacred War (596–586 BCE), action was taken against the coastal village of Cirrha, which, by virtue of its strategic position, charged exorbitant tolls for visitors to the oracle. The Council of the Amphictyons made war against the offenders, razed Cirrha to the ground, consecrated its territory to Apollo, and ordered that it henceforth be laid to waste.[212] The Second Sacred War (357–346 BCE), was overtly political in character. Beginning as a local dispute between Phocis and Thebes, it quickly escalated into nearly pan-Hellenic conflict, with Athens and Sparta allied with Phocis against Theban hegemony. In a rare act of retaliation, the Phocians occupied the Delphic sanctuary and destroyed part of it. This act led to the intervention of Philip II of Macedon into Greek affairs. He expelled the Phocians from Delphi, razed their city, and (as symbolic of his growing power over Greece) replaced them on the Delphic Amphictyonic Council in his new status as "protector" of Greece.[213]

The Delphic Amphictyony periodically served as a consultative organization for resolving inter-Hellenic disputes. Sometime this was undertaken as part of the religious functions of the League, as when inhabitants of Megara interfered with a sacred delegation (*theoroi*) from the Peloponnesus, the Council condemned the guilty individuals of sacrilege and ordered some executed and others banished.[214] A similar incident occurred in 470 BCE when some Thessalian traders had been plundered and imprisoned by the piratical inhabitants of Scyros.[215] Likewise, Sparta brought a complaint against Thebes before the Council, arguing that the Thebans had erected an improper trophy at the site of a military victory.[216] This dispute was part of a long-running litigation between the two implacably hostile city-states, the forum for which was the Amphictyonic Council.[217]

The Framing generation was not alone in believing that Greek amphictyonys represented the most sophisticated complex of treaty relations, approaching even a level of real international organization or true federal union.[218] This is unquestionably an extravagant claim. It is true that the functions of the Delphic amphictyony had far-ranging effects, including the amelioration of the conditions of conflict. Even though there was a notional sense of sovereign equality in the operations of Amphictyonic institutions, it would be misleading to consider them much more than a "primitive habit of religious fraternisation."[219] Having a restricted membership and rudimentary methods, it is difficult to consider amphictyones as an "attempt to embody the notion of international justice in an organized institution."[220] It is now impossible to believe that the Amphictyonic Council represented any form of true federal government.

There was a subtle distinction observed in ancient Greece between federal states and looser organizations of cities. Both were known by the generic term of *koinon*, which could have been used to describe virtually any sort of association. Likewise, the phrase *ethnos*, which literally meant tribe, could be used as a synonym for "nation" particularly when referring to aggregates of city-states.[221] J. A. O. Larsen says that the two most technical political terms in classical Greek, and the ones which convey definite international legal meanings, were *hegemonia symmachia*[222] and *sympoliteia*.[223]

A hegemonic symmachia was a league of states formed by a dominant city-State. In such a Greek league, the official leadership and decision-making mechanisms were in the hands of the *hegemon*. The Delian[224] and Second Athenian[225] Leagues, both established under Athens' dominance, had officials provided by that city. The Hellenic League (also known as the League of Corinth), established by Phillip II of Macedon as *hegemon*, had a facially more egalitarian form of government, led by five officers called *proëdroi*, who served not only as chairmen of the league assemblies but also as a permanent secretariat for the league administration between meetings. The Corinth League council (or *synedrion*) was composed on a proportional basis, giving greater representation to major Greek cities like Athens and Thebes.[226] It also had some limited competence to resolve inter-city disputes without reference to Macedon as hegemon, but this was sparingly exercised. The League council did, for example, assist in resolving a territorial dispute between Melos and Cimolus by referring it to arbitration by Argos.[227] But there was no question that league officials were answerable to the King of Macedon and had very limited powers.[228]

Treaties constituting hegemonic *symmachiai* were carefully crafted to both ensure the dominant role of the league leader as well as provide notional assurances of the autonomy of other parties. We have, for example, a copy of the decree establishing the Second Athenian Naval League in 378 BCE, intended to protect against Spartan aggression. It provided that:

> If anyone of the Greeks or of the barbarians dwelling upon the mainland or the islands, provided they are not subjects of the king [of Persia], wishes to become an ally of the Athenians and their allies, he may do so, preserving his freedom and autonomy, in the enjoyment of the constitution he may prefer, without receiving a garrison or governor [from Athens], and without paying tribute, upon the same conditions as the Chians, Thebans, and the other allies.... And if anyone shall make an attack upon those who have made the alliance either by land or by sea, the Athenians and the allies are to come to their rescue by land and by sea with their full strength in so far as they can.[229]

What is also significant is that, in addition to the instrument creating the Naval League, the members each concluded alliances with one another.[230]

So there was an interlocking set of obligations by treaty. And, again, make no mistake: the final say of alliance policy rested with the Athenian assembly.[231] Nor was this any form of representative, confederal government.

In contrast to these *symmachiai*, Greek federal states operated on a basis of notional sovereign equality tempered by the need of creating a unitary state. The culmination of a political union was a *sympoliteia*, in which each city granted the full rights of citizenship to the residents of every other participating city.[232] *Sympolity* as a federal union of Greek city-states conveyed not only a permanent military alliance effectuated on a basis of equality, but also a whole host of shared economic rights, which otherwise could only be conveyed by specific sorts of agreements, known generically as *enktesis* (including *isopoliteia* and *symbola*). To use Larsen's definition of a Greek federal state: it is one in which "there is a local citizenship in the smaller communities as well as a joint or federal citizenship and in which the citizens are under the jurisdiction both of federal and local authorities."[233] Examples of true federal arrangements in classical Greece would include the Boeotian confederation, which lasted from 447 to 386 BCE, and (in a second incarnation) from 336 to 246 BCE,[234] and the Achaean, Lycian and Aetolian confederations (mentioned by some of the Framers).[235]

It was manifest, for example, that federal leagues "possessed a more highly developed executive and offered more opportunities for quick action than the symmachies."[236] Most of the true federal unions in ancient Greece maintained a year-round executive office, usually a single official, called typically as a *strategos* or *archon*. Such a leader was aided by a vice president or second-in-command (the cavalry commander, or *hipparchos*), or a league secretary (*grammateus*). Usually joined with the chief magistrate was a cabinet (*synedrion*) of advisors, called variously the *boeotarchs* (in the Boeotian Confederacy), the *damiourgoi* (for the Achaeans) or the *apokletoi* (for the Aetolians). Additionally, many confederal republics had in place subsidiary boards (for the treasury and war supplies), including a body charged with the proper recording and observance of league laws, a *nomophylakes*.[237] In the Boeotian Confederacy there may well have been official bodies – elected directly by the constituent cities – to deal with religious issues (the *aphedriateuontes*), regulation of markets (*agonarchs*), and perhaps even a supreme judicial body to handle disputes between citizens or constituent league members (the *thesmophylakes*). There were also officials appointed by the federal *boule*, including the boeotarchs and *katoptai* (official auditors).[238]

A permanent secretariat was necessary because the confederation assemblies (known as a *boule* or *ekklesia*) – bringing together the delegates of the constituent cities in their representative capacity – usually met only a few times a year (twice a year for the Aetolians, quarterly for the Achaeans). For the Boeotian Confederacy, the representative institutions were uniquely arranged. For the period prior to the Macedonian invasion, the league territory was divided into eleven districts, roughly balanced between Thebes (the leading city and its environs) and distant areas. In that period, each of the constituent cities of the league was an oligarchy, and nearly half the adult male populations were disenfranchized. Each district provided the same number of troops, and made the same financial assessment to the treasury. Each district named sixty counselors who met in the federal assembly, and, most important of all, one boeotarch on the confederation council.[239] Because the assembly met only in rotating cohorts of 165 members, it was essential to have a working body that could meet regularly.

Had the Framers been aware of the Boeotian Confederacy, they would have likely added it to their list of analogous Greek leagues, and enlisted its experience for their purposes in conceiving the Constitution. The modern verdict has been favorable on the Boeotian Confederacy's success,[240] but modern historiography has validated some of the Framing generation's conclusions about the other confederations they considered. The Aetolian Confederation, mentioned in passing in *Federalist* 18,[241] was actually a model of centralization. The key decision-making organ of that league was its synedrion, which (unlike the Boeotians) had the constituent cities represented in proportion to their population. The synedrion then deputized a number of their members to serve as apokletoi, and it is these officials that Polybius and Livy reported as carrying on the bulk of the negotiations when Rome was about to conquer that part of Greece in 191 and 190 BCE.[242] The Aetolian Confederacy also apparently had well-functioning league courts, arbitrating disputes between member cities and outright settling disputes between league citizens (and ordering seizures of property by way of judgments).[243] As Larsen observes, though, "the Aetolian Confederacy was something of a paradox," insofar as its local constituents enjoyed great autonomy and the league operations were confined to foreign affairs, it still enjoyed substantial prosperity.[244]

As for the Lycian Confederacy (which flourished from 100 to 43 BCE), the league which the Framers admired because of its proportional voting system, modern philology has confirmed their conclusions, largely drawn on the account of Strabo's *Geography*.[245] It is believed that the Lycians may have had not one, but two, elected bodies for their union: a federal council (boule), and an electoral assembly (*archairesiake ekklesia*), with the latter being the representative body (with proportional representation) mentioned by Strabo. It was the electoral assembly that named the chief magistrate of the confederacy, the Lyciarch. The Lycians may have had an even more developed judiciary than the Aetolians, with records extant of multiple judges exercising different forms of jurisdiction over various kinds of disputes.[246]

That leaves the Achaean Confederacy, which Larsen rightly described as "the most important of all Greek federal states."[247] The Achaeans, like their Boeotian neighbors to the north, went through two periods of a federative republic, with the second commencing about 280 BCE, and it is the revived institution that captured the attention of the Framers. The transition, mentioned by Polybius,[248] of the league appointing one, and not two, generals, was significant for the Framing generation, who would have read Plutarch's biography of Aratus, the Achaean Confederacy's paramount leader after 251 BCE. Also, the small advisory council of ten *damiorgoi* was quite prominent in the governance of the league.[249] Additionally, there was a full assembly of the Achaean towns, which rarely met (except in emergencies), and a boule (numbering close to 300 or more), meeting as a *synodos* at regular intervals.[250] Significantly for the Framers, the constituents of the Achaean League were all democracies,[251] unlike the oligarchies of the Boeotians and the mixed systems of the Lycians and Aetolians. The Achaean Confederacy may have been the only successful ancient league constituted as a federative republic for democracies.

What most influenced the Framing generation – especially Madison and Wilson – was Polybius' statement that the Achaean constitution provided for a uniformity of laws.[252] We have evidence that the *nomographoi*, a board of commissioners charged with periodically revising the laws, was in operation during much of the life of the league.[253] There was also apparently a cadre of special judges, whose charge it was to exercise criminal jurisdiction over treasons committed against the league, as well as to dispense honors. They heard cases in small panels, sometimes even drawing foreign judges to hear particular cases where there was a potential for conflicts of interest.[254] In any event, the league institutions were primarily concerned with the management of foreign affairs and the conduct of hostilities.

The reality of ancient Greek confederations suggests that the Framers were right to consult this historic experience, even if they were grossly misguided in some of their conclusions. Putting aside the spectacular irrelevance of the Ampictyonic institutions to the problem of federative republics, it seems clear that hegemonic *symmachiai* represented the epitome of Greek power alliances, while *sympoliteiai* effectuated the unifying (almost republican) spirit of Greek intercity politics. Neither was very successful. The great hegemonic powers – Athens, Sparta, and Thebes – were never able for long to exert commanding influence over their erstwhile allies. Balance-of-power dynamics and localized tensions all but prevented this. Likewise, unifying and federalist tendencies in parts of Greece, as well as pan-Hellenic aspirations, were met with opposition by the constituent cities, jealous of their ancestral customs and prerogatives. *Symmachiai* and *sympoliteiai* were the unfulfilled dreams of two different conceptions of Greek unity.

The Framing generation had recourse to ancient history to solve the ultimate mystery of divided sovereignty – can two sovereigns subsist in the same space? For many of the Framers this was an impossibility, a version of that classical conundrum of "imperium in imperio."[255] As Thomas Tredwell observed at the New York Ratifying Convention, "[t]he idea of two distinct sovereigns in the same country, separately possessed of sovereign and supreme power, in the same matters at the same time, is as supreme an absurdity, as that two distinct separate circles can be bounded exactly by the same circumference."[256] Indeed, as Hamilton argued in *Federalist* 15:

> Let us at last break the fatal charm which has too long seduced us from the paths of felicity and prosperity.
>
> It is true, as has been before observed that facts, too stubborn to be resisted, have produced a species of general assent to the abstract proposition that there exist material defects in our national system; but the usefulness of the concession, on the part of the old adversaries of federal measures, is destroyed by a strenuous opposition to a remedy, upon the only principles that can give it a chance of success. While they admit that the government of the United States is destitute of energy, they contend against conferring upon it those powers which are requisite to supply that energy. They seem still to aim at things repugnant and irreconcilable; at an augmentation of federal authority, without a diminution of State authority; at sovereignty in the Union, and complete independence in the members. They still, in fine, seem to cherish with blind devotion the political monster of an imperium in imperio.[257]

The decisive lesson of ancient history was the possibility of splitting the "atom of sovereignty."[258] Even while Madison harbored doubts that the "plan of the Convention," and the resultant constitutional scheme, would raise "the evil of imperia in imperio"[259] and cause the ultimate dilution of national government authority, Antifederalist forces were able on this issue to mobilize opposition.[260] This was so despite the clear authority given to the states to ratify the Constitution,[261] and to authorize subsequent amendments.[262] Ultimately, in 1789, the First Congress in the course of drawing up constitutional amendments as the Bill of Rights was compelled to offer what became the Tenth Amendment: "The powers not delegated to the United States by the Constitution, nor prohibited by it to the States, are reserved to the States respectively, or to the people."[263] Athough states' rights advocates sought to strengthen this provision even more by adding a qualification that the national government could only take those powers "*expressly* delegated," this was rebuffed.[264] Despite this, Thomas Jefferson actually called the Tenth Amendment "the foundation of the Constitution,"[265] staking out a position (at least at the time) strikingly at variance with Madison's. The Tenth Amendment's reservation of state sovereignty – and the parallel provision in the Eleventh Amendment proclaiming a form of state sovereign immunity – remain to this day contentious issues, and will be considered in Chapter 4. Suffice to conclude here that the classical analogues of these amendments[266] were as notorious – and instructive – as those for the elements of federalism in the main body of the Constitution itself.

B. BICAMERALISM AND THE SENATE

Despite the fact that the entire revolutionary enterprise of the American colonies, and the first form of government under the Articles of Confederation, had been managed by a unicameral assembly – the Continental Congress – virtually none of the Framers (with the notable exception of Benjamin Franklin[267]) seriously advocated the continuance of that form of legislature. Of course, the Framers were familiar with the excesses of parliamentarianism during the English Civil War, including the periods of the Long and Rump Parliaments, where legislative and executive power was vested in one institution.[268] But in view of the fact that most of the colonies had been ruled in a bicameral fashion (with a popularly elected assembly and a governor-appointed council), at Philadelphia the Framers seemed unanimous in the view that a fundamental alteration would have to be made in the legislative organs of any national government they would create.

There was a brief flirtation with unicameralism by a handful of the new states after 1776, including Georgia, Pennsylvania, and Vermont. More than any other state of the era, Pennsylvania's experiment with legislative design reached a high level of maturity and refinement, and its rejection of unicameralism in 1790 set an influential example for other states.[269] Change was thus in the air at the Constitutional Convention at Philadelphia in 1787; the only question was what form would a new federal assembly take. Proceeding on the assumption that it would have to be broadly representative not only of the constitutive states of the confederation (as in the Articles), but also of the entire people of the nation, the Framers set to work.

The Framers knew well from the political theorists they admired about the dangers of a unified legislature, as the "most dangerous branch"[270] of government. The Athenian council (boule), as described by Aristotle, was the model most distrusted: a single, unitary body selected for one year, the leadership of which was picked by lot for even shorter terms, and which had the power to take up any issue and to decide it by a bare majority vote.[271] It is no surprise that Machiavelli's *Discourses* virtually ignores the Athenian assemblies of pure democracy, preferring instead to laud the small and elite Spartan senate (gerousia).[272] Montesquieu likewise had praise for the Spartan *ephori*, that group of leaders that held the monarchical power of the two hereditary kings in check, as a sort of protolegislature.[273] But he reserved most of his attention for the Roman and Carthaginian senates, which he viewed as being the best sort of legislative body, for so long as its members possessed "virtue" and "authority."[274]

The Framers would have likely been extensively influenced by the work of James Harrington, especially his 1656 allegorical work, *The Commonwealth of Oceana*.[275] It is a distinctive tract, because alone among English Enlightenment political writing, it emphasized a bicameral form of legislature and extols the virtues of an institution known as a "senate." Harrington discussed the ancient historical precedents of the Israelite Council of Seventy Elders (in the Old Testament) or *sanhedrin* (in the New Testament),[276] the Athenian boule,[277] Spartan gerousia,[278] Carthaginian Council of One Hundred,[279] and Roman Senate.[280] Harrington criticized the fact that the Athenian boule was selected by lot,[281] what he disparagingly called "the council of the bean."[282] The Israelite *sanhedrin* was, according to Harrington, nothing more than a self-perpetuating religious council.[283] He reserved unalloyed praise for the Lacedaemonian (Spartan) gerousia, which consisted of thirty life-members over the age of 60, elected by the people.[284] The Roman senate was larger than its Spartan counterpart, with three hundred members, and although self-perpetuating it was less oligarchical, in the sense that it was notionally open to all social cohorts, so long as an aspirant had served in the precursor magistracies, and had been approved by the censors.[285] Nevertheless, Harrington was critical of the senate of the Roman republic as being in constant conflict with plebian orders (especially over agrarian reform), and with the people's representatives, the popular tribunes.[286]

Among the Framing generation, John Adams had been one of the first to stake-out a position of hostility to a legislative branch consisting only of one chamber.[287] In a letter of March 1776, which became the basis of his pamphlet, *Thoughts on Government, Applicable to the Present State of the American Colonies*, Adams declaimed that a single assembly is subject to all the "vices, follies and frailties of an individual," leading to "hasty results and absurd judgments." Moreover, he asserted that a single assembly will tend to be corrupt or, as he put it, "is apt to be avaricious, and in time will not scruple to exempt itself from burthens which it will lay, without compunction, on its constituents." Adams then predicted that the ultimate indignity of unicameralism is that a single assembly would eventually vote itself into perpetuity.[288]

Adams expanded on these simple precepts in writing his *Defence of the Constitutions of the United States*. It must be borne in mind that Adams wrote this volume as a spirited rebuttal of the views (written in 1778) of Anne-Robert-Jacques Turgot (1727–1781), a French politician and philosopher, who was strongly critical of the constitutionalism of the new American states. Turgot, and his other French contemporaries (including Mirabeau) favored a strongly central government for America,[289] capped by a single legislative assembly.[290] Turgot concluded: "I am not satisfied, I own, with any constitutions which have as yet been framed by the different American States."[291] Grievously challenged, Adams proceeded to take up his pen (or his cudgel, depending on his mood), and the result was a nearly three hundred-page volume – part learned treatise, part screed – that was to prove somewhat influential as a basic source book on government for the Framing generation.

Consistent with his views about mixed government, Adams was concerned that a single assembly could not strike a balance between aristocratic elitism and populist faction. As Adams said, "It is from the natural aristocracy in a single assembly that the first danger is to be apprehended in the present state of manners in America.... The only remedy is to throw the rich and the proud into one group, in a separate assembly, and there tie their hands; if you give them scope with the people at large or their representatives, they will destroy all equality and liberty, with the consent and acclamations of the people themselves."[292] In support of this position, Adams relied on the well-known speech before the Roman senate of Manius Valerius, as reported in Dionysius of Halicarnassus' *Roman Antiquities*.[293] But Adams was critical of classical examples and asserted that the institutions of the Roman popular tribune and the Spartan ephors inadequately protected the interests of the popular masses against aristocratic encroachment. "It is really astonishing," Adams concluded, "that such peoples as Greeks and Romans should ever have thought four or five ephori, or a single tribune, or a college of ten tribunes, an adequate representation of themselves. If Valerius had proposed that the consul should have been made an integral part of the legislature, and that the Roman people should choose another council of two or three hundred, equally representing them, to be another integral part, he would then have seen that the appointment of a dictator could never, in any case, become necessary."[294]

The Romans, however, did offer a useful precedent to the Framers. In the institution of the overlapping functions of the comitia centuriata and the comitia tributa, some Americans perceived the principle of a divided legislature along mixed government lines.[295] Alexander Hamilton thus opined, at length, in *Federalist* 34, that

> [i]t is well known that in the Roman republic the legislative authority, in the last resort, resided for ages in two different political bodies-not as branches of the same legislature, but as distinct and independent legislatures, in each of which an opposite interest prevailed: in one the patrician; in the other, the plebian. Many arguments might have been adduced to prove the unfitness of two such seemingly contradictory authorities, each having power to ANNUL or REPEAL the acts of the other. But a man would have been regarded as frantic who should have attempted at Rome to disprove their existence. It will be readily understood that I allude to the COMITIA CENTURIATA and the COMITIA TRIBUTA. The former, in which the people voted by centuries, was so arranged as to give a superiority to the patrician interest; in the latter, in which numbers prevailed, the plebian interest had an entire predominancy. And yet these two legislatures coexisted for ages, and the Roman republic attained to the utmost height of human greatness.[296]

Adams's and Hamilton's views were certainly shared by their colleagues. James Wilson would have later cause to lecture that "the structure of the legislative power ... ought to be divided," and he asserted that "this position ... is ... one of the most important in both the theory and the practice of government."[297] "A single legislature," Wilson went on, "is calculated to unite in it all the pernicious qualities of the different extremes of bad government. It produces a general weakness, inactivity, and confusion; and these are intermixed with sudden and violent fits of despotism, injustice and cruelty."[298] So, for Wilson, the issue was not so much the degenerative effects of class warfare (as Adams feared), but, rather, the institutional dangers of concentrating legislative powers into one assembly. Or, as Luther Martin put the matter: "If gentlemen conceive that the legislative branch is dangerous, divide them into two."[299]

At the Philadelphia Convention, these ideas were put into a practical form, and were leavened with classical analogy. In the discussion on June 7 about the likely features and composition of an upper body for Congress (already being referred to as a "senate"[300]), this matter came into sharp focus. James Madison reported himself as saying:

> The use of the Senate is to consist in its proceeding with more coolness, with more system, and with more wisdom, than the popular branch. Enlarge their number and you communicate to them the vices which they are meant to correct. He differed from Mr. D[ickenson] who thought that the additional number would give additional weight to the body. On the contrary it appeared to him that their weight would be in an inverse ratio to their number. The example of the Roman Tribunes was applicable. They lost their influence and power, in proportion as their number was augmented. The reason seemed to be obvious: They were appointed to take care of the popular interests and pretensions at Rome, because the people by reason of their numbers could not act in concert; were liable to fall into factions among themselves, and to become a prey to their aristocratic adversaries. The more the representatives of the people therefore were multiplied, the more they partook of the infirmities of their constituents, the more liable they became to be divided among themselves either from their own indiscretions or the artifices of the opposite faction, and of course the less capable of fulfilling their trust.[301]

John Dickinson, in sharp contrast to the antiaristocratic view of John Adams, observed: "that the Senate ought to be composed of a large number, and that their influence from family weight and other causes would be increased thereby. He did not admit that the Tribunes lost their weight in proportion as their number was augmented. . . . If the reasoning of [Mr. Madison] was good it would prove that the number of the Senate ought to be reduced below ten, the highest number of the Tribunitial corps."[302]

The notion of a Senate as a repository of experience and wisdom – although not necessarily aristocratic virtue – was a central concern of those who advocated on behalf of the Constitution. And, for this purpose, they enlisted every scrap of ancient authority they could find. In a famous passage, James Madison in *Federalist* 63 offered this paean to the senate's virtues as an institution:

> To a people as little blinded by prejudice or corrupted by flattery as those whom I address, I shall not scruple to add, that such an institution may be sometimes necessary as a defense to the people against their own temporary errors and delusions. As the cool and deliberate sense of the community ought, in all governments, and actually will, in all free governments, ultimately prevail over the views of its rulers; so there are particular moments in public affairs when the people, stimulated by some irregular passion, or some illicit advantage, or misled by the artful misrepresentations of

interested men, may call for measures which they themselves will afterwards be the most ready to lament and condemn. In these critical moments,
how salutary will be the interference of some temperate and respectable
body of citizens, in order to check the misguided career, and to suspend the
blow meditated by the people against themselves, until reason, justice, and
truth can regain their authority over the public mind? What bitter anguish
would not the people of Athens have often escaped if their government
had contained so provident a safeguard against the tyranny of their own
passions?[303]

Madison went on to offer this conclusion from ancient history:

It adds no small weight to all these considerations, to recollect that history
informs us of no long-lived republic which had not a senate. Sparta, Rome,
and Carthage are, in fact, the only states to whom that character can be
applied. In each of the two first there was a senate for life. The constitution
of the senate in the last is less known. Circumstantial evidence makes it
probable that it was not different in this particular from the two others. It
is at least certain, that it had some quality or other which rendered it an
anchor against popular fluctuations; and that a smaller council, drawn out
of the senate, was appointed not only for life, but filled up vacancies itself.
These examples, though as unfit for the imitation, as they are repugnant
to the genius, of America, are, notwithstanding, when compared with the
fugitive and turbulent existence of other ancient republics, very instructive proofs of the necessity of some institution that will blend stability
with liberty. I am not unaware of the circumstances which distinguish the
American from other popular governments, as well ancient as modern;
and which render extreme circumspection necessary, in reasoning from
the one case to the other. But after allowing due weight to this consideration, it may still be maintained, that there are many points of similitude
which render these examples not unworthy of our attention.[304]

Concurring with his view, John Dickinson, writing as Fabius, argued that
the undoing of ancient republics occurred when popular assemblies subverted elite institutions, whether the Roman and Carthaginian senates or
the Athenian areopagus. "Though even after these encroachments had been
made," Dickinson wrote, "and ruin was spreading around, yet the remnants
of senatorial authority delayed the final catastrophe."[305]
   The Antifederalists were quick to exploit the aristocratic aspects of the
Senate. Obviously no attempt had been made to replicate the Roman or
Spartan practice of election of senators for life, and thus Noah Webster
could rightly observe that "the proposed senate for America is constituted on
principles more favorable to liberty."[306] Nevertheless, Patrick Henry scored

rhetorical points at the Virginia Ratifying Convention by noting that even as Madison and Hamilton contended that the Roman republic was at the height of its powers and liberties, its Senate still dominated the "popular" institutions of the tribunes and the comitia tributa.[307] Henry, no mean classicist himself, pointed out that the comitia tributa – although larger than the comitia centuriata – was more indefinite in its powers, could only decide matters at the initiative of the magistrates, and its legislation was (in any event) subject to senatorial approval. If followed in the Constitution, Henry contended, this was a recipe for elitist dominance of the legislature. Other Antifederalists likened the senate to the despised *decemviri*, the group of ten Roman leaders who were charged with a reform of the laws[308] (leading to the legislation of the Twelve Tables), but which evolved into a tyranny.[309]

James Bowdoin made precisely the opposite argument at the Massachusetts Convention, suggesting that the oligarchic tendencies of the Roman senate (and similar institutions) were attributable to the lack of "checks" in the Roman constitution.[310] Alexander Hamilton argued before the New York Convention that "[e]very one acquainted with the history of [the Roman] republic will recollect how powerful a check to the senatorial encroachments this small body [of popular tribunes] proved; how unlimited a confidence was placed in them by the people, whose guardians they were; and to what a conspicuous station in the government their influence at length elevated the plebians."[311]

Once it was decided in principle that there was to be an upper chamber in Congress, and that (under both the competing Virginia and New Jersey Plans[312]) the senate members would be appointed by the state legislatures, it remained to agree on numbers.[313] Consistent with Madison's and Dickinson's divergent concerns that the senate be neither too small (so as to concentrate too much power in a small number of persons) nor too large (as to be too diffuse), the agreement was that there would be two senators from each state. Two, of course, was precisely the number that each city member of the Amphictyonic League dispatched to Delphi for meetings, a fact that a few delegates were quick to remind their colleagues.[314] The important link between the composition of the senate and the confederal conception of the nation was confirmed in a final provision of the Constitution that prohibited any amendment that would be contrary to the principle "that no State, without its Consent, shall be deprived of it's [sic] equal Suffrage in the Senate."[315] Later, it was noted by Madison that "[t]he exception in favor of the equality of suffrage in the Senate, was probably meant as a palladium to the residuary sovereignty of the States, implied and secured by that principle of representation in one branch of the legislature; and was probably insisted on by the States particularly attached to that equality."[316]

Another significant element in the federalism calculus was how the salaries of senators were to be paid. There was a serious suggestion made that the states should pay the salaries of both their representatives and senators. This was even incorporated into the draft Constitution produced by the Committee of Detail in late July 1787. Oliver Ellsworth wisely objected to the provision, noting that "too much dependence on the States would be produced. . . ."[317] While Luther Martin renewed his suggestion that senators were effectively the representatives of their sending states, as under the Articles of Confederacy and with the Amphictyonic Council, the other delegates argued that "the Senate was to represent and manage the affairs of the whole, and not to be the advocates of State interests."[318]

That still left the question as to what specific functions the senate would exercise, apart from serving as a coequal chamber of the national legislature (with the requirement it assent to all legislation). These fell into a few categories: the confirmation of the President's appointment of federal officers and judges,[319] the trial of impeachments of those officials (including the President and Vice President),[320] and the advice and consent to treaties entered into by the United States.[321] On a few scores, however, those skeptical of senatorial power prevailed. For example, the initiation of impeachment proceedings was to be made solely in the House of Representatives.[322] Additionally, the Framers required that "[a]ll Bills for raising Revenue shall originate in the House of Representatives; but the Senate may propose or concur with Amendments as on other Bills."[323] Lastly, in case of the failure of the Electoral College to elect a President, the election is thrown to the House of Representatives (not the Senate), which would then vote by state delegations.[324]

Some of these aspects of senatorial authority and disability will be considered in the sections that follow, but it is important to note that some delegates at Philadelphia believed that these provisions still gave the senate too much power. Charles Pinckney was worried that if the senate had the authority to concur on treaties entered into by the President, then membership in that body ought to be confined to individuals who had been resident in America at least fourteen years. "As the Senate is to have the power of making treaties and managing our foreign affairs, there is peculiar danger and impropriety in opening its door to those who have foreign attachments. He quoted the jealousy of the Athenians on this subject who made it death for any stranger to intrude his voice into their Legislative proceedings."[325]

Hamilton was obliged, in a full number of *The Federalist*, to defend those who would criticize the power of the senate to remove federal officers, particularly the President:

> A SECOND objection to the Senate, as a court of impeachments, is, that it contributes to an undue accumulation of power in that body, tending to give to the government a countenance too aristocratic. The Senate, it is observed, is to have concurrent authority with the Executive in the formation of treaties and in the appointment to offices: if, say the objectors, to these prerogatives is added that of deciding in all cases of impeachment, it will give a decided predominancy to senatorial influence. To an objection so little precise in itself, it is not easy to find a very precise answer. Where is the measure or criterion to which we can appeal, for determining what will give the Senate too much, too little, or barely the proper degree of influence?
>
> . . .
>
> But this hypothesis, such as it is, has already been refuted in the remarks applied to the duration in office prescribed for the senators. It was by them shown, as well on the credit of historical examples, as from the reason of the thing, that the most POPULAR branch of every government, partaking of the republican genius, by being generally the favorite of the people, will be as generally a full match, if not an overmatch, for every other member of the Government.[326]

Ultimately, then, the constitutional debate about the prerogatives of the senate centered on divergent assumptions about the accumulation of power in an elite assembly.

The Framing generation's appreciation of the nature and composition of ancient senates appeared to be superior to their sketchy understanding of the operation of ancient confederal leagues. On Sparta's and Carthage's gerousia, and the various forms of Greek confederation councils[327] and the Athenian areopagus,[328] the historical data was sparse. Based on their reading of Polybius and Livy, the Framers had reliable information about the composition, procedures, and prerogatives of the Roman senate in the republican period,[329] sources that are still considered reliable today by modern philologists. This is so despite the modern conclusion that Polybius' account unduly favored aristocratic institutions in the Roman republic, including the senate.[330] Secondary sources – such as Mably's treatise, *Observations sur les Romans*, and the Abbé le Vertot's and Conyers Middleton's dissertations[331] on the Roman senate – were in wide use in the colonies, as was made clear in Noah Webster's pamphlet, *An Examination into the Leading Principles of the Constitution*.[332]

The Framers would have also been aware of the Roman republic's unique system of governance in the senate. When not summoned by a magistrate, the senate could transact some form of business under the chair of the *princeps senatus*, the most senior or most respected member. From Polybius and other sources,[333] the Framers knew that the praetors based in Rome (often the praetor urbanus) presided over the senate when conducting certain deliberations, in the absence of the consuls, who were often in the field on military campaigns and away from the city. There was thus a precedent from the Roman republic for an executive magistrate to preside over deliberative bodies and legislative assemblies. Senate actions (in the form of *senatus consultum*) were, however, subject to veto (*intercessio*) by the tribunes, or, more rarely, by a consul.[334] In the same way, the Framers designated the vice president as the president of the senate, although he was given no vote in the proceedings "unless they [the senators] be equally divided," in the event of a tie vote.[335]

The Framers were well-aware that the Roman senate had primacy over the other magistracies (including the executive power of the consuls) and the popular assemblies, in four major areas. One of these was the nearly absolute power of the purse and control of the treasury, and there was strong annalistic evidence (reported by Polybius and Livy) that the Senate controlled appropriations of funds to consuls in the field,[336] as well as public works in the city.[337] Although obviously the American Constitution devolved this power to Congress as a whole (and especially to the House to originate money bills), it has always been regarded as Senate prerogative to control government spending (more on which in Chapter 4). The second power mentioned in the classical sources was that of a judicial authority over grave public crimes.[338] This might have been thought of as analogous to the impeachment power granted in the Constitution.

Likewise, as a third prerogative, the Roman senate had the power to assign consular and proconsular provinces (*provincia*), as theaters of potential conflict and conquest, as well as announce the designation of the judicial authority of the various individuals elected as praetors, a procedure that "clearly sought to control aristocratic rivalry and to save aristocratic pride."[339] This power to allocate offices was certainly seen by the Framers as an aspect of the appointments process, and the Senate was given the exclusive power to "confirm" the nominations made by the President of Executive branch offices and judges. Lastly, the Roman senate had a unique – and well-documented – role in foreign relations, by receiving and dispatching embassies, concluding treaties, and deciding on (although not declaring) war.[340] Manifestly, this aspect of the Roman constitution counseled the Framers to vest authority to give "advice and consent" to treaties in the senate, a body of individuals who, as John Jay put it in *Federalist* 64,

> have had time to form a judgment, and with respect to whom they will not be liable to be deceived by those brilliant appearances of genius and patriotism, which, like transient meteors, sometimes mislead as well as dazzle. If the observation be well founded, that wise kings will always be served by able ministers, it is fair to argue, that as an assembly of select electors possess, in a greater degree than kings, the means of extensive and accurate information relative to men and characters, so will their appointments bear at least equal marks of discretion and discernment. The inference which naturally results from these considerations is this, that the President and senators so chosen will always be of the number of those who best understand our national interests, whether considered in relation to the several States or to foreign nations, who are best able to promote those interests, and whose reputation for integrity inspires and merits confidence. With such men the power of making treaties may be safely lodged.[341]

The senate was intended to be a unique institution in the constitutional scheme envisioned by the Framers. It was avowedly elite, if for no other reasons than the age requirements of its members[342] and their selection by state legislatures. The senate also served the dual purpose of an upper chamber in a national legislature and (at least in part) as a representative assembly of states as constituents of the Union, insofar as the equal suffrage of the states was constitutionally guaranteed in perpetuity. The unique decision-making prerogatives of the senate (over the actual appointment of most federal officials, as well as the ratification of international agreements entered into by the nation) – assured that it had a special gravitas. In almost all of these respects, the senate was clearly modeled on a classical paradigm of a deliberative body, as a necessary component of mixed government.

C. EXECUTIVE POWER

Among the most difficult of the constitutional tasks for the Framers was the conceptual design of the Executive branch and the presidency in the new national government. As has already been discussed, the delegates at Philadelphia were – in this one important respect – writing on a blank slate, because the Articles of Confederation had no formal provision for the exercise of executive power. This did not mean, of course, that it did not exist during the Revolution or its immediate aftermath. The Articles allowed Congress to establish "committees and civil offices as may be necessary for

managing the general affairs of the united states under their direction."[343]
Under this provision, Congress established a series of (at first) ad hoc committees, and then permanent bureaus, denominated as Committees on Foreign Affairs or Finance, the Board of War, and the Maritime Committee.
In 1781, these were transformed into formal departments with permanent
secretaries (who were not members of Congress) appointed to head them.[344]

The Articles also allowed for the appointment of one member of Congress
to preside over the body, and as "president" the individual could serve no
more than one year in any period of three years.[345] The Presidents of Congress
had very little institutional authority over the government, aside from their
role as Speaker of the assembly and whatever suasion they could muster
for various initiatives.[346] The Articles also allowed for a sort of executive
committee of Congress, the Committee of the States, in which one delegate from each State sat while Congress was not in session.[347] This body
could transact business during congressional recesses, but as for the actual
employment of executive power, the Articles were most circumspect: "The
committee of the states, or any nine of them, shall be authorized to execute,
in the recess of congress, such of the powers of congress as the united states
in congress assembled, by the consent of nine states, shall from time to time
think expedient to vest them with; provided that no power be delegated to
the said committee, for the exercise of which, by the articles of confederation, the voice of nine states in the congress of the united states assembled
is requisite."[348]

Robert Clinton has observed that "[w]hile the system of executive authority under the Articles had the disadvantage of divided and overlapping executive power, some argue that the system really represented an embryonic
parliamentary system of government that might have evolved along modern English parliamentary lines had its gestation not been aborted by the
adoption of the Constitution."[349] The real issue was not the formation of
a proto-Cabinet and parliamentary responsibility. Rather, the problem was
that Congress simply had no means to enforce its writ. Aside from the
Continental Army, a handful of diplomats, and some clerks, there were no
agents of executive authority for the national government. The carrying out
of congressional resolutions was left to state authorities, and, as might be
expected, state officials routinely flouted congressional enactments, decisions, and policies they did not favor. Such recalcitrance was manifested in
blocking the execution of judgments by the Court of Appeals for Maritime
Captures, interference with congressional treaty commissioners negotiat-
ing with Indian tribes, the ignoring of congressional settlements of land
disputes, the defalcation of excise tax revenues, and the subversion of state

militias seconded to the Continental Army.[350] The Articles of Confederation Congress simply had no executory teeth.

The Framing generation thus had to articulate a credible theory of energetic, but responsible, executive authority. From Livy, Cicero, and Machiavelli, the Framing generation learned that the Roman republic had quite mixed experiences with strong leaders. Machiavelli praised the Roman practice of naming dictators for one-year periods. "We can see," he observed, "that the dictatorship, as long as it was bestowed in accord with public laws and not by private authority, always benefitted the city, because it is the creation of magistrates and the granting of power by extraordinary means which harm republics, not those which are created by ordinary means."[351] Aside from this regularity in appointment, there were limits placed on the dictator's powers and "he could do nothing to curtail the government, such as taking authority away from the senate or from the people, or abolishing the city's old institutions and creating new ones."[352] But Machiavelli observed that the institution of dictatorship went into decline when the consuls, and not the senate or popular assemblies, were given the power to name the dictators, and, on occasion, appointing themselves.[353] The *lex Gabinia* of 68 BCE, granting Pompey the Great extraordinary powers to repel marauding pirates, was the beginning of the end of the Roman republic.[354] Of course, the ultimate absolutism was manifested by Julius Caesar's appointment as "dictator-for-life," of which Plutarch said that "this was indeed a tyranny avowed, since his power was not only absolute, but perpetual too."[355]

We know from the classical sources that dictators – known by their formal title, *magister populi* (master of the citizen army) – were originally conceived as an extraordinary military command to repel actual invasion or quell civil unrest, or what Livy called "fearful times (*in trepidis rebus*)", and when the "accustomed remedies (*consuetis remediis*)" were insufficient to respond.[356] This military function was symbolized also by the dictator's ability to appoint a second-in-command, the *magister equitum* (master of the horse). In addition to military functions, the dictator could actually discharge civic and religious duties, including the holding of elections and the inauguration of festivals and observances (necessary when both consuls were away from Rome).[357] Despite Machiavelli's statement, we know that dictators were always exclusively appointed by the sitting consuls to respond to a particular crisis, to serve no more than six months, and, in any event, certainly no longer than the magistrate who appointed them. There was virtually never an election of a dictator by popular assemblies.[358] As Machiavelli noted, dictators were still subject to some forms of redress for their violation of individual rights (what was called *provocatio*), and were still obliged to respect the prerogatives of the plebian tribunes, and were subject to audit and process after their term was over.[359]

For Machiavelli, the admirable Roman institution of energetic and temporary dictatorships stood in sharp contrast to the arrogation of all executive, legislative and judicial power under the decemvirate. That was the group of ten ostensible law reformers who were given plenary power in the fifth century BCE, and quickly established an autocracy and virtual tyranny.[360] During their rule, all other magistracies were abrogated, although the senate and popular assemblies continued, but with substantially reduced powers.[361] The key, for Machiavelli, to understanding "the reasons that kept the dictators good and those which made the decemvirs bad" was "th[e] safeguards...put in place to make them unable to abuse their authority."[362] Likening the Roman dictators to the Spartan kings, Machiavelli concluded that effective checks and balances on the exercise of executive authority were essential. Likewise, the Roman republic's brief flirtation (in the later fifth and early fourth centuries BCE) with replacing the two consuls with a college of up to five or more military tribunes, each endowed with consular power, was rejected as a failure.[363] Executive power had to be concentrated, not diluted, in order to be effective – and accountable.[364]

It was left to the "celebrated" Montesquieu to elaborate on the nature and control of executive authority, consistent with his famous declarations on separations of legislative, executive, and judicial powers and functions. He did enumerate executive powers as encompassing "mak[ing] peace and war, send[ing] or receiv[ing] embassies, establish[ing] the public security, and provid[ing] against invasions."[365] Montesquieu also noted that the executive power had to include the right to initiate legislation, and he admiringly noted that "[i]n some ancient commonwealths, where public debates were carried on by the people in a body, it was natural for the executive power to propose and debate in conjunction with the people, otherwise their resolutions must have been attended with a strange confusion."[366] Likewise, Montesquieu counseled that the executive needed the power to veto unsound legislation, and he cited the senate's check on some resolutions of the popular assemblies, as well as that of the plebian tribune.[367]

In addition to criticizing the ephors at Sparta as being "despotic," and the plebian tribunes exercising a "vicious" power of vetoing legislation and executive action,[368] Montesquieu advised that "the executive power ought to be in the hands of a monarch, because this branch of government, having need of despatch, is better administered by one than by many."[369] Of course, virtually all ancient models of government featured a multiple executive. Whether it was the Roman republic's two consuls, Sparta's dual monarchy and five-member ephorate, or Carthage's multiple suffetes, the goal was to spread executive power over a number of individuals in order to prevent despotism. The most extreme example was the Athenians designation of nine officers as archons (including the named archon (archon eponymous), basileus, polemarch, and six thesmothetai), as well as the separate institution of the Board of Presidents of the Council (boule), all assuming various duties and claiming different prerogatives.[370] It is no surprise that the Athenians had to institute elaborate audit and review procedures, in order to ascertain whether officials had actually competently carried out their duties without malfeasance. So with the exception of the Roman republic's occasional dictators, and the Achaean Confederacy's sole strategos,[371] ancient history was bereft of unitary executives as part of a constitutional scheme of republican or popular government.

Montesquieu's most significant observation on this subject was that while the executive ought to have "a right of restraining the encroachments of the legislative body,"[372] the obverse was not true; "it is not proper . . . that the legislative power should have a right to stay the executive; for as the execution has its natural limits, it is useless to confine it. . . . "[373] As Montesquieu also pointed out, there was a need for the legislature to engage in oversight and review of executive action, including control of the public fisc.[374] In this regard, he viewed the legislative checks on the Cretan cosmi[375] and the Spartan ephori as inadequate, while more sensible were the Roman (and, presumably also, Athenian) practice of audits of magistrates after their term in office had ended.[376] Impeachment, Montesquieu speculated, was the only other means to control executive malfeasance or autocracy, but he fretted that there was no useful model (ancient or modern) for an impeachment procedure.[377]

Indeed, the only Enlightenment political writer who appeared to endorse classical antiquity's penchant for plural and divided executive power was James Harrington, writing in his utopian work *The Commonwealth of Oceana* (1656). Harrington imagined a magistracy that included a "lord archon," a "lord strategus," and a "lord orator."[378] "These [latter] two, if you will," wrote Harrington, "may be compared unto the consuls in Rome, or the suffetes in Carthage, for their magistracy is scarcely different."[379] Likewise, Harrington's ideal government included a "first censor" and "second censor," who "derive their power of removing a senator from those of Rome."[380] He seemed also to support plural popular representatives, such as the Spartan ephors "who could question their kings," and the Roman tribunes, who "had [the] power *diem discre* to summon any . . . magistrate . . . to answer for himself unto the people."[381] Harrington's intentions for a plural executive are somewhat obscured, however, because he clearly envisioned the Lord

Archon as the ultimate and supreme legislative authority of the nation, but not as a monarch (his work was, after all, dedicated to Oliver Cromwell). Paradoxically, he seemed to endorse the Roman republic institution of a dictator, even as he noted that "there lay no appeal from the Roman dictator unto the people, which if there had, might have cost the commonwealth dear."[382]

Later English Enlightenment political theorists returned to a theme of a strong, unitary executive. As already discussed, Henry St. John Viscount Bolingbroke's *A Dissertation Upon Parties* (1734) took a strong position that the Roman republic failed not only because of corruption,[383] but also because of the lack of a strong, permanent, and accountable executive. The two Roman consuls, while exercising the power of the old elected kings, served only for a year.[384] The elected tribunes of the people were a "bullying magistracy, and often a very corrupt one."[385] The institution of the dictatorship – the extraordinary selection (by the senate or consuls) of a commander to serve six months during times of crisis – was largely intended, according to Bolingbroke, to allow the Roman aristocracy to suppress the plebians.[386] In Bolingbroke's appraisal, a strong executive in the Roman republic was virtually inimitable to the Roman constitution.[387] This was certainly a bleak picture of the classical understanding and implementation of executive power.

The Framers thus had a diverse set of ancient models and theories of executive power, combined with the intelligent commentaries of later political thinkers.[388] At the Philadelphia Convention, these were occasionally addressed, and almost invariably the office of president was referred to by the delegates as the "chief magistrate" or "first magistrate," in a very self-consciously classical mode of speaking. Indeed, this was regarded as an intentional break from English constitutionalism; the models for an energetic (but responsible and not autocratic) executive came from ancient Rome, not from contemporary Britain. Although such British rulers as Charles II, William III, and Queen Anne were highly regarded as effective, the autocratic reigns of Charles I and James II were notorious, and the Interregnum of Oliver Cromwell was deeply problematic.

Early in the Convention, discussions were had about the nature of an executive branch under a new form of government. James Wilson was quoted, on June 1, as arguing that "in his opinion so far from a unity of the Executive tending to progress towards a monarchy it would be the circumstance to prevent it. A plurality in the Executive of Government would probably produce a tyranny as bad as the thirty Tyrants of Athens, or as the Decemvirs of Rome."[389] Later, Paterson's New Jersey Plan actually proposed a multiple executive.[390] Wilson again rose and savagely critiqued this element: "In order to control the Legislative authority, you must divide it. In order to control the Executive you must unite it. One man will be more responsible than three. Three will contend among themselves till one becomes the master of his colleagues. In the triumvirates of Rome first Caesar, then Augustus, are witnesses of this truth. The Kings of Sparta, and the Consuls of Rome prove also the factious consequences of dividing the Executive Magistracy."[391]

The notion of an energetic Executive appeared to be a lightning rod of both advocacy and criticism of the Constitution. Noah Webster, writing as a "Citizen of America," believed that the assortment of powers vested in the president by the Constitution – including serving as commander-in-chief, appointing the civil officials and commissioning the military officers of the United States, sending and receiving ambassadors, making treaties, pardoning offenders,[392] informing Congress on the state of the Union and recommending needed legislation and vetoing unwise statutes,[393] as well as "tak[ing] Care that the Laws be faithfully executed"[394] – were more akin to those of the chief Roman magistrates rather than the English king from whom the American colonies had just rebelled. By the same token, Webster noted, when the president acted with the concurrence of the Senate – as with the ratification of treaties or the confirmation of official appointments – he "has powers exceeding the Roman consuls."[395] Webster conceded that the American Constitution was better conceived in this respect than its Roman counterpart because the president was elected to a longer term than the annual consuls, and by the carefully wrought electoral college mechanism, and not by direct popular election. "[I]t is impossible," Webster asserted, "that an executive officer can act with vigor and impartiality, when his office depends on the popular voice."[396]

In one respect, the American constitution directly replicated that of the Roman republic. The age requirements for the presidency (set at 35 years),[397] along-side those of other federal legislators (senators at age 30, and members of the House of Representatives at age 25),[398] was designed to promote a progression of officeholding, an American version of the *cursus honorum*. This was intended to promote a cadre of experienced leaders, and to avoid hereditary successions to office. Those who sought the office of chief magistrate (whether the consulship in Rome, or the presidency in America), were expected to have substantial experience.

The Roman constitution enunciated also a principle that executive power needed to be term-limited. A number of Roman statutes barred consuls from holding the same office twice in a decade or serving in any magistracy without a compulsory two-year refectory period.[399] The Antifederalists made much of this. The "Federal Farmer" regretted that no limit had been placed on the number of terms a president could sit, and he commented that "[t]he Roman consuls and the Carthaginian suffetes possessed extensive powers while in office, but being annually appointed, they but seldom, if ever, abused them."[400] As for the concern that term limits would deny the nation the service of a talented president, especially in times of war or national emergency, John Taylor would later write, in his *Inquiry*, that rotation of office actually improved performance: "For seven centuries Rome applied the principle to her generals, and conquered; for five, she trusted to experience and was subdued."[401] Nevertheless, Alexander Hamilton, writing in *Federalist* 25, observed that ancient polities were obliged occasionally to choose between violating a law against executive reeligibility or face imminent defeat.[402] The strong classical example of annual terms for magistrates with no chance for reelection was not adopted by the Framers, although a two-term limit was observed by every president until Franklin D. Roosevelt. An explicit limit on presidential reelection was not made in the U.S. Constitution until the Twenty-second Amendment's ratification in 1951.

Despite the indirect process of election, the president was seen by the Framers as the authentic voice of the people, although certainly not in the sense of a "plebiscitary presidency," where the Chief Magistrate was conferred with some sort of inchoate mandate.[403] It was not only, of course, that the president and vice president were the only federal officials elected by a nationwide ballot. Some of the President's powers – especially that of prosecuting criminals and vetoing dangerous or unwise laws (subject to an override by two-thirds vote of both the House and Senate[404]) – were inevitably likened to those of the Spartan ephors and Rome's plebian tribunes.[405] At the New York Ratifying Convention, Alexander Hamilton and Melancton Smith squared-off on this point, with Hamilton seeing the president as an embodiment of Spartiate and Roman institutions,[406] while Smith doubted their relevance to American society where a hereditary aristocracy was absent.[407] More significantly, the veto granted to the president is only a qualified one (it can be overridden), while that exercised by the ephors and tribunes appeared to be nearly absolute.[408]

As has already been discussed, the analogy of presidential authority to tribunitial power was imperfect. The intensely populist role for the tribunes in Roman society, as reported by Polybius,[409] had no real modern counterpart, as Smith surmised. Vetoes of legislation in the senate or comitia centuriata (dominated by patrician influences) were common, as was *intercessio* and *auxilium* on behalf of wronged citizens (which might be likened to the pardon power).[410] Less common were tribunitial obstruction of other Roman magistrates (including the consuls or praetors),[411] and the selective summons and prosecution of opponents of the plebian order.[412] The tribunes had no power to initiate real legislative or executive action, only to block the imperium exercised by another official or assembly. In this sense, the Framers realized that the president under the Constitution was an amalgam of an energetic, unitary executive and a popular representative. Indeed, the presumed Alexander White, writing under the pseudonym, "The Independent Freeholder" made just this point when he noted that:

> I shall not attempt to discuss the question, whether vesting the executive powers of government in a President and Council appointed by him, as proposed by R.H.L. [Richard Henry Lee], or in the President and Senate, as proposed by the Federal Convention would be preferable? I shall only observe, that the Convention seems to have had in view the government of Rome, the greatest and wisest republic, of which we read in history, conferring however, much less power on the President, Vice-President and Senate than the Roman Consuls and Senate enjoyed in the purest times of the republic.... [413]

All of these ideas were synthesized in Alexander Hamilton's famous discussion of executive power in *Federalist 70*. Beginning with first principles, Hamilton noted:

> Energy in the Executive is a leading character in the definition of good government. It is essential to the protection of the community against foreign attacks; it is not less essential to the steady administration of the laws; to the protection of property against those irregular and high-handed combinations which sometimes interrupt the ordinary course of justice; to the security of liberty against the enterprises and assaults of ambition, of faction, and of anarchy. Every man the least conversant in Roman story, knows how often that republic was obliged to take refuge in the absolute power of a single man, under the formidable title of Dictator, as well against the intrigues of ambitious individuals who aspired to the tyranny, and the seditions of whole classes of the community whose conduct threatened the existence of all government, as against the invasions of external enemies who menaced the conquest and destruction of Rome.[414]

Likewise, a multiplicity of executive offices – and, indeed, any dilution of that power – was a recipe for disaster in Hamilton's mind. Of course, the experience of the Roman republic was forefront in his mind, a topic he dwelled upon at some length:

> That unity is conducive to energy will not be disputed. Decision, activity, secrecy, and despatch will generally characterize the proceedings of one

man in a much more eminent degree than the proceedings of any greater number; and in proportion as the number is increased, these qualities will be diminished.

This unity may be destroyed in two ways: either by vesting the power in two or more magistrates of equal dignity and authority; or by vesting it ostensibly in one man, subject, in whole or in part, to the control and co-operation of others, in the capacity of counsellors to him. Of the first, the two Consuls of Rome may serve as an example. . . .

The experience of other nations will afford little instruction on this head. As far, however, as it teaches any thing, it teaches us not to be enamoured of plurality in the Executive. We have seen that the Achaeans, on an experiment of two Praetors, were induced to abolish one. The Roman history records many instances of mischiefs to the republic from the dissensions between the Consuls, and between the military Tribunes, who were at times substituted for the Consuls. But it gives us no specimens of any peculiar advantages derived to the state from the circumstance of the plurality of those magistrates. That the dissensions between them were not more frequent or more fatal, is a matter of astonishment, until we advert to the singular position in which the republic was almost continually placed, and to the prudent policy pointed out by the circumstances of the state, and pursued by the Consuls, of making a division of the government between them. The patricians engaged in a perpetual struggle with the plebeians for the preservation of their ancient authorities and dignities; the Consuls, who were generally chosen out of the former body, were commonly united by the personal interest they had in the defense of the privileges of their order. In addition to this motive of union, after the arms of the republic had considerably expanded the bounds of its empire, it became an established custom with the Consuls to divide the administration between themselves by lot-one of them remaining at Rome to govern the city and its environs, the other taking the command in the more distant provinces. This expedient must, no doubt, have had great influence in preventing those collisions and rivalships which might otherwise have embroiled the peace of the republic.[415]

Unitary, energetic government – at least as envisioned by Hamilton – was thus seen as having direct, ancient analogues.

Always in the background in the Framing generation's discussions of executive power was a collective fear, if not paranoia, of an unscrupulous leader who sought power by any means. The military dictator (using the modern sense of the word, not the Latin one) always lurked in the shadows, as did the more colloquial code-phrase of the "Man on Horseback." The ratification debates were replete with references to members of the classical rogues gallery of Roman tyrants: the decemvirs and Marius, Cinna, Sulla, Catiline, Augustus, and, of course, Julius Caesar.[416] In addition, contemporary tyrants – such as Oliver Cromwell – were mentioned. Thomas Jefferson, writing to Madison from Paris in 1787, just after the announcement of the Constitution's text, was concerned that the president's powers were too much like those of the Roman emperors.[417] One obvious concern was to create a presidency that would control such impulses toward despotism. This was achieved by the structural limits on the executive office, as well as the required concurrence of presidential action with congressional prerogatives. The mechanism of impeachment (to be considered in the Chapter 4) was also a necessary component of constraining presidential power. All of these institutions and features of Executive power were derived from classical precedents.

D. JUDICIAL FUNCTIONS

Of the three separate and independent branches of the federal government created by the Constitution, that leaves the judiciary for discussion. Unlike the structure of Congress (especially the institution of the Senate), and the design of the powers of the presidency, there appear to be few classical analogues to the exercise of judicial authority, and even fewer examples of such consideration by the Framers. Obviously, the Framers' substantial experience with the institutions and processes of English law as applied in the colonies undoubtedly conditioned many of their decisions in drafting the structural Constitution, and certainly the relevant provisions of the Bill of Rights. Although classical models of judiciaries were less systematically studied in the fashioning of the Constitution,[418] there were a few, and they may have exerted some influence over the Framing generation's appreciation of the proper role of judges and juries in a democratic republic.

One of these classical influences – the role of natural law as a rule of decision in court decisions – has already been mentioned here in the context of ancient political theory.[419] The place of natural law as a restraint on government interference with personal liberties has, obviously enough, been a subject of great interest in American constitutional jurisprudence. To the extent that the Constitution's Ninth Amendment appears to address this very point in its terse formulation that "[t]he Enumeration in the Constitution of certain rights shall not be construed to deny or disparage others retained by the people,"[420] it may appear to have some originalist basis. We know that many of the Framers specifically grounded their views of individual rights in a natural scheme that was largely premised on classical sources. For example,

James Wilson devoted an entire chapter in his *Law Lectures* to natural law, and relied heavily on Cicero's writings as a way to link religious precepts with natural law reasoning.[421] Wilson, along with many of the Framers, enthusiastically embraced Cicero's formulation, in *De Re Publica*, of the law as "right reason," and Wilson paraphrased Cicero's admonition with these words: "It is, indeed, a true law, conformable to nature, diffused among all men, unchangeable, eternal. By its commands, it calls men to their duty; by its prohibitions, it deters them from vice. To diminish, to alter, much more to abolish this law, is a vain attempt. Neither by the senate, nor by the people, can its powerful obligation be dissolved. It requires no interpreter or commentator."[422]

James Madison would have agreed with Wilson that, properly understood, natural law should serve as a control on overweening government authority. It was, essentially, an admittedly inchoate and abstract check and balance. Madison would have parted company with Wilson on the point that the natural law "requires no interpreter or commentator." To some degree, Madison believed, courts should play that role.[423] Speaking before the First Congress, in defending his draft of what would become the Ninth Amendment, he observed that "by enumerating particular exceptions to the grant of power, it would disparage those rights which were not placed in that enumeration, and it might follow, by implication, that those rights which were not singled out, were intended to be assigned into the hands of the General Government, and were consequently insecure."[424] In a contemporaneous letter to Thomas Jefferson, Madison observed that "[i]n our Governments the real power lies in the majority of the Community, and the invasion of private rights is chiefly to be apprehended, not from the acts of Government contrary to the sense of its constituents, but from the acts in which the Government is the mere instrument of the major number of its Constituents."[425]

All of this speaks, perhaps, to a natural law basis of the doctrine of judicial review – the structural constitutional principle that the judiciary has the power to render void statutory enactments it finds contrary to fundamental law.[426] There was certainly no instance in ancient political history of a sweeping judicial power to nullify or constrain the power of popular assemblies or deliberative bodies in this fashion, although the praetors in Rome[427] and the Areopagos in Athens[428] may have had the power to restrain executive misdeeds, and the ephors in Sparta certainly did,[429] there is no evidence that they had any authority to abrogate properly enacted legislation. Legislative, and popular, supremacy was ascendant in the political consciousness of ancient republics. Even so, the Framing generation perceived ancient sources for the structural balance to be struck between legislative power and judicial authority.

This was all a particular worry for the Framers. The Articles of Confederation had barely provided for one tribunal (to hear appeals of maritime captures), and, otherwise, Congress was completely dependent on state courts to adjudicate matters potentially involving the interests of the entire nation.[430] The real problem, as Hamilton later observed, was the inherent weakness of judicial power:

> that, in a government in which they are separated from each other, the judiciary, from the nature of its functions, will always be the least dangerous to the political rights of the Constitution; because it will be least in a capacity to annoy or injure them. The Executive not only dispenses the honors, but holds the sword of the community. The legislature not only commands the purse, but prescribes the rules by which the duties and rights of every citizen are to be regulated. The judiciary, on the contrary, has no influence over either the sword or the purse; no direction either of the strength or of the wealth of the society; and can take no active resolution whatever. It may truly be said to have neither FORCE nor WILL, but merely judgment; and must ultimately depend upon the aid of the executive arm even for the efficacy of its judgments.
>
> This simple view of the matter suggests several important consequences. It proves incontestably, that the judiciary is beyond comparison the weakest of the three departments of power; that it can never attack with success either of the other two; and that all possible care is requisite to enable it to defend itself against their attacks. It equally proves, that though individual oppression may now and then proceed from the courts of justice, the general liberty of the people can never be endangered from that quarter.... [431]

What followed from this is that there had to be in place affirmative restraints on the ability and tendency of the legislature to interfere with the proper judicial function of fairly and finally settling disputes. In other words, judicial independence from either legislative or executive meddling was essential. Among the Constitution's very few restraints on both state and federal legislative power were the prohibitions against bills of attainder and ex post facto laws.[432]

Although an "ex post facto law" purports to regulate conduct that has already occurred, a "bill of attainder," at least in English practice, was a legislative pronouncement of guilt on an individual (usually with criminal consequences), and Madison exclaimed that these "are contrary to the first principles of the social compact and to every principle of sound legislation."[433] Montesquieu had traced the origins of English bills of attainder to the

Roman practice of enacting private laws (literally *privilegia*) against specific parties.[434] The Romans had specifically disclaimed the competence of the popular assemblies to pass on the guilt of a citizen for treason (*perduellio*), without a full trial, and Cicero approved, noting that the force of a law consists in its being made for the whole community, not just one person.[435]

Hamilton, in his long discussion of judicial power in *Federalist* 78, reiterated this point and gave an inkling of at least a protozoan principle of judicial review:

> The complete independence of the courts of justice is peculiarly essential in a limited Constitution. By a limited Constitution, I understand one which contains certain specified exceptions to the legislative authority; such, for instance, as that it shall pass no bills of attainder, no ex-post-facto laws, and the like. Limitations of this kind can be preserved in practice no other way than through the medium of courts of justice, whose duty it must be to declare all acts contrary to the manifest tenor of the Constitution void. Without this, all the reservations of particular rights or privileges would amount to nothing.
>
> . . .
>
> . . . No legislative act, therefore, contrary to the Constitution, can be valid. . . .
>
> If it be said that the legislative body are themselves the constitutional judges of their own powers, and that the construction they put upon them is conclusive upon the other departments, it may be answered, that this cannot be the natural presumption, where it is not to be collected from any particular provisions in the Constitution. It is not otherwise to be supposed, that the Constitution could intend to enable the representatives of the people to substitute their WILL to that of their constituents. It is far more rational to suppose, that the courts were designed to be an intermediate body between the people and the legislature, in order, among other things, to keep the latter within the limits assigned to their authority. The interpretation of the laws is the proper and peculiar province of the courts. A constitution is, in fact, and must be regarded by the judges, as a fundamental law. It therefore belongs to them to ascertain its meaning, as well as the meaning of any particular act proceeding from the legislative body. If there should happen to be an irreconcilable variance between the two, that which has the superior obligation and validity ought, of course, to be preferred; or, in other words, the Constitution ought to be preferred to the statute, the intention of the people to the intention of their agents.
>
> Nor does this conclusion by any means suppose a superiority of the judicial to the legislative power. It only supposes that the power of the people is superior to both; and that where the will of the legislature, declared

in its statutes, stands in opposition to that of the people, declared in the Constitution, the judges ought to be governed by the latter rather than the former. They ought to regulate their decisions by the fundamental laws, rather than by those which are not fundamental.[436]

With these well-chosen words, Hamilton articulated a distinct role for the judiciary as a neutral and independent arbiter of the laws. So not only were there affirmative restraints on Congress and the state legislatures to arrogate judicial functions (through the prejudging of cases by ex post facto statutes or attainder bills), there were also more subtle structural bars. One of these, again, was the natural law derived from "free republics" (presumably both modern and ancient), which Justice Chase, in his opinion in *Calder v. Bull*, a 1798 challenge of a Connecticut statute on ex post facto grounds, was able to articulate:

The purposes for which men enter into society will determine the nature and terms of the social compact; and as they are the foundation of the legislative power, they will decide what are the proper objects of it: The nature, and ends of legislative power will limit the exercise of it. This fundamental principle flows from the very nature of our free Republican governments, that no man should be compelled to do what the laws do not require; nor to refrain from acts which the laws permit. There are acts which the Federal, or State, Legislature cannot do, without exceeding their authority. There are certain vital principles in our free Republican governments, which will determine and over-rule an apparent and flagrant abuse of legislative power; as to authorize manifest injustice by positive law; or to take away that security for personal liberty, or private property, for the protection whereof of the government was established. An ACT of the Legislature (for I cannot call it a law) contrary to the great first principles of the social compact, cannot be considered a rightful exercise of legislative authority. The obligation of a law in governments established on express compact, and on republican principles, must be determined by the nature of the power, on which it is founded. . . . The Legislature may enjoin, permit, forbid, and punish; they may declare new crimes; and establish rules of conduct for all its citizens in future cases; they may command what is right, and prohibit what is wrong; but they cannot change innocence into guilt; or punish innocence as a crime; or violate the right of an antecedent lawful private contract; or the right of private property. To maintain that our Federal, or State, Legislature possesses such powers, if they had not been expressly restrained; would, in my opinion, be a political heresy, altogether inadmissible in our free republican governments.[437]

Additionally, the Framers were concerned about legislative "revision" of court judgments. This was quite a common problem in the colonial period and early years of independence.[438] This was a practice derived from the prerogatives of the English parliament, and may well have had some ancient pedigree in the workings of the Athenian popular assemblies and the combined judicial and executive authority of the Roman emperors, consuls, and praetors. It was a tradition that the Framers conclusively broke with, as Hamilton indicated in his comment that "[a] legislature without exceeding its province cannot reverse a determination once made, in a particular case; though it may prescribe a new rule for future cases."[439]

The truly crucial elements to the Framers' development of judicial power in Article III of the Constitution were the staffing of the courts and their prescribed jurisdiction. The judges of the Supreme Court and "such inferior Courts as the Congress may from time to time ordain and establish" were to hold their "Offices during good Behaviour," and be guaranteed a "Compensation which shall not be diminished during their Continuance in Office."[440] In other words, federal judges had life tenure and substantial salary guarantees, effectively isolating them from the vagaries of politics. It was a bold stroke, one that gave the judiciary the practical and effective independence that was so necessary as, Hamilton put it, an "excellent barrier to the encroachments and oppressions of the representative body. And it is the best expedient which can be devised in any government to secure a steady, upright, and impartial administration of the laws."[441] This tenure protection, when combined with the explicit jurisdiction granted to the federal courts,[442] had the potential to create a judiciary as truly co-equal with the other branches.

Despite all of this concern over the dangers of a judiciary weakened by legislative and executive incursions, the Framers may have intended a few structural and historical limits on the judicial power. One of these was the requirement that judges, at least notionally, must follow their precedents as a means of ensuring against arbitrary and capricious rulings that would inevitably bring the courts into disrepute. Whether this was considered by the Framers as an actual constitutional constraint on judicial authority, something that has at least been mooted today,[443] it was certainly recognized. Hamilton noted in *Federalist 78* that "[t]o avoid an arbitrary discretion in the courts, it is indispensable that they should be bound down by strict rules and precedents, which serve to define and point out their duty in every particular case that comes before them. . . . "[444] Even the virulent Antifederalist, Brutus, acknowledged that judicial arbitrariness could be constrained insofar as "principles... become fixed, by a course of decisions."[445] William Cranch would later write in his preface to his edition of U.S. Supreme Court opinions that "In a government which is emphatically styled a government of laws, the least possible range ought to be left for the discretion of the judge... perhaps nothing conduces more to that object than the publication of reports. Every case decided is a check upon the judge. He can not decide a similar case differently, without strong reasons, which, for his own justification, he will wish to make public."[446]

The Framers were aware that ancient legal systems had rudimentary notions of the use of precedent, and the principle of *stare decisis*.[447] William Blackstone, in his *Commentaries on the Laws of England* (published on the eve of the American Revolution), pointed out that "[t]he Roman law, as practiced in the time of it's [sic] liberty, paid also a great regard to custom; but not so much as our law."[448] James Wilson noted in his *Lectures* that the Greeks applied a "common law... taken up by the consent of the country,"[449] although he was actually skeptical of the restraining effect that *stare decisis* should have on common law judges in America.[450]

Although the use of precedent in ancient Athenian criminal proceedings was uneven and uncritical,[451] in republican Rome consistency of judicial decisions in civil matters was largely achieved through the medium of the praetor's edict (the *ius honorarium*), an annual decree which set forth the permissible private formulary causes of action and the elements that would have to be satisfied before such suits could proceed.[452] Additionally, there was the body of imperial rescripts, as well as opinions of jurists in response to real or hypothetical situations (the *ius respondendi*).[453] These were collected, and later compiled in Justinian's *Digest*, and were often cited as authority in later disputes.[454] Criminal practice and process was more diffuse in the Roman republic, but there were mechanisms (narrated by Cicero through his forensic speeches) to ensure consistent prosecutions.[455] In the later empire, the custom of the courts (*mos iudiicorum*) was applied to procedural issues.[456] Nevertheless, we know that there never was observed a strict rule of *stare decisis* in Roman law,[457] and certainly never to the degree recognized in the English common law.

One clear restraint placed on the American judiciary by the Constitution (as well as subsequent amendments) was the jury institution,[458] and this was not only reinforced in the English common law practice, but also in ancient history. This was a significant issue at the Philadelphia Convention, and the decision not to include in the Constitution a right to a civil jury trial would hand the Antifederalist forces one of their main issues: that a despotic, life-tenured federal judiciary could trample the rights of individuals by substituting the whims and caprices of elite judges for the trustworthy verdicts of citizen juries.[459] William Grayson at the Virginia Ratifying Convention noted that weaknesses in the Roman republic's jury system led to the client system, in which plebians placed themselves in a subordinate relation to noble patricians, in order to win justice before the praetor and tribunals.[460] The "Federal Farmer" recollected that as citizen juries were forgotten in the Roman, Spartan, and Punic constitutions, so, too, were the liberties of those peoples eroded.[461]

The Framers appeared to take for granted that citizen juries were certainly part of the criminal procedures employed in ancient Athens and at Rome. James Wilson in his *Law Lectures* devoted a number of pages to this topic. Although somewhat skeptical of the large size of Athenian juries (sometimes numbering up to five hundred or a thousand), he believed that the requirement that the archons could not take a person's liberty or impose a high fine without a conviction of a citizen jury, or *eliaia*, was an important bulwark of liberty.[462] Athenian law seemed to make the distinction, as the Constitution's Fifth and Sixth Amendments later did, between petty offenses (for which a penalty could be imposed by a judge acting alone), as opposed to serious crimes, for which appeal to the eliaia could be made.[463] In the Solonic and Periclean traditions, Athenian jurors (*dicasts*) who were qualified and picked for jury service were compensated by the city (ensuring the participation of the lower orders of citizens), and were otherwise treated as officers of the state, except that they were exempted from the audit procedure of *euthyna*.[464]

Wilson was likewise complimentary of Roman criminal procedures employing juries, especially insofar as Roman juries were usually smaller (numbering typically 51), and provision being made for the challenge of members of the venire for bias.[465] In the early republic period, depending on the nature of the offense, it would be prosecuted by a praetor, tribune, or curule aedile before a popular assembly (with the members acting as a jury) or with a smaller group of assessors (*consilium*) as a lay jury before any of a number of specialized tribunals (such as for corruption, extortion, electoral fraud, or treason).[466] With Sulla's reforms of the first century BCE, court practice became more regular with the institution of permanent tribunals (*quaestiones perpetuae*),[467] and it was in this period that jury selection assumed the form that James Wilson later praised. Another civil jury institution, the *recuperatores*, with a smaller venire was instituted in this period to produce speedier verdicts.[468]

That leaves one last classical influence on the Framer's contemplation of the powers and functions of the judiciary. Madison famously commented that "[a]ll new laws, though penned with the greatest technical skill and passed on the fullest and most mature deliberation, are considered as more or less obscure and equivocal, until their meaning be liquidated and ascertained by a series of particular discussions and adjudications."[469] This was the essence of the judicial process for the Framers, but what approaches could judges employ to construe difficult laws? Alexander Hamilton wrote in favor of the use of canons on construction in the interpretation of statutes. "The[se] rules of legal interpretation," he wrote, "are rules of common sense, adopted by the courts in the construction of the laws. The true test ... of a just application of them is its conformity to the source from which they are derived."[470] Speaking to one of these interpretive canons – the presumption that a statute passed later trumps an earlier law – Hamilton tried to ascertain the "source" of the rule: "this is a mere rule of construction, not derived from any positive law, but from the nature and reason of the thing. It is a rule not enjoined upon the courts by legislative provision, but adopted by themselves, as consonant to truth and propriety, for the direction of their conduct as interpreters of the law."[471]

Hamilton also believed that these canons of construction could be applied to control "unjust and partial laws," and thereby "mitigating the severity and confining the operation of such laws."[472] James Wilson would later write, however, that although interpretive rules could be helpful, they must be followed "with the greatest circumspection[;] by indulging [them] rashly, the judges would become the arbiters, instead of being the ministers of the laws."[473] Moreover, Wilson worried that the rules "would be found at some times, too narrow; at other times, too broad. To adhere rigidly to them, at all times, would be to commit injustice under the sanction of law."[474]

Where did these canons of interpretation come from? The Framing generation would have known that they derived from classical rhetoric, especially the writings of their beloved Cicero, particularly his *de Inventione*[475] and the apocryphal *Rhetorica ad Herennium*,[476] as well as Quintilian's manual, *Institutio Oratorio*.[477] Although they may have read of these rules of construction through Blackstone,[478] the great publicist acknowledged his debt to Grotius, Pufendorf, and Vattel, who, in turn, derived their precepts from the classical sources.[479] The primary thrust of these canons was to guide the reader of any legal text – whether it be a statute, contract, will, treaty, or constitution for that matter – through a series of interpretive steps to understand the textual structure, original intent, and purposive design of the writing. The steps were formal, and depended on a natural law vision of right reason, what Robert Clinton has called a "naturalistic interpretive tradition" or declaratory approach to the law,[480] one that remained in currency until replaced by the strongly positivist jurisprudence of the early nineteenth century.

Obviously, at stake, in all of the Framing generation's debates about judicial power, and their selective use of classical precepts to advocate or refute different components of that authority, was their sense of the proper part of a judge to play in American constitutionalism. In sharp contrast to their use of ancient history in debating the virtues and vices of bicameralism or of a unified executive, the Framers' employment of classical sources for their understanding of judicial functions was far more diffuse and theoretical. Nevertheless, it was possible to derive from these materials the needed insights for a judiciary independent from legislative or executive interference, but constrained in its work by the structural institution of citizen juries and the established reason of stare decisis and canons of legal interpretation. Whether the judiciary would remain the least dangerous branch, and become the handmaiden of legislative and executive overreaching, or itself become an institution of arbitrariness and tyranny, preoccupied the attentions of the Framers and required them to use all of their classical knowledge in seeking an answer and resolution.

E. REPUBLICS AT WAR AND IN PEACE

So far in this chapter, I have looked at the classical traditions that formed both the vertical aspects of American structural constitutionalism (federalism, and the relation between the national government and the states), and the horizontal component of separation of powers between the legislative, executive, and judicial branches. That leaves for consideration what might be called the external element of the American republic's relations with other polities, which implicated nothing less than the nation's conduct of war and peace. Here, once again, the Framing generation relied upon, and discussed at length, the lessons that ancient history offered.

The Framers were all too painfully aware that the powers granted to the federal government to make and enforce treaties, conduct foreign relations, and prosecute conflicts were essential to the success of the new nation. None of the Framers were deluded in believing that the victory in the American Revolution was obtained by the strength of the colonists' arms or the superior organization of the states against British imperial might. The record of the Revolutionary period reflected just the opposite trends: fractious states, highly unwilling to give the Continental Congress (and, later, the Articles of Confederation Congress) the money, troops, and supplies necessary to conduct the rebellion. George Washington, President of the Constitutional

Convention, was particularly mindful of the weaknesses and vulnerability of the new nation. He, most of all, had known what a near run thing victory in the Revolution was.

Likewise, the Framers knew the vital significance of the American republic making and keeping its promises with other nations. The military alliance with France and financial loans from Holland had literally saved the colonists during the war. The Peace of Paris of 1783 with Britain had granted the Americans the recognition they desperately needed, and even some favorable commercial terms, in exchange for significant obligations in relation to the property of former Tory residents and London creditors. The record of the Articles of Confederation government in ensuring the United States' compliance with both its written treaty and unwritten customary international law obligations was nothing less than atrocious. This was despite the fact that the Articles granted Congress the "sole and exclusive right and power of determining on peace and war."[481] Despite this, the states thwarted the execution of the remedial clauses of the Paris Treaty, let go unpunished those who assaulted foreign diplomats, and actively interfered with Congressional negotiation with Indian tribes (then considered as like foreign nations).[482] Congress was left to meekly explain to foreign government that the "nature of the federal union" under the Articles left them powerless.[483] A number of the Framers thought this intolerable. John Jay, speaking before the Congress, complained of the Confederation government's lack of treaty enforcement powers,[484] and Edmund Randolph wrote that the Confederation "would be doomed to be plunged into war, from its wretched impotency to check offenses against" the law of nations.[485] There was thus no doubt that in 1787, the United States was militarily weak, politically divided, and diplomatically isolated.

The Framing generation was nevertheless quite troubled as how to structure the war and foreign relations powers in their Constitution. They knew that the primary role of the federal government had to be to "insure domestic Tranquility [and] provide for the common defence."[486] Nonetheless, from their readings of political philosophers they realized that the allocation of these powers, and their proper constraint, was essential if the American republic would subsist for long. On no other issue was there as much of an imperative to balance energetic national governmental authority with effective safeguards for individual liberties and the safety of the constitutional scheme. In this regard, the Framing generation seemed suspect of the model of executive authority in the English parliamentary form of government; they were particularly disposed to adopt classical models of shared executive and legislative control over the war and treaty powers.[487] The Framers would have been heedful of Polybius' admonition that republics will disintegrate quicker if they are of an expansionistic bent.[488] As Machiavelli observed, "either you discuss a republic that wishes to create an empire, like Rome, or you discuss one that is satisfied to maintain itself."[489]

The Framing generation was sharply critical of Roman imperialism, which appeared (at least for a while) to sustain the Roman republic's constitutional institutions. John Jay rhetorically questioned, in *Federalist* 5, "[h]ow many conquests did the Romans and others make in the characters of allies, and what innovations did they, under the same character, introduce into the governments of those whom they pretended to protect."[490] Hamilton went so far as to wonder whether the very nature of republics was war-like:

> Sparta, Athens, Rome, and Carthage were all republics; two of them, Athens and Carthage, of the commercial kind. Yet were they as often engaged in wars, offensive and defensive, as the neighboring monarchies of the same times. Sparta was little better than a well regulated camp; and Rome was never sated of carnage and conquest.
>
> Carthage, though a commercial republic, was the aggressor in the very war that ended in her destruction. Hannibal had carried her arms into the heart of Italy and to the gates of Rome, before Scipio, in turn, gave him an overthrow in the territories of Carthage, and made a conquest of the commonwealth.[491]

The nub of the problem for the Framers was the allure of militarism and what has later been referred to metaphorically as the "Man on Horseback," the military dictator summoned to deliver the republic from danger.[492] This was a concern with an exceedingly long intellectual pedigree. Machiavelli, in his gloss on Livy's *Histories*, warned that one of the root "cause[s] of that republic's dissolution . . . was the prolongation of military commands."[493] In the later republic, fewer and fewer Roman leaders took to heart the example of Lucius Quinctius Cincinnatus, who reluctantly assumed the dictatorship, saved Rome from disaster, and then promptly returned to his farm. Machiavelli noted that extending commands and creating permanent armies meant that "fewer men were experienced in command, and because of this, reputation became restricted to a few . . . and when a citizen was commander of an army for a lengthy period of time, he gained its support and made it his supporter, because that army forgot the senate and recognized him as its leader."[494] Hamilton noted on the floor of the Philadelphia Convention that "the election of Roman Emperors was made by the Army,"[495] and Madison made the connection between militarism and the decline of republics express when he wrote in *Federalist* 41 that "The veteran legions of Rome were an overmatch for the undisciplined valor of all other nations and rendered her the mistress of the world. Not the less true is it, that the liberties of Rome proved the final victim to her military triumphs...."[496]

Montesquieu made his warning even more clear in *The Spirit of the Laws*. Despite his acknowledgment that "once an army is established, it ought not to depend on the legislative but on the executive power; and this from the very nature of the thing, its business consisting more in action than in deliberation,"[497] nonetheless

> [t]o prevent the executive power from being able to oppress, it is requisite that the armies with which it is intrusted should consist of the people, and have the same spirit as the people, as was the cause at Rome till the time of Marius. To obtain this end, there are only two ways: either that the persons employed in the army should have sufficient property to answer for their conduct to their fellow-subjects, and be enlisted for only a year, as was customary at Rome; of if there should be a standing army, composed chiefly of the most despicable part of the nation, the legislative power should have a right to disband them as soon as it pleased.[498]

Madison echoed this point when he observed at Philadelphia: "[i]n time of actual war, great discretionary powers are constantly given to the Executive Magistrate. Constant apprehension of war, has the same tendency to render the head too large for the body. A standing military force, with an overgrown Executive will not long be safe companions to liberty. The means of defence against foreign danger, have been always the instruments of tyranny at home. Among the Romans it was a standing maxim to excite a war, whenever a revolt was apprehended."[499] The pamphleteer "Brutus" – appropriately enough – warned that "the liberties of the [Roman] commonwealth was destroyed, and the constitution overturned, by an army, led by Julius Caesar, who was appointed to the command, by the constitutional authority of that commonwealth.... A standing army effected this change, and a standing army supported it through a succession of ages...."[500] George Mason actually contemplated that a standing army could lead to a military coup, as occurred when factional riots broke out in Rome in the late republic and the senate was surrounded by 30,000 troops.[501] This comment would have struck a raw nerve; the Continental Army nearly mutinied against its Congressional pay-masters at the Newburgh encampment at the end of the Revolutionary War in 1783.[502]

These dire predictions sparked one of the most contentious debates at the Philadelphia Convention: whether the Constitution should countenance standing armies, how they were to be commanded, and general control of the warmaking power. The Framers were strongly wed to the notion that a citizen army would protect the new nation. Such a force, after all, had defeated British imperial troops and their German mercenaries. George Mason, in a speech before the Philadelphia Convention, rhapsodized that "[e]very husbandmen will be quickly converted into a soldier when he knows and feels that he is to fight not in defence of the rights of a particular family, or a prince, but for his own. This is the true construction of the *pro aris et focis* which has, in all ages, performed such wonder. It was this which in ancient times enabled the little cluster of Grecian republics to resist, and almost constantly to defeat, the Persian monarch."[503]

Nevertheless, Hamilton was skeptical about the modern relevance of citizen armies, and advocated a standing military, as he indicated in this rather discursive and ahistorical[504] passage:

[W]hy did not standing armies spring up out of the contentions which so often distracted the ancient republics of Greece?.... The industrious habits of the people of the present day, absorbed in the pursuits of gain, and devoted to the improvements of agriculture and commerce, are incompatible with the condition of a nation of soldiers, which was the true condition of the people of those republics. The means of revenue, which have been so greatly multiplied by the increase of gold and silver and of the arts of industry, and the science of finance, which is the offspring of modern times, concurring with the habits of nations, have produced an entire revolution in the system of war, and have rendered disciplined armies, distinct from the body of the citizens, the inseparable companions of frequent hostility.

There is a wide difference, also, between military establishments in a country seldom exposed by its situation to internal invasions, and in one which is often subject to them, and always apprehensive of them. The rulers of the former can have a good pretext, if they are even so inclined, to keep on foot armies so numerous as must of necessity be maintained in the latter. These armies being, in the first case, rarely, if at all, called into activity for interior defense, the people are in no danger of being broken to military subordination. The laws are not accustomed to relaxations, in favor of military exigencies; the civil state remains in full vigor, neither corrupted, nor confounded with the principles or propensities of the other state. The smallness of the army renders the natural strength of the community an over-match for it; and the citizens, not habituated to look up to the military power for protection, or to submit to its oppressions, neither love nor fear the soldiery; they view them with a spirit of jealous acquiescence in a necessary evil, and stand ready to resist a power which they suppose may be exerted to the prejudice of their rights. The army under such circumstances may usefully aid the magistrate to suppress a small faction, or an occasional mob, or insurrection; but it will be unable to enforce encroachments against the united efforts of the great body of the people.[505]

Although Hamilton spoke with some wisdom about the imperatives of modern warfare, his misty-eyed vision (shared by his contemporaries) of ancient citizen-yeoman-soldiers was quite inaccurate. Spartan hoplites and Roman legions (at least after the Punic Wars)[506] were professional standing armies; Athenian levies were nearly so (at least at the time of the Peloponnesian War).[507] Nonetheless, the Framers were persuaded that there was a strong tradition of arms-bearing and martial training that suffused classical writings, whether it was Aristotle's *Politics*[508] or Cicero's *Speeches*.[509]

As a consequence of the debates, the Constitution contained a handful of carefully crafted clauses on war powers. Congress, for example, had the power "To raise and support Armies, but no Appropriation of Money to that Use shall be for a longer Term than two Years."[510] The significant caveat on army appropriations (there was no similar restriction on Congress' power "to provide and maintain a Navy") was intended to prevent a standing army that would come to dominate the government, as Hamilton described at length in *Federalist* 26:

> The legislature of the United States will be OBLIGED, by this provision, once at least in every two years, to deliberate upon the propriety of keeping a military force on foot; to come to a new resolution on the point; and to declare their sense of the matter, by a formal vote in the face of their constituents. They are not AT LIBERTY to vest in the executive department permanent funds for the support of an army, if they were even incautious enough to be willing to repose in it so improper a confidence.
>
> ...
>
> Schemes to subvert the liberties of a great community REQUIRE TIME to mature them for execution. An army, so large as seriously to menace those liberties, could only be formed by progressive augmentations; which would suppose, not merely a temporary combination between the legislature and executive, but a continued conspiracy for a series of time. Is it probable that such a combination would exist at all? Is it probable that it would be persevered in, and transmitted along through all the successive variations in a representative body, which biennial elections would naturally produce in both houses?
>
> It has been said that the provision which limits the appropriation of money for the support of an army to the period of two years would be unavailing, because the Executive, when once possessed of a force large enough to awe the people into submission, would find resources in that very force sufficient to enable him to dispense with supplies from the acts of the legislature. But the question again recurs, upon what pretense could he be put in possession of a force of that magnitude in time of peace? If we suppose it to have been created in consequence of some domestic

insurrection or foreign war, then it becomes a case not within the principles of the objection; for this is levelled against the power of keeping up troops in time of peace. Few persons will be so visionary as seriously to contend that military forces ought not to be raised to quell a rebellion or resist an invasion; and if the defense of the community under such circumstances should make it necessary to have an army so numerous as to hazard its liberty, this is one of those calamaties for which there is neither preventative nor cure.[511]

In the same vein as the restriction on permanent appropriations for a standing army, the Constitution had sharp limitations on Congress' power over state militias.[512] The President could only command the militias "when called into the actual Service of the United States."[513] Unlike a permanent national army, the state militias were regarded as a bulwark of liberty, or, as Hamilton put it,

> What shadow of danger can there be from men who are daily mingling with the rest of their countrymen and who participate with them in the same feelings, sentiments, habits and interests? What reasonable cause of apprehension can be inferred from a power in the Union to prescribe regulations for the militia, and to command its services when necessary, while the particular States are to have the SOLE AND EXCLUSIVE APPOINTMENT OF THE OFFICERS? If it were possible seriously to indulge a jealousy of the militia upon any conceivable establishment under the federal government, the circumstance of the officers being in the appointment of the States ought at once to extinguish it. There can be no doubt that this circumstance will always secure to them a preponderating influence over the militia."[514]

The Militia Clauses thus reflected a balance of military authority between the states and the Union,[515] in the same way as the biennial appropriations requirement in the Army Clause was intended to balance executive and legislative power over a standing army. There may have also been a belief by the Framers that a citizen militia itself was an institution and organ of a free republic, capable of resisting tyranny by state or federal governments.[516] This was probably related to the notion, as derived from Polybius,[517] that the citizen assemblies of soldiers was where honors and punishments to leaders were dispensed, and ultimately the people's voice over military matters was heard.

The most difficult problem of all was how to control the war powers of the President. The key insight that the Framers made was to divide that power into two parts: declaring that war exists and then the prosecution of that conflict. So while the President was made the "Commander-in-Chief of the Army and Navy of the United States,"[518] Congress alone had the power "to declare War."[519] The Framing generation were positively obsessed with the fear that individual ambition and the drive for fame would send their leaders into ill-advised conflicts.[520] As Hamilton narrated in *Federalist 6*, even great leaders could succumb to this temptation:

> The celebrated Pericles, in compliance with the resentment of a prostitute, at the expense of much of the blood and treasure of his countrymen, attacked, vanquished, and destroyed the city of the SAMNIANS. The same man, stimulated by private pique against the MEGARENSIANS, another nation of Greece, or to avoid a prosecution with which he was threatened as an accomplice of a supposed theft of the statuary Phidias, or to get rid of the accusations prepared to be brought against him for dissipating the funds of the state in the purchase of popularity, or from a combination of all these causes, was the primitive author of that famous and fatal war, distinguished in the Grecian annals by the name of the PELOPONNESIAN war; which, after various vicissitudes, intermissions, and renewals, terminated in the ruin of the Athenian commonwealth.[521]

For these reasons it was essential that the power to actually declare war be vested in Congress. This, of course, had been done with the Articles of Confederation,[522] "in the most ample form," as Madison later observed.[523] Declarations of war had the purpose not only of restraining Executive warmongering, but also of appropriately defining the legal status of relations between nations and their citizens (including the legalization of many forms of reprisal, including naval captures of prize vessels on the high seas).[524]

The Framers would have been well aware of the ancient formalities for the declarations of war, although some have suggested that such ceremonies were regarded by them as "outdated and superfluous."[525] The Framers would have also known that under the Spartan constitution, war powers (and general responsibility for foreign relations) were split between the hereditary kings, the ephorate, and the gerousia.[526] From Thucydides' narration of the Peloponnesian War, they would have been cognizant of the problems of neutrality among Greek city-states, and the delicate nature of an open rupture in relations. From the opening pages of that history there was the example of the Athenian and Corinthian standoff in the harbor at Sybota, with neither side wishing to make the first, provocative act in the conflict, and neither side having the authority from their home assemblies to do so.[527] For the American republic, as for many ancient Greek city-states, the preservation of neutrality was an essential element of statecraft,[528] and the Framing generation was well aware of the need to provide for the legislative declaration of war, precisely to avoid an endangerment to that status.

Another element of congressional control over the war power was the fiscal authority to raise troops, build vessels, erect, and exercise legislation over "Forts, Magazines, Arsenals [and] dock-Yards,"[529] and generally provide the "sinews of war."[530] Perhaps more than anything this allocation of authority reflected the principle, enunciated by Charles Pinckney at Philadelphia, that "[t]he military shall always be subordinate to the Civil power, and no grants of money shall be made by the Legislature for supporting military Land forces, for more than one year at a time."[531] From ancient history, the Framers would have known that at least in the Roman republic, separation of military and civil authority was most imperfect. Although the consuls in command of forces in the field were notionally dependent on financial disbursements from the senate back in Rome,[532] this may not have always been an effective check on their power. In Athens, civil control over the generals (*stratgeos*) and the army and navy forces (as described in Aristotle's *Athenian Constitution*[533]) may have been more pervasive, but (what with removals for incompetence or malfeasance, annual audits, and potential criminal prosecutions) with disastrous consequences on the war-making capacities of the city.

Perhaps even more important to the Framers in preserving the United States' neutrality as a weak nation in a world of avaricious international relations, the legislative control over war declaration tended to protect the good faith of the new nation. John Jay fretted about this in *Federalist 3*: "The JUST causes of war, for the most part, arise either from violation of treaties or from direct violence. America has already formed treaties with no less than six foreign nations, and all of them, except Prussia, are maritime, and therefore able to annoy and injure us. She has also extensive commerce with Portugal, Spain, and Britain, and, with respect to the two latter, has, in addition, the circumstance of neighborhood to attend to."[534] So, as already noted, the Framing generation was very much preoccupied with ensuring that the new country would observe the rules of the laws of nations, a modern embodiment of Cicero's notion of *bona fides*.

In the context of war declarations, Cicero observed that "[t]he only excuse ... for going to war is that we may live in peace unharmed. ... [N]o war is just, unless it is entered upon after an official demand for satisfaction has been submitted, or warning has been given and a formal declaration made."[535] The Roman republic was a pious polity and the war declaration ceremonial, presided over by an aristocratic sacerdotal College of Fetials,[536] was exacting. The actual decision to initiate hostilities was vested in the senate and comitia centuriata.[537] Livy's and Polybius' histories are replete with examples of where the republic's fortunes faltered because it initiated hostilities on pretextual or legally flimsy grounds. In the well-known morality tale of Rome's Second Samnite War (c. 321 BCE), the moral advantage swung back and forth with every violation of the law of nations committed by the parties.[538] Popular action and accountability for the commencement of a just war was not only the Ciceronian ideal, but was manifested throughout Roman republican history. It is, as John Adams observed in his gloss on Polybius in his *Defence of the Constitutions*, that the Roman people "determine concerning peace and war."[539]

In the Constitution, the Framers enshrined a recognition of the new nation's dependence on international law, and the good faith obligation to keep the nation's promises.[540] After all, Congress was given the power "to define and punish . . . Offenses against the Law of Nations . . . ,"[541] and as John Jay noted "[i]t is of high importance to the peace of America that she observe the laws of nations towards all these powers."[542] Or, as Hamilton put it even more directly, "The Union will undoubtedly be answerable to foreign powers for the conduct of its members. And the responsibility for an injury ought ever to be accompanied with the faculty of preventing it."[543] Although it is by no means certain the Framers had in mind the Roman law concept of *jus gentium*, when referring to the "law of nations,"[544] this assumption has been commented on by contemporary courts and scholars.[545]

The leading exponent of a vigorous, classical notion of *fides* in the American constitutionalism of the foreign affairs power was undoubtedly James Wilson. As was later discussed by counsel in the 1819 Supreme Court case of *Sturges v. Crowninshield*, in the private law context of debt obligations:

> The judges of the state courts, and of this court, have confessed that there is in these words, "impairing the obligation of contracts," an inherent obscurity. Surely, then, here, if anywhere, the maxim must apply, semper in obscuris quod minimum est sequimur. They are not taken from the English common law, or used as a classical or technical term of our jurisprudence, in any book of authority. No one will pretend, that these words are drawn from any English statute, or from the states' statutes, before the adoption of the constitution. Were they, then, furnished from that great treasury and reservoir of rational jurisprudence, the Roman law? We are inclined to believe this. The tradition is, that Mr. Justice WILSON, who was a member of the convention, and a Scottish lawyer, and learned in the civil law, was the author of this phrase. If, then, these terms were borrowed

from the civil code, that code presents us with a system of insolvency in its cessio bonorum; and yet, as it is said by Gibbon, "the goddess of faith was worshipped, not only in the temples, but in the lives of the Romans."[546]

James Wilson in his *Law Lectures* provided the most coherent contemporary account of the United States' international law obligations. Much of it was based on Cicero's declamations in his *De Legibus* and *De Officiis*.[547] The primary themes were the place of friendship and trust between nations, and the universality of certain rules.[548] "A state," Wilson wrote, "which violates the sacred faith of treaties, violates not only the voluntary, but also the natural and necessary law of nations; for we have seen that, by the law of nature, the fulfilment of promises is a duty as much incumbent upon states as upon men."[549] Finally, Wilson concluded with this rhetorical flourish: "The corruption of the best things and institutions, however, always degenerates into the worst. The citizens of Carthage prostituted the character of their republic to such a degree, that if we may believe the testimony of the enemy, *Punica fides* became proverbial, over the ancient world, to denote the extreme of perfidy.... In the great chart of global credit, we hope to see the American placed as the very antipode of Carthaginian faith."[550]

From these practical and theoretical considerations, Wilson made a powerful argument for the concentration of foreign affairs powers in the federal government. Wilson noted that "[w]ith a policy, wiser and more profound, because it shuts the door against foreign intrigues with the members of the union, no state comprehended within our national government, can enter into any treaty, alliance, or confederation."[551] In addition to this element, the Constitution vested substantial foreign affairs power in the national government and, reciprocally, denied the states much influence in that external sphere.[552]

The other novel aspect of the Constitution's handling of the foreign affairs power was the allowance that the President "shall have the Power, by and with the Advice and Consent of the Senate, to make treaties, so long as two thirds of the Senators present concur."[553] This was a unique grant of initiative to the President, checked by a supermajority requirement in the upper body of Congress.[554] It was all completely consistent with the particular role to be played by the Senate and the nature of treaties, as Hamilton noted in *Federalist 75*:

[T]he particular nature of the power of making treaties indicates a peculiar propriety in that union [between the President and Senate]. Though several writers on the subject of government place that power in the class of executive authorities, yet this is evidently an arbitrary disposition; for if we attend carefully to its operation, it will be found to partake more of the legislative than of the executive character, though it does not seem strictly to fall within the definition of either of them. The essence of the legislative authority is to enact laws, or, in other words, to prescribe rules for the regulation of the society; while the execution of the laws, and the employment of the common strength, either for this purpose or for the common defense, seem to comprise all the functions of the executive magistrate. The power of making treaties is, plainly, neither the one nor the other. It relates neither to the execution of the subsisting laws, nor to the enaction of new ones; and still less to an exertion of the common strength. Its objects are CONTRACTS with foreign nations, which have the force of law, but derive it from the obligations of good faith. They are not rules prescribed by the sovereign to the subject, but agreements between sovereign and sovereign. The power in question seems therefore to form a distinct department, and to belong, properly, neither to the legislative nor to the executive. The qualities elsewhere detailed as indispensable in the management of foreign negotiations, point out the Executive as the most fit agent in those transactions; while the vast importance of the trust, and the operation of treaties as laws, plead strongly for the participation of the whole or a portion of the legislative body in the office of making them.[555]

The Framers may well have believed that by requiring that the senate give its "advice and consent" on an international agreement that it was bestowing the same substantial treaty powers enjoyed by the Roman Senate.[556] John Jay, writing in *Federalist* 64, certainly implied this position.[557] In the early practice of the American republic, Presidents did seek the senate's collective "advice" *before* concluding an agreement, and later submitting it for consent, although President Washington quickly curtailed this practice.[558] To the extent that the Framers followed the classical precedent of the Roman republic, they clearly intended that the senate have a definitive role in the negotiation of treaties. The "advice" element of the Advice and Consent Clause was not some mere surplusage in the Framers' original intent, but had definitive classical analogues in the prerogatives of the Roman, Spartan, and Punic senates.

Viewing the totality of the Framing generation's understandings about the war and foreign relations powers, there seems no doubt that ancient historical influences pervaded their thinking in making some crucial decisions about the allocation of these competences between the federal and state governments, and between Congress and the President. The structure of the war power's division of authority, the embrace of the guidance of the law of nations, and the procedures of treaty-making all speak to a number of classical analogues and models. At bottom was the Framers' belief that the new republic had to have a vigorous and unified approach to war and peace, and that personal ambition (as with all political spheres and decisions) had to be effectively constrained. Much was at stake in these decisions as to the external face of the structural Constitution. The Framers knew that the future life of the American republic could well depend on how well government institutions managed foreign affairs and conflict. Ancient history provided one set of milestones for that experience.

FOUR

MODERN RESONANCES

So FAR, THIS VOLUME HAS SHOWN THAT THE LESSONS OF ANCIENT history enriched and conditioned the Framing generation's appreciation of the political theory of constitutionalism as well as the crucial elements of the American charter. The Framers' use of classical authority for these purposes was eclectic and selective, anecdotal and abstract. Depending on the kind of argument being advanced, members of the Framing generation felt perfectly comfortable in citing ancient jurists for natural law truths, classical historians for the constitutional life of specific Mediterranean polities as well as of confederal leagues, and ancient political philosophers for enduring insights into human government. As I think I have shown, some of the Framers were quite prepared to engage in close textual readings and glosses of ancient texts, and to attempt to reach narrowly drawn historical conclusions about the advisability of various kinds of institutional features for constitutional governance.

Although all of this makes a proof of the influence of antiquity on the making of the structural Constitution, I am mindful that for some academic lawyers and constitutional historians there is an additional intellectual step to be taken in this argument. That is to assess whether the Framers' discussions of classical antiquity had any affect on specific doctrines of constitutional law that are significant *today*. This double demand of contemporary relevance and doctrinal specificity would, for example, tend to preclude discussion of the broad constitutional principles of federalism and separation of powers. Although there is substantial contemporary jurisprudence by the Supreme Court in patrolling the institutional prerogatives of Congress, the Executive, and the courts, and some of this makes use of the Framing generation's intent, most of the real work of the Court in this realm is carried on in very particular niches.[1] It is to these interstices of constitutionalism that I now turn.

In selecting current constitutional disputes, and the possible relevance of the Framers' use of ancient history in resolving them, I was guided by a few criteria. One was to amplify Chapter 3's discussion of the broad features and institutions of American constitutionalism. Specific doctrines need to be seen in their wider institutional context. So, for example, when I presently consider the constitutional principle of sovereign immunity for states of the Union, that dovetails nicely with some elements of the Framers' architecture of federalism. The institutional interplay between Congress and the President is manifesting itself in the continued debates about the doctrine of executive privilege and other officerial immunities for the Presidency, the constitutionality of the line-item veto, and the role of impeachment in ensuring executive accountability. Likewise, the place of the judiciary in the constitutional scheme has been raised in the context of the role of judicial review in patrolling state–federal relations, as well as the meaning of the Constitution's guarantee of republican government for states.

A second criterion I employed was to have a mix of live and quiescent constitutional disputes to consider. While debates are currently raging about the historic underpinnings of state sovereign immunity, war powers, and line-item vetoes, my musings on reform of the Electoral College and the meaning of the Guarantee Clause, although timely, are certainly not presented in the context of current Supreme Court cases. My last touchstone for treatment of the following constitutional controversies was at least the possibility of brevity and conciseness. I am mindful that each of the issues I will be considering – including sovereign immunity and federalism, war powers, and executive privileges – has been the subject of full-length book treatments.[2] I cannot hope to plumb the depths of these controversies, and that is not my task here. Rather, it is to briefly sketch the contours of the modern controversy and then to identify the relevant meditations of the Framers and their use of ancient wisdom.

I am quite mindful that this challenge carries my book into very dangerous straits, indeed. Implicit in the charge is some overarching principle of historic causality that would allow an investigator to assert that distinctive rules of constitutional law, or particular methodologies of constitutional interpretation, can be properly and legitimately traced back to antiquity. I absolutely decline such an intellectually ruinous invitation, preferring, instead, a more modest course (which I have maintained over the previous Chapters) of allowing the Framers to speak for themselves when they are reciting or employing ancient sources, to evaluate how their use of classical authority squares with our current understandings of ancient political institutions, and, finally, to determine whether the invocations of antiquity had a material impact on specific decisions made in the design of the Constitution at Philadelphia in 1787, and its subsequent ratification and implementation.

All of this, I suppose, begs the question of the proper role of originalism and original intent in constitutional adjudication,[3] a matter I hope to address in this book's final chapter. I would observe here that so long as I was operating at the rarefied heights of the theory and broad features of American constitutional order, I supposed the practical consequences of originalism mattered less. Now that I am narrowing the expository aperature of this topic to particular constitutional provisions and doctrines, where specific interpretations of the Framers' intent lead to distinctively divergent outcomes, suddenly, my academic and antiquarian interest in classical history might really matter. It is in this caustic and unforgiving intellectual milieu that I hope to make my final – if qualified – proof of classical models in the making of the Constitution.

A. SOVEREIGN IMMUNITY AND FEDERALISM

The Framers clearly conceived a delicate balance of power between the national government and that of the separate states. As has already been recounted in some detail, the Constitution of 1787 contains a number of structural features that place the institutions of the national government within the control of the states. Among these was that the state legislatures would elect members of the federal Senate,[4] and would generally control the qualifications of electors for House members as well as for the President (through the Electoral College).[5] On the other hand, the Constitution clearly enabled the Congress to legislate on matters of national concern,[6] and that where there was a variance between federal law (properly adopted) and state law, federal law was supreme.[7] Lastly, for certain legal spheres, the Constitution specifically disabled state competence, including the ability to independently wage war, conduct foreign policy, issue money, and affect private rights through bills of attainder, ex post facto laws, or impairments of contract.[8] So even before the constitutional revolution that followed the Civil War amendments, which began the process of selectively incorporating the substantive provisions of the federal Bill of Rights as against the states, there was already a precedent for the balancing of federal and state law-making ability. Nevertheless, there was one important trump card held by the states: the implied limitation in the enumeration of Congress' law-making powers,[9] and the Tenth Amendment's delphic reminder that "[t]he powers not delegated to the United States by the Constitution, nor prohibited by it to the States, are reserved to the States respectively, or to the people."[10]

The political and rights-based aspects of federalism were clearly manifest to the Framers. As James Madison famously observed – at great length – in *Federalist* 39:

> In order to ascertain the real character of the government, it may be considered in relation to the foundation on which it is to be established; to the sources from which its ordinary powers are to be drawn; to the operation of those powers; to the extent of them; and to the authority by which future changes in the government are to be introduced.
>
> On examining the first relation, it appears, on one hand, that the Constitution is to be founded on the assent and ratification of the people of America, given by deputies elected for the special purpose; but, on the other, that this assent and ratification is to be given by the people, not as individuals composing one entire nation, but as composing the distinct and independent States to which they respectively belong. It is to be the assent and ratification of the several States, derived from the supreme authority in each State,-the authority of the people themselves. The act, therefore, establishing the Constitution, will not be a NATIONAL, but a FEDERAL act....
>
> The next relation is, to the sources from which the ordinary powers of government are to be derived. The House of Representatives will derive its powers from the people of America; and the people will be represented in the same proportion, and on the same principle, as they are in the legislature of a particular State. So far the government is NATIONAL, not FEDERAL. The Senate, on the other hand, will derive its powers from the States, as political and coequal societies; and these will be represented on the principle of equality in the Senate, as they now are in the existing Congress. So far the government is FEDERAL, not NATIONAL. The executive power will be derived from a very compound source....
>
> The difference between a federal and national government, as it relates to the OPERATION OF THE GOVERNMENT, is supposed to consist in this, that in the former the powers operate on the political bodies composing the Confederacy, in their political capacities; in the latter, on the individual citizens composing the nation, in their individual capacities. On trying the Constitution by this criterion, it falls under the NATIONAL, not the FEDERAL character; though perhaps not so completely as has been understood. In several cases, and particularly in the trial of controversies to which States may be parties, they must be viewed and proceeded against in their collective and political capacities only. So far the national countenance of the government on this side seems to be disfigured by a few

federal features. But this blemish is perhaps unavoidable in any plan; and the operation of the government on the people, in their individual capacities, in its ordinary and most essential proceedings, may, on the whole, designate it, in this relation, a NATIONAL government.

But if the government be national with regard to the OPERATION of its powers, it changes its aspect again when we contemplate it in relation to the EXTENT of its powers. The idea of a national government involves in it, not only an authority over the individual citizens, but an indefinite supremacy over all persons and things, so far as they are objects of lawful government. Among a people consolidated into one nation, this supremacy is completely vested in the national legislature. Among communities united for particular purposes, it is vested partly in the general and partly in the municipal legislatures. In the former case, all local authorities are subordinate to the supreme; and may be controlled, directed, or abolished by it at pleasure. In the latter, the local or municipal authorities form distinct and independent portions of the supremacy, no more subject, within their respective spheres, to the general authority, than the general authority is subject to them, within its own sphere. In this relation, then, the proposed government cannot be deemed a NATIONAL one; since its jurisdiction extends to certain enumerated objects only, and leaves to the several States a residuary and inviolable sovereignty over all other objects.

. . . .

The proposed Constitution, therefore, is, in strictness, neither a national nor a federal Constitution, but a composition of both. In its foundation it is federal, not national; in the sources from which the ordinary powers of the government are drawn, it is partly federal and partly national; in the operation of these powers, it is national, not federal; in the extent of them, again, it is federal, not national; and, finally, in the authoritative mode of introducing amendments, it is neither wholly federal nor wholly national.[11]

The Madisonian vision of federalism had as its centerpiece an accommodation of the political interests of the states, even while the national government had a range of independent action. Particularly noteworthy was Madison's reflection on the way in which the laws of the national government were supposed to operate directly on all citizens, without the intermediary effect of state action, or, as he put it, "that in [truly federal regimes] the powers operate on the political bodies composing the Confederacy, in their political capacities; in [national governments], on the individual citizens composing the nation, in their individual capacities."[12]

Despite the careful attention given by the drafters of the Constitution to these elements of federalism, many decisive problems were left unanswered in the constitutional text. The chief of these was the sovereign immunity that states enjoyed in the tribunals of the federal government. The constitutional immunity intimated here is of a specific nature: that states cannot be sued by "individual citizens" in federal court, even in seeking vindication of rights granted by the federal Constitution or properly enacted statutes (which, under the Supremacy Clause, would be binding against the state governments). At stake in this debate was nothing less than the capacity of the national government to effectively enforce the rights of national citizens, against the (sometimes) recalcitrant interests of the individual states.

At the Philadelphia Convention this issue arose in only a tangential way, and chiefly in the form of abstract discussions involving the relative power of the state and federal governments. Even in these isolated passages, references to classical antiquity were common in staking out the positions of the participants. Not surprisingly, Alexander Hamilton took the view that state power would be eroded over time. "As States," he further asserted, "they should be abolished. But [there might be] the necessity of leaving in them, subordinate jurisdictions. The examples of Persia and the Roman Empire, cited by (Mr. Wilson) were, he thought in favor of his doctrine: the great powers delegated to the Satraps and proconsuls, having frequently produced revolts, and schemes of independence."[13] In contrast, James Wilson's point (alluded to by Hamilton) was much more modest: that "[a]ll large Governments must be subdivided into lesser jurisdictions,"[14] not that state sovereignty should be extinguished altogether. Wilson observed at an earlier juncture in the Convention that "[t]he state governments ought to be preserved – the freedom of the people and their internal good police depends on their existence in full vigor – but such a government can only answer local purposes – That it is not possible a general government, as despotic as even that of the Roman emperors, could be adequate to the government of the whole without this distinction."[15]

The debate at Philadelphia about the role of the states as sovereign entities in the new confederal union thus resonated with the same concerns the American colonists had with the ancient analogues for the treatment of colonies by their mother country.[16] In the pivotal June 6 debate about the mode of popular elections for members of the House of Representatives, Madison made one of his usual forays into "observations . . . verified by the histories of every country, ancient and modern," and he noted: "[w]hat a source of oppression was the relation between the parent cities of Rome, Athens, and Carthage, and their respective provinces: the former possessing the power and the latter being sufficiently distinguished to be separate objects of it?"[17] So, unlike Hamilton, Madison was apparently making a strong argument for the continued sovereignty of the states, as distinct from the federal union.

In the most pointed exchange on the Convention floor about state sovereign immunity, James Wilson and James Madison combined to recommend that among the powers of the national government would be the creation of "inferior tribunals," in addition to the Supreme Court. Although this provision ultimately made its way into the Constitution,[18] and is a significant basis for the federal judiciary, many delegates recognized the impact that additional layers of federal courts and federal judges might have on states' rights. Pierce Butler wasted no time in rising in criticism: "The people will not bear such innovations," he retorted, "The States will revolt at such encroachments. Supposing such an establishment to be useful, we must not venture to it." Not resisting the temptation to turn one of Madison's classical references against him, Butler finished with this rhetorical flourish: "We must follow the example of Solon who gave the Athenians not the best Government he could devise; but the best they would receive."[19]

As has already been narrated, the Philadelphia Convention struck a delicate compromise between the sovereignty of the confederal regime and the preexisting state governments.[20] There simply was no agreement over the actual sovereign status of the individual states.[21] This controversy extended to later historiographic disputes about the Founding moment. In Yates's notes of the debate of June 29, 1787, he has Madison declaring that "[t]he states never possessed the essential rights of sovereignty. These were always vested in congress."[22] Madison was later obliged – in the midst of his election campaign for President in 1808 – to disavow these remarks,[23] and indicate that they were a legal nonsense; after all, the second Article of Confederation had provided that the states retained their "sovereignty, freedom and independence, and every Power, Jurisdiction and right...."[24] Even before the Constitutional Convention, states had asserted sovereign immunity in proceedings brought by citizens of other states, and had prevailed on such arguments.[25] After the Constitution's adoption, some states did not resist federal court jurisdiction in cases involving foreign nationals or the citizens of other states.[26]

That there was some evident confusion on the part of the Framers as to the sovereign immunity of the states was borne out by one of the first cases decided by the U.S. Supreme Court, *Chisholm v. Georgia*,[27] just a few years after the founding of the republic. The issue squarely presented there was whether states were amenable to suit in the Supreme Court on the instance of a private citizen of another state. In a curious turn of events, Chisholm was represented by the then-sitting Attorney General of the United States,

Edmund Randolph, who had ably served at the Philadelphia Convention.[28] Georgia refused to enter an appearance before the Court, which consisted of John Jay (as Chief Justice), James Iredell, James Wilson, John Blair, and William Cushing. Both Blair and Wilson had been delegates at Philadelphia. Jay and Iredell had been ardent supporters of the Constitution in their respective state ratifying conventions, and, of course, Jay was the third author of *The Federalist* essays. In short, the Supreme Court bench in 1794 was a microcosm of the Framing generation, including some of its brightest legal lights.

In a 4–1 decision (with Iredell in dissent), the *Chisholm* Court ruled in a series of seriatim opinions that the states had, under the plan of the Convention, no sovereign immunity in the federal tribunals. What is significant for present purposes is the extent to which historical considerations played a role in the argument and decision in *Chisholm* as it bore on the nature of state sovereignty under the Constitution, and central to these was references to classical antiquity. The pattern was set by Edmund Randolph in his argument to the Court, in which (at one and the same time) he reviewed and disclaimed the experience of ancient confederations:

> Are not peace and concord among the States two of the great ends of the Constitution? To be consistent, the opponents of my principles must say, that a State may not be sued by a foreigner. What? Shall the tranquility of our country be at the mercy of every State? Or, if it be allowed, that a State may be sued by a foreigner, why, in the scale of reason, may not the measure be the same, when the citizen of another State is the complainant? Nor is the history of confederacies wholly deficient in analogy; although a very strict one is scarcely to be expected. A parade of deep research into the Amphyctionic Council, or the Achaean league, would be fruitless, from the dearth of historical monuments. With the best lights they would probably be found, not to be positively identical with our union. So little did they approach to a National Government, that they might well be destitute of a common judicatory. So ready were the ancient Governments to merge the injuries to individuals in a State quarrel, and so certain was it, that any judicial decree must have been enforced by arms, that the mild form of a legal discussion could not but be viewed with indifference, if not contempt. And yet it would not be extravagant to conjecture, that all civil causes were sustained before the Amphyctionic Council. What we know of the Achaean confederacy, exhibits it as purely national, or rather consolidated. They had common Magistrates taken by rotation, from the towns; and the amenability of the constituent cities to some Supreme Tribunal, is as probable as otherwise. But, in fact, it would be a waste of time, to dwell upon these obscurities. To catch all the semblances of confederacies, scattered

through the historic page, would be no less absurd, than to search for light in regions of darkness, or a stable jurisprudence in the midst of barbarity and bloodshed.[29]

Using these historic data, and combining it with the clear language of the Constitution's grant of judicial power to the federal courts under Article III,[30] Randolph was able to make a powerful textual claim for federal jurisdiction over private suits against even unconsenting states.

Randolph's straightforward textual argument won at least two votes; Justices Blair and Cushing drafted short opinions concurring in that thrust. Chief Justice Jay and Justice Wilson felt obliged to go further and explore the historic and theoretical premises of the American union. Although Jay tended to emphasize the feudal vestiges of sovereign immunity that (he held) were swept away by the Constitution,[31] Justice Wilson (like Professor Wilson) could not resist the wholesale use of classical learning to fashion his holding. The central tenet of Wilson's opinion was that, under the Constitution, the people of the United States had formed a new nation that fundamentally altered the calculus of sovereignty preexisting under the Continental Congress and Articles of Confederation.[32] The classical underpinnings of Wilson's judgment are made clear from the outset of his opinion: he quotes Cicero for the proposition that

> Man, fearfully and wonderfully made, is the workmanship of his all perfect Creator: A State; useful and valuable as the contrivance is, is the inferior contrivance of man; and from his native dignity derives all its acquired importance. When I speak of a State as an inferior contrivance, I mean that it is a contrivance inferior only to that, which is divine: Of all human contrivances, it is certainly most transcendantly excellent. It is concerning this contrivance that Cicero says so sublimely, "Nothing, which is exhibited upon our globe, is more acceptable to that divinity, which governs the whole universe, than those communities and assemblages of men, which, lawfully associated, are denominated States. Let a State be considered as subordinate to the People: But let every thing else be subordinate to the State."[33]

Classical antiquity thus provided support for Wilson's theory – so often expressed in his writings[34] – of popular sovereignty, which, he believed, was antithetical to the sovereign immunity of the individual states of the Union.

Additionally, the experience of Greek governing institutions confirmed for Wilson that sovereigns were amenable to suit. "I am," Wilson intoned, "to examine this question by the laws and practice of different States and Kingdoms. In ancient Greece, as we learn from Isocrates, whole nations defended their rights before crowded tribunals. Such occasions as these excited, we are told, all the powers of persuasion; and the vehemence and enthusiasm of the sentiment was gradually infused into the Grecian language, equally susceptible of strength and harmony. In those days, law, liberty, and refining science, made their benign progress in strict and graceful union: The rude and degrading league between the bar and feudal barbarism was not yet formed."[35] Additionally, Wilson noted that "Other States have instituted officers to judge the proceedings of their Kings: Of this kind were the Ephori of Sparta. . . . "[36]

In the rhetorical climax of his opinion, Wilson declaimed:

Concerning the prerogative of Kings, and concerning the sovereignty of States, much has been said and written; but little has been said and written concerning a subject much more dignified and important, the majesty of the people. The mode of expression, which I would substitute in the place of that generally used, is not only politically, but also (for between true liberty and true taste there is a close alliance) classically more correct. On the mention of Athens, a thousand refined and endearing associations rush at once into the memory of the scholar, the philosopher, and the patriot. When Homer, one of the most correct, as well as the oldest of human authorities, enumerates the other nations of Greece, whose forces acted at the siege of Troy, he arranges them under the names of their different Kings or Princes: But when he comes to the Athenians, he distinguishes them by the peculiar appellation of the PEOPLE of Athens. The well known address used by Demosthenes, when he harrangued and animated his assembled countrymen, was 'O Men of Athens.' With the strictest propriety, therefore, classical and political, our national scene opens with the most magnificent object, which the nation could present. 'The PEOPLE of the United States' are the first personages introduced. Who were those people? They were the citizens of thirteen States, each of which had a separate Constitution and Government, and all of which were connected together by articles of confederation. To the purposes of public strength and felicity, that confederacy was totally inadequate. A requisition on the several States terminated its Legislative authority: Executive or Judicial authority it had none. In order, therefore, to form a more perfect union, to establish justice, to ensure domestic tranquillity, to provide for common defence, and to secure the blessings of liberty, those people, among whom were the people of Georgia, ordained and established the present Constitution.[37]

James Wilson thus offered an intelligible doctrine of state sovereignty and sovereign immunity, grounded in classical political theory and historic practice.[38] As he had earlier reached the conclusion in his *Law Lectures*, "[i]n controversies, to which the state or nation is a party, the state or nation itself ought to be amenable before the judicial powers."[39]

Perhaps Edmund Randolph had it right and there was no real experience of ancient confederacies that was useful on the matter of state sovereign immunity. After all, Madison in *Federalist* 45 intimated such a conclusion, even while warning of the inevitable centrifugal forces affecting all confederal republics:

> We have seen, in all the examples of ancient and modern confederacies, the strongest tendency continually betraying itself in the members, to despoil the general government of its authorities, with a very ineffectual capacity in the latter to defend itself against the encroachments. Although, in most of these examples, the system has been so dissimilar from that under consideration as greatly to weaken any inference concerning the latter from the fate of the former, yet, as the States will retain, under the proposed Constitution, a very extensive portion of active sovereignty, the inference ought not to be wholly disregarded. In the Achaean league it is probable that the federal head had a degree and species of power, which gave it a considerable likeness to the government framed by the convention. The Lycian Confederacy, as far as its principles and form are transmitted, must have borne a still greater analogy to it. Yet history does not inform us that either of them ever degenerated, or tended to degenerate, into one consolidated government. On the contrary, we know that the ruin of one of them proceeded from the incapacity of the federal authority to prevent the dissensions, and finally the disunion, of the subordinate authorities. These cases are the more worthy of our attention, as the external causes by which the component parts were pressed together were much more numerous and powerful than in our case; and consequently less powerful ligaments within would be sufficient to bind the members to the head, and to each other.[40]

Madison, Wilson, and Randolph may have all been correct in one respect. The history of ancient Greek confederations does reveal that the constituent components of the unions were not necessarily protected by sovereign immunity. A common problem confronted by the Achaean, Lycian, Boeotian, and Thessalian confederacies was the handling of private disputes between merchants seeking to import or export grain, duty-free, into member cities, even while wheat embargoes were being enforced by the cities and the confederacy. These disputes were heard by the *damiourgoi* of the Acahaen Confederacy (a committee of the League synedrion) or the *hyloros* of the Thessalian Confederacy,[41] without regard to the immunity of the defendant city. This lack of immunity by member cities in cases involving private suits was in addition to them being susceptible to actions by the confederal union itself to receive taxes collected on behalf of the union.[42]

That any of the intellectual premises for the Framing generation's understandings of state sovereign immunity matter today, turns on an historic accident. In the immediate aftermath of the *Chisholm* decision, state authorities rallied for a constitutional change that was achieved in 1795 with the ratification of the Eleventh Amendment, which provided "The Judicial power of the United States shall not be construed to extend to any suit in law or equity, commenced or prosecuted against one of the United States by Citizens of another State, or by Citizens or Subjects of any Foreign State."[43] What exactly was intended by this alteration – and particularly whether it was supposed to merely overturn the narrow holding of *Chisholm*, or to enshrine a constitutional principle of state sovereign immunity that ostensibly existed even before the Constitution's adoption – remains an extremely contentious issue, one that has preoccupied today's Supreme Court for the past decade. In large measure, this current constitutional debate turns on what the Framing generation's understanding was of state sovereign immunity, or, put another way, what precisely was the "plan of the Convention" in this regard?[44]

It is a debate that the Justices of today's Supreme Court and academic commentators have very self-consciously styled as an historical inquiry.[45] This discourse reached a historicist peak in the Supreme Court's 1999 decision in *Alden v. Maine*, ruling that the Congress could not subject states to suits by private parties in their own courts without their consent. The majority in *Alden*, written by Justice Kennedy, went on to hold that the states' immunity from suit is a fundamental aspect of the sovereignty they enjoyed before the Constitution's ratification and is retained today except as altered by the plan of the Convention or certain constitutional amendments. Under the federal system established by the Constitution, the states retain a "residuary and inviolable sovereignty,"[46] and they are not relegated to the role of mere provinces or political corporations, but retain the dignity, though not the full authority, of sovereignty. The *Alden* majority held, relying on Justice Iredell's dissent in *Chisholm* and not Jay's or Wilson's majority views, that the "founding generation"[47] considered immunity from private suits central to this dignity. It also held that the Eleventh Amendment's text and history suggest that Congress acted not to change, but to restore, the original constitutional design. Because the Amendment confirmed rather than established sovereign immunity as a constitutional principle, it followed that

that immunity's scope is demarcated not by the text of the Eleventh Amendment alone but by "fundamental postulates implicit in the constitutional design."[48]

The dissent in *Alden* (written by Justice Souter, and joined by Justices Stevens, Breyer, and Ginsburg) proceeded to attack the historical basis for what they described as the majority's "natural law" characterization of sovereign immunity as the dominant motif of thinking by the Framing generation.[49] Tracing the course of the Framers' thinking about sovereignty from the pre-Revolutionary period up to the adoption of the Eleventh Amendment, Justice Souter concluded that the predominant view of that time was that there was no inherent principle that states were immune from private suits either in their own tribunals or those of a confederal entity to which they belonged. Although the *Alden* dissent made no direct mention of the Framers' use of classical authority on this point, it did gloss the views of legal philosophers known to the Framers – including Baldus, Bodin, Pufendorf, Hobbes, and Locke[50] – in order to conclude "that the doctrine of sovereign immunity is not the rationally necessary or inherent immunity of the civilians, but the historically contingent, and to a degree illogical, immunity of the common law. But if the Court admits that the source of sovereign immunity is the common law, it must also admit that the common law doctrine could be changed by Congress. . . . "[51]

Also considered by the *Alden* dissent is the historic pedigree of sovereign immunity in Roman law. As Justice Souter observed:

> The doctrine that the sovereign could not be sued by his subjects might have been thought by medieval civil lawyers to belong to jus gentium, the law of nations, which was a type of natural law; or perhaps in its original form it might have been understood as a precept of positive, written law. The earliest source for this conception is a statement of Ulpian's recorded in the Digest, I.3.31, and much interpreted by medieval jurists, "Princeps legibus solutus est"; "The emperor is not bound by statutes." Through its reception and discussion in the continental legal tradition, where it related initially to the Emperor, but also eventually to a King, to the Pope, and even to a city-state . . . this conception of sovereign immunity developed into a theoretical model applicable to any sovereign body.[52]

Juxtaposed with this ostensible support for an ancient pedigree of the doctrine "the King can do no wrong," Justice Souter was careful to note an extract from Justinian's *Code*: "Furthermore, the very idea of dignity ought also to imply that the State should be subject to, and not outside of, the law. It is surely ironic that one of the loci classici of Roman law regarding the imperial prerogative begins with (and is known by) the assertion that it is appropriate to the Emperor's dignity that he acknowledge (or, on some readings, at least claim) that he is bound by the laws."[53]

The essential ancient bases of sovereign immunity were thus the Roman law derived from imperial rescripts and the experience of confederal republics. This knowledge was available to members of the Framing generation, and as discussed here, did influence their conclusions about the immunities available to states under the Constitution. How all of this matters today may well be seen in the role of judges in divining the intent of the Framers and the legitimacy of courts in monitoring the boundaries of federalism and the balance of power between states and the national government. Without entering the treacherous debate as to whether the political safeguards of federalism – the role of states in actually constituting the national government and the practicalities of modern party politics in protecting states' rights – are adequate or not,[54] judicial review of federalism questions will continue. Although the U.S. Supreme Court has sent mixed signals as to the proper justiciability of such disputes,[55] the recent trend has been for the Court to demarcate the limits of the states' Eleventh Amendment sovereign immunities, as well as Congress' power to impose restrictions on state activities under the Commerce Clause and the Enforcement Clause of the Fourteenth Amendment, and to commandeer the functions of state officials under the Tenth Amendment.

Whether the debate is framed in the idiom of political or structural safeguards to states' rights, or in terms of specific constitutional doctrines of federalism, there remains the relevance of the Framing generation's use of political history, and ancient history in particular. Even the propriety of using such historical and comparative knowledge can be a bone of contention. In *Printz v. United States*,[56] raising the question of whether Congress could constitutionally command state executive officers to enforce a federal law, Justice Scalia (writing for the majority striking down the law and upholding the state sovereignty interest presented in the case) savagely replied to the dissent's contrary use of history:

> Justice BREYER's dissent would have us consider the benefits that other countries, and the European Union, believe they have derived from federal systems that are different from ours. We think such comparative analysis inappropriate to the task of interpreting a constitution, though it was of course quite relevant to the task of writing one. The Framers were familiar with many federal systems, from classical antiquity down to their own time; they are discussed in Nos. 18–20 of *The Federalist*. Some were (for the purpose here under discussion) quite similar to the modern 'federal'

systems that Justice BREYER favors. Madison's and Hamilton's opinion of such systems could not be clearer. The Federalist No. 20, after an extended critique of the system of government established by the Union of Utrecht for the United Netherlands, concludes:

> "I make no apology for having dwelt so long on the contemplation of these federal precedents. Experience is the oracle of truth; and where its responses are unequivocal, they ought to be conclusive and sacred. The important truth, which it unequivocally pronounces in the present case, is that a sovereignty over sovereigns, a government over governments, a legislation for communities, as contradistinguished from individuals, as it is a solecism in theory, so in practice it is subversive of the order and ends of civil polity...."

.... The fact is that our federalism is not Europe's. It is "the unique contribution of the Framers to political science and political theory."[57]

So the ultimate question for Justice Scalia is whether the American experience of divided and dual sovereignty is so unique as to render irrelevant the Framers' use of comparative history as a basis for modern judicial review in federalism decisions. Given the Supreme Court's strong thrust toward originalism, it has to be that the Framing generation's employment of classical knowledge in designing this aspect of the structural Constitution remains germane.

Indeed, it was the classical sources available to the Framers that really provided any precedent for the operation of leagues, and such interstitial details of the constitutional design as sovereign immunity. After all, English constitutional doctrine was of no help: Great Britain was effectively a unitary state under the doctrine of parliamentary supremacy. To ignore the Framers' discussion of the history and practices of ancient confederations – no matter how obtuse and obscure – is to turn a blind eye to a crucial source of original intent of federalism.

B. EXECUTIVE PRIVILEGES AND ACCOUNTABILITY

If any classical theme resonated with the Framers it was the fear of tyranny. As has already been narrated, the Framing generation was positively obsessed with designing a scheme of government that minimized the chances that an organ of the state would assume a position of dominance over the others, and then proceed to derogate individual liberties. Oftentimes, of course, the Framers spoke of legislative overreaching, the danger that an unscrupulous majority of lawmakers would enact laws to further their own interests and be injurious to the commonweal. In this regard, the President as chief magistrate and executive, was intended as a check on Congressional oppression.

All of this may explain why there were so few provisions in the Constitution that granted specific personal privileges to particular officeholders, and this was only done with great reluctance by the Framers. One of these was the legislative privilege of not being subject to arrest, "except for Treason, Felony and Breach of the Peace," and "for any Speech and Debate in either House, they shall not be questioned in any other Place."[58] This has meant, in practice, that federal legislators are cloaked with a general immunity from private suit for actions taken in their official, legislative capacity, although they have only a limited immunity from criminal prosecution.[59] Likewise, the life tenure given to federal judges, and the security of compensation in their salaries,[60] was intended as a necessary protection of the independence of judges from political forces.[61] These forms of legislative and judicial privileges were established, in large measure, from the experience of English constitutionalism, and particularly the parliamentary struggles against the Crown.[62]

In this context, it was perhaps unsurprising that there was no parallel provision in the Constitution granting any form of executive privilege to the Presidency. Aside from the laconic Vesting Clause of Article II that "[t]he executive Power shall be vested in a President . . . ,"[63] nothing even intimates of executive privilege.[64] As James Wilson was reported as having said before the Pennsylvania ratifying convention, this was intentional. "The executive power," he said, "is better to be trusted when it has no screen . . . [the President cannot] hide either his negligence or inattention . . . not a single privilege is annexed to his character; far from being above the laws, he is amenable to them in his private character as a citizen, and in his public character by impeachment."[65] For many members of the Framing generation the crucial power of the Presidency, indeed, the one that defined the office, was the responsibility "to take Care that the Laws be faithfully executed."[66] James Wilson, as chairman of the Committee of Detail at the Philadelphia Convention was the one who introduced the phrase "executive Power" into the draft, and he clearly intended it in a narrow sense of the responsibility to ensure that Congress' laws were enforced.[67]

If the Framers intended the President to enjoy certain, unenumerated executive privileges, they would have been operating at variance with classical models of governance, which had been quite explicit in granting officeholders certain prerogatives. In the Roman republic, all magistrates were imbued with *potestas*, and those of the highest rank (the consuls, praetors, and dictators) had the further quality of *imperium*, which allowed for certain ceremonial forms of status, including the insignia of the *fasces* (the bundles of rods and axes) carried by the lictors, the folding chair (*sella curulis*) upon which they transacted official business, and the bordered toga.[68] The only

Roman officials who were allowed an actual form of immunity as a privilege were the plebian tribunes who, along with their junior colleagues (the plebian aediles), were endowed with sacrosanctity – they literally could not be touched or obstructed in their official duties.[69]

Modern constitutional doctrine has tended to follow the Framers' profound aversion toward executive privileges. Most contemporary disputes have revolved around Presidential claims of secrecy in executive actions and consultations, and the Supreme Court has usually ruled against such privileges.[70] Although it has been held that a President enjoys civil immunity from suit for acts taken while in office,[71] in a recent case, the Court ruled that a sitting President enjoyed no temporary immunity from civil proceedings for actions arising before entry into office.[72] Today, disputes revolving around executive privilege tend to congregate in areas of dominant presidential authority, particularly the commander-in-chief power and control over foreign policy.[73]

One of these areas is the war power. Under the Constitution's strict formulation of this legislative power, it is seemingly not required to have Presidential concurrence for a declaration of war, and the veto power is inapplicable (in the same way that a President cannot veto a proposed constitutional amendment).[74] This appears odd, since ultimately the President is charged with prosecuting any conflict as commander-in-chief. As has been pointed out by some recent commentators, the lack of a requirement for presidential concurrence in declarations of war is consistent with the Framing generation's concerns about the allure of fame, an affliction that can strike both legislators and chief executives.[75] Members of early Congresses clearly acknowledged that the power to declare war was unaffected by any executive privilege.[76] In 1812, James Madison issued a Proclamation announcing the outbreak of war with Great Britain, in these terms: "Whereas the Congress of the United States, by virtue of the constituted authority vested in them, have declared by their act bearing date the 18th day of the present month that war exists between the United Kingdom of Great Britain and Ireland and the dependencies thereof and the United States of America and their Territories. . . ."[77]

The strangeness of not having a declaration of war subject to a presidential veto makes slightly more sense when seen in the context of the procedures used by the Roman republic. The power to initiate hostilities was constitutionally reserved to the comitia centuriata, which met on the Campus Martius outside the city walls. As Polybius noted, "the people have the power of approving or rejecting laws, and what is most important of all, they deliberate on the question of war and peace. Further in the case of alliances, terms of peace, and treaties, it is the people who ratify all of these or the reverse."[78] Obstruction, in the form of a veto, by a plebian tribune over a war decree (*rogatio*) was apparently an impossibility.[79] Although a war declaration would have to be submitted to the assembly by a consul, and be concurred in by the college of fetials – the quasireligious officials who ensured that the proper procedure was followed[80] – no other form of executive sanction was necessary. This was the procedure used to initiate the Second Punic War and the war against Macedon.[81]

So it appears that the Framers followed classical analogues in limiting some forms of executive privileges, and structuring the exercise of the war power. Ultimately, though, control of a President with tyrannical tendencies would not be resolved through the ascertainment of the Chief Executive's privileges and immunities. Removal from office would be the last means to ensure accountability. The Framers were thus particularly intrigued with the process of impeachment of magistrates in ancient times, although the political practices of Great Britain in the seventeenth century were certainly more immediate, and relevant.[82] Alexander Hamilton observed that "by making the executive subject to impeachment, the term monarchy cannot apply. These elective monarchs have produced tumults in Rome...."[83] Madison likewise emphasized the fact that the President was subject to impeachment at any time during his time in office.[84] The clear analogue for this was the Athenian practice of investigation and audit of officeholders. As James Wilson noted in his *Lectures*, impeachments in ancient Greece "were prosecuted for great and public offenses, by which the commonwealth was brought in danger. They were not referred to any court of justice, but were prosecuted before the popular assembly, or before the senate of five hundred."[85] Wilson even traced the practice of impeachment back to the democratic practices of ancient Germanic tribes, as reported by Tacitus.[86] The Framers would have also been aware that the hereditary kings of Sparta were subject to removal by the ephors and gerousia.[87]

In any event, the Athenian processes of impeachment and audit, as ordained in the Laws of Solon, and mentioned by Aristotle,[88] were well-documented.[89] In the Athenian assembly (ekklēsia), a regular vote was taken every prytany (36 days or so) as to whether the elected officials of the city were discharging their duties properly. This was called a *epikheirotonia*.[90] If the vote was in the negative, the official was deposed from office (*apokheirotonia*) and a trial immediately ensued, usually under the *eisangelia* (treason) or *graphe* (ordinary) procedure. There were a number of famous examples of such impeachments, including that of Pericles for alleged embezzlement in 430 BCE (mentioned in Thucydides[91]), and that of the generals commanding the Athenian fleet at Arginousai in 406 BCE (narrated at some length by Xenophon[92]). Pericles was found guilty of the charges brought against him, fined, but was reelected to the office he had previously held. The Athenian strategoi were not so fortunate; those who returned to Athens for the procedure were convicted of official misfeasance, condemned to death, and executed.

In another set of procedures, the Athenian boule could regularly supervise and investigate the activities of individuals in office, and, if dissatisfied, could fine or remove the officer. A subcommittee of the boule, the *logistai*, audited the accounts of officials every prytany.[93] Such a proceeding could also be initiated by a nonmember of the boule, and this was also called an eisangelia (although not to be confused with the special judicial procedure of treason charges before the ekklesia).[94]

The other important mechanism by which the Athenians ensured the accountability of their public officials was by the audit of their administrations, conducted after their term of office was over. This was called the *euthyna*, or "straightening," a reference to the inquiry as to whether an official had been "straight" or "crooked" in his public administration.[95] The typical euthyna proceeded in distinct stages. The first was a financial audit, led by ten *logistai* (auditors), assisted by ten *synegoroi* (speakers, or prosecutors). A former officeholder could be found guilty at this stage of embezzlement, bribe-taking, or financial negligence.[96] Next came a general review of an official's conduct in office, led by ten *euthynoi*, each assisted by two *paredroi* (assessors), all drawn from the membership of the council, or boule. If the euthynoi had cause to believe that misconduct had occurred, his task was to refer the charges for trial before a regular jury, if it was a private offense, or to the *thesmothetai* (six of the nine archons), if it was a public one.[97] This was exactly the procedure used in the audit initiated by Demosthenes and Timarkhos, to accuse Aeschines in his conduct of the Athenian diplomatic mission of 343 BCE, immortalized in Demosthenes speech, *On the False Embassy*.[98] Likewise, there were the famous denunciations of Aristides by Themistocles,[99] as well as the strategos Cimon's acquittal (in 463 BCE) of Pericles' charges that he had accepted a bribe from the King of Macedon.[100] In any event, the Athenian institution of euthyna had a long history in that city's political life, one that the Framers were undoubtedly familiar with through such canonical works as Plutarch, Demosthenes, and Thucydides. Athenian inscription evidence[101] confirms this historiographic view from the literary sources.

Lastly, there was the Athenian practice of ostracism. It was supposedly initiated by Clesithenes in 508 BCE to protect the nascent Athenian democracy against politicians that would gain too much power.[102] The ecclesia voted once a year whether to ostracize an individual, the vote being taken on shards of pottery (*ostrakon*) and requiring at least 6,000 ballots being cast.[103] Once ostracized, an individual was exiled from the city for ten years, although without the loss of civic rights, and could return after that time without any political disability or shame. Ostracism was a purely political sanction. An individual could be ostracized without having committed a crime; it was necessary only that the person be considered dangerous. History records at least nine actual cases of ostracism, all directed against politically prominent families (for example, both Pericles' father and uncle had been ostracized).[104]

Legal institutions for official accountability were probably less developed in the Roman republic than in democratic Athens, but they did exist and were the subject of commentary. The Roman *lex repetundarum* apparently provided for the audit of magistrates, after their year in office was concluded,[105] and would have been similar to the Athenian euthyna. The difference was that under the Roman constitution, magistrates were immune from process while they held office. As for investigations of officials in office, we know that some consuls were subject to investigations by a praetor (usually the one presiding over the corruption court), sometimes at senate instigation, and joined by the plebian tribunes and aediles (protected by sacrosanctity).[106]

Another check on consular or dictatorial power was the legal process of *provocatio*, which prevented the arbitrary detention or injury of a citizen without just cause, and demanded that the magistrate show cause as to his official conduct. This procedure – an ancient analogue of habeas corpus – was effective to deter some forms of official misconduct, except in times of grave emergency when the senate had decreed in advance that the magistrates "were to defend the Republic and ensure that it come to no harm,"[107] by which was meant that the action of provocatio was suspended. As Mommsen has famously contended, provocatio was designed to be the legal antidote to the Roman magistrate's imperium.[108] And, as more recent historians have observed, the institution of provocation, when combined with the tribunitial power of intercessio, and senate-ordered inquiries (*quaestio*), made consuls – and even dictators[109] – think twice before abusing the powers of their office. These caveats were understood by the Framers,[110] and this connection between habeas corpus and ancient Roman practice was made express in an 1807 debate in the House of Representatives, concerning a bill to suspend the writ of habeas corpus for three months, in the wake of the Burr conspiracy.[111]

The relevance of these ancient precedents to the American practice of impeachments can also readily be seen. In the aftermath of the impeachment proceedings during the Clinton Administration, the modalities of presidential removal under the U.S. Constitution still remain quite contentious. The constitutional predicate of the President (or any office-holder) having committed "Treason, Bribery, or other high Crimes and Misdemeanors,"[112] is one source of difficulty. At the Philadelphia Convention it was suggested in a resolution offered by Edmund Randolph that the President be removable for "mal practice or neglect of duty,"[113] and later by George Mason that the grounds for impeachment include "malad-ministration."[114] Madison objected to these formulation as "so vague,"[115] and the current text was adopted. James Wilson in his *Law Lectures* referred to "high misdemeanors" as "malversation in office,"[116] which could have extended to any corrupt behavior. What seems to be clear, though, is that the Framers self-consciously considered, and rejected, some aspects of the classical *epikheirotonia, euthyna*, and *provocatio* procedures – which allowed sanctions of officeholders for mere negligence in the conduct of their duties. They certainly rejected the Athenian idea of ostracism and exile on the mere suspicion of hubris.[117] The "high crimes and misdemeanors" formulation in the American Constitution has generally been regarded as requiring, at a minimum, affirmative misdeeds in office.[118]

Another constitutional difficulty is the proper interpretation of the clause providing that "Judgment in cases of impeachment shall not extend further than to removal from office, and disqualification to hold and enjoy any office of honor, trust, or profit under the United States; but the party convicted shall, nevertheless, be liable and subject to indictment, trial, judgment, and punishment according to law."[119] One question that has arisen is whether an individual is subject to retrospective impeachment, after leaving office. An elucidation is to be found in *Federalist* 69, where Hamilton observes that

> The President of the United States would be liable to be impeached, tried, and, upon conviction of treason, bribery, or other high crimes or misde-meanors, removed from office; and would afterwards be liable to prosecu-tion and punishment in the ordinary course of law. The person of the king of Great Britain is sacred and inviolable; there is no constitutional tribunal to which he is amenable; no punishment to which he can be subjected without involving the crisis of a national revolution. In this delicate and important circumstance of personal responsibility, the President of Con-federated America would stand upon no better ground than a governor of New York, and upon worse ground than the governors of Virginia and Delaware.[120]

Hamilton's references to the constitutions of Virginia and Delaware may be significant, because under those instruments the state governors were only subject to impeachment until *after* removal from office.[121]

That a President, or other federal officer or judge, might be impeached after leaving office, thus precluding the individual from prospectively holding any "office of honor, trust, or profit," has been controversial.[122] This appeared to be the understanding of the Framers, and at least of some Presidents. John Quincy Adams proclaimed on the floor of the House of Representatives (where he served with distinction after leaving the presidency), "I hold myself, so long as I have the breath of life in my body, amenable to impeachment by this House for everything I did during the time I held any public office."[123] Joseph Story in his *Commentaries on the Constitution* was skeptical of after-office impeachment.[124] Nonetheless, the better view – and the one consistent with the Framing generation's understanding of the classical sources – was that individuals could be impeached after holding office.[125]

The clear lessons of ancient political history – well-known to the Framers and articulated in the constitutional debates – was that officeholders were always accountable for their actions. This was consistent with the Framing generation's belief in the honor that came with public service. As with anything in political life, if one's conduct in office could bring fame, it could also bring obloquy. It is, as Alexander Hamilton wrote in *Federalist* 65, that courts of impeachment "could doom to honor or to infamy the most confidential and the most distinguished characters of the community" and could lead an individual to "perpetual ostracism from the esteem and confidence, and honors . . . of his country. . . . "[126] The Impeachment Clauses of the Constitution were an embodiment not only of a Roman law concept of infamy,[127] but also the wider classical notion of honor and fame in public service. The lessons of the Spartan, Athenian, and Roman republics was that even the commonwealth's highest officers were not immune from investigation and sanction, and were always subject to review and sanction for their official misdeeds.

C. LINE-ITEM VETOES

For the last twenty years, one of the most contentious debates in American constitutional governance has centered on granting the President a line-item veto over congressional spending enactments, thus enabling the executive branch to specifically reject certain spending items, without the necessity of vetoing an entire piece of legislation. Although there is little evidence that the Framers considered such a power, it is clear that the constitutional text does not support such authority. The Constitution provides that "[e]very Order, Resolution or Vote to which the Concurrence of the Senate and House of Representatives may be necessary . . . shall be presented to the President . . . ;

and before the Same shall take Effect, shall be approved by him, or being disapproved by him shall be repassed by two thirds of the Senate and House of Representatives, according to the Rules and Limitations prescribed in the Case of a Bill."[128] This, the Presentment Clause, has to be read with the constitutional requirement that "[n]o Money shall be drawn from the Treasury, but in Consequence of Appropriations made by Law."[129] Proponents of a line-item veto – which has been granted to a number of governors in state constitutions – do observe that such authority does not literally violate the Treasury Clause (because the president is not unilaterally spending unappropriated money, but, rather, choosing *not* to spend it). Nevertheless, the constitutional scheme appears to contemplate that the presidential veto is an all-or-nothing proposition; the executive cannot pick-and-choose among spending measures.

The Supreme Court has ruled that short of a constitutional amendment, proposals to institute a Presidential line-item veto via legislation would be impermissible. In *Clinton v. City of New York*,[130] the Court ruled that a congressional grant to the president of line-item recission or cancellation authority in the 1996 Line-Item Veto Act[131] violated the Presentment Clause. The Court, Justice Stevens writing, noted that the Act amounted to an unconstitutional transfer of fiscal power to the executive branch by giving the President authority to selectively rescind spending (or tax exemptions) he did not approve of, and thus to amend properly enacted Acts of Congress without actually using the constitutionally mandated procedure of "return" or veto.[132] As the Supreme Court observed:

> Although the Constitution expressly authorizes the President to play a role in the process of enacting statutes, it is silent on the subject of unilateral Presidential action that either repeals or amends parts of duly enacted statutes.
>
> There are powerful reasons for construing constitutional silence on this profoundly important issue as equivalent to an express prohibition. The procedures governing the enactment of statutes set forth in the text of Article I were the product of the great debates and compromises that produced the Constitution itself. Familiar historical materials provide abundant support for the conclusion that the power to enact statutes may only "be exercised in accord with a single, finely wrought and exhaustively considered, procedure." Our first President understood the text of the Presentment Clause as requiring that he either "approve all the parts of a Bill, or reject it in toto."[133]

Although the dissent in *Clinton v. City of New York* argued that the power granted by the Line-Item Veto Act was a permissible delegation of congressional authority to the President to simply decline to spend appropriated money,[134] it also considered whether the line-item veto would aggrandize executive power at the expense of Congress. In this regard, Justice Breyer noted: "Nor can one say the Act's grant of power 'aggrandizes' the Presidential office. The grant is limited to the context of the budget. It is limited to the power to spend, or not to spend, particular appropriated items, and the power to permit, or not to permit, specific limited exemptions from generally applicable tax law from taking effect. These powers ... resemble those the President has exercised in the past on other occasions."[135] Although both the dissent and majority relied on the contemporary understandings of the Framing generation to settle this question,[136] the dissent took issue with a literalist reading of the Constitution, which did not take into account fundamental changes in the nature of American government over the past two centuries:

> Congress cannot divide [a spending] bill into thousands, or tens of thousands, of separate appropriations bills, each one of which the President would have to sign, or to veto, separately. Thus, the question is whether the Constitution permits Congress to choose a particular novel means to achieve this same, constitutionally legitimate, end.
>
> Chief Justice Marshall, in a well-known passage, explained, "To have prescribed the means by which government should, in all future time, execute its powers, would have been to change, entirely, the character of the instrument, and give it the properties of a legal code. It would have been an unwise attempt to provide, by immutable rules, for exigencies which, if foreseen at all, must have been seen dimly, and which can be best provided for as they occur." This passage ... calls attention to the genius of the Framers' pragmatic vision, which this Court has long recognized in cases that find constitutional room for necessary institutional innovation.[137]

The line-item veto initiative thus places in sharp relief problems of constitutional change, and the place of history in allowing the meaning of a constitutional text to evolve.

Although framed as a constitutional question, it is also a story of political accountability and congressional-presidential competition. Advocates of the line-item veto articulate a view that the President needs additional legal tools to cancel unwise spending measures, without incurring the political costs of vetoing entire spending bills, and thus potentially paralyzing the entire operations of the government. Under this theory, Congress has come under the thrall of special interest lobbies and has essentially abdicated fiscal restraint, and so it requires the President – as the embodiment of the popular will – to counteract unwise spending policies and cancel pork-barrel, special-interest appropriations.

On the other side of the ledger is a set of assertions about constitutional principle and the necessity of ensuring legislative supremacy over federal government spending: the "power of the purse," as it is almost invariably referred to today. As Hamilton observed in *Federalist* 58, in referring to the power of the House of Representatives to originate money bills, but which is equally applicable to congressional control of spending:

> They, in a word, hold the purse – that powerful instrument by which we behold, in the history of the British Constitution, an infant and humble representation of the people gradually enlarging the sphere of its activity and importance, and finally reducing, as far as it seems to have wished, all the overgrown prerogatives of the other branches of the government. This power over the purse may, in fact, be regarded as the most complete and effectual weapon with which any constitution can arm the immediate representatives of the people, for obtaining a redress of every grievance, and for carrying into effect every just and salutary measure.[138]

As some members of the Framing generation realized, legislative power over spending had a far older political pedigree than the British constitution and the prerogatives of Parliament. It dated back to the established authority of the senate in the Roman republic.

As Polybius observed in his discussion of separation of powers in the Roman constitution, the senate had "control of the treasury, all revenue and expenditure being regulated by it. For with the exception of payments made to the consuls, the quaestors are not allowed to disburse for any particular object without a decree of the senate. And even the item of expenditure which is far heavier and more important than any other – the outlay every five years by the censors on public works, whether constructions or repairs – is under the control of the senate, which makes a grant to the censors for the purpose."[139] The senate controlled the appointment of the quaestors charged with management of the treasury in Rome, and heard their regular accountings of the republic's finances.[140] Additionally, by statutes and decrees passed by the senate, controls were placed on the spending and receipt of funds.[141]

Does the classical experience of legislative control over spending in the Roman republic have any bearing on the contemporary line-item veto debate? The answer is, surprisingly, yes, owing to the efforts of one current legislator. In an extraordinary set of floor speeches and published remarks[142] made in 1985 and 1993 (when Congress was considering, respectively, a line-item veto constitutional amendment and statute), Sen. Robert C. Byrd of West Virginia offered a detailed historic account of the Roman republic and its constitutional decline.[143] The primary thrust of Sen. Byrd's speeches was his belief that the Roman republic's progressive failings could be attributed to the senate's willingness to transfer spending power to the consuls and other magistrates. Acknowledging his debt to Montesquieu's volume, *Considerations on the Causes of the Greatness of the Roman and Their Decline*, Sen. Byrd consistently used Roman precedents as the basis for his opposition to a variety of constitutional changes that he regarded as unwarranted and dangerous.[144] Moreover, Sen. Byrd has ably made the argument that the Framing generation was substantially influenced by classical history and political theory.[145]

Senator Byrd's classical historiography of the Roman republic's constitution is a curious blend of folksy moralism and instrumental insight. Although it was not lost on him that the Roman senate was, first and foremost, an aristocratic and elite institution (with plebian appointments to the body only occurring in any great numbers during the Second Punic War),[146] he nonetheless saw it as the bulwark of Roman liberties. The popular assemblies and plebian tribunes do not appear to him to be effective checks on tyranny or despotism.[147] Rather, it was the prestige (*auctoritas*) of the senate as an institution – and the collective wisdom of its members (which, Byrd correctly notes, had all served as former magistrates) – which gave that body effective control over the republic's foreign policy and finances.[148]

Following the fairly standard historical account, Byrd traces the beginnings of the Roman senate's decline to the popular reforms of the Gracchi brothers, Tiberius and Gaius Sempronius Gracchus in the second century BCE.[149] Acting simultaneously as tribunes and land-commissioners in the years 133, 123, and 122, the Gracchi sought to advance an ambitious and popular program of agrarian reform and land redistribution, immigration restrictions, and fiscal policy changes – including the limitation of senatorial power over raising and spending funds in the provinces.[150] Tiberius Gracchus went so far as to depose his tribunitial colleague, Octavius, on the ground that he was not sufficiently supportive of the reforms and thus was not discharging the will of the people.[151] Although the Gracchi were challenged by senators anxious to preserve their institutional power,[152] and both were actually assassinated by senatorial-led conspiracies, the senate acquiesced in the limitation of their fiscal authority in a way that set an adverse precedent for the future. In short, the Gracchi led a popular movement, one that the conservative Polybius recognized meant that "the senate is afraid of the masses and must pay attention to the popular will."[153] Cicero was more blunt in his assessment: the Gracchi's actions "through the tribunate [led to] a complete revolution in the State," contributing to the later fall of the Roman republic.[154]

Senator Byrd is even less charitable in his analysis: "both of the Gracchi brothers were earnest patriots, but in their efforts to overcome the opposition to their measures they had followed a course that shook the foundations of the Roman Constitution, and presented a direct challenge to the Senate's control of the government. The Senate, as a result, lost greatly in prestige and authority."[155] From this populist moment (led by the opportunistic general, Gaius Marius) came a reactionary backlash with Sulla's dictatorship in 82 BCE, and with this the senate proceeded to derogate more authority to strong leaders. It was, as Sen. Byrd observed "a slow decline which would be followed, in time, by the decline of the republic. It would be a slow process, brought about by bloody civil wars, the overextension of the territorial administration of the Roman Government, the growing influence of the military and military leaders, the continuing erosion of the Senate's power and authority, and the gradual corrosion of old Roman virtues and the Roman character."[156]

There is little indication whether Sen. Byrd's appeals to the Framers' understandings of ancient history gained much traction in persuading his senate colleagues as to the public wisdom of line-item vetoes.[157] Of course, the 1996 statute legislatively enacting that innovation was adopted over his objection, even though it was struck down by the Supreme Court. But in the other contexts in which Sen. Byrd has raised Roman constitutionalism – particularly the proposed adoption of constitutional *amendments* on line-item vetoes, balanced budgets, and victim rights – his pleas for caution may have been heeded, for in none of those instances did Congress recommend a constitutional change. Irrespective of the historiographic defects in Sen. Byrd's simplistic narration of the decline of the Roman republic's constitution, the primary lesson is that one branch of government has to be chary in transferring power and authority to another, even in circumstances of the greatest political expediency.

The line-item veto debate touches as well on another aspect of potential executive power. That is the President's competence to suspend or dispense with the enforcement of any law he regards as unconstitutional, and not merely a spending appropriation he regards as fiscally unwise. With a long history traced to the English kings' relations with Parliament,[158] the executive prerogative of dispensation cannot likely be viewed as having been adopted by the Framers. The Take Care Clause of Article II appears to brook no possibility of the President choosing to selectively enforce only certain laws.[159] Although some of the state ratification conventions proposed, as part of the Bill of Rights, a provision expressly barring the President's dispensing power,[160] it may have been regarded that such was unnecessary in view of the Take Care Clause.[161]

These issues were certainly known to the Framing generation. In the 1806 case of *United States v. Smith*, a prosecution arising under the Neutrality Act, the defendants essentially pleaded that their actions had been authorized by President Jefferson, and thus no prosecution could proceed. Justice William Paterson, a prominent delegate at the Philadelphia Convention, unequivocally rejected this argument, holding that "[t]he president of the United States cannot control the statute, nor dispense with its execution, and still less can he authorize a person to do what the law forbids. If he could, it would render the execution of the laws dependent on his will and pleasure; which is a doctrine that has not been set up, and will not meet with any supporters in our government. In this particular, the law is paramount. Who has dominion over it? None but the legislature; and even they are not without their limitation in our republic."[162] Even in this realm of war and peace, executive prerogatives had their limit, as Justice Paterson observed. "This instrument [the Constitution], which measures out the powers and defines the duties of the President, does not vest in him any authority to set on foot a military expedition against a nation with which the United States is at peace."[163] In conclusion, Justice Paterson stated that "the law under consideration is absolute" and "requires universal obedience."[164]

Line-item vetoes and presidential refusals to enforce questionable statutes are just the leading examples of today's recrudescence of executive prerogatives. As has been suggested in the context of federalism and executive privileges, the Framers were certainly not writing on a blank slate when it came to presidential authority. In some respects, the Framers' intended the presidency as the antithesis of the British monarchy's hereditary, arbitrary, and unaccountable practices. To the extent that the model of power exercised by Roman magistrates under the republic was apparent to the Framing generation (and it certainly seems that it was), it is certainly useful to employ that evidence in any contemporary separation-of-powers dispute.

D. THE ELECTORAL COLLEGE

In the wake of the controversial presidential election of 2000, there were renewed calls for revisiting the role of the electoral college under the Constitution. Much ink has been spilt considering possible abolition of that institution,[165] and putting in its place the direct, popular election of the president. It may be significant to consider the historic conditions under which the Framing generation adopted the electoral college, and also to appreciate some of the classical analogues for a system of indirect selection of a chief magistrate in a confederal government.

For starters, there is no question that the electoral college as finally enshrined in the Constitution's Article II was a matter of extensive debate.[166] It was, by far and away, the most controversial issue considered at the Philadelphia Convention. James Wilson observed that "[t]his subject has greatly divided the House, and will also divide people out of doors. It is in truth the most difficult of all on which we have had to decide."[167] Although some in Philadelphia, most notably Wilson, forcefully and skillfully advocated the idea of direct, popular election of the president,[168] these initiatives were rebuffed by delegates deeply skeptical of the ability of individual candidates to curry national favor, and the capacity of the American people to make such a choice.[169] Moreover, they were fearful that a president elected in such a fashion would be "inviting demagoguery and possibly dictatorship as one man claimed to embody the Voice of the American People."[170] Most significantly of all, a direct popular ballot for president would have gravely disadvantaged southern, slaveholding states who (obviously) would not allow their slaves to vote in such a election.[171] So fully implicated in the Constitutional Convention's debates on the mode of selecting the Union's chief magistrate were all the sublimated issues that could have potentially derailed altogether the constitutional moment: voter qualifications, slavery, sectional rivalry, and federalism.

James Wilson quickly realizing that direct popular election of the president was a political nonstarter among his colleagues, and, moreover, that left to their own devices they would default to presidential selection by the national legislature, an option Wilson feared would subvert a government of separate and distinct branches. Indeed, on a number of occasions the Convention resolved to have Congress pick the president, only later to reconsider the motion.[172] So Wilson cleverly proposed a compromise scheme of each state being divided into districts, the people of which would choose an elector who then, in turn, would pick the president.[173] Although this plan was quickly rejected (again as being too populist), the idea persisted. It inspired Oliver Ellsworth's suggestion that state legislatures could appoint the presidential electors,[174] and formed the basis of the compromise arrangement offered by a special committee of eleven delegates in the closing days of the Convention.

Under the adopted recommendation, each state was to "choose its electors in such manner as its legislature may direct,"[175] the key proposal earlier made by Ellsworth. Each state could appoint a number of electors equal to their total representation in Congress (the number of Representatives, plus two Senators).[176] To the extent that slave states were favored under the three-fifth's compromise, they were proportionately better represented, as were smaller states. Thus were the interests of slavery and federalism supported by the scheme. To prevent (as James Wilson wrote) "cabal and intrigue," the electors were to assemble in their own states on a date established by Congress, and to vote (by secret ballot transmitted to The National Capital) for two persons, one of whom could not be a citizen of their state, a partial antidote to concerns of local favoritism.[177] As a further safeguard of independence and rectitude, "no Senator or Representative, or Person holding an Office of Trust or Profit under the United States, shall be appointed an Elector." The individual receiving the highest vote became president, provided the candidate received a majority vote of all the electors.[178]

If no candidate received a majority in the electoral college balloting, the House of Representatives was to select the president from among the five candidates receiving the highest vote.[179] The Philadelphia delegates believed that with the multiplicity of candidates (they had not considered that political parties and factions would tend to concentrate the field), and sectional rivalries, that the default legislative mechanism would become the chief means of presidential selection. To counteract the fear that a combination of a few large states in the House would control the selection process for the presidency, the Constitution provides that the voting in the House would be by state contingents, not by individual representatives, and that a majority vote of all states would be required for election.[180] So in the final mechanism for presidential selection, the House of Representatives proceeds on a one state—one vote principle, consistent with a voting assembly of a confederal union.

Few of the delegates at Philadelphia believed that this arrangement, born of political compromise, was an elegant or wholly satisfactory mechanism. Nearly alone among the Framers, James Madison attempted to ascribe some theoretic coherence to the presidential election plan, as part of his discussion in *Federalist* 39 on the federal and national features of the Constitution:

> The executive power will be derived from a very compound source. The immediate election of the President is to be made by the States in their political characters. The votes allotted to them are in a compound ratio, which considers them partly as distinct and coequal societies, partly as unequal members of the same society. The eventual election, again, is to be made by that branch of the legislature which consists of the national

representatives; but in this particular act they are to be thrown into the form of individual delegations, from so many distinct and coequal bodies politic. From this aspect of the government it appears to be of a mixed character, presenting at least as many FEDERAL as NATIONAL features.[181]

James Wilson later wrote in his *Law Lectures* that "[i]t is well worth our while to mark the sedulous attention, with which intrigues, and cabals, and tumults, and convulsions, in the election of our first magistrate, are avoided, nay, we trust, rendered impracticable, by the wise provisions introduced into our national constitution."[182]

The entire electoral college concept was thus intended to strike a delicate balance between populism (direct election) and elitism (filtration of the peoples' desires through preexisting governmental institutions and leaders). It also marked a substantial compromise, as Madison himself noted, between state interests (with state legislatures selecting the manner of appointment of the electors, leaving open the possibility of a popular ballot) and national prerogatives (with the House of Representatives, acting in state unit blocs, having the last word). Today, however, the electoral college appears to some to be a true anachronism, and an antidemocratic one. With the election in 2000 of a President who did not (like John Quincy Adams in 1826 and Rutherford B. Hayes in 1876) receive a plurality of the popular vote, the legitimacy of the electoral college is in question. Although the practical reality of modern party politics makes the electoral college significant insofar as presidential elections are transformed into fifty separate races (one for each state, the popular vote winner typically getting all of that states' electors), the real effect is to cripple third-party movements and transfer substantial power to states with smaller populations.[183]

It is perhaps understandable that most modern commentators in looking at the electoral college institution, as part of the broader constitutional clauses on presidential selection, have concluded that the Framers cut these provisions out of whole cloth, and that it would be best for all concerned to scrap it. At least in its historical premises, that may well be a mistaken view. For at least a number of the Framers recognized that a system of indirect election of magistrates was a classical legacy. Alexander Hamilton, James Wilson, and James Madison were on record at the Philadelphia Convention as seeing the electoral college mechanism as an improvement upon ancient procedures – whether it was the comitia centuriata's election of consuls, the designation of leaders in Greek confederations, or the Praetorian Guard's selection of a Roman emperor.[184]

The most sustained set of observations were made by Noah Webster, who offered this comparison of the American presidential election procedure and that of one of the "best constitutions that ever existed in Europe, the Roman...."[185] Webster noted:

> In ancient Rome, the king was elective, and so were the consuls, who were the executive officers in the republic. But they were elected by the body of the people, in their public assemblies; and this circumstance paved the way for such excessive bribery and corruption as are wholly unknown in modern men. The president of the United States is also elective; but by a few men – chosen by the several legislatures – under their inspection – separated at a vast distance – and holding no office under the United States. Such a mode of election almost precludes the possibility of corruption.[186]

So in Webster's mind, election of Roman magistrates was defective precisely because of popular involvement. Or, as he also put it, no "executive officer can act with vigor and impartiality, when his office depends on the popular voice."[187]

In contrast to Webster's harsh portrayal, what we know of voting assemblies during the Roman republic suggests an orderly procedure, one largely dictated by statute and custom.[188] The annual magisterial elections occurred (prior to Sulla's regime) in February and early March, with the new consuls to taking office (after making the prescribed oath to uphold the laws) at the commencement of the consular year, on the Ides of March.[189] After 154 BCE, elections occurred in July (with entry into office in January), in order that more citizens from the surrounding provinces could attend and successful candidates had time to prepare for their office. Notice of the precise date of a vote in the comitia centuriata (for elections of consuls, praetors, and censors) or in the comitia tributa (for elections of aediles, quaestors and minor officials[190]) had to be given in the city and environs three market-days (seventeen calendar days) before (what was known as a *trinundinum*).[191] Voting assemblies began with prayers and the taking of auspices, and then candidates could make short speeches.[192] Voting within tribes and centuries was, after the late second century BCE, conducted by secret ballot (*suffragia*), with the elector dropping a tablet (*puncta*), bearing the preferred candidate's abbreviated name, or a distinctively colored pebble (*psēphoi*), into a supervised bin.

As has already been noted, both the comitia centuriata and comitia tributa used a form of weighted and segmented voting, which tended to privilege certain interests in elections. Although the tribal assembly was not divided by socioeconomic status, balloting was done by each individual tribe. It was thus necessary for any successful candidate to be the "first-past-the-post": the first- or second-place votegetter in eighteen of the thirty-five tribes. The order in which tribal votes was announced was determined by lot. This meant that the first candidate to "cross the post," may not necessarily have had the most tribes supporting them.[193]

Likewise, in the original organization of the comitia centuriata by Servius Tullius at the beginning of the republic, balloting proceeded through each of the 193 military cohorts. It began with the eighteen cavalry (*equites*) centuries, proceeding next to the five classes of infantry (*pedites*), organized by property and equipage, and concluding with the five unarmed centuries of artisans, musicians, and other *proletarii*. Once again, it required a consular or praetorian candidate to get majorities in ninety-eight centuries. So if the propertied classes – including the eighteen cohorts of cavalry and the eighty centuries comprising the first class of heavy infantry – were in agreement on a candidate, that individual was elected, and the remaining contingents were not even polled for their votes.[194] In the Servian conception (as reported by Cicero), the comitia centuriata was "to prevent the great masses from having the greatest power,"[195] or as Livy put it, "[g]radations were established so that no one would seem to be excluded from the vote and yet all the strength would rest with the leading men of the state."[196] Even when the comitia centuriata was ostensibly reformed in the mid-third century BCE, this weighted voting system persisted. Under the new scheme, in order to be elected, a candidate would have had to achieve majorities in cohorts of not only the first rank of wealth, but also some in the second (and, perhaps, third) classes.[197] Weighted voting and supermajority requirements were often a feature of voting in classical assemblies.

The other possible source of classical inspiration for the electoral college was the practices of ancient Greek federative states in selecting their executive leadership. These were certainly noticed by John Adams in his *Defence of the Constitutions of the United States*.[198] In those Greek federal unions that featured an independent and accountable chief magistrate who was more than a ceremonial figure[199] – including the Arcadian, Aetolian, Achaean, and Lycian Confederacies – this chief executive was known usually as the archon or strategos. His second-in-command was called the hipparchos, and the secretary of the confederacy was known as the grammateus. These officials of the Achaean League, for example, were all elected annually by special meetings (*synodoi*) of the assemblies (ekklesia) comprising the league members, as well as (occasionally) the league councils (boule).[200] In the Achaean and Aetolian Confederation boules, representation was proportional to the size and population of the constituent cities; in the ekklesia it may have been that votes were taken by constituent cities, and not by counting heads.[201] It is possible that in the Aetolian League, a candidate for strategos had to receive concurring votes in both the assembly and council.[202] Polybius and Livy's narration of events in Greece between 220 and 150 BCE are replete with references to such elections,[203] and members of the Framing generation were quite aware of this history.[204]

The Framing generation was thus able to draw on classical precedents to at least make a colorable claim that the electoral college had virtues aside from being a necessary political compromise. Indirect election of the high magistrates of the Roman republic or the leading Greek confederacies was accomplished through special voting assemblies in which votes were weighted based on the strength and wealth of the city constituents or social cohorts represented. Elaborate measures were often taken in antiquity to protect the process from internal corruption (by candidates and their factions) or external influence (by other polities), although the Framers would have known from their reading of Polybius and Livy that this was often unsuccessful. Particularly significant is the dual role of different assembly institutions (the comitia centuriata and comitia tributa in the Roman republic, and boules and ekklesia in the Greek federations) as providing a check on abuses in the selection process. In this fashion, the balance struck between presidential selection by the electoral college, as opposed to the House of Representatives, is illustrative.

Even within the electoral college institution itself, the aspect of dividing national authority over presidential elections (with Congress establishing the dates for elections and other modalities) from that of the state legislatures (in selecting the manner in which electors will be chosen), although intensely controversial in the 2000 election,[205] may well have some intrinsic merit. Most critically, the fact that the electoral college process demands that any presidential candidate seek broad national support by campaigning in many states, it is certainly reminiscent of the cohort voting system in the comitia centuriata, although (obviously) without the class and wealth distinctions of that body. Classical writers (and the Framers who read them) understood that the voting procedures in these bodies could produce peculiar outcomes, resulting in the popular will being sometimes frustrated. That this was regarded as acceptable by the Framing generation, in order to ensure greater security for the commonwealth, may be one of antiquity's most significant bequests for American constitutionalism.

E. REPUBLICAN GOVERNMENT

That leaves for consideration the one clause of the Constitution that most probably embodies the Framers' debt to classical antiquity. Although I have already discussed how the political ethos of civic republicanism imbued the

Framing generation with a critical intellectual tool for conceiving of a new constitutional order,[206] it is important to realize that the drafters and ratifiers of the Constitution were not content to leave it as a mere background principle. Rather, it was placed in the constitutional text itself, in this somewhat enigmatic clause: "The United States shall guarantee to every State in this Union a Republican Form of Government and shall protect each of them against invasion; and on Application of the Legislature, or of the Executive (when the Legislature cannot be convened) against domestic Violence."[207] This provision has been justifiably called "striking"[208] and "elusive"[209] and "loose and indefinite."[210] At the outset, though, one must distinguish the different elements of this provision. For my purposes here, I propose to analytically separate the first portion of the Guarantee Clause (which actually establishes the standard of "Republican Form of Government") from the remaining two components (which "protect" states from invasions and public unrest). As will become evident, when this provision was drafted, these different elements were, in fact, regarded as distinct.[211]

What is of interest here, though, is what the Framing generation's conception of a "republican government" for the states was and how they intended it to be implemented and enforced within the established constitutional scheme of federalism. By its very placement in Article IV of the Constitution, where other "housekeeping" issues of federalism were addressed,[212] the clear message is that the Guarantee Clause was intended as an essential part of the compact made by states as a condition of entry into the Union. The very grammar and structure of the provision enshrines a federal system of co-equal and co-sovereign national and state governments.[213] So, under one reading of the Guarantee Clause, the provision (along with the later-adopted Tenth Amendment) acts as a limit and break on federal intrusions into state sovereignty.[214]

But the Guarantee Clause's importance must really be divined in reference to what is being vouchsafed by the federal government: a republican form of government in each state. As originally contemplated by James Madison in his 1787 working paper, *Vices of the Political System of the United States*, the purpose of the provision was to protect against "internal violence" and the potential threat that factions within a state would seek an overthrow of the legitimate government.[215] Some of Madison's colleagues were more interested, however, in having the Constitution prevent the reemergence of monarchical and authoritarian forms of government in the states.[216] Upon consulting with Edmund Randolph, his fellow Virginian, the first proposal for an outline of the Constitution made at Philadelphia in May 1787 was merely that "a Republican Government and the territory of each State . . . ought to be guaranteed by the United States to each State."[217] Many of the other delegates at Philadelphia believed that the Madison-Randolph formulation of the Guarantee Clause in the Virginia Plan represented too much of an intrusion into state autonomy and sovereignty.[218] Luther Martin and Elbridge Gerry were vociferous in their criticism of the draft provision, claiming that it would give the Union "a dangerous and unnecessary power" and would result in the "letting loose [of] myrmidons of the U[nited] States on a State without its own consent."[219] Yet other delegates were concerned that the draft Guarantee Clause went too far in the *other* direction, and would have the effect of obliging the federal government to uphold and support the objectionable laws of some jurisdictions.[220] Gouverneur Morris and Rufus King announced that they could not stomach a provision that would constitutionally and perpetually recognize either the institution of slavery or limited voting franchises, both common in many states.[221] The final version of the Clause, largely crafted at the suggestion of James Wilson,[222] carried with it the constructive ambiguity of what values of "republican government" were to be protected by the Constitution.

At the state ratifying conventions, the Guarantee Clause was given substantial regard by delegates viewing the Constitution as a possible infringement on state sovereignty. It was employed by Federalist forces as a way to deflect criticism. Jasper Yeates, a Federalist at the Pennsylvania ratifying convention, noted that the Clause was superior to anything that could be introduced in a Bill of Rights, and thus "assure[d] us of the intention of the framers [of] this constitution to preserve the individual sovereignty and independence of the States inviolable."[223] At the Massachusetts convention, the provision was construed to mean that "each state shall choose such republican form of government as they please, and Congress solemnly engage themselves to protect it from every kind of violence, whether of faction at home or enemies abroad."[224] These views were largely reflected in both the Federalist and Antifederalist pamphlets and broadsides of the time,[225] although the anonymous "Impartial Examiner" was skeptical on this score:

> It is true, "the United States shall guarantee to every state in this union a republican form of government:" yet they do not guarantee to the different states their present forms of government, or the bill of rights thereto annexed, or any of them; and the expressions are too vague, too indefinite to create such a compact by implication. It is possible that a "republican

form" of government may be built upon as absolute principles of despotism as any oriental monarchy ever yet possessed. I presume that the liberty of a nation depends, not on planning the frame of government, which merely consists in fixing and delineating the powers thereof; but on prescribing due limits to those powers, and establishing them upon just principles.[226]

The federalism aspects of the Guarantee Clause aside, what remains to comprehend is what the Framing generation actually understood a "republican form of government" to encompass, or, perhaps, more accurately, what it precluded. John Adams would later write in 1807 that "I confess I never understood it [the Guarantee Clause] and I believe no man ever did or ever will.... The word [republic] is so loose and indefinite that successive predominant factions will put glosses and constructions upon it as different as light and darkness."[227] Adams's contemporaries were not so circumspect in expressing their views.

One bedrock principle of republicanism was that the people ultimately control their rulers. As James Madison put it, a republic is a "government which derives all its powers directly or indirectly from the great body of the people.... It is *essential* to such a government that it be derived from the great body of society, not from an inconsiderable proportion or a favored class of it."[228] Hamilton agreed when he noted that a "fundamental maxim of republican government... requires that the sense of the majority should prevail."[229] Or, as Justice James Wilson put the matter in his opinion in *Chisholm v. Georgia*, a "short definition" of republican government is "one constructed on th[e] principle that the Supreme Power resides in the body of the people."[230] This sentiment was certainly echoed during the ratification debates.[231]

Clearly counterpoised with this antimonarchical principle was an equally antidemocratic one: that government had to be accomplished through a "scheme of representation."[232] As put famously by Madison, in *Federalist* 10, this is "the delegation of the Government... to a small number of citizens elected by the rest...."[233] This was echoed by none other than Patrick Henry, the ardent Antifederalist speaking at the Virginia ratifying convention, "The delegation of power to an adequate number of representatives, and an unimpeded reversion of it back to the people, at short periods, form the principal traits of a republican government."[234]

Some of the Framers recognized the paradoxical status of republicanism poised between monarchy and mobocracy. Nathaniel Gorham at Philadelphia raised the specter of the "man on horseback" when he declaimed: "an enterprising Citizen might erect the standard of Monarchy in a particular

State, might gather together partisans from all quarters, might extend his views from State to State, and threaten to establish a tyranny over the whole and the General Government [would] be compelled to remain an inactive witness of its own destruction."[235] Alexander Hamilton, in *Federalist* 21, made a sly appeal based on recent events in Massachusetts with Shay's Rebellion, noting the necessity of

> repelling those domestic dangers which may sometimes threaten the existence of the State constitutions, must be renounced. Usurpation may rear its crest in each State, and trample upon the liberties of the people, while the national government could legally do nothing more than behold its encroachments with indignation and regret. A successful faction may erect a tyranny on the ruins of order and law, while no succor could constitutionally be afforded by the Union to the friends and supporters of the government. The tempestuous situation from which Massachusetts has scarcely emerged, evinces that dangers of this kind are not merely speculative. Who can determine what might have been the issue of her late convulsions, if the malcontents had been headed by a Caesar or by a Cromwell? Who can predict what effect a despotism, established in Massachusetts, would have upon the liberties of New Hampshire or Rhode Island, of Connecticut or New York?[236]

And James Madison offered this extended discussion of the double dangers of monarchical authoritarianism and exuberant democracy leading to mob rule:

> It may possibly be asked, what need there could be of such a precaution, and whether it may not become a pretext for alterations in the State governments, without the concurrence of the States themselves. These questions admit of ready answers. If the interposition of the general government should not be needed, the provision for such an event will be a harmless superfluity only in the Constitution. But who can say what experiments may be produced by the caprice of particular States, by the ambition of enterprising leaders, or by the intrigues and influence of foreign powers? . . . [I]f the general government should interpose by virtue of this constitutional authority, it will be, of course, bound to pursue the authority. But the authority extends no further than to a GUARANTY of a republican form of government, which supposes a pre-existing government of the form which is to be guaranteed. As long, therefore, as the existing republican forms are continued by the States, they are guaranteed by the federal Constitution. Whenever the States may choose to substitute other republican forms, they have a right to do so, and to claim the federal guaranty for the latter. The only restriction imposed on them is, that they

shall not exchange republican for antirepublican Constitutions; a restriction which, it is presumed, will hardly be considered as a grievance. . . .

At first view, it might seem not to square with the republican theory, to suppose, either that a majority have not the right, or that a minority will have the force, to subvert a government; and consequently, that the federal interposition can never be required, but when it would be improper. But theoretic reasoning, in this as in most other cases, must be qualified by the lessons of practice. Why may not illicit combinations, for purposes of violence, be formed as well by a majority of a State, especially a small State as by a majority of a county, or a district of the same State. . . .

Is it true that force and right are necessarily on the same side in republican governments? May not the minor party possess such a superiority of pecuniary resources, of military talents and experience, or of secret succors from foreign powers, as will render it superior also in an appeal to the sword? May not a more compact and advantageous position turn the scale on the same side, against a superior number so situated as to be less capable of a prompt and collected exertion of its strength? Nothing can be more chimerical than to imagine that in a trial of actual force, victory may be calculated by the rules which prevail in a census of the inhabitants, or which determine the event of an election! May it not happen, in fine, that the minority of CITIZENS may become a majority of PERSONS, by the accession of alien residents, of a casual concourse of adventurers, or of those whom the constitution of the State has not admitted to the rights of suffrage?. . . .

In cases where it may be doubtful on which side justice lies, what better umpires could be desired by two violent factions, flying to arms, and tearing a State to pieces, than the representatives of confederate States, not heated by the local flame? To the impartiality of judges, they would unite the affection of friends. Happy would it be if such a remedy for its infirmities could be enjoyed by all free governments; if a project equally effectual could be established for the universal peace of mankind![237]

It is hard to tell from this passage whether Madison is more worried about mob rule or political juntas or men-who-would-be-king. In another number of *The Federalist* he focuses his ire on a renewed aristocracy, where he notes: "Could any further proof be required of the republican complexion of this system, the most decisive one might be found in its absolute prohibition of titles of nobility, both under the federal and the State governments; and in its express guaranty of the republican form to each of the latter."[238] In yet another, he chastises "popular government," noting that in Greece, only the Achaean League could avoid its "tempestuous . . . disorders" because they "tempered by the general authority and laws of the confederacy."[239] But the

Framing generation believed that the Guarantee Clause vindicated certain aspects of republican virtue. At the Massachusetts ratifying convention a number of delegates expressed the hope that the Guarantee Clause would ensure that "wisdom, virtue, and order" would prevail over "licentiousness," "avarice," and "tyranny" and so prevent the rise of another "Sulla [or] Caesar" from the "tumult of the people."[240]

A crucial linchpin of the Framers' concern for guaranteeing republican government was the ancient concern that confederations including polities with different forms of government could not long endure. Madison also made this point as a preface to his remarks in *Federalist* 43 on the dangers of military adventurers and mob escapades:

> In a confederacy founded on republican principles, and composed of republican members, the superintending government ought clearly to possess authority to defend the system against aristocratic or monarchial innovations. The more intimate the nature of such a union may be, the greater interest have the members in the political institutions of each other; and the greater right to insist that the forms of government under which the compact was entered into should be SUBSTANTIALLY maintained. But a right implies a remedy; and where else could the remedy be deposited, than where it is deposited by the Constitution? Governments of dissimilar principles and forms have been found less adapted to a federal coalition of any sort, than those of a kindred nature. "As the confederate republic of Germany," says Montesquieu, "consists of free cities and petty states, subject to different princes, experience shows us that it is more imperfect than that of Holland and Switzerland." "Greece was undone," he adds, "as soon as the king of Macedon obtained a seat among the Amphictyons." In the latter case, no doubt, the disproportionate force, as well as the monarchical form, of the new confederate, had its share of influence on the events.[241]

Likewise, in his *Law Lectures*, James Wilson referred to Montesquieu's history and commented that "[a] confederate republick should consist of states, whose government is of the same nature.... Hence we may see the propriety and wise policy of that wise article... which provides that [the United States] shall guaranty to every state in the union a republican form of government."[242] The historic example of King Philip of Macedon's subversion of the Amphictyonic Council was a staple at the state ratifying conventions.[243] So, too, were Julius Caesar's and his successors' (including Augustus') subversion of the institutions of the Roman republic. Although the traditional offices of the consuls, tribunes, and censors persisted, as well as the republican assemblies (including the senate), they were stripped of power by the Roman emperors. The "appearance and forms" of republican government subsisted in Rome, but not the reality.[244]

A counterpoint to the requirement of uniformity in forms of government was that a confederation of republics lent themselves to a higher degree of cohesion and national purpose. As Pelatiah Webster discussed in his pamphlet criticizing the work of the arch-Antifederalist, Brutus, and his exploitation of Montesquieu's small republic maxim,

> The Romans rose, from small beginnings, to a very great extent of territory, population and wisdom; I don't think their constitution of government, was near so good as the one proposed to us, yet we find their power, strength, and establishment, were raised to their utmost height, under a republican form of government.... The Carthagenians [sic] acquired an amazing degree of strength, wealth, and extent of dominion under a republican form of government. Neither they or the Romans, owed their dissolution to any causes arising from that kind of government; 'twas the party rage, animosity, and violence of their citizens, which destroyed them both; it weakened them, 'til the one fell under the power of their enemy, and was thereby reduced to ruin; the other changed their form of government, to a monarchy which proved in the end, equally fatal to them.[245]

The demands of uniformity and cohesion in the form of government taken by the component states of the Union led to the Framers' concerns about the basic attributes of those governments. The Full Faith and Credit Clause of Article IV of the Constitution required that each state recognize and enforce "the public Acts, records, and judicial proceedings of every other State,"[246] and the following provision extended to "the citizens of each State ... all Privileges and Immunities of Citizens in the Several States."[247] Resonating with their knowledge of the Achaean League, the Framers believed these provisions essential to a federative union.[248]

Two additional elements stood out as requirements of republican government: separation of powers between the branches and an independent judiciary. As noted by later courts[249] and commentators,[250] the relevant question was the form of constitutional governance taken by states at the time of the Founding. Madison believed the principles of separation of powers and federalism worked hand-in-hand:

> In a single republic, all the power surrendered by the people is submitted to the administration of a single government; and the usurpations are guarded against by a division of the government into distinct and separate departments. In the compound republic of America, the power surrendered by the people is first divided between two distinct governments, and

then the portion allotted to each subdivided among distinct and separate departments. Hence a double security arises to the rights of the people. The different governments will control each other, at the same time that each will be controlled by itself.[251]

For Hamilton, there were ancient lessons to be drawn on the republican virtues of divided power, especially executive authority:

THERE is an idea, which is not without its advocates, that a vigorous Executive is inconsistent with the genius of republican government.... Every man the least conversant in Roman history, knows how often that republic was obliged to take refuge in the absolute power of a single man, under the formidable title of Dictator, as well against the intrigues of ambitious individuals who aspired to the tyranny, and the seditions of whole classes of the community whose conduct threatened the existence of all government, as against the invasions of external enemies who menaced the conquest and destruction of Rome....

The Roman history records many instances of mischiefs to the republic from the dissensions between the Consuls, and between the military Tribunes, who were at times substituted for the Consuls. But it gives us no specimens of any peculiar advantages derived to the state from the circumstance of the plurality of those magistrates. That the dissensions between them were not more frequent or more fatal, is a matter of astonishment, until we advert to the singular position in which the republic was almost continually placed, and to the prudent policy pointed out by the circumstances of the state, and pursued by the Consuls, of making a division of the government between them.[252]

Whether the Guarantee Clause demands a formal separation of powers between the branches of state governments counts among the modern mysteries of this constitutional provision. Some recent courts have weighed in on this issue. One of these was in a challenge to the constitutionality of section 1983, the key provision of the Civil Rights Act, adopted in the wake of the Civil War. In doubt was whether the Act abrogated the common law immunity of state judges for official acts taken in the regular performance of their duties. In a passage that the Third Circuit frankly indicated was dicta, it concluded that "[t]he framers of the Constitution clearly evinced their belief that a separate and independent judiciary is an indispensable element of a republican form of government. We believe that abrogation of judicial immunity by Congress would destroy the independence of the judiciary in the various States, and consequently deprive them of a republican form of government."[253] No court has gone so far to rule that innovations in state government – such as judicial involvement in legislative redistricting[254] or the exercise by a governor of legislative power to reorganize the state executive branch[255] – constituted an impermissible violation of the separation of powers principle enshrined in the Guarantee Clause.

In making this determination, courts have reached strikingly different conclusions about whether the separation-of-powers principle can be legitimately subsumed as part of republican government. The Colorado Supreme Court, after conducting a rather desultory review of the Philadelphia debates, ratifying conventions, and *Federalist Papers* decided that the Framers were concerned only about the reinvigoration of monarchical institutions and suppressing unrest.[256] That court particularly relied on Madison's statements in *Federalist* 39 and 43 that it was merely "SUFFICIENT for such a [republican] government that the persons administering it be appointed, either directly or indirectly by the people,"[257] and, in any event, "[w]henever the States may choose to substitute other republican forms, they have a right to do so, and to claim the federal guaranty for the latter...."[258] The Kansas Supreme Court was, however, far more searching in its review of the original intent of the Guarantee Clause, appreciating the philosophical and intellectual background of the provision, and made this inference:

> As indicated in the foregoing analysis of the debates of the federal convention, it was no accident that discussions of the republican form of government and of the expressed guaranty to the states were perfunctory in character. However, the Federalist Papers are replete with references to separation of power as a fundamental concept of a free government. In fact, one of the attacks made upon the proposed constitution as drafted by the federal convention was that it violated the doctrine of separation of powers which was considered intrinsic to a free republican government. The concept of a republican form of government and by implication the doctrine of separation of powers were the underlying assumption upon which the framework of the new government was developed. In reaching this conclusion, this court holds that the doctrine of separation of powers is an inherent and integral element of the republican form of government, and separation of powers, as an element of the republican form of government, is expressly guaranteed to the states by Article IV, Section 4 of the Constitution of the United States.[259]

These two constructions of the Guarantee Clause thus turned on the particular court's ability to comprehend the deep meaning and purpose of the provision, in light of the Framing generation's understanding of republican government.

A second prominent aspect of the puzzle that is the modern construction of the Guaranty Clause is that it appears to be beyond the reach of judicial enforcement, at least by federal courts. This result is an application of the "political question" doctrine enunciated by the U.S. Supreme Court to avoid adjudication of certain kinds of disputes, which are constitutionally consigned to the political branches of the federal government – Congress and the Presidency. It is also a peculiar legacy of one of the few documented cases of political revolution in the United States: the so-called "Dorr War," in which a popular movement of disenfranchised and under-represented citizens in Rhode Island rose-up in the 1840s and supplanted the existing regime, placed in power by the colonial Charter of 1663 (Rhode Island had never adopted a constitution after the Revolution).[260] When the legal status of these events was adjudicated by the Supreme Court in *Luther v. Borden*,[261] the Court declared itself powerless to rule on which was the legitimate government of the state, and thus to practically enforce the Republican Government guarantee:

> Under this article of the Constitution it rests with Congress to decide what government is the established one in a State. For as the United States guarantee to each State a republican government, Congress must necessarily decide what government is established in the State before it can determine whether it is republican or not. And when the senators and representatives of a State are admitted into the councils of the Union, the authority of the government under which they are appointed, as well as its republican character, is recognized by the proper constitutional authority. And its decision is binding on every other department of the government, and could not be questioned in a judicial tribunal.[262]

Of course, the *Luther* Court never explained the textual basis for its abdication of judicial authority in construing the Guarantee Clause. Nothing in the constitutional provision textually commits such questions to the political branches; quite the contrary, its placement in Article IV, rather than Article I (Congress' powers) is highly suggestive of the opposite conclusion.[263]

The Guaranty Clause is not, as some might assume, a dead-letter, however. At least in terms of federal power, there remains the possibility of Congress and the Executive enforcing some strictures of republican government as against the states, without necessarily resorting to the expedient of seeking to militarily intervene to quell civil unrest upon the application of the state legislature or governor (assuming such permission would be granted). Rather, it is possible to imagine that Congress would have the power to legislate pursuant to the Guarantee Clause certain substantive standards of governance that states would be obliged to obey, as with the federal government's attempts to blunt some aspects of the peculiar theocracy that governed Utah in the late nineteenth century.[261] Of course, the political question bar only affects *federal* courts. One can see that there has been, and will continue to be, robust litigation in state tribunals as to whether certain constitutional innovations are consistent with republican government.

One of these implicates the third, and final, problem in the contemporary construction of the Guarantee Clause. This is its applicability as a check against state voter initiatives, referenda, and plebiscites, which made laws (as distinct from state constitutional amendments) without recourse to the legislature and a governor's signature. Although such popular law-making measures comprise only a tiny portion of all laws adopted in the land,[265] they have been the subject of substantial controversy. Part of the debate has been whether such voter initiatives, when conducted without the sanction of the legislature, are violative of the Guarantee Clause insofar as they insinuate a popular and democratic mode of government in place of a republic's representative scheme.[266] Although the U.S. Supreme Court,[267] and a number of state supreme courts,[268] have rejected such challenges on a variety of grounds, they have on very rare occasions succeeded[269] and are continually asserted.[270]

Recognizing that the proper resolution of this issue turns on the original understanding of "republican government," at least one commentator has sought to canvass the classical record that the Framing generation had available to it. Relying primarily on John Adams's discussions of ancient popular government in his *Defence of the Constitutions of the United States*, Robert Natelson has concluded that the Framers would have inevitably regarded popular referenda as a legitimate form of republican law-making, and not some sort of impermissible democratic novelty.[271] It was Adams who reported on the various processes for submitting legislative matters to the people in Carthage,[272] Athens,[273] Rome,[274] and Sparta.[275] Even Adams recognized that there were definitive checks on popular law-making. In Athens, there were elaborate procedures for submission of bills to smaller and more selective tribunals (the areopagus and nomothetai) for approval, even after a favorable vote in the ekklesia or boule.[276] At Sparta, the popular assembly had only the power to grant or deny a proposal made by the gerousia.[277] The Roman republic observed customs (including the *ius agendi cum populo*), which limited the ability of popular assemblies to initiate their own legislation, save with the consent of the presiding officer (the consuls for the comitia centuriata and comitia tributa; the plebian tribune for the concilium plebis) and (at least, during the period of Sulla's reforms) the concurrence of the senate.[278]

So while Natelson makes a strong case certainly for the relevance of clas-sical authority for the original intent of the Guarantee Clause, it is by no means clear that he reaches the correct interpretation based on ancient political practices. Although Athenian democracy undoubtedly reflected a democratic principle of popular governance captured by voter referenda, it was clear that that model was not looked upon with favor by the Framing generation, and was not at all seen as a "republican form of government."[279] The Framers were also well aware that the Spartan and Roman popular assemblies were sharply circumscribed in their power to initiate legislation without *both* submission by an elected official *and* subsequent approval by another body, usually the senate or gerousia. Notwithstanding Natel-son's colorful claim that the Roman plebescita reflects a pure act of popular governance,[280] that is not borne out by the classical sources.[281] Although he may well be correct that popular referenda and initiatives are fully consis-tent with republican government as we today understand that phrase, it is by no means certain that the Framing generation would have been quick to use ancient history and classical modes of government in support of that proposition.

The Guarantee Clause thus remains a conundrum in a constitutional text full of riddles. As I have tried to make clear in this chapter, to the extent that originalism helps at all in the explication of difficult constitutional provi-sions to novel circumstances, it is essential that the full drafting and ratifying history be recounted and (especially, as I argue here) the complete intellec-tual engagement of the Framers with ancient history and political practice. The constitutional clauses I have glossed here simply make less sense with-out that classical overlay. Whether it is the historical basis of state sovereign immunity, the possibility of presidential vetoes of war declarations and after-term impeachments, the propriety of the line-item veto and electoral college reform, or the consistency of popular referenda with "republican govern-ment," all turn on a deep cognizance of the Framers' instrumental use of ancient authority, legitimacy, wisdom, and experience.

FIVE

THE CLASSICAL CONSTITUTION

GORDON WOOD HAS CALLED THE AMERICAN CONSTITUTION OF 1787 an "intrinsically . . . aristocratic document, designed to check the democratic tendencies of the period" and the "end to classical politics."[1] In the final pages of this book, I might legitimately question whether the Constitution is, indeed, a classical work. Even more relevantly, it should be considered whether the Constitution marks a defining transition between classical modes of governance and the modern, democratic, and representational styles of government that were predicted by Jefferson and Madison. When viewed in this way, it matters less to see the Framing generation through a prism of class and economic distinctions, than it is to view the Framers' intellectual ethos through the lens of the ideas they held in common. Among these attitudes were certainly their collective experience in resisting, and then defeating, British imperial designs. Also of importance was their tolerant, but devout, religiosity, as well as their commitment to the rule of law (and particularly the ideal of the common law and English civil liberties). Lastly, and as I have emphasized here, was the Framing generation's inculcation in, and devotion to, the classical ideals of civic responsibility, public honor, and republican government.

As I have acknowledged at the outset, it would be easy to dismiss the influence of the classical tradition on the Framing generation as some peculiar and pretentious residuum of the elite culture of the times. Indeed, in the modern historiography of the intellectual life of the early republic, that is precisely the prevalent view: that classicism was a mere window dressing to the pragmatic, hard-knuckled politics of the period.[2] In the same fashion, these same historians have tended to discount the religious fervor of the times. We have thus managed to make a caricature of the Framers and rendered them as we would prefer to see them as ourselves today. In this version of the Framing mythos, the individuals who act in our national nativity scene read only Enlightenment political literature, speak only in a pragmatic political argot, and think only in terms of class, money, and power. These are, after all, things we can comprehend today. In accordance with this view, when the script of the Framing morality play veers off into unexpected pieces of dialogue – as when the Framers speak of God's providence and the role of churches in the new society, or of classical models of government and republican virtues – our modern, internal dramaturge excises those scenes, or, worse yet, annotates them as irrelevant. As an exercise in recollection, this book has sought to return to the roots of our understanding of the Founding moment.

The relevance of the classical tradition to the Constitution's framing is not just a story of elite culture in late colonial and early republic America. As I suggested in Chapter 1, the same depth of classical training and affinity was shared both by those who advocated and opposed the new Constitution. Federalists and Antifederalists were often united in their recourse to ancient history and the classical precedents of government.[3] They often reached, of course, opposite conclusions as to the advisability of structuring government institutions in particular ways (based on their reading of the classical record), but both sides of the debate employed the same classical metaphors, similes, texts, and legends in making their points. If any intellectual current was marginalized in the debates in Philadelphia or in the state ratification conventions it was the views of the anticlassicists. Despite the respect that such individuals as Benjamin Franklin, Benjamin Rush, Benjamin Randall, and Rufus King were otherwise accorded, when they sought to discount or ridicule the pertinence of classicism in the making of the Constitution, they were politely – but firmly – ignored.

It would also be easy, but quite mistaken, to suggest that the Framers used classical models of government to fashion only the "aristocratic" or "elite" elements of the Constitutional scheme. This view is suggestive of a notion that classicism provided a clever intellectual cover for those who wanted to perpetuate class distinctions in America, to control the vibrant democracy that was formed in the crucible of the Revolution. Once again, there is no correlation between those who advanced popular democracy at the Constitutional Convention and those who also eschewed classical models. Quite the contrary: the most consistent and effective advocate in Philadelphia for popular governance in the Constitution's provisions for electing representatives and leaders was James Wilson, also one of the most prominent classicists. It has to be credited that classicism was instrumental in the development of two crucial elements in the structural Constitution: (1) the role of the Senate as a check on a popularly elected assembly[4] and (2) the selection of the nation's chief magistrate.

There is no doubt that Spartan, Punic, and Roman history provided the crucial support for the institution of the Senate – which was clearly intended by the Framers as an elite institution. It appears that the decision to have two senators perpetually elected from each State was directly modeled on the plan of Greek city-state representation on the Amphictyonic Council. No Framer believed that the American Senate should be a hereditary aristocratic assembly, like the British House of Lords. Rather, the archetype was Spartan and Roman practices in choosing senators based on age, experience, and prior service as a magistrate. Just as plebians served in the Roman senate (although admittedly not in large numbers until the late republic period), so, too, the American senate would be open to qualified individuals of all classes and backgrounds. Despite James Wilson's best efforts to win direct, popular election of the president, he believed (along with Madison) that the electoral college system – perhaps premised on Roman voting assemblies – was best calculated to give effect to popular preferences, while, at the same time, ensuring against sectional rivalries and outright electoral corruption.

Another criticism of the role of classicism in making the Constitution was the intellectual succor it gave to the Framers in seeing their creation as a set of structural safeguards, rather than as an affirmative set of liberties or rights vested in the people. As the Framing generation was quite well aware, ancient polities had virtually no conception of individual rights. At its epitome, classical government existed only for the common weal. Liberal philosophy was purely the product of the modern Enlightenment mind. As I have already suggested here, the Framers would have found it odd to differentiate the "structural" Constitution that was the essence of their project, from the "rights" Constitution that we have come to believe (by virtue of the later Bill of Rights) was really their object. It was taken as an article of faith by both Federalists and Antifederalists that the best protection of individual liberty was a government that governed least – with decisions being made at the most local and immediate level practicable – and when government did act it did so in a responsible and accountable fashion. The federalism and separation-of-powers bundles of provisions in the Constitution were clearly intended to restrain government by directing certain kinds of actions to those decision makers in the best position to make them in a capable fashion. This decision-forcing aspect of the Constitution ratcheted both "up" and "down" in the federalism sense: state governments were given authority over many issues of the daily lives of citizens, whereas the national government had plenary authority especially in the high affairs of state: commerce, finance, diplomacy, and war. Likewise, decision-making authority was deflected in a "horizontal" manner between different branches of the national government. Especially significant was the allocation of different components of the taxation, appointments, treaty-making, and war-making powers between the popular House of Representatives, the elite senate, and the chief magistrate of the Presidency.

Even before the provisions of the Bill of Rights were deliberated in the aftermath of the state ratification debates, the main body of the Constitution contained many subtle, substantive aspects that served as structural safeguards on individual liberties. The enumeration of the limited powers of the federal Congress was assuredly one of these. In the contemplation of the federal courts, the restraints imposed on inherent judicial powers – including the jury institution, the doctrine of *stare decisis*, and the proper use of canons of statutory construction – all had significant classical antecedents, although English common law considerations were prevalent. In a similar fashion, the Constitution's express renunciation of certain pathologies of legislation – including ex post facto laws, impairments of contract, and bills of attainder – were vitally significant and were informed by the Framers' aversion not only to British parliamentary excesses but also to those of Greek democratic assemblies.

Although the dichotomy between the structural constitution and rights constitution is a false one, an anachronism that the Framers would have disavowed, it may reveal a real tension between viewing the Constitution as a classical instrument of divided and republican government, or as an Enlightenment vehicle for the vindication of individual liberties and personal freedoms. Of course, to state this tension in the way that I just have may well mischaracterize the problem, for there can be no doubt that to the extent that the Framers conceived of liberty, it was exclusively in the negative sense of individuals and social cohorts being free of government restrictions and coercions. This is certainly consistent with the lessons the Framing generation derived from classical antiquity's accounts of resistence to tyranny. The Framers thus conceived the Constitution as a rights charter that protected citizens from government intrusion, while granting no entitlements to government largesse. The conferral of such benefits was left to the political process itself, and thus subject to the safeguards of the structural constitution. In these respects, the *real* Enlightenment conception of liberty – the one the Framers understood and embraced – was actually quite consistent with the classical vision of a limited republican government.

Of course, that raises the quite uncomfortable problem of the Framers' insistence on extolling classical republican virtues. These included the discipline, austerity, rectitude, and caution of citizens and leaders alike, the public's avoidance of avarice, luxury, and dissipation, and a common commitment to the public good. It is perhaps no surprise that John Adams began his *Defence of the Constitutions of Government the United States* with a gloss on Cicero's aphorism, *"respublica est res populi."*[5] As James Madison pithily noted, "[n]o theoretical checks, no form of government can render us secure. To suppose that any form of government will secure liberty or happiness without any virtue in a people, is a chimerical idea."[6] The Framing generation's rhetoric of classicism was thus suffused with these values and aspirations,[7] and perhaps this is what makes us uneasy today in sensing that the Framers may have actually *believed* in all of this. As articulated in this way, classical republican virtues appear to be communitarian ideals, and may well pose a challenge to the rights-based, liberal Constitution many tend to embrace. To the extent that contemporary American material culture – with its emphasis on urban life, commercial economies, and entrepreneurial spirit – is at such a remove from the simple agrarian vision of classical republicanism, the Framers' ideals appear to be quaint, if not downright silly.[8]

Imposing a libertarian-communitarian construct on the classical thinking of the Framing generation may well be pointless because classical texts and ancient history did not merely suggest that the only public virtue was subservience to a notional public good. If anything, the Framers may well have believed, more than they publicly admitted, that the notion of "mixed government," with different social cohorts (including the aristocracy and populace) being balanced and poised for national purposes, was accurate. Although Jefferson and Madison came to repudiate such elitist notions as a "natural aristocracy" (at least in their later political writings, although not in their private correspondence), both admitted that public goods could never be equally distributed in a society that respected and valued talent. The Framers also constantly alluded to positive stories of ancient personages who sought fame and honor by affirmatively exercising effective leadership. And although unbridled ambition and demagoguery were obviously bad, the Framers were as much concerned about making a government that was lethargic, unresponsive, and unable to unleash the creative and dynamic energies of its citizens, than a regime that was despotic. The Framers' contemplation of the operations of the Executive branch under the control of a single, nationally elected and politically independent official, as well as the conduct of the nation's foreign relations and war-making capacity, was premised on the ancient lesson of harnessing – and controlling – the aspirations of different individuals and social groups.

How much, then, of an intellectual debt does the Constitution – as distinct from the Framers – owe to antiquity? Aside from the broad structural themes of federalism and separation-of-powers, classicism assuredly provided the needed insights to dissuade the Framers from adopting a unicameral assembly, multiple executives, or a dependent judiciary. If one looks to the actual provisions of the constitutional document, probably the most classically inspired clauses are: those requiring minimum ages for federal office holders;[9] those constituting the senate and endowing it with special authority in the area of appointments and treaties;[10] the unitary Presidency as selected by the electoral college;[11] the congressional control of declarations of war;[12] defining and punishing offenses against the law of nations;[13] the vice president as president of the Senate;[14] the president's pardon power;[15] the possibility of retrospective impeachments;[16] the granting of full faith and credit to sister-state acts, records, and judgments;[17] the prohibition of attainders;[18] the suspension of writs of habeas corpus only in times of grave emergency;[19] and the guarantee to the states of republican government.[20] Each of these provisions had manifest classical antecedents, clearly recognized by the Framers and discussed during the course of the Philadelphia Convention or the state ratifying debates.

No claim is being made here that classical antiquity provided the chief inspiration of the constitutional text. Such an assertion would be historically unsupportable and laughably simplistic. Rather, my point is that the Framers' appreciation of ancient history has to be taken into account in any intelligible interpretation of the original intent of the Constitution. The Framing generation's use of classical authority in designing not only the broad contours of the constitutional scheme and drafting particular clauses, but also in rejecting plausible alternatives, should be considered as a coequal body of originalist literature. It should rightfully be placed on a par with the Framers' use of Enlightenment political philosophy, their religious beliefs, their training in the common law, and their pragmatic political attitudes. Far from being epiphenomenal and irrelevant, the Framing generation's use of antiquity was instrumental and deeply rooted in what they viewed as the proper role of history in human affairs.

In this, virtually all of the Framers were agreed. The Framing generation was more apt to pay homage to Clio than to other Enlightenment deities.[21] John Dickinson casually noted at Philadelphia that "experience must be our only guide. Reason may mislead us."[22] In *The Federalist*, Alexander Hamilton could declare that history was "the least fallible guide of human opinions,"[23] and James Madison said simply that history was "the oracle of truth."[24] Patrick Henry, perhaps the Antifederalists' most fervent voice, announced to the Virginia assembly that "I have but one lamp by which my feet are guided, and that is the lamp of experience. I know of no way of judging the future but by the past."[25]

Although the Framers clearly valued historical wisdom, they sometimes did not realize that as an "oracle" it could speak in garbled tones, and as a "guide" it could, indeed, deceive. Nowhere is this more spectacularly demonstrated than in the Framing generation's use of classical antiquity for the instrumental purposes of political precedent. In putting their trust in sometimes corrupted texts and faulty translations, and by relying on dubious secondary sources, the Framers were often seriously misled in some of their historical conclusions. The amount of attention the Framers devoted to the practices of the Amphictyonic League, which they erroneously regarded as a protozoan "United States of Greece" (as per the writings of the Abbé de Mably), were totally wasted. Modern classical philologists have all but ruled out the relevance of that religious institution as a model for Greek federal government. In a similar vein, having made up their minds that Athenian political institutions were fatally infected with the virus of demagoguery and inconstancy, the Framers tended to selectively ignore those parts of the historical record (especially from such reliable sources as Thucydides) that placed the effectiveness of those bodies in a more favorable light. Somewhat less egregiously, the Framers were wont to creatively fill in some of the details of the Roman constitution based on Cicero's hortatory observations, even though they were not necessarily supported by the historical texts of Polybius, Livy, and Tacitus, much less the archaeological evidence of inscriptions.

It would be easy to ridicule the instrumental classicism of the Framers and to declare it a precursor to the current phenomenon of "law office history,"[26] or to use Martin Flaherty's memorable turn-of-phrase, "History Lite."[27] Given the primary sources that were at their disposal, even by today's standards of philology, archaeology, and classical studies, the Framers did a reputable job in trying to make sense of antiquity. The best classicists among the Framing generation – Adams, Dickinson, Hamilton, Jefferson, Madison, Pinckney, Randolph, Webster, Wilson, and Wythe – attempted to resolve problems in the original texts, to cross-read different accounts of the same historic events or institutions, and to derive broad conclusions about ancient statecraft from a wide array of sources. These Framers tended to read critically, and were not necessarily quick to accept some ancient axiom at face value. Lastly, and most important of all, they all knew the limits of the classical canon and the true social, economic, and political differences between life in ancient Greece and Rome and the American experience.

The fact that the members of the Framing generation were careful readers of classical literature did not make them any less instrumental in their uses of ancient history. Profoundly influenced by the Whig school of politics and historiography, it was only natural that they would seek to draw parallels between ancient political conditions and their own. Although the classics could impart wisdom and pleasure, the Framers perused ancient history and political philosophy chiefly as a means to a clearly prescribed end: the founding of a new Order to national life. They would have been unapologetic about their utilitarian desire to marshal evidence of ancient political institutions in their search for the enduring truths of human governance.

So one can hardly be critical of "law office history," when it is clear that Framers like James Madison were quite prepared to enlist historical (including classical) scholarship in the service of politics. As time went on, Madison's views about the uses of history in American constitutional life also changed. As Carl Richard has noted, by the time of the Nullification Crisis of the 1830's – one of the major sectional disputes prior to the Civil War – in the closing days of Madison's life,[28] Madison knew he occupied a privileged place as the last living member of the Framing generation: "Madison understood that American political debate was no longer a search for truth, with the history of nations as a guide, but a search for legitimacy, with the hallowed Constitution as the authority.... Madison's role had shifted from that of a scholar, whose task was to distill the wisdom of the ages, to that of a high priest, whose duty was to recount the intent of the demigods."[29] So, just as the Greeks valued past history (as *patrioi nomoi*), and the Romans had respected "the ways of our fathers" (*mos maiorum*), Americans came to regard the Founding moment as almost a mythic beginning.[30]

The Framing generation's debate over the political relevance of ancient history is thus substantially similar to today's discussions about the role of the Framers' original intent in constitutional interpretation. The only thing that has changed is the relevant canon of texts. It seems odd, but the prevailing mode of contemporary constitutional construction is to divine the intent of the Framers in drafting and ratifying particular textual provisions. As Justice Clarence Thomas has observed, the original understanding of the constitutional text is "what the delegates at the Philadelphia Convention and the state ratifying conventions understood it to mean."[31] Or, as Justice Antonin Scalia put it, originalism requires that "[t]he Constitution means now what its text reasonably conveyed to intelligent and informed people at the time it was drafted and ratified."[32] Putting aside questions of whether the views of the Constitution's drafters should be privileged, or open to public scrutiny as those of the ratifiers in the state conventions,[33] originalism demands a fidelity to the creators of our constitutional order, if for no other reason than to give the Constitution's text an historical anchor and the national compact some social legitimacy.[34]

Of course, originalism as an interpretive approach, cannot, and does not, purport to reach definitive conclusions about constitutional meaning. The embrace of originalism has been critiqued by some as Burkean and as a reactionary tendency to promote conservative values and social traditions. And it is ironic that those judges (including Justices Scalia and Thomas) who espouse originalism for the Constitution eschew the use of legislative intent in construing statutes. Moreover, the current Supreme Court has been by no means consistent in its use of original intent in various provisions of the Constitution. For those clauses bearing on federalism and state sovereign immunity, including the Tenth and Eleventh Amendments, the contemporary Supreme Court has staked-out what it acknowledges is an interpretation that may well run counter to what the Framers actually *intended*, but one that advances the essential *purpose* of state sovereignty under the "Plan of the Convention." What is perhaps most surprising of all is that a majority of the Court, in its search for original intent, might dismiss as irrelevant the Framers' own comparative and historical engagement with constitutionalism. As Justice Scalia recently opined in *Printz v. United States*, "We think such comparative analysis inappropriate to the task of interpreting a constitution, though it was of course quite relevant to the task of writing one. . . . The fact is that our federalism is not Europe's. It is 'the unique contribution of the Framers to political science and political theory.'"[35]

Although Justice Scalia might be justified in excoriating comparative approaches to *modern* constitutionalism, insofar as the Framing generation very self-consciously made a comparative analysis of constitutional governance, especially depending on classical models and insights, I would argue that this has to figure in any contemporary appreciation of original intent. Some broad features of the structural Constitution (particularly those dealing with federalism and states' rights), and some specific provisions (most notably the "advice" portion of the Treaty Clause, the retrospective element of the Impeachment Clause, and the entirety of the Republican Government Guarantee Clause), simply make no sense without knowing what the Framers knew about ancient history and political practices. To fashion an original intent for these provisions based on only a superficial reading of the Framers' sense of English constitutional history or of colonial-era or

Articles of Confederation-period politics would lead to strange and bizarre results, ones quite unintended by the Framing generation.

So, comparative constitutionalism has something to offer not only for the making of constitutions, but also their interpretation. If originalism is going to be consistently and legitimately espoused as a means of constitutional construction, then the complete *mentalité* of the Framing generation needs to be observed. If it matters what "intelligent and informed people" of the Framing generation understood the Constitution to mean, it would be folly to exclude from the analysis the crucial element of the educational background, historical sensibilities, and political fears of those people. As I have suggested here, classicism and ancient history were crucial components of those understandings and beliefs, and were every bit as significant as the Framers' economic interests, their religious values, and their confidence in the rule of law and the promise of liberty.

Without necessarily endorsing the originalism that is often expounded as a means for constitutional interpretation, one can embrace the classical heritage of the Constitution on its own terms. The American constitutional experiment has actually proven itself as durable as that of the Lycurgan constitution at Sparta, that of the Roman and Punic republics, or that of the Achaean and Aetolian Confederacies. Two centuries may not seem an extended period of time, but, in the currents of history, few republics have subsisted for so long under one consistent form of government. The genius of the Framing generation in creating such a robust form of government – one that has survived sectional rivalry and civil war, vast territorial expansion and emergence into Great Power status, and amazing economic, social, and cultural changes – would have been appreciated by their classical forebears. As Polybius noted in his narrative of the rise of the Roman republic, "the chief cause of success or the reverse in all matters is the form of a state's constitution."[36] So instead of seeing the American Founding moment as exclusively the making of a new world order – a *Novus Ordo Seclorum* – we may do well to recognize its ancient precedents, and its classical legacy.

NOTES

PREFACE

1. Dinesh D'Souza, WHAT's So GREAT ABOUT AMERICA (Washington, DC: Regnery, 2002).

2. For elaboration of this distinction between the "structural Constitution" and the "rights Constitution," see see Akhil R. Amar, *The Bill of Rights as a Constitution*, 100 YALE L. J. 1131, 1132, 1201 (1991); Steven G. Calabresi and Kevin H. Rhodes, *The Structural Constitution: Unitary Executive, Plural Judiciary*, 105 HARV. L. REV. 1153, 1153–54 (1992).

3. See J. G. A. Pocock, THE MACHIAVELLIAN MOMENT: FLORENTINE POLITICAL THOUGHT AND THE ATLANTIC REPUBLICAN TRADITION (Princeton: Princeton University Press, 1975); See also Paul A. Rahe, REPUBLICS ANCIENT AND MODERN: CLASSICAL REPUBLICANISM AND THE AMERICAN REVOLUTION, at 9–10, 136–62 (Chapel Hill: University of North Carolina Press, 1992); Gordon S. Wood, THE CREATION OF THE AMERICAN REPUBLIC, 1776–1787 (Chapel Hill: University of North Carolina Press, 1969); Michael P. Zuckert, NATURAL RIGHTS AND THE NEW REPUBLICANISM, at 150–83 (Princeton: Princeton University Press, 1994); Robert E. Shalhope, *Toward a Republican Synthesis: The Emerging of an Understanding of Republicanism in American Historiography*, 29 WMQ 49 (1972); David Wootton, *The Republican Tradition: From Commonwealth to Common Sense*, in REPUBLICANISM, LIBERTY AND COMMERCIAL SOCIETY, 1649–1776, at 11, 13–26 (David Wootton, ed.; Palo Alto: Stanford University Press, 1994).

The "republican hypothesis" has been attacked by those who would reestablish Lockean liberalism as the theoretical centerpiece of the American Revolution. See, for example, Joyce Appleby, LIBERALISM AND REPUBLICANISM IN THE HISTORICAL IMAGINATION (Cambridge, Mass.: Harvard University Press, 1992); John Patrick Diggins, THE LOST SOUL OF AMERICAN POLITICS; VIRTUE, SELF-INTEREST AND THE FOUNDATIONS OF LIBERALISM (Chicago: University of Chicago Press, 1986); Isaac Kramnick, *Republican Revisionism Revisited*, 87 AM. HIST. REV. 629 (1982).

For consensus views and intellectual histories of this debate, see Alan Gibson, *Ancients, Moderns and Americans: the Republicanism-Liberalism Debate*

Revisited, 21 Hist. of Political Thought 261 (2000); Jeffrey C. Isaac, *Republicanism v. Liberalism? A Reconsideration*, 9 id., 349 (1988); Lance Banning, *Jeffersonian Ideology Revisited: Liberal and Classical Ideas in the New American Republic*, 42 WMQ 11 (1987); Jean Yarbrough, *Republicanism Reconsidered: Some Thoughts on the Foundation and Preservation of the American Republic*, 41 Rev. of Politics 61 (1979); Isaac Kramnick, Republicanism and Bourgeois Radicalism: Political Ideology in Late 18th Century England and America (Ithaca: Cornell University Press, 1990); Max M. Edling, A Revolution in Favor of Government: Origins of the U.S. Constitution and the Making of the American State, 31–46 (Oxford: Oxford University Press, 2003); Thomas L. Pangle, The Spirit of Modern Republicanism: The Moral Vision of the American Founders and the Philosophy of Locke 7–39 (Chicago: University of Chicago Press, 1988).

4. M. N. S. Sellers, American Republicanism: Roman Ideology and the United States Constitution 20 (Houndmills: MacMillan, 1994). For additional intellectual histories on this point, see Charles R. Kesler, *The Founders and the Classics*, in The Revival of Constitutionalism (James W. Muller, ed.; Lincoln: University of Nebraska Press, 1988); E. Christian Kopff, *Open Shutters on the Past: Rome and the Founders*, in Vital Remnants: America's Founding and the Western Tradition, at 71, 71–73, 94–96 (Gary L. Gregg, II, ed.; Wilmington: ISI Books, 1999); Meyer Reinhold, Classica Americana: The Greek and Roman Heritage in the United States, at 40, 283–95 (Detroit: Wayne State University Press, 1984); Carl J. Richard, The Founders and the Classics: Greece, Rome and the American Enlightenment 1–11 (Cambridge, Mass.: Harvard University Press, 1994); Louis J. Sirico, Jr., *The Federalist and the Lessons of Rome*, 75 Miss. L. J. 431 (2006).

5. Bernard Bailyn, The Ideological Origins of the American Revolution, at 26 (enlarged ed., Cambridge, Mass.: Belknap Press of Harvard University Press, 1992).

6. Russell Kirk, *What Did Americans Inherit from the Ancients?* in America's British Culture, at 95, 96 (New Brunswick: Transaction, 1985) (original emphasis). See also Robert N. Clinton, *A Brief History of the Adoption of the United States Constitution*, 75 Iowa L. Rev. 891, 897–98 (1990) (reflecting some skepticism of influence of classical republican values); Paul A. Rahe, *Antiquity Surpassed: The Repudiation of Classical Republicanism*, in Republicanism, Liberty, supra note 3, at 231.

7. Clinton Rossiter, Seedtime of the Republic: The Origin of the American Tradition of Political Liberty, at 356–57 (New York: Harcourt Brace, 1953). See also Paul Eidelberg, The Philosophy of the American Revolution: A Reinterpretation of the Intentions of the Founding Fathers (New York: Free Press, 1968).

8. See Bailyn, supra note 5, at 22–54.

9. See Gilbert Chinard, *Polybius and the American Constitution*, 1 JHI 38 (1940), reprinted in The American Enlightenment, at 217, 235–37 (Frank Shuffleton, ed.; New York: University of Rochester Press, 1993); Richard Gummere, The American Colonial Mind and the Classical Tradition, at 174,

n. 5 (Cambridge, Mass.: Harvard University Press, 1963); Kopff, supra note 4, at 94–96.

10. For this (perhaps) extreme view, see Gummere, supra note, at 173–90, and for a defense, see Richard, supra note 4, at 3–4.

11. One of the conventions respected in this book will be lengthy quotations from the original sources written by members of the Framing generation. This will include extracts from the Philadelphia and state ratifying Conventions, as well as published judicial decisions of the period. My practice of lengthy quotation will particularly apply to The Federalist, the series of essays published in 1787 and 1788 by James Madison, Alexander Hamilton, and John Jay to persuade the citizens of New York to ratify the Constitution.

For reasons that will be explained below, *The Federalist Papers* offer one of the best sources for insights into the Framers' appreciation of the classics. But because of the complex narrative structure of the essays – including obtuse sentence constructions and discursive arguments – it is imperative that the relevant portions of the Papers be quoted at length, or else the true thrust of the essayists' views will be lost. See also Bernard Bailyn, To Begin The World Anew: The Genius and Ambiguities of the American Founders, at 100–07 (New York: Knopf, 2003)

12. See David J. Bederman, Classical Canons: Rhetoric, Classicism and Treaty Interpretation (Aldershot: Ashgate, 2001); id., International Law in Antiquity (Cambridge, UK: Cambridge University Press, 2001).

13. See Jack N. Rakove, Original Meanings: Politics and Ideas in the Making of the Constitution, at 42 (New York: Knopf, 1997); Paul Brest, *The Misconceived Quest for the Original Understanding*, 60 B. U. L. Rev. 204 (1980); Peter J. Smith, *The Marshall Court and the Originalist's Dilemma*, 90 Minn. L. Rev. 612 (2006).

CHAPTER 1. THE FRAMERS' CLASSICAL EDUCATION AND WORLD VIEW

1. See Perry Miller, The New England Mind: The Seventeenth Century, at 86 (Cambridge, Mass.: Harvard University Press, 1954) (which notes that literacy rates approached 90 percent in well-settled regions).

2. See, for example, Charles A. Beard, An Economic Interpretation of the Constitution of the United States (New York: Free Press, 1935); Joseph J. Ellis, Founding Brothers – The Revolutionary Generation (New York; Knopf, 2000); Charles S. Sydnor, American Revolutionaries in the Making: Political Practices in Washington's Virginia (New York: Free Press, 1952).

For standard summary biographies of those who attended the Philadelphia Convention, see M. E. Bradford, Founding Fathers (2nd rev. ed.) (Lawrence, Kansas: University Press of Kansas, 1994).

3. See U.S. Const. Preamble ("We the People of the United States. . . . "); Resolution by the Constitutional Convention of Sept. 17, 1787 (noting that "Conventions of Delegates, chosen in each State by the People thereof. . ." would ratify the Constitution).

4. See, for example, H. T. Parker, The Cult of Antiquity and the French Revolutionaries (Chicago: University of Chicago Press, 1965).

5. Charles A. Beard and Mary R. Beard, 1 THE RISE OF AMERICAN CIVILIZATION, at 485–86 (New York: MacMillan, 1927).

6. The leading sources remain, Richard Gummere, THE AMERICAN COLONIAL MIND AND THE CLASSICAL TRADITION (Cambridge, Mass.: Harvard University Press, 1963); Meyer Reinhold, CLASSICA AMERICANA: THE GREEK AND ROMAN HERITAGE IN THE UNITED STATES (Detroit: Wayne State University Press, 1984); Carl J. Richard, THE FOUNDERS AND THE CLASSICS: GREECE, ROME AND THE AMERICAN ENLIGHTENMENT (Cambridge, Mass.: Harvard University Press, 1994).

7. See Richard, supra note 6, at 12.

8. See Gummere, supra note 6, at 58.

9. See Edgar W. Knight, 1 A DOCUMENTARY HISTORY OF EDUCATION IN THE SOUTH BEFORE 1860, at 511 (Chapel Hill: University of North Carolina Press, 1949).

10. See Richard, supra note 6, at 13.

11. See Gummere, supra note 6, at 61.

12. See Werner W. Jaeger, PAIDEIA: THE IDEALS OF GREEK CULTURE (Gilbert Highet transl., 2nd ed.; New York: Oxford University Press, 1945).

13. There are just a handful of instances of girls being classically instructed. Ezra Stiles, President of Yale, examined Lucinda Foote (age 12 years) and issued her a certificate saying that if she had been a boy she could have entered the freshman class at Yale. See Gummere, supra note 6, at 59.

14. See Reinhold, CLASSICA AMERICANA, supra note 6, at 26 (noting that Boston Latin School (founded in 1635), dropped its residency requirement from seven years to four years in 1789).

15. Robert Middlekauff, ANCIENTS AND AXIOMS: SECONDARY EDUCATION IN EIGHTEENTH-CENTURY NEW ENGLAND, at 76–77 (New Haven, Yale University Press, 1963). See also Sheldon D. Cohen, A HISTORY OF COLONIAL EDUCATION, 1607–1776 (New York: John Wiley, 1974); THEORIES OF EDUCATION IN EARLY AMERICA, 1655–1819 (Wilson Smith, ed.; New York: Bobbs-Merrill, 1973); Lorraine Smith Pangle and Thomas L. Pangle, THE LEARNING OF LIBERTY: THE EDUCATIONAL IDEAS OF THE AMERICAN FOUNDERS (Lawrence: University Press of Kansas, 1993).

16. See ESSAYS ON EDUCATION IN THE EARLY REPUBLIC, at 65 (Frederick Rudolph, ed.; Cambridge, Mass.: Harvard University Press, 1965).

17. See Richard, supra note 6, at 13.

18. See Richard, supra note 6, at 13; Reinhold, CLASSICA AMERICANA, supra note 6, at 26. See also Rexine, *The Boston Latin School Curriculum in the Seventeenth and Eighteenth Centuries*, 72 CJ 261, 265 (1977).

19. See Richard, supra note 6, at 13–14 (describing the writings of John Clarke, who was sharply critical of teaching methods of Latin and Greek).

20. See Richard, supra note 6, at 17–18.

21. See James Axtell, THE SCHOOL UPON A HILL: EDUCATION AND SOCIETY IN COLONIAL NEW ENGLAND, at 187–88 (New Haven: Yale University Press, 1974).

22. Edwin A. Miles, *The Old South and the Classical World*, 48 NORTH CAROLINA HISTORICAL REVIEW 262 (1971) (quoting William Hooper of the University of North Carolina in 1832).

23. See Richard, supra note 6, at 15–17.

24. See Patrick Critwell, *The Eighteenth Century: A Classical Age?* 7 ARION 117–18 (Spring 1968).
25. Id. See also Richard, supra note 6, at 14–15.
26. Richard, supra note 6, at 16.
27. See Axtell, supra note 21, at 186–87.
28. See Gummere, supra note 6, at 58.
29. Silvio A. Bedini, THOMAS JEFFERSON: STATESMAN OF SCIENCE, at 16 (New York: MacMillan, 1990).
30. See Bernard Bailyn, EDUCATION IN THE FORMING OF AMERICAN SOCIETY: NEEDS AND OPPORTUNITIES FOR STUDY (Chapel Hill: University of North Carolina Press, 1960); Lawrence A. Cremin, AMERICAN EDUCATION: THE COLONIAL EXPERIENCE, 1607–1783, at 506–09 (New York: Harper & Row, 1970); Carl F. Kaestle, PILLARS OF THE REPUBLIC: COMMON SCHOOLS AND AMERICAN SOCIETY, 1780–1860 (New York: Hill & Wang, 1983).
31. See Evarts B. Greene, THE REVOLUTIONARY GENERATION, 1763–1790, at 122–23 (New York: MacMillan, 1943); Beverly McAnear, *College Founding in the American Colonies*, 42 MISSISSIPPI VALLEY HISTORICAL REVIEW 22 (1955); Reinhold, CLASSICA AMERICANA, supra note 6, at 27, 43.
32. Samuel Eliot Morrison, 1 HARVARD COLLEGE IN THE SEVENTEENTH CENTURY, at 81 (Cambridge, Mass.: Harvard University Press, 1936) (spelling and punctuation modernized).
33. See Richard Hofstadtler and Wilson Smith, 1 AMERICAN HIGHER EDUCATION: A DOCUMENTARY HISTORY, at 54, 117 (Chicago: University of Chicago Press, 1962). See also Edwin C. Broome, A HISTORICAL AND CRITICAL DISCUSSION OF COLLEGE ADMISSION REQUIREMENTS (New York: Macmillan, 1903).
34. See Gummere, supra note 6, at 56–57.
35. See Gilbert Chinard, HONEST JOHN ADAMS, at 11–12 (Boston: Little Brown, 1933); C. Bradley Thompson, JOHN ADAMS AND THE SPIRIT OF LIBERTY, at 24–32 (Lawrence: University Press of Kansas, 1998); Forrest McDonald, ALEXANDER HAMILTON: A BIOGRAPHY, at 11–12 (New York: W. W. Norton, 1979).
36. See Gummere, supra note 6, at 66. See also James J. Walsh, EDUCATION OF THE FOUNDING FATHERS OF THE REPUBLIC (New York: Fordham University Press, 1935).
37. See Gummere, supra note 6, at 75.
38. OLD FAMILY LETTERS, at 456 (A. Biddle, ed.; Philadelphia, 1892) (letter to Benjamin Rush, in which Adams is mimicking Witherspoon's Scots brogue). See also Gummere, supra note 6, at 73.
39. See Hofstadtler and Smith, 1, supra note 33, at 141; Gummere, supra note 6, at 72.
40. Gummere, supra note 6, at 64.
41. See Varnum L. Collins, PRESIDENT WITHERSPOON: A BIOGRAPHY (Princeton: Princeton University Press, 1925).
42. Gummere, supra note 6, at 74.
43. See Colyer Meriwether, OUR COLONIAL CURRICULUM, 1607–1776 (Washington, DC: Capital Pub. Co., 1907); Frederick Rudolph, CURRICULUM: A HISTORY OF AMERICAN UNDERGRADUATE COURSE SINCE 1636 (San Francisco: Jossey-Bass, 1977).
44. Gummere, supra note 6, at 65.

45. See Joe W. Kraus, Book Collections of Five Colonial College Libraries: A Subject Analysis 284 (Ph.D. dissertation, University of Illinois, 1960).

46. See Thomas G. Wright, LITERARY CULTURE IN EARLY NEW ENGLAND, 1620–1730, at 149–50 (New Haven: Yale University Press, 1920). See also Reinhold, CLASSICA AMERICANA, supra note 6, at 28–30.

47. See Gummere, supra note 6, at 63.

48. See http://whigclio.princeton.edu/~historian (visited Aug. 2, 2002) for links to the official history of the (now) combined American-Whig Cliosophic Society. See also James McLachlan, *Classical Names, American Identities: Some Notes on College Students and the Classical Tradition in the 1770s*, in CLASSICAL TRADITIONS IN EARLY AMERICA, at 87–91 (John W. Eadie, ed.; Ann Arbor: Center for the Coordination of Ancient and Modern Studies, 1976).

49. Robert Middlekauff, *A Persistent Tradition: The Classical Curriculum in Eighteenth-Century New England*, 18 WMQ (3rd ser.) 65 (Jan. 1961).

50. See Edwin A. Miles, *The Young American Nation and the Classical World*, 35 JHI 265 and n. 25 (Apr.–June 1974).

51. See David J. Bederman, CLASSICAL CANONS: RHETORIC, CLASSICISM AND TREATY INTERPRETATION, at 11–21 (Aldershot, UK: Ashgate, 2001); Stephen Botein, *Cicero as Role Model for Early American Lawyers: A Case Study of Classical "Influence,"* 73 CJ 318 (1978).

52. See Paul Lewis, THE GRAND INCENDIARY: A BIOGRAPHY OF SAMUEL ADAMS, at 10 (New York: Dial Press, 1973). See also Gummere, supra note 6, at 114–17.

53. See Gummere, supra note 6, at 71.

54. See Gummere, supra note 6, at 71.

55. See John M. Murrin, *The Legal Transformation: The Bench and Bar of Eighteenth-Century Massachusetts*, in COLONIAL AMERICA: ESSAYS IN POLITICS AND SOCIAL DEVELOPMENT, at 540 (Stanley N. Katz and John M. Murrin, eds., 3rd ed.; New York, 1983); M. M. Klein, *The Rise of the New York Bar: The Legal Career of William Livingston*, 15 WMQ 334 (1958).

56. See Mark Warren Bailey, *Early Legal Education in the United States: Natural Law Theory and Law as a Moral Science*, 48 J. LEGAL EDUC. 311–12 (Sept. 1998).

57. See *Massachusetts Legal Education in Transition, 1766–1840*, 17 AJLH 27, 38 (1973).

58. See Alfred Zantzinger Reed, TRAINING FOR THE PUBLIC PROFESSION OF LAW, at 276–78 (New York, 1921).

59. See Bailey, supra note 56, at 313.

60. See Harold J. Berman, *The Origins of Historical Jurisprudence: Coke, Selden, Hale*, 103 YALE L. J. 1651 (1994); Harold J. Berman and Charles J. Reid, Jr., *The Transformation of English Legal Science: From Hale to Blackstone*, 45 EMORY L. J. 437 (1996); Charles F. Mullett, *Coke and the American Revolution*, 12 ECONOMICA 457 (1932).

61. See Edward Coke, FIRST PART OF THE INSTITUTES OF THE LAWS OF ENGLAND: OR, COMMENTARIES UPON LITTLETON (1628). Thomas Jefferson, recalling the 1760s when he was reading for the bar, said "Coke Lyttleton was the universal elementary book of law students." A. Smith, VIRGINIA LAWYERS, 1680–1776: THE BIRTH OF AN AMERICAN PROFESSION, at 75 (1967) (unpublished

Ph.D. dissertation, Johns Hopkins University). See also Jenni Parrish, *Law Books and Legal Publishing in America, 1760–1840*, 72 LAW LIBRARY J. 355 (1979).

62. William Blackstone, 1 COMMENTARIES ON THE LAWS OF ENGLAND, at *35–36 (all citations to Blackstone in this volume are from the authoritative Clarendon Press edition of 1765, as reprinted; page references are to this "star edition"). See also Alan Watson, *The Structure of Blackstone's* Commentaries, 97 YALE L. J. 795 (1988) (tracing the influence of Justinian's *Institutes* on Blackstone's project).

63. See 1 DIARY AND AUTOBIOGRAPHY OF JOHN ADAMS, at 173–74 (L. H. Butterfield, ed.; Cambridge, Mass.: Harvard University Press, 1961).

64. See Paul M. Hamlin, LEGAL EDUCATION IN COLONIAL NEW YORK, at 197–200 (New York, 1939). Carew's English translation of Barbeyrac's principal relevant essay, titled *An Historical and Critical Account of the Science of Morality*, was printed as a preface to several editions of the Kennet translation of Pufendorf, OF THE LAW OF NATURE AND NATIONS. See Barbeyrac, *Preface to the Fourth Edition of Pufendorf*, OF THE LAW OF NATURE AND NATIONS, at 1–88 (Kennet, transl., London: J. Walthoe, ed., 4th ed., 1729) (introduced by a translation of the second iteration of Barbeyrac's essay). See also Herbert A. Johnson, IMPORTED EIGHTEENTH-CENTURY LAW TREATISES IN AMERICAN LIBRARIES 1700–1799, at 18–19 (Knoxville: University of Tennessee Press, 1978).

65. See David J. Bederman, *Reception of the Classical Tradition in International Law: Grotius' De Jure Belli Ac Pacis*, 10 EMORY INT'L L. REV. 1 (1996). See also Zuckert, supra note 3 (pr.), at 126–49.

66. See *Triquet v. Bath*, 3 Burr., at 1478, 1481, 97; Eng. Rep., at 936, 938 (K. B. 1764) (L. J. Mansfield), ("the law of nations was to be collected from the practice of different nations and . . . the authority of Grotius, Barbeyrac, Bynkershoek, Wiquefort," and others). See also R. H. Helmholz, *Use of the Civil Law in Post-Revolutionary American Jurisprudence*, 66 TUL. L. REV. 1649 (1992); Peter Stein, *The Attraction of the Civil Law in Post-Revolutionary America*, 52 VA. L. REV. 403 (1966).

67. See Bailey, supra note 56, at 323.

68. See Bailey, supra note 56, at 324. See also John H. Langbein, *Chancellor Kent and the History of Legal Literature*, 93 COLUM. L. REV. 547, 569–70 (1993).

69. See Anton-Herman Chroust, THE RISE OF THE LEGAL PROFESSION IN AMERICA (Norman Okla.: University of Oklahoma Press, 1965); Gerald W. Gawalt, THE PROMISE OF POWER: THE LEGAL PROFESSION IN MASSACHUSETTS, 1760–1840 (Wesport, Conn.: Greenwood Press, 1979); Reed, supra note 58.

70. See also Paul D. Carrington, *Teaching Law and Virtue at Transylvania University: The George Wythe Tradition in the Antebellum Years*, 41 MERCER L. REV. 673 (1990).

71. See Langbein, supra note 68.

72. Charles Warren, A HISTORY OF THE AMERICAN BAR, at 347 (Boston: Little Brown, 1911) (quoting Hampton L. Carson, AN HISTORICAL SKETCH OF THE LAW DEPARTMENT OF THE UNIVERSITY OF PENNSYLVANIA (Philadelphia, 1882)). See also Stephan A. Conrad, *The Rhetorical Constitution of "Civil Society" at the Founding: One Lawyer's Anxious Vision*, 72 IND. L. J. 335 (1997).

73. Advertisement of King's College, in Charters, Acts of the Legislature, Official Documents and Records, at 32 (John B. Pine, comp.; New York, 1920).

74. See Bailey, supra note 56, at 318–19 (noting that James Kent's lectures at Columbia were often undersubscribed), at 322–23 (observing that college lectures on moral philosophy, typically taken in a student's senior year, were among the most popular of the offerings).

75. Robert Ferguson, Law and Letters in American Culture, at 5 (Cambridge, Mass.: Harvard University Press, 1984).

76. "Twenty-five of the fifty-six signers of the Declaration of Independence, thirty-one of the fifty-five members of the Constitutional Convention, and thirteen of the first sixteen presidents were lawyers." Ferguson, supra note 75, at 11.

77. Gilbert Chinard, *Polybius and the American Constitution*, 1 JHI 38 (1940), reprinted in The American Enlightenment, at 217, 219 (Frank Shuffleton, ed.; New York: University of Rochester Press, 1993).

78. Hofstadtler and Smith, supra note 33, at 220.

79. See Richard, supra note, 6, at 23.

80. See letter to Peter Carr, Aug. 19, 1785, 8 Papers of Thomas Jefferson, at 407 (Julian P. Boyd, ed.; Princeton: Princeton University Press, 1950–present); letter to Thomas Mann Randolph, Aug. 27, 1786, 10 id., at 305. See also Gilbert Chinard, *Thomas Jefferson as Classical Scholar*, 18 Johns Hopkins Alumni Magazine 291 (1929–1930); Louis B. Wright, *Thomas Jefferson and the Classics*, 87 Proc. Am. Philosophical Soc'y 223 (1943–1944).

81. See Reinhold, Classica Americana, supra note 6, at 30. John Adams would later reminisce that "Some thirty years ago I took upon me the severe task of going through all [Plato's] works. With the help of two Latin translations, and one English and one French translation, and comparing of the most remarkable passages with the Greek, I labored through the tedious toil." See The Adams–Jefferson Letters (Lester J. Cappon, ed.; Chapel Hill: University of North Carolina Press, 1959) (July 16, 1814).

82. See Gummere, supra note 6, at 174.

83. See Cary H. Conley, The First English Translators of the Classics (New Haven: Yale University Press, 1927); Francis O. Matthiessen, Translation, an Elizabethan Art (Cambridge, Mass.: Harvard University Press, 1931); Tom B. Jones, *The Classics in Colonial Hispanic America*, 70 Transactions Am. Philological Ass'n 37 (1939).

84. Samuel Miller, 2 Brief Retrospect on the Eighteenth Century, at 273, 434–36 (New York, 1803).

85. See M. N. S. Sellers, American Republicanism: Roman Ideology and the United States Constitution, at 21 (Houndmills: MacMillan, 1994).

86. See Federalist 301 (No. 47) (Madison). Also influential was Montesquieu's *Considerations in the causes of greatness of the Romans and their decline* (authoritative ed., 1748) (David Lowenthal, transl.; New York: Free Press, 1965).

87. See George Kennedy, *Classical Influences on* The Federalist, in Classical Traditions in Early America, supra note 48, at 119, 127; The Classick Pages: Classical Reading of Eighteenth-Century Americans, at 153–221 (Meyer Reinhold ed.; University Park, Penn.: Pennsylvania State University,

1975); Sellers, supra note 85, at 257, n. 9. Ferguson's work is specifically cited by John Adams in his discussion of ancient Rome in *Defence of the Constitutions*, 4 THE WORKS OF JOHN ADAMS, at 521, n. 1 (Boston: Little Brown, 1856).

88. See Kennedy, supra note 87, at 128. Fragments of *De Re Publica* had been available from the Middle Ages, but the complete text was only discovered in the early 1800s. John Adams apparently had access to part of the work because he did cite it in his *Defence of the Constitutions*. See 4 WORKS OF JOHN ADAMS, supra note 87, at 296, n. 1.

89. See Kennedy, supra note 87, at 128.

90. See Reinhold, CLASSICK PAGES, supra note 87.

91. For example, James Otis, one of the leading advocates of the American revolution published, in 1760, a volume titled, THE RUDIMENTS OF LATIN PROSODY, WITH A DISSERTATION ON LETTERS, AND THE PRINCIPLES OF HARMONY, IN POETIC AND PROSAIC COMPOSITION, COLLECTED FROM THE BEST WRITERS. Otis used a number of ancient references in his significant tract, *The Rights of British Colonies Asserted and Proved* (1764). See also Gummere, supra note 274, at 101.

92. 9 THE WRITINGS OF THOMAS JEFFERSON 463 (New York: G. Putnam & Sons, 1892).

93. 10 WORKS OF JOHN ADAMS, supra note 87, at 102. See also Reinhold, CLASSICK PAGES, supra note 87, at 126 (recounting the famous correspondence between Adams and Jefferson in 1814 on Plato's legacy). See also Eric Nelson, THE GREEK TRADITION IN REPUBLICAN THOUGHT, at 200–01 (Cambridge, UK: Cambridge University Press, 2004).

94. See John Corrigan, THE HIDDEN BALANCE: RELIGION AND THE SOCIAL THEORIES OF CHARLES CHAUNCY AND JONATHAN MAYHEW (New York: Cambridge University Press, 1987).

95. See Charles F. Mullett, *Classical Influences on the American Revolution*, 35 CJ 92, 99, n. 17 (1939–1940).

96. See Aristotle, POLITICS 207 (H. Rachkam, transl., 1932; Loeb Classical Library reprint, 1990) (passage 1279a).

97. See Reinhold, CLASSICK PAGES, supra note 87, at 118; Gummere, supra note 6, at 175–76; Pangle, SPIRIT, supra note 3 (pr.), at 68–72.

98. See 4 ADAMS WORKS, supra note 87, at 106, 435–63, 469–78.

99. Reinhold, CLASSICK PAGES, supra note 87, at 82.

100. Thomas Woody, THE EDUCATIONAL VIEWS OF BENJAMIN FRANKLIN, at 67–68 (New York: McGraw-Hill, 1931). See also Pangle, SPIRIT, supra note 3 (pr.), at 289, n. 17 (discussing Xenophon's influence on Franklin).

101. See Parker, supra note 4, at 17–21.

102. But see Thomas L. Pangle, *The Classical Challenge to the American Constitution*, 66 CHI.–KENT L. REV. 145, 147 (1990) (suggesting that Xenophon was "probably the most widely read and cited classical political theorist at the time of the Founding."); Pangle, SPIRIT, supra note 3 (pr.), at 25, 29.

103. 4 ADAMS WORKS, supra note 87, at 258.

104. 2 ADAMS FAMILY CORRESPONDENCE, at 307 (L. H. Butterfield, ed.; Cambridge, Mass.: Harvard University Press, 1963–1973) (letter of Aug. 11, 1777) (spelling and orthography modernized).

105. See, for example, Chinard, supra note 77.
106. See Gummere, supra note 6, at 177–78.
107. 4 ADAMS WORKS, supra note 87, at 435.
108. See 1 THE HISTORY OF THE VIRGINIA FEDERAL CONVENTION OF 1788, at 174 (Richmond: Virginia Historical Society, 1890).
109. D. A. Russell, PLUTARCH, at preface (London: Duckworth, 1962).
110. Mullett, supra note 95, at 100.
111. Of course, the defenders of British imperial policies in North America were just as apt to rely on classical sources in support of their positions. Thomas Hutchinson, the conservative governor of Massachusetts prior to the revolutionary events, was an accomplished classicist, and often quoted Plutarch. See Gummere, supra note 274, at 110–13.
112. Plutarch, 6 LIVES 261 (B. Perrin, transl., 1914; Loeb Classical Library reprint, 1968) (*Timoleon*, pr. 1).
113. Cotton Mather, 1 MAGNALIA CHRISTI AMERICANA, at 27 (1702) (Hartford, 1830). See also Gustaaf van Cromphout, *Cotton Mather as Plutarchan Biographer*, 46 AM. LIT. 465 (1974).
114. THE AUTOBIOGRAPHY OF BENJAMIN FRANKLIN, at 58 (Leonard W. Labaree, ed.; New Haven: Yale University Press, 1964).
115. See Reinhold, CLASSICA AMERICANA, supra note 6, at 255.
116. See id., at 255–57.
117. See 4 ADAMS FAMILY CORRESPONDENCE, supra note 104, at 117.
118. Reinhold, CLASSICK PAGES, supra note 87, at 99. See also Blair Worden, *Marchmont Needham and English Republicanism*, in REPUBLICANISM, LIBERTY, supra note 3 (pr.), at 45, 52.
119. See Mullett, supra note 282, at 102 (noting that Josiah Quincy regarded Tacitus as "elegant and instructive" and "masterly"). John Adams highly esteemed Sallust, however. See Richard, supra note 6, at 25. See Moses Hadas, *Introduction*, COMPLETE WORKS OF TACITUS ix, xix (Alfred John Church and William Jackson Brodribb, transl., Moses Hadas, ed.; 1942) (describing Tacitus as an "aristocrat with a nostalgic admiration of the Republic and contempt for a populace and nobility alike corrupted by slavery.").
120. 18 WRITINGS OF THOMAS JEFFERSON 255 (Washington, DC: GPO, 1905). See also Mullett, supra note 95, at 102–03. The other known example of a Framer insisting on the classical education for a girl was Aaron Burr's daughter, Theodosia. See also Linda K. Kerber, WOMEN OF THE REPUBLIC: INTELLECT AND IDEOLOGY IN REVOLUTIONARY AMERICA, at 215, 218 (Chapel Hill: University of North Carolina Press, 1980). See also James Wilson's remark, before the Pennsylvania ratifying convention, that Tacitus was "a profound politician." 2 Elliot at 423.
121. See Reinhold, CLASSICK PAGES, supra note 87, at 73. See also Jean M. Yarbrough, AMERICAN VIRTUES: THOMAS JEFFERSON ON THE CHARACTER OF A FREE PEOPLE, at 19–20, 153–65 (Lawrence: University Press of Kansas, 1998) (on the influence of Seneca on Jefferson).
122. 4 ADAMS WORKS, supra note 87, at 295. See also Worden, in REPUBLICANISM, LIBERTY, supra note 3 (pr.), at 52–53.

123. 1 THE WORKS OF JAMES WILSON, at 377 (Robert Green McCloskey, Cambridge, Mass.: Harvard University Press, 1967) (The Nature and Philosophy of Evidence).

124. 2 ADAMS–JEFFERSON LETTERS, supra note 81, at 433 (letter of July 5, 1814).

125. 12 JEFFERSON WRITINGS, supra note 92, at 343.

126. See Gummere, supra note 6, at 176–77.

127. See Gummere, supra note 6, at 122–25.

128. See Sellers, supra note 85, at 21.

129. Mullett, supra note 95, at 97.

130. Kennedy, supra note 87, at 119.

131. See Douglass Adair, *The Authorship of the Disputed* Federalist Papers, 1 WMQ (3rd ser.), at 97–98 (1944). See also Karl-Friedrich Walling, REPUBLICAN EMPIRE: ALEXANDER HAMILTON ON WAR AND FREE GOVERNMENT, at 6–7 (Lawrence: University Press of Kansas, 1999); Wilbur Samuel Howell, EIGHTEENTH-CENTURY BRITISH LOGIC AND RHETORIC, at 441–691 (Princeton: Princeton University Press, 1971).

132. See Kennedy, supra note 87, at 134.

133. Id., at 137–38. One might note that Madison also used the rhetorical device of inserting a speech into an essay. See FEDERALIST No. 54.

134. See Adair, supra note 131, at 250; Walling, supra note 131, at 106.

135. See Kennedy, supra note 87, at 121–22.

136. For standard biographies, see Imogene E. Brown, AMERICAN ARISTIDES: A BIOGRAPHY OF GEORGE WYTHE (Rutherford, NJ: Farleigh-Dickinson University Press, 1981); Robert Bevier Kirtland, GEORGE WYTHE: LAWYER, REVOLUTIONARY, JUDGE (New York: Garland, 1986). See also David N. Mayer, THE CONSTITUTIONAL THOUGHT OF THOMAS JEFFERSON, at 4–6 (Charlottesville: University Press of Virginia, 1994).

137. See Richard, supra note 6, at 36.

138. See Richard J. Hoffman, *Classics in the Courts of the United States,* 1790–1800, 22 AJLH 55, 59 (1978) (calculating that Wythe cited twenty-four ancient authors). Compare with Parker, supra note 4, at 18–19 (who tabulates the classical references made by French revolutionary figures in legislative debates and significant newspapers and pamphlets).

139. See *Commonwealth v. Caton,* 9 Va. (4 Call) 5 (1782).

140. See William N. Eskridge, *All About Words: Early Understandings of the "Judicial Power" in Statutory Interpretation, 1776–1806,* 101 COLUM. L. REV. 990, 1106 (2001); Matthew P. Harrington, *Judicial Review Before John Marshall,* 72 GEO. WASH. L. REV. 51 (2003); Helen K. Michael, *The Role of Natural Law in Early American Constitutionalism: Did the Founders Contemplate Judicial Enforcement of "Unwritten" Individual Rights?* 69 N. C. L. REV. 421, 452 (1991); Suzanna Sherry, *The Founders' Unwritten Constitution,* 54 U. CHI. L. REV. 1127, 1143 (1987); William Michael Treanor, *Judicial Review Before* Marbury, 58 STAN. L. REV. 455 (2005); Gordon S. Wood, *The Origins of Judicial Review Revisited, or How the Marshall Court Made More Out of Less,* 56 WASH. AND LEE L. REV. 787 (1999).

141. It is, for example, the motto of the Supreme Court of Georgia. See http://www2. state.ga.us/Courts/Supreme/ (visited Aug. 5, 2002).

142. See Hoffman, supra note 138, at 61–63.

143. See, for example, *Dandridge v. Lyon*, Wythe, at 123, 125 (Va. Ch. 1791), 1791 WL 262 ("The Roman civil law, the authority of which, if not decisive, is respectable") (citing J. Inst. 1.2.20.7); *Woodson v. Woodson*, Wythe, at 129, 131 (Va. Ch. 1791), 1791 WL 489 (citing Code Just. 4.24.1–3). For more on the use of Roman law sources, see materials cited at note 66 with text.

144. See *Aylett v. Minnis*, Wythe, at 219, 231 (Va. Ch. 1793), 1793 WL 2, rev'd, 1 Va. (1 Wash.) 300 (1794) (calling for a body of civil law equal to the "code, pandects, institutes, and novels."). See also Hoffman, supra note 138, at 71–73.

145. See 1 Wilson Works, supra note 123, at 69 ("Of the Study of Law in the United States"), id., 270 ("Of Man, as a Member of the Great Commonwealth of Nations"), 2 id., at 773 (July 4, 1788 oration to celebrate the adoption of the Constitution). See also Page Smith, James Wilson: Founding Father, 1742–1798, at 8, 315 (Chapel Hill: University of North Carolina Press, 1956).

146. See 2 U.S. (2 Dall.) 419, 462 (1793).

147. See Hoffman, supra note 138, at 64, 84.

148. The story is recounted in Livy, 1 History of Rome, at 189 (B. O. Foster transl., 1929; Loeb Classical Library reprint 1988) (passage i.54).

149. See Gummere, supra note 6, at 8–9.

150. See Gilbert Chinard, Thomas Jefferson, The Apostle of Americanism, at 175 (Boston: Little Brown, 1929).

151. 11 Thomas Jefferson Papers, supra note 80, at 286.

152. Gummere, supra note 6, at 174.

153. See Gummere, supra note 6, at 174.

154. Gummere, supra note 6, at 16.

155. See 1 The Papers of Alexander Hamilton, at 390–407 (Harold C. Syrett, ed.; New York: Columbia University Press, 1961–1979). See also 12 id., at 500–01 ("Catullus" No. 3) (Likening Caesar as a Whig and Cato as a Tory).

156. See 11 id., at 545.

157. See Richard, supra note 6, at 24.

158. See Milton Embick Flower, John Dickinson: Conservative Revolutionary (Charlottesville: University Press of Virginia, 1983); Charles J. Stille, *The Life and Times of John Dickinson*, 1732–1808, reprinted in 13 Memoirs of the Historical Society of Pennsylvania, at 14–19 (1891) (Burt Franklin rep.; New York, 1969). See also Robert G. Natelson, *The Constitutional Contributions of John Dickinson*, 108 Penn. St. L. Rev. 415 (2003) ["Natelson, Dickinson"]; James H. Hutson, *John Dickinson at the Federal Constitutional Convention*, 40 WMQ 256 (1983).

159. See Mullett, supra note 95, at 93, n. 1 (discussing Dickinson's use of Joannes Stobaeus's works in his *Essay on the Constitutional Power of Great Britain over the Colonies in America* (1774)); Gummere, supra note 6, at 107–110 (Dickinson's use of classical references in *Pennsylvania Farmer*); Natelson, Dickinson, supra note, at 440, 445–47.

160. See Richard, supra note 6, at 35–36.

161. See Merrill D. Peterson, JAMES MADISON: A BIOGRAPHY IN HIS OWN WORDS, at 16, 18 (New York: Harper and Row, 1974). See also Kennedy, supra note 87, at 136.

162. See 1 THE PAPERS OF JAMES MADISON 5 (Robert A. Rutland, ed.; Chicago: University of Chicago Press and Charlottesville: University Press of Virginia 1962); Richard, supra note 6, at 25.

163. See 1 PAPERS OF JAMES MADISON, supra note, at 1–6, 17–18, 21–22, 35–41.

164. See Jack N. Rakove, ORIGINAL MEANINGS: POLITICS AND IDEAS IN THE MAKING OF THE CONSTITUTION, at 42 (New York: Knopf, 1997); Lance Banning, THE SACRED FIRE OF LIBERTY: JAMES MADISON AND THE FOUNDING OF THE AMERICAN REPUBLIC (Ithaca: Cornell University Press, 1995); Gary Rosen, AMERICAN COMPACT: JAMES MADISON AND THE PROBLEM OF FOUNDING (Lawrence: University Press of Kansas, 1999).

165. See *Notes on Ancient and Modern Confederacies,* 9 JAMES MADISON PAPERS, supra note 162, at 3.

166. See Richard, supra note 274, at 31.

167. See Gummere, supra note 6, at 56. See also Donald L. Smith, JOHN JAY: FOUNDER OF A STATE AND NATION (New York: Teachers College Press, Columbia University, 1968); Richard Brandon Morris, JOHN JAY, THE NATION, AND THE COURT (Boston: Boston University Press, 1967).

168. Adams's later recalled that, as a child, he announced to his father that he no longer wanted to study Latin. His father promptly sent him out to dig ditches for 2 days. John dutifully returned to his books, and he ruefully noted, "If I have gained any distinctions, it has been owing to the two days' labor in that abominable ditch." Chinard, HONEST JOHN ADAMS, supra note 35, at 11.

169. See 2 WORKS OF JOHN ADAMS, supra note 87, at 86 (diary entry of May 31, 1760); 3 ADAMS DIARY, supra note 63, at 262. See also Richard, supra note 6, at 21.

170. See 2 WORKS OF JOHN ADAMS, supra note 87, at 149.

171. Adams's DEFENCE appears in 4 id.

172. See Chinard, supra note 77, at 221. See also Thompson, supra note 35, at 251–58 (discussing contemporary reactions to the *Defence of the Constitutions*).

173. Defence, 4 WORKS OF JOHN ADAMS, supra note 87, at 435 (original emphasis).

174. See Henry Adams, *Harvard College, 1796–1797,* in HISTORICAL ESSAYS, at 84 (London, 1891). See also Richard, supra note 6, at 25, 32–34, 37.

175. See Linda K. Kerber, FEDERALISTS IN DISSENT: IMAGERY AND IDEOLOGY IN JEFFERSONIAN AMERICA, at 121–22 (Ithaca: Cornell University Press, 1970).

176. 1 LETTERS OF BENJAMIN RUSH, at 518 (L. H. Butterfield ed.; Princeton: Philosophical Society, 1951) (letter of June 19, 1789). See also THE SPUR OF FAME: DIALOGUES OF JOHN ADAMS AND BENJAMIN RUSH, 1805–1813 (Douglas[s] Adair and John A. Schulz, eds.; San Marino, Calif.: Huntington Library, 1966).

177. See Thomas Jefferson, COMMONPLACE BOOK: A REPERTORY OF HIS IDEAS ON GOVERNMENT (Gilbert Chinard, ed.; Baltimore: Johns Hopkins University Press, 1926). See also Richard, supra note 6, at 26.

178. See 2 WORKS OF JOHN ADAMS, supra note 87, at 430.

179. Mullett, supra note 95, at 94.

180. See Karl Lehmann, THOMAS JEFFERSON: AMERICAN HUMANIST 34, 75 (Chicago: University of Chicago Press, 1964).

181. See Richard, supra note 6, at 27–28.

182. 2 ADAMS–JEFFERSON CORRESPONDENCE, supra note 81, at 350 (letter of July 9, 1813).

183. 14 WRITINGS OF THOMAS JEFFERSON, supra note 92, at 200 (letter to Thomas Cooper, Oct. 17, 1814).

184. 15 id., at 207 (letter to John Brazier, Aug. 24, 1819).

185. See Richard, supra note 6, at 29–30.

186. Thomas Jefferson, NOTES ON THE STATE OF VIRGINIA, Query XIV, in WRITINGS OF THOMAS JEFFERSON, at 273 (Merrill Peterson, ed.; New York: Library of America, 1984).

187. Wilson Smith, *Thomas Jefferson's Design for his State University, 1818*, in THEORIES OF EDUCATION IN EARLY AMERICA, 1655–1819, at 329 (Wilson Smith, ed.; New York: Bobbs-Merrill, 1973).

188. Gummere, supra note 6, at 191. See also Yarbrough, supra note 121, at 153–65 (Jefferson as Epicurean).

189. Id., at 197.

190. 2 ADAMS–JEFFERSON CORRESPONDENCE, supra note 81.

191. THE SNARE BROKEN 43 (2nd ed., Boston, 1766). See also Gummere, supra note 6, at 175.

192. See Maynard Smith, *Reason, Passion and Political Freedom in* The Federalist, 22 JOURNAL OF POLITICS 528 (1960). See also Martin Diamond, *Democracy and* The Federalist, 53 AM. POL. SCI. REV. 67 (1959); David L. Wardle, *Reason to Ratify: The Influence of John Locke's Religious Beliefs on the Creation and Adoption of the United States Constitution*, 26 SEATTLE U. L. REV. 291 (2002).

193. See FEDERALIST, at 314 (No. 49) (Madison).

194. Kennedy, supra note 87, at 133.

195. Reinhold, CLASSICA AMERICANA, supra note 6, at 24.

196. See, for example, Bailyn, Education, supra note 30, at 33–36; Daniel J. Boorstin, THE LOST WORLD OF THOMAS JEFFERSON, at 213–25 (New York: Holt, 1948); Louis B. Wright, *The Purposeful Reading of Our Colonial Ancestors*, 4 JOURNAL OF ENGLISH LITERARY HISTORY 85 (1937).

197. Reinhold, CLASSICA AMERICANA, supra note 6, at 32.

198. See id. (quoting Horace, *Ars Poetica*, line 343).

199. Pa. Const. of 1776, § 44; N. C. Const. of 1776, art. 41.

200. See Reinhold, CLASSICA AMERICANA, supra note 6, at 33–34.

201. See Richard Peters, A SERMON ON EDUCATION, WHEREIN SOME ACCOUNT IS GIVEN OF THE ACADEMY ESTABLISHED IN THE CITY OF PHILADELPHIA, at 25 (Philadelphia, 1751) (spelling and orthography modernized). See also Hubertis M. Cummings, RICHARD PETERS, PROVINCIAL SECRETARY AND CLERIC, 1704–1776 (Philadelphia: University of Pennsylvania Press, 1944).

202. 15 JEFFERSON WRITINGS, supra note 92, at 209.

203. See Reinhold, CLASSICA AMERICANA, supra note 6, at 131–36.

204. 2 RUSH LETTERS, supra note 176, at 1066.

205. Id., at 1073.

206. 10 WORKS OF JOHN ADAMS, supra note 87, at 105 (letter of June 16, 1814).

207. See Reinhold, CLASSICA AMERICANA, supra note 6, at 36, 123–28.
208. 1 RUSH LETTERS, supra note 176, at 491.
209. Benjamin Rush, *An enquiry into the Utility of a knowledge of the Latin and Greek languages as a branch of liberal Studies, with hints of a plan of liberal instruction, without them, accommodated to the present state of society, manners and government in the United States*, 5 AMERICAN MUSEUM 525 (1789).
210. 1 Rush Letters, supra note 176, at 604 (original emphasis).
211. U.S. Const. Art. I, § 8, cl. 8. See also Malla Pollack, *What is Congress Supposed to Promote?: Defining "Progress" in Article I, Section 8, Clause 8 of the United States Constitution, or Introducing the Progress Clause*, 80 NEB. L. REV. 754 (2001); Edward Walterscheid, *To Promote the Progress of Science and Useful Arts: The Background and Origin of the Intellectual Property Clause of the United States Constitution*, 2 J. INTELL. PROP. L. 1, 26–27 (1994).
212. 1 RUSH LETTERS, supra note 176, at 619.
213. Reinhold, CLASSICA AMERICANA, supra note 6, at 35–36.
214. Forrest McDonald, NOVUS ORDO SECLORUM: THE INTELLECTUAL ORIGINS OF THE CONSTITUTION (Lawrence: University Press of Kansas, 1985) (citing 1 Farrand, at 87, 103, 125, 135, 137 151–53, 204, 254, 285, 290, 305, 317, 319, 399–402).
215. See Kennedy, supra note 87, at 133.
216. See 1 Farrand, at 50, 65–66, 153, 233.
217. William Smith, A GENERAL IDEA FOR THE COLLEGE OF MIRANIA, at 27, 30, 76 (New York, 1753).
218. Reinhold, CLASSICA AMERICANA, supra note 6, at 38.
219. Id. See also Kenneth B. Murdock, *Clio in the Wilderness: History and Biography in Puritan New England*, 24 CHURCH HISTORY 221 (1955).
220. Henry Steele Commager, *Leadership in Eighteenth-Century and Today*, 90 DAEDALUS 659 (1961).
221. 1 LETTERS OF MEMBERS OF THE CONTINENTAL CONGRESS, at 526 (Edmund C. Burnett, ed.; Washington, DC: Carnegie Institute 1921–1936); 2 id., at 67, 228. See also Rosen, supra note 164, at 110; Charles Howard McIlwain, CONSTITUTIONALISM: ANCIENT AND MODERN, at 14, 23 (Ithaca: Cornell University Press, 1940).
222. 1 Farrand, at 423.
223. Id., at 424.
224. *Page v. Pendleton*, Wythe 215 (Va. Ch. 1793).
225. See id., all references to ancient dates shall be to "Before Common Era" (BCE). "Anno Domini" (AD) dates will be rendered "Common Era" (CE).
226. See Tacitus, ANNALES 243 (John Jackson transl., 1931; Loeb Classical Library reprint, 1979) (passage i.1).
227. Andrew Lintott, THE CONSTITUTION OF THE ROMAN REPUBLIC, at 27–39 (Oxford: Clarendon Press, 1999).
228. See id., at 31–34. The founding of the city of Rome (*ab urbe condita*) is traditionally given as 753 BCE. Kings ruled in Rome for nearly 200 years. See also Pangle, Spirit, supra note 3 (pr.), at 56.
229. See 1 Livy, supra note 148, at 289–94, 303–07 (passages ii.23, ii.27).
230. See William A. Galston, *The Use and Abuse of Classics in American Constitutionalism*, 66 CHI.-KENT L. REV. 47, 53–54 (1990); Charles R. Kesler, FEDERALIST

10 *and American Republicanism*, in Saving the Revolution: The Federalist Papers and the American Founding, at 13, 19, 33 (Charles R. Kesler,
ed.; New York: Free Press, 1987) (discussing Plutarch, *Publicola* x.1–6); Pangle,
Spirit, supra note 3 (pr.), at 43; Rosen, supra note 164, at 111–12.

231. See Robert E. Shalhope, The Roots of Democracy: American Thought
and Culture, 1760–1800, at 27–47 (Boston: Twayne, 1990).

232. See Gummere, supra note 6, at 116. See also Linda K. Kerber, *The Republican Ideology of the Revolutionary Generation*, 37 Am. Q. 474 (1985); Michael
Allen Gillespie, *Massachusetts*, in Ratifying the Constitution, at 138, 140
(Michael Allen Gillespie and Michael Lienesch, eds.; Lawrence: University Press
of Kansas, 1989).

233. Reinhold, Classica Americana, supra note 6, at 253. See also Paul Cartledge,
The Spartans: The World of the Warrior-Heroes of Ancient Greece
(Woodstock, NY: Overlook Press, 2003); Richard, supra note 6, at 73.

234. Federalist, at 57 (No. 6) (Hamilton). See also Richard, supra note 274, at
73–74.

235. See Letters from a Farmer in Pennsylvania to the Inhabitants of
the British Colonies, letter III (Philadelphia, 1768). See also Rahe, supra
note 3 (pr.), at 136–62.

236. See Mullett, supra note 95, at 102–03; Richard, supra note 6, at 80–81.

237. Federalist, at 38 (No. 2) (Jay).

238. Id., at 39.

239. Federalist, at 128 (No. 18) (Madison (with Hamilton)).

240. Federalist, at 107 (No. 15) (Hamilton).

241. See Philip Abbott, *What's New in the* Federalist Papers, 49 Pol. Res. Q. 525, 531
(1996). See also Gerald Stourzh, Alexander Hamilton and the Idea of
Republican Government, at 178–79 (Palo Alto: Stanford University Press,
1970); Diamond, supra note 192, at 67–68; Thompson, supra note 35, at 41–
42. See also Aristotle, Athenian Constitution, infra note 175 (ch. 2), at
21 (passage iv) (Draco's decrees), 23 (passage v) (Solon's constitution), 61
(passage xx) (Cleisthenes' laws); Plutarch, *Solon*, passage xviii.

242. Federalist, at 231 (No. 37) (Madison).

243. Diamond, supra note 192, at 132 (quoting Federalist, at 314 (No. 49) (Madison)).

244. Federalist, at 230–31 (No. 37) (Madison).

245. See Rakove, supra note 164, at 3.

246. See id., at 3–7.

247. Irving Brant, James Madison, Father of the Constitution, 1787–1800
(1950). See also Larry D. Kramer, *Madison's Audience*, 112 Harv. L. Rev. 611
(1999) (for the influence of Madison's political theory); James H. Hutson,
The Creation of the Constitution: The Integrity of the Documentary Record, 65
Tex. L. Rev. 1 (1986) (for more on the secrecy rules at the Convention and
after); Vason Kesavan and Michael Stokes Paulsen, *The Interpretive Force of the
Constitution's Secret Drafting History*, 91 Geo. L. J. 1113 (2003).

248. Harry C. Payne, The Philosophes and the People, at 61–62 (New Haven:
Yale University Press, 1976).

249. Noah Webster, Citizen of America, reprinted in Ford, Pamphlets, infra note
46 (ch. 2), at 29 (Oct. 10, 1787).

250. Federalist, at 231–33 (No. 38) (Madison).
251. Id., at 232. See also Kennedy, supra note 87, at 131–32; Rakove, supra note 164, at 56; Rosen, supra note 164, at 110–12.
252. Wood, supra note 3 (pr.), at 606–15.
253. Douglass Adair, *Fame and the Founding Fathers*, in Fame and the Founding Fathers, at 3, 8, 11 (Trevor Colbourn, ed.; New York: Norton, 1974). See also The Spur of Fame: Dialogues of John Adams and Benjamin Rush, 1805–1813 (John A. Schutz and Douglass Adair, eds.; Indianapolis: Liberty Fund, 2001); Peter McNamara, The Noblest Minds: Fame, Honor and the American Founding (Lanham: Rowan & Littlefield, 1999).
254. 2 Farrand, at 53.
255. 1 Works of James Wilson, supra note 123, at 405.
256. Federalist, at 437 (No. 72) (Hamilton).
257. Id., at 440. See also Stourzh, supra note 241, at 104.
258. 6 Works of John Adams, supra note 87, at 234 (*Discourses on Davila: a Series of Papers on Political History*).
259. See, for example, Leo Braudy, The Frenzy of Renown: Fame and Its History, at 51 (New York: Oxford University Press, 1986); Michael Lienesch, New Order of the Ages: Time, the Constitution, and the Making of Modern Political Thought (Princeton: Princeton University Press, 1988); Bruce Miroff, *John Adams: Merit, Fame and Political Leadership*, 48 J. Pol. 116 (1986); William Michael Treanor, *Fame, the Founding and the Power to Declare War*, 82 Corn. L. Rev. 695, 729–39 (1997).
260. See Chinard, supra note 77, at 219; Lintott, supra note 227, at 252. See also Machiavelli, *Discourses on Livy*, passage i. 9–10.
261. See Adair, Fame, supra note 253, at 13.
262. See Aristotle, Nicomachaean Ethics 217 (H. Rackham transl. 1926; Loeb Classical Library reprint, 1982) (passages iv.3.1123b–1125a).
263. Cicero, De Officiis 65–67 (Walter Miller transl., 1913; Loeb Classical Library reprint, 1990) (passage ii.26)
264. See Adair, Fame, supra note 253, at 13–14 (quoting Jefferson letter of Jan. 16, 1811).
265. See Spur of Fame, supra note 176, at 180–82 (letter of June 21, 1811).
266. See 2 Livy, supra note 148, at 81–101 (passages iii.24–29).
267. See Garry Wills, Cincinnatus: George Washington and the Enlightenment (Garden City: Doubleday, 1984).
268. See Richard, supra note 6, at 69–72. See also 2 Works of James Wilson, supra note 123, at 716.
269. See Writings of Thomas Jefferson, supra note 92, at 913 (letter to John Adams, Dec. 13, 1787), 916 (letter to James Madison, Dec. 20, 1787).
270. See U.S. Const. Amend. XXII, § 1.
271. See McLachlan, supra note 48, at 86. See also Gordon S. Wood, *Classical Republicanism and the American Revolution*, 66 Chi.–Kent L. Rev. 13, 22–29 (1990).
272. See Bailey, supra note 56, at 327–28.
273. *New England Quarterly Magazine*, Sept. 1802, at 125 (quoted at Kerber, supra note 175, at 118).
274. See Gummere, supra note 6, at 13. ("Classical history supplied sobriquets favorable or unfavorable to an extent that grows almost wearisome.")

275. See Kate M. Rowland, 1 THE LIFE OF GEORGE MASON, 1725–1792, at 169 (New York: G. P. Putnam & Sons, 1892).

276. 10 WORKS OF JOHN ADAMS, supra note 87, at 272.

277. See Richard, supra note 6, at 68–69.

278. See id., at 70.

279. Fisher Ames, *A Eulogy on General George Washington*, in EULOGIES AND ORATIONS ON THE LIFE AND DEATH OF GENERAL GEORGE WASHINGTON 153 (Boston: Manning & Loring, 1800) (delivered Feb. 19, 1800).

280. Xenophon, MEMORABILIA 95–103 (E. Marchant transl. 1923; Loeb Classical Library reprint, 1979) (passages ii.1.21–34).

281. Reinhold, CLASSICA AMERICANA, supra note 6, at 150.

282. 1 DIARY AND AUTOBIOGRAPHY OF JOHN ADAMS, supra note 63, at 72. See also 2 id., 75 (entry of Dec. 31, 1772); Defence, 6 WORKS OF JOHN ADAMS, supra note 87, at 206.

283. See James McLachlan, The Choice of Hercules: *American Student Societies in the Early 19th Century*, in 2 THE UNIVERSITY IN SOCIETY 449, 488–92 (Lawrence Stone, ed.; Princeton: Princeton University Press, 1974).

284. See 2 ADAMS FAMILY CORRESPONDENCE, supra note 104, at 96–97 (letter by Abigail Adams, Aug. 14, 1776).

285. *Curious Dissertation on the Valuable Advantages of a Liberal Education*, NEW-JERSEY MAGAZINE AND MONTHLY ADVERTISER, January 1787, at 52–53 (quoted in Reinhold, CLASSICA AMERICANA, supra note 6, at 143).

286. Quoted in Paul M. Spurlin, MONTESQUIEU IN AMERICA, 1760–1801, at 261 (Baton Rouge: Louisiana State University Press, 1940).

287. WASHINGTON'S FAREWELL ADDRESS: THE VIEW FROM THE TWENTIETH CENTURY, at 25 (Burton I. Kaufman, ed.; Chicago: University of Chicago Press, 1969); Matthew Spalding, A SACRED UNION OF CITIZENS: GEORGE WASHINGTON'S FAREWELL ADDRESS AND THE AMERICAN CHARACTER (Lanham: Rowman & Littlefield, 1996).

288. Clinton Rossiter, SEEDTIME OF THE REPUBLIC: THE ORIGIN OF THE AMERICAN TRADITION OF POLITICAL LIBERTY, at 137–39, 144–46, 429–37 (New York: Harcourt Brace, 1953).

289. See Hoffman, supra note 138, at 67–68. See, generally, PAMPHLETS OF THE AMERICAN REVOLUTION, 1750–1776 (Bernard Bailyn, ed.; Cambridge, Mass.: Harvard University Press, 1965); TRACTS OF THE AMERICAN REVOLUTION, 1763–1776 (Merrill Jensen, ed.; Indianapolis: Bobbs-Merrill, 1967).

290. See Parker, supra note 4, at 3–7, 146, 177.

291. See Stanley M. Elkins, THE AGE OF FEDERALISM (New York: Oxford University Press, 1993).

292. FEDERALIST, at 423 (No. 70) (Hamilton). See also Walling, supra note 131, at 125.

293. Kerber, supra note 175, at 120.

294. 3 THE LIFE AND WORKS OF THOMAS PAINE, at 33 (William M. Van der Weyde, ed.; New Rochelle: Thomas Paine National Historical Association, 1925) (*The American Crisis*, No. 5).

295. 1 THE COMPLETE WRITINGS OF THOMAS PAINE, at 387 (Philip S. Foner, ed.; New York: Citadel Press, 1945) (*The Rights of Man*) (1792).

296. See Rahe, *Antiquity Surpassed,* in REPUBLICANISM, LIBERTY, supra note 3 (pr.), at 233, 237–41.
297. 1 Farrand, at 401 (June 25).
298. 1 Farrand, at 449 (June 28).
299. 1 Farrand, at 451 (June 28).
300. 2 Elliot, at 69.
301. 4 Elliot, at 192.
302. 4 Eliiot, at 174.
303. See Mullett, supra note 95, at 235–36.
304. 2 Elliot, at 68–69.
305. 3 Elliot, at 209.
306. 2 Elliot, at 422; reprinted in 2 WORKS OF JAMES WILSON, supra note 123, at 762.
307. Letter from Deane to John Jay, Nov. 1780, cited in Edmund S. Morgan, *The Puritan Ethic and the American Revolution,* 24 WMQ (3rd ser.) 3, 27 (1967). See also Drew R. McCoy, THE ELUSIVE REPUBLIC: POLITICAL ECONOMY IN JEFFERSONIAN AMERICA, at 10, 77 (Chapel Hill: University of North Carolina Press, 1980).
308. Letters of Cassius, No. 1, *The Massachusetts Gazette,* Sept. 18, 1787, reprinted in ESSAYS ON THE CONSTITUTION OF THE UNITED STATES PUBLISHED DURING ITS DISCUSSION BY THE PEOPLE 1787–1788, at 5, 6 (Paul Leicester Ford, ed.; Brooklyn: Historical Printing Club, 1892). See also Pangle, SPIRIT, supra note 3 (pr.), at 35.
309. William Vans Murray, *Political Sketches,* 2 AMERICAN MUSEUM 228 (Sept. 1787). See also Alexander de Conde, *William Van Murray's* Political Sketches: *A Defence of the American Experiment,* 41 MISS. VALLEY HIST. REV. 623 (1954–1955).
310. 2 WORKS OF JAMES WILSON, supra note 123, at 762. See also id., at 774.
311. See 4 PAPERS OF ALEXANDER HAMILTON, supra note 155, at 140. See also Walling, supra note 131, at 85.
312. FEDERALIST, at 72 (No. 9) (Hamilton). See also Rakove, supra note 164, at 153; Rahe, supra note 3 (pr.), at 581–83.
313. FEDERALIST, at 385 (No. 63) (Madison). See also Sirico, supra note 4 (pr.), at 473–76.
314. Richard, supra note 6, at 233.
315. Richard, supra note 6, at 233–34. See also Herbert J. Storing, WHAT THE ANTIFEDERALISTS WERE FOR, at 53–63 (Chicago: University of Chicago Press, 1981) [1 CAF 53–63].
316. See Middlekauff, supra note 15, at 90–91.
317. McDonald, supra note 214, at xi.
318. E. Christian Kopff, *Open Shutters on the Past: Rome and the Founders,* in VITAL REMNANTS: AMERICA'S FOUNDING AND THE WESTERN TRADITION, at 71, 74 (Wilmington: ISI Books, 1999).
319. Middlekauff, supra note 15, at 193.
320. Richard, supra note 6, at 118.
321. 1 THE PAPERS OF JOHN ADAMS, at 200 (Robert J. Taylor, ed.; Cambridge, Mass.: Harvard University Press, 1977-) (Feb. 19, 1767).

322. Richard M. Gummere, *John Dickinson: Classical Penman on the Revolution*, 52 CJ 83 (Nov. 1956).
323. See Richard, supra note 6, at 120.
324. See Aristotle, Nicomachaean Ethics, supra note 262, at 315 (passage v.10.14). ("all law is universal but about some things it is not possible to make a universal statement which shall be correct.")
325. Cicero, De Legibus 381 (Clinton Walker Keyes transl., 1928; Loeb Classical Library reprint, 1988) (passage ii.4.10); see also Cicero, De Re Publica, at 211 (Clinton Walker Keyes transl., 1928; Loeb Classical Library reprint, 1988) (passage iii.22.33) ("there will not be different laws at Rome and at Athens, or different laws now and in the future, but one eternal and unchangeable law will be valid for all nations and all times."). See also 1 Works of James Wilson, supra note 123, at 145 (who, in his lecture on Natural Law, quotes Cicero).
326. See Reinhold, Classica Americana, supra note 6, at 97; Bailey, supra note 56, at 323–28. For a complete discussion of Grotius's and Pufendorf's influence on English Enlightenment political thought, see Zuckert, supra note 3 (pr.), at 97–149, 188–95, 248–52.
327. Bailey, supra note 56, at 327. See also C. P. Courtney, *Montesquieu and Natural Law*, in Montesquieu's Science of Politics: Essays on The Spirit of the Laws, at 41 (David W. Carrithers, Michael A. Mosher, and Paul A. Rahe, eds.; Lanham: Rowman & Littlefield, 2001).
328. Declaration of Independence, para. 2 (1776) ("that all Men are created equal, that they are endowed by their Creator with certain unalienable Rights, that among these are Life, Liberty, and the Pursuit of Happiness. . . . ").
329. 3 Works of John Adams, supra note 87, at 462 (*Dissertation on the Canon Law and Feudal Law*).
330. See Declaration of Independence, para. 1 (1776) ("WHEN in the Course of human events, it becomes necessary for one people to dissolve the political bands which have connected them with another, and to assume among the powers of the earth, the separate and equal station to which the Laws of Nature and of Nature's God entitle them. . . . "). See also Edward S. Corwin, The "Higher Law" Background of American Constitutional Law (Ithaca: Cornell University Press, 1955); Charles F. Mullett, Fundamental Law and the American Revolution, 1760–1776 (New York: Columbia University Press, 1933); Benjamin Fletcher Wright, American Interpretations of Natural Law (Cambridge, Mass.: Harvard University Press, 1931); Pangle, Spirit, supra note 3 (pr.); Zuckert, supra note 3 (pr.).
331. Thomas Jefferson, Writings, at 422, 423 (Merrill D. Patterson, ed.; Library of Am. Ed., 1984) (Opinion on the French Treaties) (Apr. 28, 1793).
332. See Robert Lowry Clinton, *The Supreme Court Before John Marshall*, 27 J. Sup. Ct. Hist. 222, 228–30 (2002).
333. Chinard, supra note 77, at 221. For Montesquieu's general influence, see Montesquieu's Science, supra note 327.
334. Id.
335. For the debate on whether John Locke or the Scottish school of Common Sense Philosophy most influenced the Declaration of Independence, compare Garry Wills, Inventing America: Jefferson's Declaration of Independence (Garden City: Doubleday, 1978); with Ronald Hamowy, *Jefferson*

and the Scottish Enlightenment: A Critique of Garry Wills's Inventing America: Jefferson's Declaration of Independence, 36 WMQ 503 (1979). See also Harold J. Berman, *The Impact of the Enlightenment on American Constitutional Law,* 4 YALE J. L. AND HUM. 311 (1992); Pauline Maier, AMERICAN SCRIPTURE: MAKING THE DECLARATION OF INDEPENDENCE (New York: Alfred A. Knopf, 1997).

336. See Parker, supra note 4.

337. See Bernard Bailyn, THE IDEOLOGICAL ORIGINS OF THE AMERICAN REVOLUTION at 150–57 (Cambridge, Mass.: Belknap Press of Harvard University Press, enlarged ed., 1992). See also [Justice] Stephen Breyer, ACTIVE LIBERTY: INTERPRETING OUR DEMOCRATIC CONSTITUTION, at 3–5 (New York: Knopf, 2006) (discussing philosophy of Benjamin Constant's *Liberty of the Ancients Compared with that of the Moderns* (1819)).

338. See Mullett, supra note 282, at 104; Zuckert, supra note 3 (pr.), at 175–83, 187–319; Rahe, Antiquity Surpassed, in REPUBLICANISM, LIBERTY, supra note 3 (pr.), at 233, 235 (discussing the writings of John Trenchard, Walter Moyle, and Jean Louis de Lolme).

339. See Bailyn, supra note 337, at 31. See also J. G. A. Pocock, THE ANCIENT CONSTITUTION AND THE FEUDAL LAW (Cambridge, UK: Cambridge University Press, 1957).

340. Herbert Butterfield, THE WHIG INTERPRETATION OF HISTORY, at 11 (New York: Norton Library ed., 1965).

341. See Perry Miller, *From the Covenant to the Revival,* in 1 RELIGION IN AMERICAN LIFE: THE SHAPING OF AMERICAN RELIGION, at 322 (James W. Smith and A. Leland Jamison, eds.; Princeton: Princeton University Press, 1961); Pangle, SPIRIT, supra note 3 (pr.), at 78–85.

342. Kopff, supra note 318, at 90.

343. Jefferson to Peter Carr, Aug. 10, 1787, in THE LIFE AND SELECTED WRITINGS OF THOMAS JEFFERSON (A. Koch and W. Peden, eds.; New York: Random House, 1944).

344. See Marci A. Hamilton, *James Madison and the Distrust of Power,* in CELEBRATING MADISON: A COLLECTION OF SCHOLARLY ESSAYS (Charlottesville: University of Virginia Press, 2002); id., *Free? Exercise,* 42 WM. AND MARY L. REV. 823 (2001); John Witte, Jr., RELIGION AND THE AMERICAN CONSTITUTIONAL EXPERIMENT: ESSENTIAL RIGHTS AND LIBERTIES (Boulder: Westview Press, 1999).

345. 4 WORKS OF JOHN ADAMS, supra note 87, at 15. A thorough and searching review of the Whig tradition in constitutional thought – including such writers as Marchamont Nedham, James Harrington, Henry Neville, John Trenchard, Thomas Gordon, and David Hume – is beyond the scope of this volume.

346. Jefferson Works, supra note 331, at 1501 (letter to Henry Lee, May 8, 1825). See also Yarbrough, supra note 121, at 24–25.

CHAPTER 2. CLASSICAL POLITICAL MODELS AND THE FOUNDERS

1. Hannah Arendt, ON REVOLUTION, at 197 (New York: Viking Press, 1963). See also id., at 13–14, 20, 119, 139–215 (for more on Arendt's views on the classical sources of American revolutionary political theory).

2. 3 WORKS OF JOHN ADAMS, supra note 87 (ch. 1), at 454 (*On the Canon Law and Feudal Law*).

3. 7 id., at 593.

4. William Livingston, THE INDEPENDENT REFLECTOR, at 279 (1753) (Milton M. Klein, ed.; Cambridge, Mass.: Harvard University Press, 1963).

5. Douglass G. Adair, *Experience Must be Our Only Guide: History, Democratic Theory, and the United States Constitution*, in REINTERPRETATION OF THE AMERICAN REVOLUTION, 1763–1789, at 405 (Jack P. Greene, ed.; New York: Harper & Row, 1968) (emphasis in original).

6. Reinhold, CLASSICA AMERICANA, supra note 6 (ch. 1), at 100. See also Rahe, *Antiquity Surpassed*, in REPUBLICANISM, LIBERTY, supra note 3 (pr.), at 233; Vincent M. Bonventre, *A Classical Constitution: Ancient Roots of our National Charter*, 59 N.Y. STATE BAR. J. 10 (Dec. 1987).

7. 1 Farrand, at 110 (June 4) (Madison's notes).

8. Reinhold, CLASSICA AMERICANA, supra note 6 (ch. 1), at 97.

9. See, generally, John R. Galvin, THREE MEN OF BOSTON (New York: Crowell, 1976); Frank W. Grinnell, JAMES OTIS AND HIS INFLUENCE AS A CONSTRUCTIVE THINKER (Boston: Bostonian Society, 1936).

10. See James Otis, THE RIGHTS OF THE BRITISH COLONIES ASSERTED AND PROVED (Boston, 1764), reprinted in Bailyn, 1 PAMPHLETS OF THE AMERICAN REVOLUTION, supra note 289 (ch. 1), at 437.

11. See James Otis, A VINDICATION OF THE BRITISH COLONIES (Boston, 1765), reprinted in 1 id., 570.

12. John Dickinson, LETTERS FROM A FARMER IN PENNSYLVANIA TO THE INHABITANTS OF THE BRITISH COLONIES, letter III (Philadelphia, 1768).

13. See Thomas Hutchinson, THE HISTORY OF THE COLONY OF MASSACHUSETTS BAY (Boston, 1764) (rep., New York: Arno Press, 1972). See also William Pencak, AMERICA'S BURKE: THE MIND OF THOMAS HUTCHINSON (Washington: University Press of America, 1982); Andrew S. Walmsley, THOMAS HUTCHINSON AND THE ORIGINS OF THE AMERICAN REVOLUTION (New York: New York University Press, 1999).

14. 2 THE WRITINGS OF SAMUEL ADAMS, at 262 (Harry Alonzo Cushing, ed.; Boston, 1908; rep. New York: Octagon Books, 1968) (Oct. 28, 1771).

15. Jefferson, COMMONPLACE BOOK, supra note 177 (ch. 1), at 181.

16. 1 HAMILTON PAPERS, supra note 155 (ch.1), at 53 ("A Full Vindication of the Measures of Congress").

17. 1 id., 104 ("*The Farmer Refuted* ") (a response to a 1775 Tory tract by Rev. Samuel Seabury, LETTERS OF A WESTCHESTER FARMER (Clarence H. Vance ed.; White Plains, NY: Westchester County Historical Society, 1930)). See also Gummere, supra note 6 (ch. 1), at 113. See also Walling, supra note 131 (ch. 1), at 29–30.

18. Declaration of Independence, para. 2 (1776).

19. 1 THE PAPERS OF GEORGE MASON, at 435 (Robert A. Rutland, ed.; Chapel Hill: University of North Carolina Press, 1970) (letter of Oct. 2, 1778) (punctuation modernized).

20. 2 PAPERS OF JOHN ADAMS, supra note 321 (ch. 1), at 311 (March 6, 1775).

21. Id., at 312.

22. Pliny, NATURAL HISTORY (passage iii.3) (using, as an example, the province of Baetica, and listing the towns and their respective status). See also Lintott, supra note 227 (ch. 1), at 50; C. Nicolet, THE WORLD OF THE CITIZEN IN REPUBLICAN ROME, at 21–44 (P. S. Falla, transl.; Berkeley: University of California Press, 1980).

23. Dionysius of Halicarnassus, ROMAN ANTIQUITIES, at 45 (Ernest Cary and Edward Spelman, transl.; 1937; Loeb Classical Library reprint, 1990) (passage iii.11.1).

24. See Thucydides, 1 HISTORY OF THE PELOPONNESIAN WAR, at 7, 25 (C. F. Smith, transl., 1919; Loeb Classical Library reprint, 1991) (passages i.2.6, i.12.4).

25. See 2 id., 165 (passage iii.92) (Spartan establishment of a colony at Heraclea in Trachis).

26. See 1 id., 5 (passage i.2.2) (tenuousness of trade and communications in archaic Greece); 1 id., 15 (passage i.8.3); 3 id., 185 (passage vi.2.6) (Phoenicians established trade colonies in Sicily).

27. See 1 id., 23 (passage i.12.3) (Dorian settlement of Peloponnesus); 2 id., 285 (passage iv.42.2) (Aeolian settlement of Corinth); 3 id., 15 (passage v.9.1) (speech of Brasidas); 4 id., 111 (passage vii.57.2) (structure of alliances in Athenian invasion of Sicily based on tribal allegiances).

28. See Richard, supra note 6, at 76 (discussing Richard Bland's 1766 *An Inquiry into the Rights of the British Colonies*, which discusses this incident in Thucydides).

29. See David J. Bederman, INTERNATIONAL LAW IN ANTIQUITY, at 177 (Cambridge, UK: Cambridge University Press, 2001).

30. See 1 Thucydides, supra note 24 (ch. 2), at 25 (passage i.13.4).

31. See id., at 43–47, 79 (passages i.24–25, i.44). See also David Cartwright, A HISTORICAL COMMENTARY ON THUCYDIDES, at 27 (Ann Arbor: University of Michigan Press, 1997).

32. Id., at 43–45 (passages i.24.3–5).

33. Id., at 45 (passages i.24.6–7).

34. Id., at 45–47 (passages i.25.3–4).

35. Id., at 47–49 (passages i.26.3–4).

36. See id., at 49–51 (passage i.27).

37. See id., at 51–55 (passages i.28–30).

38. Id., at 61 (passage i.34.1).

39. Id., at 69 (passages i.38.1–3).

40. See Cartwright, supra note 31, at 28 (glossing passage i.29), 31 (passage i.38).

41. See 1 Thucydides, supra note 24, at 95 (passage i.56) (Corinthian colony at Potidaea was a tributary of rival Athens); 2 id., 109 (passage iii.61) (Plataeans refused to accede to leadership of Thebes, and allied with Athens, leading to the destruction of the town by Theban and Spartan forces).

42. See Charlotte Elizabeth Goodfellow, ROMAN CITIZENSHIP; A STUDY OF ITS TERRITORIAL AND NUMERICAL EXPANSION FROM THE EARLIEST TIME TO THE DEATH OF AUGUSTUS (Lancaster, Pa.: Lancaster Press, 1935); Nicolet, supra note 22, at 30–44; Edward Togo Salmon, ROMAN COLONIZATION UNDER THE REPUBLIC (London: Thames & Hudson, 1969); A. N. Sherwin-White, THE ROMAN CITIZENSHIP (2nd ed.; Oxford: Clarendon Press, 1973).

43. See 12 Livy, supra note 148 (ch. 1), at 207–11, 319 (passages xli.8.6–12; xlii.10.3). See also Deryck J. Piper, *Latins and the Roman Citizenship in Roman Colonies: Livy 34, 42, 5–6; Revisited*, 36 HISTORIA 38 (1987); R. E. Smith, *Latins and the Roman Citizenship in Roman Colonies: Livy, 34, 42, 5–6*, 44 JRS 18, 20 (1954).

44. See Patrick Le Roux, *La question des colonies latines sous l'Empire*, 17 KTEMA 183 (1992).

45. 3 Elliot, at 282.

46. John Dickinson, *Letters of Fabius* (No. VIII) (Wilmington, 1788) (original emphasis), reprinted in PAMPHLETS ON THE CONSTITUTION OF THE UNITED STATES, at 208 (Paul Leicester Ford, ed.; Brooklyn, 1888; rep. New York: Capo Press, 1968).

47. See 2 Herodotus, HISTORIES 105–10 (A. D. Godley, transl., 1920; Loeb Classical Library reprint, 1969) (passages iii.80–82).

48. See Aristotle, POLITICS, supra note 96 (ch. 1), at 477–83 (passage v.10).

49. There are other classical sources for the theory of mixed constitutions. See Aristotle, POLITICS, supra note 96 (ch. 1), at 129–65, 308–39, 345–53, 497–503 (passages 1269a–73b, 1278b–80a, 1293a–96b, 1298a–b, 1318b–19a). Additionally, Aristotle's pupil, Diecaerchus of Messana, wrote a book on the subject (now lost), titled *Tripolitkōn*, mentioned in other sources, including Cicero, LETTERS TO ATTICUS, at 175 (E. O. Winstedt, transl. 1918; Loeb Classical Library reprint, 1987) (passage xiii.32.2).

50. See Edwin Graeber, DIE LEHRE VON DER MISCHVERFASSUNG BEI POLYBIOS (Bonn: H. Bouvier, 1968); Paul Pédech, LA MÉTHODE HISTORIQUE DE POLYBE (Paris: Société d'édition "Les Belles Lettres," 1964); C. O. Brink and F. Walbank, *The Construction of the Sixth Book of Polybius*, 4 CQ 97 (1954); Thomas Cole, *The Sources and Composition of Polybius VI*, 13 HISTORIA 478 (1964); Wilfried Nippel, PUBLIC ORDER IN ANCIENT ROME 142–53 (Cambridge, UK: Cambridge University Press, 1995).

51. 3 Polybius, HISTORIES 269 (W. R. Paton, transl., 1923; Loeb Classical Library reprint, 1975) (passages vi.2.2–3). See also 1 id., at 3–5 (passage i.1.5) (for virtually the same point, made in the opening pages of the *History*). See also J. M. Alonso-Núñez, *The Mixed Constitution in Polybius*, 97 ERANOS 11 (1999); Mary F. Williams, *Polybius on Wealth, Bribery and the Downfall of Constitutions*, 14(4) ANCIENT HIST. BULL. 131 (2000).

52. 3 Polybius, supra note, at 273–77 (passages vi.3; v.4).

53. See Plato, 1 LAWS 225 (R. G. Bury transl., 1926; Loeb Classical Library reprint, 1984) (passage 693e) (a state should balance its monarchic and democratic elements, for "a State which does not partake of these can never be rightly constituted."). See also Frank W. Walbank, in *Polybius and the Roman State*, 5 GRBS 239, 247–48 (1964).

54. 3 Polybius, supra note 303, at 277 (passage vi.5.1).

55. See Kurt von Fritz, THE THEORY OF THE MIXED CONSTITUTION IN ANTIQUITY, at 73–75 (New York: Columbia University Press, 1954; rep. New York: Arno Press, 1975).

56. See G. W. Trompf, THE IDEA OF HISTORICAL RECURRENCE IN WESTERN THOUGHT: FROM ANTIQUITY TO THE REFORMATION, at 4–59 (Berkeley: University of California Press, 1979); Stephan Podes, *Polybius and His Theory of*

Anacylosis: Problems of Not Just Ancient Political Theory, 12 HISTORY OF POLIT-ICAL THOUGHT 577 (1991); F. W. Walbank, *The Idea of Decline in Polybius*, in NIEDERGANG: STUDIEN ZU EINEM GESCHICHTLICHEN THEMA, at 41 (Reinhart Koselleck and Paul Widmer, eds.; Stuttgart: Klett-Cotta, 1980); F. W. Walbank, 1 A HISTORICAL COMMENTARY ON POLYBIUS, at 637–45, 647–49 (Oxford: Oxford University Press, 1967) [hereinafter "Walbank"].

57. 3 Polybius, supra note 51, at 385 (passage vi.51.4).

58. See id., at 283–89 (passages vi.7–9).

59. Id., at 289 (passage vi.9.10). This same point is made by Cicero, DE RE PUB-LICA, supra note 325 (ch. 1), at 69 (passage i.28) ("For the primary forms already mentioned degenerate easily into the corresponding perverted forms, the kind being replaced by a despot, the aristocracy by an oligarchical faction, and the people by a mob and anarchy; but whereas these forms are frequently changed into new ones, this does not usually happen in the case of the mixed and evenly balanced constitution except through great faults in the governing class.").

60. 3 Polybius, supra note 51, at 289–91 (passage vi.10). See Walbank, supra note 56, at 659–63.

61. See Alonso, supra note 51, at 12. See also Walbank, supra note 56, at 645.

62. See Eugène N. Tigerstedt, 2 THE LEGEND OF SPARTA IN CLASSICAL ANTIQUITY, at 113–30 (Stockholm: Almqvist & Wiksell, 1965). Cf. Lintott, supra note 227 (ch. 1), at 16–17 (arguing that although Spartan constitution was "imposed," Roman constitution was "organic"). To the same effect, see Cicero, DE RE PUBLICA, supra note 325 (ch. 1), at 111 (passage ii.1.2) ("Cato used to say that our constitution was superior to those of other States on account of the fact that almost every one of the other commonwealths had been established by one man.... [O]ur own commonwealth was based upon the genius, not of one man, but of many; it was founded, not in one generation, but in a long period of several centuries, and many ages of men."). See also Walbank, supra note 56, at 662–63.

63. See 3 Polybius, supra note 51, at 383 (passage vi.49). See also Walbank, supra note 56, at 731.

64. See 3 Polybius, supra note 51, at 385 (passage vi.51).

65. Compare id., at 379 (passages vi.48.2–8) (Sparta) with pp. 373–77 (passages vi.46–47) (Crete) and pp. 393–95 (passages vi.56.1–5) (Carthage).

66. See von Fritz, supra note 55, at 98–100. See also Walbank, supra note 56, at 726–28.

67. See von Fritz, supra note 55, at 102–05. See also Cartledge, supra note 233 (ch. 1); Paul Cartledge, *Spartan Institutions in Thucydides*, in THE LANDMARK THUCYDIDES, at 589, 590 (Robert B. Strassler, ed.; New York: Free Press, 1996) (for a summary of Spartan political bodies at the time of the Peloponnesian War); Paul Cartledge, *Spartan Justice, or the State of the Ephors*, 3 DIKE 5 (2000); Walbank, supra note 56, at 731–32, 734–35. See also Rahe, supra note 3 (pr.), at 166–83; Antony Andrewes, *The Government of Classical Sparta*, in ANCIENT SOCIETY AND INSTITUTIONS: STUDIES PRESENTED TO VICTOR EHRENBERG ON HIS 75TH BIRTHDAY, at 1 (Oxford: Blackwell, 1966). See also Cicero, DE RE PUBLICA, supra note 325 (ch. 1), at 159 (passage ii.28).

68. See Cicero, DE RE PUBLICA, supra note 325 (ch. 1), at 169 (passage ii.33.58); Aristotle, Politics, supra note 96 (ch. 1), at 141–43, 321–23 (passages 1270b17–25; 1294b13–41).

69. See Xenophon, CONSTITUTION OF THE LACEDAEMONIANS, at 161–63, in SCRIPTA MINORA (E. C. Marchant transl., 1925; Loeb Classical Library reprint, 1968) (passage viiii).

70. See 3 Herodotus, supra note 47, at 263–65 (passage vi.57.5); 1 Thucydides, supra note 24, at 37 (passage i.20.3); 3 Polybius, supra note 51, at 373 (passage vi.45.5); Carol G. Thomas, *On the Role of the Spartan Kings*, 23 HISTORIA 257 (1974).

71. See 3 Herodotus, supra note 47, at 231 (passage vi.82); 1 Thucydides, supra note 24, at 221 (passage i.131); 10 Plutarch, supra note 112 (ch. 1), at 27–29, 43–49 (*Agis*, xi. 4–5; xix–xxi) (recounting King Agis's execution); id., at 71–73 (*Cleomenes*, x. 3–6). See also Rahe, supra note 3 (pr.), at 174–75; Ephraim David, *The Trial of Spartan Kings*, 32 RIDA (3rd ser.) 131 (1985); H. W. Parke, *The Deposing of Spartan Kings*, 39 CQ 106 (1945).

72. See 3 Herodotus, supra note 47, at 199 (passage vi.52.8); Aristotle, POLITICS, supra note 96, at 145–49 (passages 1271a25–26); 4 Plutarch, supra note 112 (ch. 1), at 293–95, 301–03 (*Lysander*, xxii, xxiv).

73. Xenophon, Constitution of the Lacadaemonians, supra note 69, at 163 (passage viii.4). See also Andrewes, supra note 67, at 13–14.

74. See Paul A. Rahe, *The Selection of Ephors at Sparta*, 29 HISTORIA 385 (1980); P. J. Rhodes, *The Selection of Ephors at Sparta*, 30 HISTORIA 498 (1981); H. D. Westlake, *Reelection to the Ephorate?*, 17 GRBS 343 (1976).

75. See 3 Polybius, supra note 51, at 373 (passage vi.45.5); 1 Plutarch, supra note 112 (ch. 1), at 283–87 (*Lycurgus*, xxvi); 5 id., at 9–11 (*Agesilaus*, iv); 10 id., at 25 (*Agis*, xi. 1) (noting that the power of the gerousia lay in "previously determining which laws should be proposed to the people.").

76. See von Fritz, supra note 55, at 108–14. See also Ephraim David, SPARTA BETWEEN EMPIRE AND REVOLUTION (404–243 B.C.): INTERNAL PROBLEMS AND THEIR IMPACT ON CONTEMPORARY GREEK CONSCIOUSNESS (New York: Arno Press, 1981); Pavel Oliva, SPARTA AND HER SOCIAL PROBLEMS (Iris Urwin-Lewitová transl.; Prague: Academia, 1971).

77. Isocrates 91 (George Norlin transl., 1928; Loeb Classical Library reprint, 1980) (*Nicoles*, passage iii.24).

78. Aristotle, POLITICS, supra note 96 (ch. 1), at 157 (passage ii.8; 1272b).

79. 3 Polybius, supra note 51, at 385 (passage vi.51.2).

80. See 4 id., at 145 (passage x.18.1); 6 id., 361 (passage xxxvi.4.6). See also Justinus, EPITOME (passage xix.2.6). See also A. Heuss, in Joseph Vogt, ROM UND KARTHAGO: EIN GEMEINSCHAFTSWERK, at 111 (Leipzig: Koehler & Amelang, 1943).

81. See 9 Livy, supra note 148 (ch. 1), at 399–401 (passage xxxiii.46).

82. See von Fritz, supra note 55, at 119–22. This view was shared by John Adams in his Defence of the Constitutions, in 4 WORKS OF JOHN ADAMS, supra note 87 (ch. 1), at 470–72.

83. 3 Polybius, supra note 51, at 295–97 (passages vi.11.11–13). See also Fergus Millar, THE ROMAN REPUBLIC IN POLITICAL THOUGHT, at 23–36 (Hanover, N.H.: University Press of New England, 2002) ["Millar, Political Thought"].

84. 3 Polybius, supra note 51, at 297–303 (passages vi.12–14). See also A. H. J. Greenidge, Roman Public Life, at 245–48 (New York: MacMillan, 1901, rep. 2003).
85. 3 Polybius, supra note 51, at 293 (passage vi.11.3).
86. See id., at 293–95 (passages vi.11.4–10). See also Walbank, supra note 56, at 673–75.
87. 3 Polybius, supra note 51, at 303 (passage vi.15.1).
88. Id., at 311 (passages vi.18.7–8).
89. Id., at 309 (passage vi.18.1).
90. See id., at 293 (passage vi.11.2). For more on the Second Punic War, see The Second Punic War: a reappraisal (Tim Cornell, Boris Rankov, and Philip Sabin, eds.; London: Institute of Classical Studies, School of Advanced Study, University of London, 1996); Nigel Bagnall, The Punic Wars (London: Hutchinson, 1990); Brian Caven, The Punic Wars (New York: St. Martin's Press, 1980); Adrian Keith Goldsworthy, The Punic Wars (London: Cassell, 2000).
91. See F. W. Walbank, *Polybius on the Roman Constitution*, 36 CQ 73, 75 (1943); id., *Polybius and the Roman State*, 5 GRBS 239, 252–55 (1964) (critiquing thesis that Polybius was arguing that Roman imperialism was leading to constitutional decline). See also 1 Dionysius, supra note 23 (passage ii.7.7) (speech of Manius Valerius).
92. 3 Polybius, supra note 51, at 397–99 (passage vi.57). See also Cicero, De Legibus, supra note 325 (ch. 1), at 465–67 (passages iii.i.6–8).
93. See Lintott, supra note 227 (ch. 1), at 18, 94–146. See also T. Corey Brennan, 1 The Praetorship of the Roman Republic, at 3–57 (Oxford: Oxford University Press, 2000).
94. See Lintott, supra note 227 (ch. 1), at 18–20, 65–88.
95. See id., at 25.
96. See also von Fritz, supra note 55, at 220–52.
97. Lintott, supra note 227 (ch. 1), at 199. See also H. H. Scullard, From the Gracchi to Nero: A History of Rome from 133 BC to AD 68 (London: Merithen, 1959); von Fritz, supra note 55, at 158–78 (considering Roman senatorial powers and concluding that Polybius may have deliberately understated them).
98. See Cicero, De Re Publica, supra note 325 (ch. 1), at 173 (passage ii.36.61); at 175 (passage ii.37.63).
99. See E. Stuart Staveley, *The Constitution of the Roman Republic 1940–54*, 5 Historia 74, 75–84 (1956); von Fritz, supra note 55, at 160. See also Cicero, De Re Publica, supra note 325 (ch. 1), at 149–51 (passage ii.22) (for the origins of these assemblies).
100. See Jolowicz and Nicholas, infra note 177, at 24–30, 86–88; Wolfgang Kunkel, An Introduction to Roman Legal and Constitutional History, at 22 (J. M. Kelly transl., 2nd ed.; Oxford: Oxford University Press, 1973); Nicolet, supra note 22, at 207–34, 281–85.
101. See Lintott, supra note 227 (ch. 1), at 40–63.
102. See id., at 198–99, 204–07. See also Cicero's suggestion that the use of secret, written ballots, instead of *viva voce* voting, was a "silent assertor of liberty."

Cicero, De Lege Agraria, at 373–75 (John Henry Freese, transl., 1930; Loeb Classical Library reprint, 1967) (passage ii.2); Cicero, De Legibus, supra note 325 (ch. 1), at 503–05 (passage iii.17).

103. See Lintott, supra note 227 (ch. 1), at 207–13.

104. See id., at 220–32. See also Neal Wood, Cicero's Social and Political Thought, at 159–75 (Berkeley: University of California Press, 1991).

105. See, generally, Fritz Taeger, Die Archaeologie des Polybius (Stuttgart, 1922); von Fritz, supra note 55, at 123–54.

106. See Cicero, De re Publica, supra note 325 (ch. 1), at 101–05 (passages i.44–45) (extolling monarchy over other forms of government); at 177–79 (passage ii.65).

107. See id., at 183 (passage ii.42) (mixed constitution is the "most splendid conceivable").

108. See Cicero, De Legibus, supra note 325 (ch. 1), at 485 (passages iii.10; iii.19). See also Nelson, supra note 93 (ch. 1), at 57–59.

109. See id., at 461–75 (passages iii.2–5).

110. For more on Cicero's political life, see Anthony Everett, Cicero (New York: Random House, 2003); Christian Habicht, Cicero the politician (Baltimore: Johns Hopkins University Press, 1990); D. L. Stockton, Cicero: a political biography (London: Oxford University Press, 1971). See also Henrik Mouritsen, Plebs and Politics in the Late Roman Republic (Cambridge, UK: Cambridge University Press, 2001).

111. See Richard, supra note 6 (ch. 1), at 127–30; Pangle, Spirit, supra note 3 (pr.), at 62–72.

112. Passages from Machiavelli and Montesquieu were extracted by John Adams in his Defence on the Constitutions of the United States, in 4 Works of John Adams, supra note 87 (ch. 1), at 416–20, 423–27. See also Thompson, supra note 35 (ch. 1), at 113–19, 136–40.

113. See Niccolò Machiavelli, Discourses on Livy, at 23–26 (Julia Conway Bondanella and Peter Bondanella, transl.; Oxford: Oxford University Press, 1997). See also Lintott, supra note 227 (ch. 1), at 236–37; Millar, Political Thought, supra note 83, at 64–79; A. Momigliano, Polybius' Reappearance in Western Europe, in Essays in Ancient and Modern Historiography, at 79 (Oxford: Oxford University Press, 1977); Harvey C. Mansfield, Jr., Machiavelli's New Modes and Orders: A Study of the Discourses on Livy, at 34–41 (Ithaca: Cornell University Press, 1979); Peter Onuf and Nicholas Onuf, Federal Union, Modern World: The Law of Nations in the Age of Revolutions, 1776–1814, at 41–45 (Madison: Madison House, 1993).

114. Machiavelli, supra note 113, at 23, 26.

115. See id., at 26–28. See Mansfield, Machiavelli, supra note 113, at 39–40.

116. See Machiavelli, supra note 113, at 28–31 ("One should, therefore, criticize Roman government more sparingly and consider that the many good effects that came out of that republic were produced only by the best causes. If these disturbances were the cause for the creation of the tribunes, they deserve the highest praise, because besides giving to the people its role in democratic administration, the tribunes were established as the guardians of Roman

liberty...."). See also Mansfield, MACHIAVELLI, supra note 113, at 44–45; 4 Plutarch, supra note 112 (ch. 1), at 131–33 (*Coriolanus*, vii).

117. See Lintott, supra note 227 (ch. 1), at 243.
118. See Machiavelli, supra note 113, at 31–32. See also Mansfield, MACHIAVELLI, supra note 113, at 48–50.
119. See Lintott, supra note 227 (ch. 1), at 109–15; Staveley, supra note 99, at 101–07.
120. See Lintott, supra note 227 (ch. 1), at 95–96. See also 1 Livy, supra note 148 (ch. 1), at 275 (passage ii.18.4) (first appointment of a dictator); 3 Plutarch, supra note 112 (ch. 1), at 127–31 (*Fabius*, iv) (Fabius's appointment as dictator); von Fritz, supra note 55, at 209–19.
121. See Lintott, supra note 227 (ch. 1), at 96–98, 107–12.
122. Machiavelli, supra note 113, at 32.
123. See id., at 36–37. See also Lintott, supra note 227 (ch. 1), at 239–40; Mansfield, MACHIAVELLI, supra note 113, at 46–47, 51–52, 199.
124. See Baron de Montesquieu, 1 THE SPIRIT OF THE LAWS (Thomas Nugent, transl., J. V. Prichard, rev.; New York: Appleton, 1900). For more on Montesquieu's life and times, see Isaiah Berlin, MONTESQUIEU (London: Oxford University Press, 1955); Elie Carcassonne, MONTESQUIEU ET LE PROBLÈME DE LA CONSTITUTION FRANÇAISE AU XVIII E SIÈCLE (Paris: Les Presses Universitaires de France, 1927); Mark Hulliung, MONTESQUIEU AND THE OLD REGIME (Berkeley: University of California Press, 1976); Robert Shackleton, MONTESQUIEU; A CRITICAL BIOGRAPHY (London: Oxford University Press, 1961); Thomas L. Pangle, MONTESQUIEU'S PHILOSOPHY OF LIBERALISM: A COMMENTARY ON THE SPIRIT OF THE LAWS, at 121–26 (Chicago: University of Chicago Press, 1973); Montesquieu's Science, supra note 327 (ch. 1), at 69 (Paul A. Rahe, *Forms of Government: Structure, Principle, Object and Aim*), 109 (David W. Carrithers, *Democratic and Aristocratic Republics: Ancient and Modern*).
125. See 1 Montesquieu, supra note 124, at 9.
126. See 1 id., at 23–34.
127. See Anne M. Cohler, MONTESQUIEU'S COMPARATIVE POLITICS AND THE SPIRIT OF AMERICAN CONSTITUTIONALISM, at 75–85 (Lawrence: University of Kansas Press, 1988); Paul O. Carrese, THE CLOAKING OF POWER: MONTESQUIEU, BLACKSTONE, AND THE RISE OF JUDICIAL ACTIVISM, at 131–38 (Chicago: University of Chicago Press, 2003); Donald S. Lutz, THE ORIGINS OF AMERICAN CONSTITUTIONALISM, at 142–47 (Baton Rouge: Louisiana State University Press, 1988) (charting Montesquieu's influence on the Framers by analyzing citation frequency); Nelson, supra note 93 (ch. 1), at 155–76; Rahe, Antiquity Surpassed, in REPUBLICANISM, LIBERTY, supra note 3 (pr.), at 233, 248.
128. See 1 Montesquieu, supra note 124, at 217. See also Carrithers, in Montesquieu's SCIENCE, supra note 327 (ch. 1), at 128–34.
129. FEDERALIST, at 57 (No. 6) (Hamilton).
130. Id., at 257 (No. 41) (Madison). See also id., at 53 (No. 5) (Jay) ("how many conquests did the Romans and others make in the character of allies, and what innovations did they under the same character introduce into the governments of those whom they pretended to protect.").

131. 1 Montesquieu, supra note 124, at 202–03.
132. 1 id., at 214. See also Breyer, supra note 337 (ch. 1); Philip Pettit, Repub-
     licanism: A Theory of Freedom and Government 27–36 (Oxford:
     Clarendon Press, 1997); Chaim Wirszubski, Libertas as a political idea
     at Rome during the late Republic and early principate (Cambridge,
     UK: Cambridge University Press, 1960).
133. 1 Montesquieu, supra note 124, at 181. See also Cohler, supra note 127, at 81–83.
134. Harvey C. Mansfield, Taming the Prince: The Ambivalence of Modern
     Executive Power, at 158–64 (New York: Free Press, 1989) (discussing Milton's
     1649 *Eikonoklastes*, Nedham's 1656 *The Excellencie of a Free State*, Filmer's 1657
     An Examination of the Political Part of Mr. Hobbs his Leviathan, and Dallison's
     1646 *The Royalist's Defense*). See also Blair Worden, *Marchamont Nedham
     and the Beginnings of English Republicanism, 1649–1656*, in Republicanism,
     Liberty, supra note 3 (pr.), at 45; Donald S. Lutz, *The Relative Influence
     of European Writers on Late Eighteenth-Century American Political Thought*,
     78 Am. Pol. Sci. Rev. 189 (1984); Karl Walling, *Was Hamilton a Machiavel-
     lian Statesman?*, 57 Rev. of Politics 419 (1995); Paul Rahe, *Thomas Jeffer-
     son's Machiavellian Political Science*, 57 id., 447 (1995); Paul A. Rahe, *Jefferson's
     Machiavellian Moment*, in Reason and Republicanism: Thomas Jeffer-
     son's Legacy of Liberty, at 53 (Gary L. McDowell and Sharon L. Noble,
     eds.; Lanham: Rowan & Littlefield Publishers, 1997); Thompson, supra note 35
     (ch. 1), at 113–19, 309, n. 23; Felix Raab, The English Face of Machiavelli
     (Toronto: University of Toronto Press, 1964); Mayer, supra note 136 (ch. 1), at
     69–74.
135. See Mansfield, Taming, supra note, at 153–58.
136. See Mansfield, Taming, supra note 134, at 158–78. See M. M. Goldsmith, *Liberty,
     Virtue, and the Rule of Law, 1689–1770*, in Republicanism, Liberty, supra
     note 3 (pr.), 197, 198 (glossing Hobbes's statement in *Leviathan* concerning
     the "glorious histories and the sententious politics of the ancient popular
     governments of the Greeks and Romans, amongst whom kings were hated
     and branded with the name of tyrants, and popular government (though no
     tyrant was ever so cruel as a popular assembly) passed by the name of liberty.");
     Rahe, *Antiquity Surpassed*, in Republicanism, Liberty, supra note 3 (pr.), at
     252 (discussing Hobbes's statement that ancient writers were "the maintainers
     of the Greek, and Roman Anarchies").
137. See id., at 184–211. See also Pangle, Spirit, supra note 3 (pr.), at 131–275; Rahe,
     supra note 3 (pr.), at 291–520.
138. See James Harrington, The Commonwealth of Oceana and A System of
     Politics, at 34, 38 (J. G. A. Pocock ed.; Cambridge, UK: Cambridge University
     Press, 1992). See also Blair Worden, *James Harrington and* The Commonwealth
     of Oceana, 1656; and id., *Harrington's* Oceana: *Origins and Aftermath, 1651–
     1660*, in Republicanism, Liberty, supra note 3 (pr.), at 82, 111.
139. See Harrington, supra note, at 65–66 (citing Thucydides viii.66). See also Rahe,
     Antiquity Surpassed, in Republicanism, Liberty, supra note 3 (pr.), at 256–
     60.
140. See Harrington, supra note 138, at 149–50 (citing Cicero, Pro Flacco, iv.9 and
     vii.16), 163–66.

141. See Bolingbroke, Political Writings vii–xxix (David Armitage ed.; Cambridge, UK: Cambridge University Press, 1997). See also Rahe, Antiquity Surpassed, in Republicanism, Liberty, supra note 3 (pr.), at 264–68.

142. Bolingbroke, supra note, at 125.

143. Id., at 127–28 (quoting 3 Tacitus, Annals, supra note 226 (ch. 1), at 57 (passage iv.33.1) ("All nations and cities are ruled by the people, the leading inhabitants, or a single person. The form of a republic chosen and made up from these elements is easier to praise than to produce, while, if it does arise, it will not last long.")).

144. Id., at 143 ("of the three simple forms of government, the monarchical, the aristocratical, and the democratical, Rome wanted the first. . . . Rome had a nobility and commonalty, but no magistracy fitted by its institution to answer the purposes of that supreme magistrate. . . . ").

145. See id. (quoting 1 Livy, supra note 148 (ch. 1), at 353 (passage ii.41.3)). See also Nelson, supra note 93 (ch.1), at 49–68.

146. Bolingbroke, supra note 141, at 130. See Blair Worden, *Republicanism and Restoration, 1660–1683*, in Republicanism, Liberty, supra note 3 (pr.), at 139, 183–84 (discussing the works of Nedham, Harrington, and Moyle on the issue of social conflicts in the Roman republic).

147. William Blackstone, 1 Commentaries on the Laws of England *50 (spelling modernized).

148. Id. (citing Tacitus, *Histories*, i. 4).

149. See id., at *50–52.

150. Id., *52. See also Francis Dunham Wormuth, The Origins of Modern Constitutionalism (New York: Harper, 1979); M. J. C. Vile, Constitutionalism and Separation of Powers, at 33–43 (Oxford: Clarendon Press, 1967); Carrese, supra note 127, at 124–49; William Kristol, *The Problem of Separation of Powers*: Federalist, at 47–51, in Kesler, supra note 230 (ch. 1), at 100, 104–06 (discussing Montesquieu); Thomas G. West, *The Rule of Law in* The Federalist, in id., at 150, 154–62.

151. David Hume, Politics as Science (1777) and On Some Remarkable Customs (1777), in Essays, Moral, Political and Literary, at 16, 371–73 (Eugene F. Miller, ed.; rev. ed., 1987).

152. See Richard, supra note 6 (ch. 1), at 132–39.

153. See Thornton Anderson, Creating the Constitution: The Convention of 1787 and the First Congress, at 24 (University Park: Pennsylvania State University Press, 1993); Chinard, supra note 77 (ch. 1), at 221; Correa Moylan Walsh, The Political Science of John Adams: a Study in the Theory of Mixed Government and the Bicameral System, at 307 (New York: G. P. Putnam, 1915).

154. 4 Works of John Adams, supra note 87 (ch. 1), at 435.

155. See 11 Papers of Thomas Jefferson, supra note 80 (ch. 1), at 159 (letter of Feb. 16, 1787) (list of favored classical texts); Thomas Jefferson, Notes on The State of Virginia, at 128–29 (1787) (William Peden, ed.; Chapel Hill, University of North Carolina Press, 1955); Richard, supra note 6 (ch. 1), at 131.

156. FEDERALIST, at 389 (No. 63) (Madison). See also Rahe, supra note 3 (pr.), at 573–616; Vile, supra note 150, at 131–92.

157. See 1 Farrand 299–300, 308, 424, 432 (remarks by Alexander Hamilton). For an extended and outstanding discussion of Montesquieu's influence on Hamilton in this regard, see Carrese, supra note 127, at 185–210.

158. See 2 Elliot, at 68 (Dr. Willard) (Massachusetts convention) ("republics had soon degenerated into aristocracies"); 3 id., at 19 (Mr. Nicholas) (Virginia convention) (favorably noting system of balances introduced into the Roman government by the "creation of tribunes of the people").

159. See Chinard, supra note 77 (ch. 1), at 221–25.

160. 4 WORKS OF JOHN ADAMS, supra note 87 (ch. 1), at 443. For Rousseau's influence, see Nelson, supra note 93 (ch. 1), at 183–93.

161. Id., at 440 (emphasis in original).

162. Id.

163. Id., at 298.

164. See 2 ADAMS DIARY AND AUTOBIOGRAPHY, supra note 63 (ch. 1), at 58 (citing 2 Tacitus, ANNALES, supra note 226 (ch. 1), at 57 (passage iv.33.1)). See also Rahe, *Antiquity Surpassed*, in REPUBLICANISM, LIBERTY, supra note 3 (pr.); Thompson, supra note 35 (ch. 1), at 123, 140–47.

165. See 4 WORKS OF JOHN ADAMS, supra note 87 (ch. 1), at 285 ("We shall learn to prize the checks and balances of a free government, . . . if we recollect the miseries of Greece, which arose from its ignorance of them.").

166. 6 id., at 399.

167. 2 Elliot, at 434, 474, 523–24. See also 1 WORKS OF JAMES WILSON, supra note 123 (ch. 1), at 303 (*Of Government*). See also Pangle, SPIRIT, supra note 3 (pr.), at 114–15.

168. See Richard, supra note 6, at 143–46. See also 2 CAF 272–73 (Letters from a Federal Farmer No. VII) (Jan. 3, 1788) (questioning whether the plebian tribunes really represented the peoples' interests).

169. See Richard, supra note 6, at 152–53. See also Thompson, supra note 35 (ch. 1), at 216–19.

170. 15 WRITINGS OF THOMAS JEFFERSON, supra note 92 (ch. 1), at 65–66 (letter to Isaac Tiffany) (Aug. 26, 1816). See also 15 id., 234–35 (letter to John Adams) (Dec. 10, 1819) (Cicero, Cato, and Brutus "had no ideas of government themselves, but of their degenerate Senate, nor the people of liberty, but of the factious opposition of their tribunes.").

171. See Richard, supra note 6, at 154–57.

172. See THE MIND OF THE FOUNDER: SOURCES OF THE POLITICAL THOUGHT OF JAMES MADISON, at 507 (Marvin Meyers, ed.; New York: Bobbs-Merrill, 1973).

173. See John Taylor [of Caroline], AN INQUIRY INTO THE PRINCIPLES OF THE GOVERNMENT OF THE UNITED STATES, at 41–80 (1814) (rep.; New Haven: Yale University Press, 1950). See also Richard, supra note 6 (ch. 1), at 151–53.

174. Aristotle, POLITICS, supra note 96 (ch. 1), at 343–45 (passages 1297b–98a).

175. Aristotle, THE ATHENIAN CONSTITUTION, at 127, 143–47, 171–73 (H. Rackham, transl., 1935; Loeb Classical Library reprint, 1996) (passages xlv, liii, lxiii).

176. See Rahe, supra note 3 (pr.), at 166–78. See also the discussion in Rahe, supra, at notes 69–76 with text.

177. The best works on this subject remain T. Robert and S. Broughton, THE MAGISTRATES OF THE ROMAN REPUBLIC (Chico, Calif.: Scholars Press, 1984–1986); Michael H. Crawford, THE ROMAN REPUBLIC (Cambridge, Mass.: Harvard University Press, 1993); Greenidge, supra note 84; H. F. Jolowicz and Barry Nicholas, HISTORICAL INTRODUCTION TO THE STUDY OF ROMAN LAW (3rd ed.; Cambridge, UK: Cambridge University Press, 1972); Lintott, supra note 227 (ch. 1); Francesco de Martino, STORIA DELLA COSTITUZIONE ROMANA (Naples: E. Jovene, 1958–1967); Fergus Millar, *The political character of the Classical Roman Republic, 200–151 B.C.*, 74 JRS 1 (1984); Theodor Mommsen, RÖMISCHES STAATSRECHT (Leipzig, 1887–1888).

178. See Jolowicz and Nicholas, supra note 177, at 33–34; Lintott, supra note 227 (ch. 1), at 86–88; Kunkel, supra note 100, at 20. See also Tacitus, ANNALS, supra note 226 (ch. 1), at 57 (passage iv.32) (indicating that there was "a free scope of digression" in political discussion in the republic Senate).

179. See Greenidge, supra note 84, at 158–61, 250–55; Jolowicz and Nicholas, supra note 177, at 18–24; Kunkel, supra note 100, at 9–13; Nicolet, supra note 22, at 224–26; Staveley, supra note 99, at 84–90.

180. See Cicero, DE DOMO (passages xli, l); Cicero, PHILIPPICS, at 153 (D. R. Shackelton Bailey transl.; Chapel Hill: University of North Carolina Press, 1986) (passage v.8).

181. See RES GESTAE DIVI AUGUSTI (passages xxxiv.1, xxxiv.3). See also Lintott, supra note 227 (ch. 1), at 3–5 (for more on the role of custom in the formation of the Roman constitution). Or, as Varro wrote in his treatise *On Customs* (as reported by Macrobius), custom is "a pattern of thought which has evolved to become a regular practice." Macrobius (passage iii.8.9).

182. See Lintott, supra note 227 (ch. 1), at 97–99; Greenidge, supra note 84, at 167–71, 189–90.

183. See Lintott, supra note 227 (ch. 1), at 96–99, 147–62; Jolowicz and Nicholas, supra note 177, at 46–47; Kunkel, supra note 100, at 15–16; Staveley, supra note 99, at 107–12. See also Cicero, DE LEGIBUS, supra note 325 (ch. 1), at 467 (passage iii.3.9).

184. See Jolowicz and Nicholas, supra note 177, at 48–49; Staveley, supra note 99, at 90–101. The office of praetor may have preexisted the consuls. See Brennan, supra note 93, at 54–57; Jolowicz and Nicholas, supra note 177, at 8; Kunkel, supra note 100, at 15.

185. See Lintott, supra note 227 (ch. 1), at 100. For more on the role of the censors, see Brennan, supra note 93, at 58–97; Jolowicz and Nicholas, supra note 177, at 51–54; Greenidge, supra note 84, at 216–33; Nicolet, supra note 22, at 73–88. See also 2 Plutarch, supra note 112 (ch. 1), at 125 (*Camillus*, xiv) (office of censor "esteem[ed] [as] sacred"); 347–59 (*Cato the Elder*, xvi–xix) (Cato's term as censor); 5 id., at 169–71 (*Pompey*, xxii) (role of censors in examining and discharging military officers); 10 id., at 373–77 (*Flamininus*, xviii–xix) (Flamininus as censor). For Montesquieu's writing on the institution of the censors, see Carrithers, in Montesquieu's SCIENCE, supra note 327 (ch. 1), at

152, n. 27 (discussing Montesquieu's 1734 *Considerations on the Causes of the Greatness of the Romans and their Decline*).

186. See Cicero, DE RE PUBLICA, supra note 325 (ch. 1), at 167 (passage ii.31.55). See also A. Drummond, *Some Observations on the Order of Consuls' Names*, 56 ATHENAEUM 80 (1978).

187. See Lintott, supra note 227 (ch. 1), at 101–02.

188. See id., at 104–05. See also Greenidge, supra note 84, at 191, 197–98.

189. See Lintott, supra note 227 (ch. 1), at 104–06.

190. See, generally, Bruce W. Frier, THE RISE OF THE ROMAN JURISTS: STUDIES IN CICERO'S PRO CAECINA (Princeton: Princeton University Press, 1985).

191. See Brennan, supra note 93, at 125–35; Jolowicz and Nicholas, supra note 177, at 78–82.

192. See Lintott, supra note 227 (ch. 1), at 104–05. See also Fergus Millar, THE CROWD IN ROME IN THE LATE REPUBLIC (Ann Arbor: University of Michigan Press, 1998); Alexander Yakobson, ELECTIONS AND ELECTIONEERING IN ROME: A STUDY IN THE POLITICAL SYSTEM OF THE LATE REPUBLIC (Stuttgart: Verlag, 1999); Karl-J. Hölkeskamp, *The Roman Republic: Government of the People, by the People, for the People?*, 19 SCRIPTA CLASSICA ISRAELICA 203 (2000) (review essay of Millar). See also Cicero, DE RE PUBLICA, supra note 325 (ch. 1), at 169 (passage ii.33); 2 Plutarch, supra note 112 (ch. 1), at 195–99, 203–07 (*Camillus*, xxxix, xl, and xlii).

193. Cicero, PHILIPPICS, supra note 180, at 177 (passage v.48); Cicero, DE LEGE AGRARIA 373 (John Henry Freese, transl., 1930; Loeb Classical Library reprint, 1967) (passage ii.2); 10 Plutarch, supra note 112 (ch. 1), at 325 (*Flamininus*, ii) (Flamininus exceptionally elected consul, although under age 30 and without prior office). See also the *Lex agraria*, reprinted in 1 ROMAN STATUTES, at 2 (M. H. Crawford, ed.; London: Institute of Classical Studies, University of London, 1996).

194. See Jolowicz and Nicholas, supra note 177, at 79; Lintott, supra note 227 (ch. 1), at 144–46; Tom Holland, RUBICON: THE LAST YEARS OF THE ROMAN REPUBLIC, at 101 (New York: Doubleday, 2003).

195. See Lintott, supra note 227 (ch. 1), at 55–61. See also Kunkel, supra note 100, at 11–12; Nicolet, supra note 22, at 250–81.

196. See Kunkel, supra note 100, at 21, n.1.

197. See the *Lex latina tabulae Bantinae*, line 23, reprinted in 1 ROMAN STATUTES, supra note 193, at 7. See also 10 Livy, supra note 148, at 163 (passage xxxvi.3.3). See also Kunkel, supra note 100, at 19; Greenidge, supra note 84, at 263–67.

198. Compare 1 Livy, supra note 148 (ch. 1), at 221 (passages ii.1.10–11) (suggesting that plebians sat in the senate from the beginning) with Pierre Willems, LE SÉNAT DE LA RÉPUBLIQUE ROMAINE. SA COMPOSITION ET SES ATTRIBUTIONS (Louvain, 1885; rep., Aalen: Scientia-Verlag, 1968) (suggesting this only occurred by the last decades of the fifth century BCE). See Jolowicz and Nicholas, supra note 177 (ch. 2), at 32–33.

199. See 2 Mommsen, supra note 177, at 377, 421; Lintott, supra note 227 (ch. 1), at 68–72, 117–19; Kunkel, supra note 100, at 18 (who notes that only exconsuls could serve as censors); Nicolet, supra note 22, at 82–88.

200. See 1 Gellius, ATTIC NIGHTS, at 303 (John C. Rolfe, transl.; New York: G. Putnam's Sons, 1927) (passage iii.18.8).

201. See Jolowicz and Nicholas, supra note 177 (ch. 2), at 43–45; Kunkel, supra note 100, at 19; Greenidge, supra note 84, at 269–72. See also 10 Plutarch, supra note 112 (ch. 1), at 373 (*Flamininus*, xviii) (censors name first member of the senate).

202. See Holland, supra note 194, at 102; Jolowicz and Nicholas, supra note 177, at 54–55; von Fritz, supra note 55, at 197–204.

203. See 8 Plutarch, supra note 112 (ch. 1), at 331–33 (*Cato the Younger*, passage xl).

204. See 6 Livy, supra note 148 (ch. 1), at 349–51 (passage xxv.3.13); 7 id., at 7–13 (passages xxvi.2.7–3.12); 13 id., at 31 (passages xliii.8.2–3).

205. See Ernst Badian, Tribuni Plebis *and* Res Publica, in IMPERIUM SINE FINE: T. ROBERT S. BROUGHTON AND THE ROMAN REPUBLIC, at 187 (Jerzy Linderski, ed.; Stuttgart: Franz Steiner Verlag, 1996). See also 9 Plutarch, supra note 112 (ch. 1), at 543–47 (*Gaius Marius*, xxix).

206. 3 Polybius, supra note 51, at 307 (passage vi.16.4); 8 Plutarch, supra note 112 (ch. 1), at 281–83 (*Cato the Younger*, xx). See also Walbank, supra note 56, at 691–92.

207. See R. Rillinger, *"Loca intercessionis"und Legaismus in der späten Republik*, 19 CHIRON 481 (1989); von Fritz, supra note 55, at 207–09; Greenidge, supra note 84, at 176–80.

208. See 7 Livy, supra note 148 (ch. 1), at 223–25 (passages xxvii.6.2–11).

209. See 7 Plutarch, supra note 112 (ch. 1), at 473–77 (*Caesar*, xiv); 2 Livy, supra note 148 (ch. 1), at 71 (passage iii.20.8). See also Lintott, supra note 227 (ch. 1), at 125–28; Kunkel, supra note 100, at 16.

210. See Cicero, DE LEGIBUS, supra note 325 (ch. 1), at 469 (passage iii.3.9); 1 Livy, supra note 148 (ch. 1), at 325 (passages ii.33.1, iii.55.6–7); 4 Dionysisus, supra note 23, at 121–23 (passages vi.89.2–4). See also Lintott, supra note 227 (ch. 1), at 123–24.

211. See 5 Plutarch, supra note 112 (ch. 1), at 167 (*Pompey*, xxi). See also Holland, supra note 194, at 103.

212. One important limit on the legislative power of the popular assemblies was that the senate had to give its approval, or auctoritas, for the measure to enter into force. See von Fritz, supra note 55, at 195–96.

213. 4 WORKS OF JOHN ADAMS, supra note 87 (ch. 1), at 284.

214. Id., at 440. One scholar disputes this. See Greenidge, supra note 84, at 179 (citing Livy).

215. See 1 Dionysius, supra note 23 (passage ii.7.7).

216. 4 WORKS OF JOHN ADAMS, supra note 87 (ch. 1), at 447–48. See also Thompson, supra note 35 (ch. 1), at 212–22.

217. See, generally, William B. Gwyn, THE MEANING OF THE SEPARATION OF POWERS; AN ANALYSIS OF THE DOCTRINE FROM ITS ORIGIN TO THE ADOPTION OF THE UNITED STATES CONSTITUTION (New Orleans: Tulane University Press, 1965).

218. Montesquieu, supra note 124, at 182. See also Cohler, supra note 127, at 161–69; Carrese, supra note 127, at 43–47.

219. See Benjamin F. Wright, *The Origin of Separation of Powers in America*, 13 ECONOMICA 169, 171–76 (1933).

220. See Gerhard Casper, SEPARATING POWER: ESSAYS ON THE FOUNDING PERIOD, at 11–12 (Cambridge, Mass.: Harvard University Press, 1997).

221. See Mass. Const. of 1780, First Part, Art. XXX ("In the government of this Commonwealth, the legislative department shall never exercise the executive and judicial powers, or either of them: The executive shall never exercise the legislative and judicial powers, or either of them: The judicial shall never exercise the legislative and executive powers, or either of them: to the end it may be a government of laws and not of men."), reprinted in 3 THE FEDERAL AND STATE CONSTITUTIONS, COLONIAL CHARTERS, AND OTHER ORGANIC LAWS OF THE STATES, TERRITORIES, AND COLONIES NOW OR HERETOFORE FORMING THE UNITED STATES OF AMERICA, at 1888, 1893 (Francis N. Thorpe, ed.; 1909) [hereinafter State Constitutions]. Compare N.C. Const. of 1776, reprinted in 5 STATE CONSTITUTIONS, supra, at 2787, 2787 (providing that "the legislative, executive, and supreme judicial powers of government, ought to be forever separate and distinct from each other"), Va. Const. of 1776, reprinted in 7 STATE CONSTITUTIONS, supra, at 3812, 3813 (providing that "the legislative and executive powers of the State should be separate and distinct from the judiciary"), id., reprinted in 7 STATE CONSTITUTIONS, supra, at 3812, 3815 (providing that the "legislative, executive, and judiciary department, shall be separate and distinct, so that neither exercise the powers properly belonging to the other"), and Ga. Const. of 1777, art. I, reprinted in 2 STATE CONSTITUTIONS, supra, at 777, 778 (providing that the "legislative, executive, and judiciary departments shall be separate and distinct, so that neither exercise the powers properly belonging to the other"). But see Jefferson's observations of the relative absence of separation of powers in the first state constitutions, in his NOTES ON THE STATE OF VIRGINIA, supra note 155.

222. N.H. Const. of 1784, Art. XXXVII, reprinted in 4 STATE CONSTITUTIONS, at 2457.

223. See U.S. Const. Art. I, § 1 ("All legislative powers herein granted shall be vested in a Congress of the United States which shall consist of a Senate and House of Representatives"); Art. II, § 1 ("The executive Power shall be vested in a President of the United States of America"); Art. III, § 1 ("The judicial Power of the United States shall be vested in one supreme court, and in such inferior Courts as the Congress may from time to time ordain and establish."). The literature on the original intent of the vesting clauses is vast. See, for example, Steven G. Calabresi, The vesting clauses as power grants, 88 Nw. U. L. REV. 1377 (1994); Steven G. Calabresi and Kevin H. Rhodes, The Structural Constitution: Unitary Executive, Plural Judiciary, 105 HARV. L. REV. 1153 (1992); Edward S. Corwin, The Steel Seizure Case: A Judicial Brick Without Straw, 53 COLUM. L. REV. 53 (1953); Bruce Ledewitz, The Uncertain Power of the President to Execute the Laws, 46 TENN. L. REV. 757 (1979); Joseph P. Verdon, Note, The vesting clauses: the Nixon test and the pharaoh's dreams, 78 VA. L. REV. 1253 (1992).

224. See 1 Farrand, at 98, 100, 139–40 (the legislative, executive and judicial department "ought to be distinct and independent"). See also Clinton, BRIEF HISTORY, supra note 6 (pr.), at 902–03; Banning, supra note 164 (ch. 1), at 135, 168, 184; James T. Barry, III, The Council of Revision and the Limits of Judicial Power, 56 U. CHI. L. REV. 235 (1989).

225. 1 Farrand, at 138. See also Cohler, supra note 127, at 160–61.
226. 5 U.S. (1 Cranch), at 137 (1803). See also sources at supra note 140 (ch. 1).
227. FEDERALIST, at 301 (No. 47) (Madison).
228. Id.
229. Id., at 304.
230. See id., at 308.
231. FEDERALIST, at 308 (No. 48) (Madison).
232. Id.
233. See Garry Wills, EXPLAINING AMERICA: THE FEDERALIST, at 100 (New York: Penguin Books, 1981).
234. See, generally, Thomas L. Pangle, *The Classical Challenge to the American Constitution*, 66 CHI.-KENT L. REV. 145, 153–66 (1990); Clinton, BRIEF HISTORY, supra note 6 (pr.), at 897–98.
235. 1 Montesquieu, supra note 124, at 146, 153. See Judith Sklar, *Montesquieu and the New Republicanism*, in MACHIAVELLI AND REPUBLICANISM, at 265 (Cambridge, UK: Cambridge University Press, 1990).
236. Machiavelli, supra note 113, at 32.
237. FEDERALIST, at 73 (No. 9) (Madison). See also Rakove, supra note 164 (ch. 1), at 153–54.
238. See George Clinton, *Letters of Cato III*, NEW YORK JOURNAL (Oct. 25, 1787), reprinted in Ford, ESSAYS, supra note 308 (ch. 1), at 255, 256.
239. *"Brutus" I*, NEW YORK JOURNAL, Oct. 18, 1787, reprinted in 1 THE DEBATE ON THE CONSTITUTION: FEDERALIST AND ANTIFEDERALIST SPEECHES, ARTICLES AND LETTERS DURING THE STRUGGLE OVER RATIFICATION, at 171 (New York: Library of America, 1993). See also Walling, supra note 131 (ch. 1), at 101–02.
240. Samuel Bryan, CENTINEL, No. 14, Feb. 5, 1788, reprinted in 16 DOCUMENTARY HISTORY OF THE RATIFICATION OF THE CONSTITUTION, at 37 (Merrill Jensen, John P. Kaminski, and Gaspare J. Saladino, eds.; Madison: State Historical Soc'y, 1976).
241. *Agrippa XII*, THE MASSACHUSETTS GAZETTE, Jan. 7, 1788, reprinted in Ford, ESSAYS, supra note 308 (ch. 1), at 91.
242. *Americanus I*, DAILY ADVERTISER (New York), Nov. 2, 1787, reprinted in 1 id., 227, 227–28 (original emphasis).
243. Id., at 228–29.
244. *Americanus III*, DAILY ADVERTISER (New York), Nov. 30, 1787, reprinted in 1 id., 437.
245. Id.
246. Id., at 438.
247. Id.
248. Id., at 438, 439.
249. See Bederman, supra note 29, at 31–35 (Greek *poleis* as exclusionary institutions).
250. A CITIZEN OF AMERICA (Philadelphia, Oct. 17, 1787), reprinted in 1 DEBATE ON THE CONSTITUTION, supra note 239, at 129, 158–59 n.*.
251. Id. See also Nelson, supra note 93 (ch. 1), at 213–19; Yarbrough, supra note 121 (ch. 1), at 102–52.

252. Interestingly, *Federalist* (No. 10) was published just a few days after the Americanus letter. See id., at 227 (*Americanus I*, published Nov. 2, 1787), 404 (FEDERALIST (No. 10), published Nov. 22, 1787), 437 (*Americanus III*, published Nov. 30, 1787).

253. For an intellectual history of the impact of *Federalist* (No. 10), see Douglass Adair, *The Tenth Federalist Revisited*, 8 WMQ 48 (1951); David F. Epstein, THE POLITICAL THEORY OF THE FEDERALIST (Chicago: University of Chicago Press, 1984); J. Christopher Jennings, *Madison's New Audience: The Supreme Court and the Tenth Federalist Visited*, 82 B. U. L. REV. 817 (2002); Larry D. Kramer, *Madison's Audience*, 112 HARV. L. REV. 611, 613–14 (1999); Thomas L. Pangle, *The* Federalist Papers' *Vision of Civic Health and the Tradition out of which that Vision Emerges*, 38 WESTERN POL. Q. 577 (1986).

254. FEDERALIST, at 83 (No. 10) (Madison).

255. Other pamphleteers intimated as much, including Pelatiah Webster, who had little truck for the Antifederalists' insistence on applying Montesquieu's small republic axiom at every available turn: "And when he [Brutus, a prominent opponent of the Constitution] has run himself out of breath with his dreary declamation, he comes to the conclusion he set out with, viz. That the Thirteen States are too big for a republican government. . . . " Pelatiah Webster, *The Weakness of Brutus Exposed*, Nov. 4, 1787, reprinted in Ford, PAMPHLETS, supra note 303 (ch. 2), at 122.

256. See Kennedy, supra note 87 (ch. 1), at 123–24; Richard, supra note 6 (ch. 1), at 141; Stourzh, supra note 241 (ch. 1), at 55.

257. FEDERALIST, at 100 (No. 14) (Madison). See also Banning, supra note 164 (ch. 1), at 227–28.

258. See McDonald, supra note 214 (ch. 1), at 285–87.

259. *Agrippa XII*, MASSACHUSETTS GAZETTE (Boston), Jan. 11, 15, 18, 1788, reprinted in 1 DEBATES ON THE CONSTITUTION, supra note 239, at 764; 4 CAF 71.

260. FEDERALIST, at 327 (No. 52) (Madison). See also Epstein, supra note 253, at 118–25; Rahe, *Antiquity Surpassed*, in REPUBLICANISM, LIBERTY, supra note 3 (pr.), at 233, 251–56; Kesler, FEDERALIST (No. 10), in Kesler, supra note 230 (ch. 1), at 35.

261. Hanna Fenichel Pitkin, *Representation*, in POLITICAL INNOVATION AND CONCEPTUAL CHANGE, at 133 (Terence Ball, James Farr, and Russell L. Hanson, eds.; Cambridge, UK: Cambridge University Press, 1989).

262. FEDERALIST, at 386 (No. 63) (Madison). See also Rahe, *Antiquity Surpassed*, in REPUBLICANISM, LIBERTY, supra note 3 (pr.), at 233, 151–56; Kesler, FEDERALIST (No. 10), in Kesler, supra note 230 (ch. 1), at 35.

263. See FEDERALIST, at 243–46 (No. 39) (Madison). See also Vincent Ostrom, THE POLITICAL THEORY OF A COMPOUND REPUBLIC: A RECONSTRUCTION OF THE LOGICAL FOUNDATIONS OF AMERICAN DEMOCRACY AS PRESENTED IN THE FEDERALIST (Blacksburg, Va.: Public Choice, VPI & SU, 1971).

264. See Onuf and Onuf, supra note 113, at 80–84.

265. Meyer Reinhold, *From Classical Republicanism to Modern Republicanism in the American Revolution*, 10 STUDI ITALIANI DI FIOLOGIA CLASSICA 513, 514 (1992).

266. See Rahe, supra note 3 (pr.), at 29; Richard, supra note 6 (ch. 1), at 239; Sellers, supra note 85 (ch. 1), at 172–74, 207; Yarbrough, supra note 121 (ch. 1), at 71–81.

267. J. R. Howe, Jr., THE CHANGING POLITICAL THOUGHT OF JOHN ADAMS, at 164 (Princeton: Princeton University Press, 1966); Thompson, supra note 35 (ch. 1), at 192–201.

268. 1 Farrand, at 424 (June 26). See also Rahe, supra note 3 (pr.), at 651–59.

269. See Oscar and Lilian Handlin, 1 LIBERTY IN AMERICA, 1600–1760 (New York: Harper & Row, 1986).

270. Adams, 4 WORKS OF JOHN ADAMS, supra note 87 (ch. 1), at 470.

271. *Agrippa XII*, MASSACHUSETTS GAZETTE (Boston), Jan. 15, 1788, reprinted in 1 DEBATES ON THE CONSTITUTION, supra note 239, at 764; 4 CAF 95. See also Walling, supra note 131 (ch. 1), at 177.

272. A CITIZEN OF PHILADELPHIA, THE WEAKNESSES OF BRUTUS EXPOSED (Philadelphia; Nov. 8, 1787), reprinted in 1 DEBATES ON THE CONSTITUTION, supra note 239, at 187.

273. FEDERALIST, at 57 (No. 6) (Hamilton).

274. See id. See also Walling, supra note 131 (ch. 1), at 179–82.

275. See Adams, *Defence of the Constitutions*, 4 WORKS OF JOHN ADAMS, supra note 87 (ch. 1), at 470–72; *A Cumberland County Mutual Improvement Society Addresses the Pennsylvania Minority*, CARLISLE GAZETTE, Jan. 2, 1788, reprinted in 1 DEBATES ON THE CONSTITUTION, supra note 239, at 563. ("The republic of Venice, by the progressive and almost imperceptible encroachments of the nobles, has at length degenerated into an odious and permanent aristocracy.")

276. 3 Polybius, supra note 51, at 385 (passage vi.51).

277. 3 id., at 395 (passages vi.56.2–4).

278. See 3 id., at 387 (passages vi.52.4–6). See also Cicero, DE RE PUBLICA, supra note 325 (ch. 1), at 117–19 (passage ii.4) (discussing the corruption of maritime and commercial cities).

279. See Galston, supra note 230 (ch. 1), at 49–52.

280. FEDERALIST, at 71–72 (No. 9) (Hamilton). See also Pangle, SPIRIT, supra note 3 (pr.), at 43–44, 46–47.

281. 2 Elliot, at 8.

282. FEDERALIST, at 342 (No. 55) (Madison). See also Bruce Ackerman, WE THE PEOPLE: FOUNDATIONS 180 (Cambridge, Mass.: Belknap Press of Harvard University Press, 1991); Onuf and Onuf, supra note 113, at 81; Reinhold, REPUBLICANISM, supra note 265, at 517.

283. 3 Polybius, supra note 51, at 369–71 (passages vi.44.3 and 8).

284. See 3 id., at 255–57 (passages v.106.6–8); 5 id., at 115 (passage xviii.14.10); 6 id., at 135–37 (passages xxx.20.1–7).

285. See Jennifer Tolbert Roberts, ATHENS ON TRIAL: THE ANTI-DEMOCRATIC TRADITION IN WESTERN THOUGHT (Princeton: Princeton University Press, 1994); id., *Thinking About Democracy: Ancient Greece and Modern America*, 25 PROLOGUE 137 (1993); Martin Ostwald, *Popular Sovereignty and the Problem of Equality*, 19 SCRIPTA CLASSICA ISRAELICA 1 (2000); Philip Brook Manville, THE ORIGINS OF CITIZENSHIP IN ANCIENT ATHENS, at 3–34 (Princeton: Princeton University Press, 1990).

286. FEDERALIST, at 81 (No. 10) (Madison).
287. Id., at 386 (No. 63) (Madison) (original emphasis). See also 5 CAF 18 (*Essays by a Farmer No. II*) (Feb. 29, 1788) (describing Solon's constitution for Athens, which subsisted only a few years, until unsettled by the tyrant, Pisistratus).
288. Adams, *Defence of the Constitution*, in 4 WORKS OF JOHN ADAMS, supra note 87 (ch. 1), at 488–49. See also Richard, supra note 6 (ch. 1), at 137–38.
289. See Aristotle, ATHENIAN CONSTITUTION, supra note 175, at 119 (passage xlii.1); Rahe, supra note 3 (pr.), at 192–93.
290. See Aristotle, ATHENIAN CONSTITUTION, supra note 175, at 121 (passage xliii.1). See also Alan I. Boegehold, *The Athenian Government in Thucydides*, in THE LANDMARK THUCYDIDES, at 577 (New York: Free Press, 1996).
291. See G. E. M. de Ste Croix, *The Constitution of the Five Thousand*, 5 HISTORIA 1 (1956); Charles Hignett, A HISTORY OF THE ATHENIAN CONSTITUTION TO THE END OF THE FIFTH CENTURY B.C. (Oxford: Clarendon Press, 1970); Douglas M. MacDowell, THE LAW IN CLASSICAL ATHENS, at 24–29 (Ithaca: Cornell University Press, 1978); Manville, supra note 285, at 17–20, 194–97; Peter John Rhodes, THE ATHENIAN BOULE (Oxford: Clarendon Press, 1985).
292. 1 Montesquieu, supra note 124, at 201. See also Rob Atkinson, *Reviving the Roman Republic: Remembering the Good Old Cause*, 71 FORDHAM L. REV. 1187 (2003).

CHAPTER 3. CONSTITUTION-MAKING AND ANCIENT HISTORY

1. FEDERALIST, at 181 (No. 28) (Hamilton). To the same effect was Madison's observation that "Ambition must be made to counteract ambition." FEDERALIST, at 322 (No. 51) (Madison).
2. U.S. Const. Amend. 10 ("The powers not delegated to the United States by the Constitution, nor prohibited by it to the States, are reserved to the States respectively, or to the people.").
3. Id., Art. I, § 9, cl. 2.
4. Id., Art. I, § 9, cl. 3.
5. Id., Art. IV, cl. 3.
6. Id., Art. I, § 10, cl. 1.
7. Id., Art. III, § 2, cl. 3.
8. Id., Art. III, § 3.
9. Id., preamble.
10. The exceptions are id., art. I, § 2 (three-fifths compromise on apportionment in the House of Representatives); id., Art. I, § 9, cl. 1 (limits on Congress' power to legislate on the slave trade); id., Art. I, § 9, cl. 4 (capitation tax clause); id., Art. IV, § 2, cl. 3 (fugitive slave clause). See Paul Finkelman, *The Founders and Slavery: Little Ventured, Little Gained*, 13 YALE J. L. AND HUMAN. 413, 426–39 (2001). Voting qualifications for electors of federal office-holders are mentioned at id., art. I, § 2, cl. 1 (electors for House of Representatives).
11. U.S. Const. Art. I, § 3, cl. 1.
12. See id., amend. 17, cl. 1. The amendment provided also that "The electors in each state [for Senators] shall have the qualifications requisite for electors of the most numerous branch of the State legislatures." Id. See also

Ralph A. Rossum, FEDERALISM, THE SUPREME COURT AND THE SEVEN-
TEENTH AMENDMENT: THE IRONY OF CONSTITUTIONAL DEMOCRACY (Lanham, Md.: Lexington Books, 2001).

13. Id., Art. II, § 1, cls. 2–4; Amend. 12.
14. FEDERALIST, at 214 (No. 35) (Hamilton).
15. See MacDowell, supra note 291 (ch. 2), at 174; Manville, supra note 285 (ch. 2), at 124–209.
16. See 13 Livy, supra note 148 (ch. 1), at 293–95 (passages xlv.15.1–3). See also Lintott, supra note 227 (ch. 1), at 51–52. See also L. R. Taylor, ROMAN VOTING ASSEMBLIES (Ann Arbor: University of Michigan Press, 1966).
17. See 1 Livy, supra note 148 (ch. 1), at 149–55 (passages i.42–i.43.13). See also Nicolet, supra note 22 (ch. 2), at 264–67.
18. Cicero, DE RE PUBLICA, supra note 325 (ch. 1), at 149 (passage ii.39); 2 Dionysius, supra note 23 (ch. 2), at 321–37 (passages iv.16–21); 4 id., 319–23 (passages vii.59.2–8); 4 Plutarch, supra note 112 (ch. 1), at 167 (*Coriolanus*, xx). See also Lintott, supra note 227, at 55–61; L. Grieve, *The Reform of the Comitia Centuriata*, 34 HISTORIA 278 (1985); L. R. Taylor, *The Centuriate assembly before and after the Reform*, 78 AJP 337 (1957); Millar, Political Thought, supra note 83 (ch. 2), at 43–46.
19. See Kunkel, supra note 100 (ch. 2), at 12.
20. See P. A. Brunt, ITALIAN MANPOWER, 225 B.C.–A.D. 14, at 376 (Oxford: Claren-don Press, 1971); Greenidge, supra note 84 (ch. 2), at 299–315; Nicolet, supra note 22 (ch. 2), at 48–56 (providing detailed figures from various sources).
21. See Appian, ROMAN HISTORY: CIVIL WAR 17–29 (passages i.8–13) (Horace White, transl., 1913) (Loeb Classical Library reprint, 1979)(narrating the passage of Tiberius Gracchus' agrarian bill). See also 10 Plutarch, supra note 112 (ch. 1), at 159–75 (*Tiberius Gracchus*, viii–xiii).
22. A CITIZEN OF AMERICA [NOAH WEBSTER], AN EXAMINATION INTO THE LEADING PRINCIPLES OF THE FEDERAL CONSTITUTION (Philadelphia, Oct. 17, 1787), reprinted in DEBATES ON THE CONSTITUTION, supra note 239 (ch. 2), at 129, 143 n.*; and in Ford, PAMPHLETS, supra note 46 (ch. 2), at 43 n.*.
23. See id., REPRINTED IN DEBATES ON THE CONSTITUTION, supra note 239 (ch. 2), at 157; and in Ford, PAMPHLETS, supra note 46 (ch. 2), at 58.
24. For an English translation, see Charles-Louis Montesquieu, CONSIDERATIONS ON THE CAUSES OF THE GREATNESS OF THE ROMANS AND THEIR DECLINE (David Lowenthal, transl.; New York: Free Press, 1965).
25. Id., at 93.
26. See Two ENGLISH REPUBLICAN TRACTS (Caroline Robbins, comp.; London: Cambridge University Press, 1969). See also Millar, POLITICAL THOUGHT, supra note 83 (ch. 2), at 102–06; Nelson, supra note 93 (ch. 1), at 134–38; M. M. Goldsmith, *Liberty, Virtue and the Rule of Law*, 1689–1770, in REPUBLICANISM, LIBERTY, supra note 3 (pr.), at 197, 206–07.
27. Edward S. Corwin, *The Pelatiah Webster Myth*, in THE DOCTRINE OF JUDICIAL REVIEW, at 111, 116 (Princeton: Princeton University Press, 1914).
28. See 2 Farrand, at 201.
29. 1 WORKS OF JAMES WILSON, supra note 123 (ch. 1), at 403.
30. Id., at 405.

31. U.S. Const. Art. I, § 2, cl. 1. See also Eidelberg, supra note 7 (pr.), at 52–77.
32. See Works of James Wilson, supra note 123 (ch. 1), at 407–11 (discussing constitutions of Massachusetts, Connecticut, New York, New Jersey, Maryland, South Carolina, and Georgia).
33. Federalist, at 291 (No. 45) (Madison).
34. Id., at 326 (No. 52) (Madison). See also Jeffrey Rosen, Divided Suffrage, 12 Const. Comment. 199 (1995).
35. Federalist, at 78 (No. 10) (Madison).
36. The most famous articulation of this view can be found in Charles A. Beard, An Economic Interpretation of the Constitution of the United States (New York: Free Press, 1935).
37. 2 Farrand, at 371 (Aug. 22) (spelling and punctuation modernized).
38. Id., at 370 (spelling and punctuation modernized).
39. Id., at 372.
40. See Thomas Jefferson to John Holmes, Apr. 22, 1820, in 15 Writings of Thomas Jefferson, supra note 92 (ch. 1), at 249 (paraphrasing Suetonius, Lives of the Caesars (Tiberius, xxv)).
41. See Orlando Patterson, Slavery and Social Death: A Comparative Study, at vii (Cambridge, Mass.: Harvard University Press, 1982).
42. 23 U.S. (10 Wheat.) 66 (1825).
43. I have elsewhere compared Story's and Marshall's treatment of slavery and the natural/positive law divide in David J. Bederman, The Spirit of International Law, at 6–7 (Athens: University of Georgia Press, 2002).
44. 23 U.S. at 103 and n.13 (citing "Domat, Loix Civ. Prel. tit. 2. § 2. Wood's Inst. Imp. and Civ. Law, Introd. 93. Grotius, de J. B. ac P. C. 2. c. 5. § 27. Puffend. b. 3. 2. § 8. 1 Rutherf. b. 1. c. 20. p. 474. Bynk. Quaest. Jur. Pub. l. 1. c. 3. p. 20. Du Ponceau's Transl."). The quoted language is from Justinian's Institutes and is translated: "Slavery is an institution of the law of nations [ius gentium] by which, contrary to the law of nature, a person is subjected to the dominion of another." Institutes of Justinian, passage 1.3.2.
45. Thomas Jefferson, Notes on the State of Virginia, at 138–43 (1787) (William Peden, ed.; Chapel Hill: University of North Carolina Press, 1955).
46. See id.
47. See MacDowell, supra note 291 (ch. 2), at 79–82.
48. See, for example, M. I. Finley, Ancient Slavery and Modern Ideology, at 81 (London: Chatto & Windus, 1980); Holland, supra note 194 (ch. 2), at 166–67 (discussing the philosopher Posidonius's observations on Roman slavery); G. E. M. de Ste. Croix, The Class Struggle in the Ancient Greek World (London: Duckworth, 1981); Michael H. Jameson, Agriculture and Slavery in Classical Athens, 73 CJ 122 (1977); Victor Davis Hanson, Warfare and Agriculture in Ancient Greece (Berkeley: University of California Press, 1998). See also 4 Plutarch, supra note 112 (ch. 1), at 177–79 (Coriolanus, xxiv) (concerning gentle treatment of slaves).
49. See Ellen Meiksins Woods, Agricultural Slavery in Classical Athens, 8 Am. J. Ancient Hist. 1 (1983).
50. See P. A. Brunt, Social Conflicts in the Roman Republic (London: Chatto & Windus, 1971); Keith Hopkins, Conquerors and Slaves (Cambridge, UK: Cambridge University Press, 1978).

51. See K. R. Bradley, SLAVERY AND SOCIETY AT ROME (Cambridge, UK: Cambridge University Press, 1994); W. W. Buckland, THE ROMAN LAW OF SLAVERY (Cambridge, UK: Cambridge University Press, 1908); O. Robleda, IL DIRITTO DEGLI SCHIAVI NELL'ANTICA ROMANA (Rome: Gregoriana Press, 1976); Wolfgang Zeev Rubinsohn, DIE GROSSEN SKLAVENAUFSTÄNDE DER ANTIKE: 500 JAHRE FORSCHUNG (Darmstadt: Wissenschaftliche Buchgesellschaft, 1993); GREEK AND ROMAN SLAVERY (Thomas Wiedemann, ed.; London: Croom Helm, 1981); Alan Watson, ROMAN SLAVE LAW, at 1–22 (Baltimore: Johns Hopkins University Press, 1987); John Madden, *Slavery in the Roman Empire: numbers and origins*, 3 CLASSICS IRELAND 109 (1996).

Roman slavery was also viewed in this light by David Hume. See OF THE POPULOUSNESS OF ANCIENT NATIONS (1777), in Hume, supra note 151 (ch. 2), at 388–96.

52. See 12 WRITINGS OF THOMAS JEFFERSON, supra note 92 (ch. 1), at 217 (Jefferson to Joel Barlow) (Dec. 25, 1808); 16 id., 124 (to unidentified correspondent) (Oct. 25, 1825).

53. See Edward Gibbon, 1 THE HISTORY OF THE DECLINE AND FALL OF THE ROMAN EMPIRE 266 (New York: Begelow, Brown, 1854). But cf. Thomas R.R. Cobb, AN INQUIRY INTO THE LAW OF NEGRO SLAVERY IN THE UNITED STATES OF AMERICA lxix–lxxxv (1858) (Paul Finkelman ed.; Athens: University of Georgia Press, 1999) (quoting ancient authors and asserting that classical slavery was more brutal than American institution).

54. Seneca, 1 MORAL ESSAYS, at 421 (John W. Basore, transl.; 1928) (Loeb Classical Library reprint, 1985) (*Clementia*, i.24.1). See also F. Favory, *Clodius et le péril servile: fonction du thème servile dans le discours polémique cicéronien*, 8 INDEX 173 (1979).

55. Pliny, 1 LETTERS, at 213 (Betty Radice, transl.; 1969) (Loeb Classical Library reprint, 1972) (*Epistles*, iii.14).

56. See Xenophon, OECONOMICUS (E.C. Marchant, transl., 1938) (Loeb Classical Lib. rep. 1968).

57. U.S. Const. Art. IV, § 2, cl. 3 ("No Person held to Service or Labour in one State, under the Laws thereof, escaping into another, shall, in Consequence of any Law or Regulation therein, be discharged from such Service or Labour, but shall be delivered up on Claim of the Party to whom such Service or Labour may be due.").

58. Id., Art. I, § 9, cl. 1 ("The Migration or Importation of such Persons as any of the States now existing shall think proper to admit, shall not be prohibited by Congress prior to the year one thousand eight hundred and eight. . . . ").

59. Id., Art. I, § 8, cl. 15 (Congress has the power to call "forth the Militia" to "suppress Insurrections"); Art. IV, § 4 ("The United States shall . . . protect each of them against Invasion; and on Application of the Legislature, or of the Executive (when the Legislature cannot be convened) against domestic Violence.").

60. Id., Art. I, § 2, cl. 3 ("Representatives and direct Taxes shall be apportioned among the several States, according to their respective Numbers, which shall be determined by adding the whole Number of free Persons, including those bound to Service for a Term of Years, and excluding Indians not taxed, three fifths of all other Persons."). For Madison's somewhat peculiar, and socratic

defense of the compromise, see FEDERALIST, at 336–40 (No. 54) (Madison). In truth, the three-fifths formula had its origins in provisions adopted by the Continental Congress in 1783.

61. See Finkelman, supra note 10, at 414 ("The success of the slave owners at the Convention was sweeping."), at 425–39. See also Paul Finkelman, AN IMPERFECT UNION: SLAVERY, FEDERALISM AND COMITY (Chapel Hill: University of North Carolina Press, 1981); id., *Slavery and the Constitutional Convention*, in BEYOND CONFEDERATION: ORIGINS OF THE CONSTITUTION AND AMERICAN NATIONAL IDENTITY. at 188, 216 (Richard Beeman, Stephen Botein, and Edward C. Carter, II, eds.; Chapel Hill: University of North Carolina Press, 1987); William H. Freehling, *The Founding Fathers and Slavery*, 77 AHR 81 (1972); Gary Wills, "NEGRO PRESIDENT": JEFFERSON AND THE SLAVE POWER (Boston: Houghton Mifflin, 2003).

62. Clinton, BRIEF HISTORY, supra note 6 (pr.), at 892. See also Douglas G. Smith, *An Analysis of Two Federal Structures: The Articles of Confederation and the Constitution*, 34 SAN DIEGO L. REV. 249 (1997); Rosen, supra note 164 (ch. 1), at 42–47; Walling, supra note 131 (ch. 1), at 50–52.

63. Art. Confed. XIII. See also *Oneida Indian Nation of New York v. New York*, 649 F. Supp. 420, 428 (N.D. N.Y. 1986); *Oneida Indian Nation of Wisconsin v. New York*, 691 F.2d 1070, 1095 n.21 (2d Cir. 1982).

64. Art. Confed. III. A previous draft of the Articles provided that "[t]he said Colonies unite themselves so as never to be divided by any Act whatever, and hereby several enter into a firm League of Friendship with each other. . . . " 5 Cont. Cong. 546–54, at Art. II. This provision emphasized the perpetual nature of the union among the states. However, the language was dropped.

65. Art. Confed. II. The earlier, 1776, version of this clause was more modest in scope, providing that "Each Colony shall retain and enjoy as much of its present Laws, Rights and Customs, as it may think fit, and reserved to itself the sole and exclusive Regulation and Government of its internal police, in all matters that shall not interfere with the Articles of this Confederation." 5 Cont. Cong. 675.

66. See Art. Confed. IX (enumerating, *inter alia*, the power of Congress to declare war, entering treaties and alliances, sending and receiving ambassadors, establishing rules for maritime captures, adjudicating land disputes between States, controlling intercourse with the Indian tribes, fixing weights and measures, inaugurating a postal service, and commissioning military officers).

Doubts later arose about the extent of powers of the Articles of Confederation Congress over some of these areas of authority. See, for example, *Oneida Indian Nation of New York v. New York*, 649 F. Supp. 420, 428–44 (N.D. N.Y. 1986) (ruling that Congress did not have the authority to block certain kinds of purchases of Indian lands). Cf. FEDERALIST, at 268–69 (No. 42) (Madison) ("The regulation of commerce with the Indian tribes is very properly unfettered from two limitations in the Articles of Confederation, which render the provision obscure and contradictory."). See also Clinton, BRIEF HISTORY, supra note 6 (pr.), at 893–94.

67. See Art. Confed. VIII, cl. 2 (states retained power of taxation); id., Art. IX, cl. 1 (Congress could not prohibit the states from imposing "imposts and duties on foreigners" or "prohibiting the exportation or importation of any species

of goods or commodities whatsoever."). This accounts for James Madison's comment that

> If the new Constitution be examined with accuracy and candor, it will be found that the change which it proposes consists much less in the addition of new powers to the Union, than in the invigoration of its original powers. The regulation of commerce, it is true, is a new power; but that seems to be an addition which few oppose, and from which no apprehensions are entertained. The powers relating to war and peace, armies and fleets, treaties and finance, with the other more considerable powers, are all vested in the existing Congress by the Articles of Confederation. The proposed change does not enlarge these powers; it only substitutes a more effectual mode of administering them.

FEDERALIST, at 293 (No. 45) (Madison). See also Smith, supra note 62, at 285–88.

68. Art. Confed. IX, cl. 5.
69. See Henry J. Bourguignon, THE FIRST FEDERAL COURT: THE FEDERAL APPELLATE PRIZE COURT OF THE AMERICAN REVOLUTION, 1775–1787 (Philadelphia: American Philosophical Society, 1977).
70. Art. Confed. IX, cl. 2.
71. Id., Art. V, cl. 1 ("For the more convenient management of the general interests of the united states, delegates shall be annually appointed in such manner as the legislature of each state shall direct, to meet in Congress on the first Monday in November, in every year, with a power reserved to each state, to recall its delegates, or any of them, at any time within the year, and to send others in their stead, for the remainder of the Year.").
72. Id., Art. V, cls. 2 and 3. ("[N]or shall any person, being a delegate, be capable of holding any office under the united states, for which he, or another for his benefit receives any salary, fees or emolument of any kind. . . . Each state shall maintain its own delegates in a meeting of the states, and while they act as members of the committee of the states.")
73. 28 Cont. Cong., at 388 (May 23, 1785) (resolution of the Commonwealth of Massachusetts that Members of Congress be debarred from appointment "to any office of trust or profit, under the said [united] states, during the term for which he shall have been so elected a member of Congress").
74. Art. Confed. V, cl. 4.
75. Id., Art. X ("The committee of the states, or any nine of them, shall be authorized to execute, in the recess of congress, such of the powers of congress as the united states in congress assembled, by the consent of nine states, shall from time to time think expedient to vest them with; provided that no power be delegated to the said committee, for the exercise of which, by the articles of confederation, the voice of nine states in the congress of the united states assembled is requisite.").
76. See Smith, supra note 62, at 270–72, 291–93.
77. See Madison's comment in *Federalist* (No. 43) that "A compact between independent sovereigns, founded on ordinary acts of legislative authority, can pretend to no higher validity than a league or treaty between the parties." FEDERALIST, at 279–80 (No. 43) (Madison). See also, Chief Justice John Marshall's famous observation in *McCulloch v. Maryland,* that "To the formation of a league, such as was the confederation, the State sovereignties were certainly

competent. But when, 'in order to form a more perfect union,' it was deemed necessary to change this alliance into an effective government, possessing great and sovereign powers, and acting directly on the people, the necessity of referring it to the people, and of deriving its powers directly from them, was felt and acknowledged by all." 17 U.S. (4 Wheat.) 316, 404 (1819).

Ironically, the *McCulloch* decision was the subject of sharp attacks, including one published in Richmond, Virginia newspapers under the pen-name of "Amphictyon," probably written by Judge William Brockenbrough. See JOHN MARSHALL'S DEFENSE OF *McCULLOCH v. MARYLAND* 53, 55 (Gerald Gunther, ed.; Palo Alto: Stanford University Press, 1969).

78.   6 Cont. Cong. 1102 (Aug. 1, 1776).
79.   See id., 1102–03, 1104.
80.   Id., at 1103 (spelling and punctuation modernized).
81.   Id., at 1105.
82.   See the remarks of Dr. Benjamin Rush, see id., at 1104, and see James Wilson, id., at 1105–06.
83.   See 9 Cont. Cong. 779–81 (Oct. 7, 1777).
84.   Id., at 781.
85.   Id., at 782.
86.   Clinton, BRIEF HISTORY, supra note 6 (pr.), at 896.
87.   FEDERALIST, at 247 (No. 40) (Madison).
88.   See Herbert Aptheker, EARLY YEARS OF THE REPUBLIC, at 37 (New York: International Publishers, 1976) (there were "clear evidences of inadequacies were present and were recognized by all elements of the revolutionary coalition"); Max Farrand, THE FRAMING OF THE CONSTITUTION OF THE UNITED STATES, at 47 (New Haven: Yale University Press, 1913) (the weaknesses of the general government "were self-evident and there seems to have been a general unanimity of sentiment in favor of the reforms proposed"); Gordon S. Wood, *Interests and Disinterestedness in the Making of the Constitution*, in BEYOND CONFEDERATION: ORIGINS OF THE CONSTITUTION AND AMERICAN NATIONAL IDENTITY, at 69, 72 (Richard Beeman et al., eds.; Chapel Hill: University of North Carolina Press, 1987) ("[b]y 1787 almost every political leader in the country, including most of the later Antifederalists, wanted something done to strengthen the Articles of Confederation").
89.   FEDERALIST, at 105–06 (No. 15) (Hamilton).
90.   A Plebian [Melancthon Smith], *An Address to the People of the State of New York: Shewing the Necessity of Making Amendments to the Constitution, Proposed for the United States, Previous to its Adoption*, at 11 (1788), reprinted in Ford, PAMPHLETS, supra note 46 (ch. 2), at 99. For other sources, see the excellent compilation at Smith, supra note 62, at 253 and nn. 9 and 10.
91.   FEDERALIST, at 251 (No. 40) (Madison). Madison also cautioned that the Articles may have concentrated too much power in the hands of Congress: "The present Congress can make requisitions to any amount they please, and the States are constitutionally bound to furnish them; they can emit bills of credit as long as they will pay for the paper; they can borrow, both abroad and at home, as long as a shilling will be lent. Is an indefinite power to raise troops dangerous? The Confederation gives to Congress that power also; and they have

already begun to make use of it.... The existing Congress, without any such control, can make treaties which they themselves have declared, and most of the States have recognized, to be the supreme law of the land." FEDERALIST, at 238 (No. 38) (Madison).

92. Wood, supra note 3 (pr.), at 359. Indeed, Edward Corwin speculated that the Articles of Confederation "might easily have come to support an even greater structure of derived powers than the Constitution of the United States does at this moment." Edward S. Corwin, *The Progress of Constitutional Theory Between the Declaration of Independence and the Meeting of the Philadelphia Convention*, 30 AHR 511, 529 (1925).

93. See Machiavelli, supra note 113 (ch. 2), at 145–47 (mentioning Demetrius, Philip of Macedon, and Athenian League).

94. See Philip A. Hamburger, *Natural Rights, Natural Law, and American Constitutions*, 102 YALE L. J. 907, 914 n.24 (1993); Bruce Ackerman and Neal Katyal, *Our Unconventional Founding*, 62 U. CHI. L. REV. 475, 554 (1995); Smith, supra note 62, at 264–68.

95. See Samuel Pufendorf, 2 DE JURE NATURAE ET GENTIUM LIBRI OCTO (On the Law of Nature and of Nations), at 1046–48 (James Brown Scott ed.; C. H. Oldfather and W. A. Oldfather, transl.; Washington, DC: Carnegie Endowment, 1934) (originally published 1688).

96. 2 id., at 1047 ("[t]he case is entirely different with the treaties that appear in systems, the purpose of which is that distinct states may intertwine for all time the prime interests of their safety, and on that score make the exercise of certain parts of the supreme sovereignty depend upon the mutual consent of their associates. For there is a great difference between 'I will bring you aid in this war, and we will consider in concert how we shall attack the enemy', and 'No one of us who have entered this society will exercise his right of peace and war, save with the common consent of all.'").

97. Id.

98. 2 id., at 1048 (citing Polybius' discussion of Philip of Macedon's interventions in the affairs of his Greek allies).

99. Emmerich de Vattel, LE DROIT DES GENS, OU, PRINCIPES DE LA LOI NATURELLE: APPLIQUÉS À LA CONDUITE ET AUX AFFAIRES DES NATIONS ET DES SOUVERAINS (*The Law of Nations or the Principles of Natural Law*) (Charles G. Fenwick transl.; Washington, DC: Carnegie Foundation, 1916).

100. See Onuf and Onuf, supra note 113 (ch. 2), at 5, 11 (1993) ("Vattel enjoyed enormous prestige and influence in Europe and America" and that Vattel's *Law of Nations* "was unrivaled ... in its influence on the American founders"); Charles G. Fenwick, *The Authority of Vattel*, 7 AM. POL. SCI. REV. 395 (1913). See also Thomas H. Lee, *Making Sense of the Eleventh Amendment: International Law and State Sovereignty*, 96 N.W. U. L. REV. 1027, 1061–67 (2002).

101. See Vattel, supra note 99, at 250–51.

102. Id.

103. See Vattel, supra note 99 (editor's introduction) (quoting Franklin as writing of Vattel's treatise that "It came to us in good season, when the circumstances of a rising State make it necessary frequently to consult the Law of Nations.") (quoting 2 WHARTON'S THE REVOLUTIONARY DIPLOMATIC CORRESPONDENCE,

at 64). See also Max Farrand, THE FATHERS OF THE CONSTITUTION: A CHRON-
ICLE OF THE ESTABLISHMENT OF THE UNION, at 48–51 (New Haven: Yale
University Press, 1921).

104. Vattel, supra note 99, at 12.
105. 1 Montesquieu, supra note 124 (ch. 2), at 153–54.
106. See 2 id., at 674–75 (criticizing Solon's law and the ordinance of the Amphictyonic League about the destruction of towns and diversion of waters).
107. See FEDERALIST, at 74 (No. 9) (Hamilton).
108. Id., at 76. See also id., at 291 (No. 45) (Madison) ("the states would remain
constituent and essential parts of the federal government.").
109. Id., at 323 (No. 51) (Madison).
110. 2 Farrand, at 92–93 (Yates's notes) (July 23).
111. 1 WORKS OF JAMES WILSON, supra note 123 (ch. 1), at 262–63.
112. See, generally, Smith, supra note 62, at 312–13.
113. Richard, supra note 6 (ch. 1), at 104.
114. Alexander Hamilton had written on the subject as early as 1778 and 1781. See 1
THE WORKS OF ALEXANDER HAMILTON 217, 246 (H. C. Lodge, ed.; New York:
G. P. Putnam's Sons). See John Adams, 1 DEFENCE OF THE CONSTITUTIONS
OF THE UNITED STATES OF AMERICA, at 296, 298, 305 (rep. New York: De
Capo Press, 1971) (mentioning the Achaean Confederacy).
115. 9 JAMES MADISON PAPERS, supra note 162 (ch. 1), at 3.
116. See 8 id., at 11, 266, 472, 501 (letters in which Madison explained to his corre-
spondents his scholarly project).
117. For concerns about dating of the final completion of the Notes, see 9 id., at 22,
n.1.
118. See Rakove, supra note 164 (ch. 1), at 55, 191; Banning, supra note 164 (ch. 1),
at 115, 219.
119. See 9 JAMES MADISON PAPERS, supra note 162 (ch. 1), at 4. See also 4 CAF 153
(Essays by Helvidius Priscus) (Dec. 27, 1787) (discussing Lycian League).
120. See id., at 23, n.4.
121. Id.
122. See, generally, André Aymard, LES ASSEMBLÉES DE LA CONFÉDÉRATION
ACHAIENNE: ÉTUDE CRITIQUE D'INSTITUTIONS ET D'HISTOIRE (Rome:
L'Erma di Bretschneider, 1967) [Aymard, Achaean Confederation]; id., LES
PREMIERS RAPPORTS DE ROME ET DE LA CONFÉDÉRATION ACHAIENNE (198–
189 AVANT J.C.) (Rome: L'Erma di Bretschneider, 1970).
123. 9 JAMES MADISON PAPERS, supra note 162 (ch. 1), at 7 (editors' emendation).
124. Id. (citing Félice and the Conde d'Albon's *Discours sur l'histoire, le gouvernment*
(Geneva, 1782)).
125. Id., at 24, n.16.
126. Id., at 8.
127. Compare this with the view of John Dickinson, writing as Fabius, reprinted
in Ford, PAMPHLETS, supra note 46 (ch. 2), at 188, 191–94, 201–02 (quoting
Polybius extensively).
128. John Adams, 1 DEFENCE OF THE CONSTITUTIONS OF THE UNITED STATES
OF AMERICA, at 296, 298, 305 (rep.; New York: De Capo Press, 1971). See also 10
Plutarch, supra note 112 (ch. 1), at 275–77 (*Philopoemen*, viii) (on the formation
and history of the Achaean League).

129. 9 JAMES MADISON PAPERS, supra note 162 (ch. 1), at 5–6 (quoting Aeschines, SPEECHES, at 245–47 (Charles Darwin Adams transl., 1919; Loeb Classical Library reprint, 1988) (*De falsa legatione*, passage 115)).

130. Id., at 6 (citing Félice, Plutarch's *Cimon*, and Demosthenes' *Oration on the Crown*).

131. Id. (citing Plutarch's *Themistocles*).

132. Id., at 7.

133. Id. See also Hans Beck, *"The Laws of the Fathers" versus "The Laws of the League": Xenophon on Federalism*, 96 CLASSICAL PHILOLOGY 355 (2001).

134. See 9 JAMES MADISON PAPERS, supra note 162 (ch. 1), at 6–7.

135. Id., at 4.

136. Rakove, supra note 164 (ch. 1), at 55.

137. See id., at 191.

138. See 1 Farrand, at 282 (June 18).

139. See Clinton, supra note 6 (pr.), at 898–905. See also Eidelberg, supra note 7 (pr.), at 40–51.

140. 1 Farrand, at 285 (June 18) (Madison's notes).

141. Id. See also Hamilton's speech at the New York ratifying convention, 2 Elliot, at 234; 2 CAF 333 (Letters of a Federal Farmer No. XVII) (Jan. 23, 1788) ("The Amphictionic council . . . have not possessed sufficient powers to controul the members of the republic in a proper manner.")

142. 1 Farrand, at 296 (Yates's notes).

143. Id., at 319–20 (June 19) (Madison's notes). See also Lance Banning, *The Practicable Sphere of the Republic*, in BEYOND CONFEDERATION, supra note 61, at 162, 164–87.

144. 1 Farrand, at 326 (Yates' notes). To the same effect was Madison's later speech at the Virginia Ratifying Convention, 3 Elliot, at 129–30 (June 6, 1788).

145. Id., at 328.

146. Id., at 329.

147. Id., at 343 (June 20) (Madison's notes).

148. Id., at 439 (June 27) (Yates' notes).

149. Id., at 441. To the same effect was Martin's later "Genuine Information," tabled before the Maryland legislature in November 1787. See 3 id., at 172, 184.

150. 1 id., at 454 (June 28) (Yates' notes). See also Gummere, supra note 6 (ch. 1), at 182; 2 CAF 37.

151. See Chapter 1, at Note 299 with text.

152. 1 Farrand, at 447–49 (June 28) (Madison's notes).

153. Id., at 485 (June 30) (Madison's notes).

154. See 9 JAMES MADISON PAPERS, supra note 162 (ch. 1), at 4.

155. See Clinton, supra note 6 (pr.), at 905. See also Forrest McDonald, STATES' RIGHTS AND THE UNION, at 15–25 (Lawrence: University of Kansas Press, 2000).

156. See 12 PAPERS OF THOMAS JEFFERSON, supra note 80 (ch. 2), at 274 (Oct. 24, 1787); 1 DEBATES ON THE CONSTITUTION, supra note 239 (ch. 2), at 192, 196 ("Without a check in the whole over the parts, our system involves the evil of imperia in imperio. . . . The want of some such provision [such as a negative on state laws] seems to have been mortal to the antient Confederacies, and to be the disease of the modern. Of the Lycian Confederacy little is known. That

of the Amphyctions is well known to have been rendered of little use whilst it lasted, and in the end to have been destroyed by the predominance of the local over the federal authority. The same observation may be made, on the authority of Polybius, with regard to the Achaean League."). See also Mayer, supra note 136 (ch. 1), at 91–94.

157. FEDERALIST, at 76 (No. 9) (Hamilton) (emphasis in original). See also Sellers, supra note 85 (ch. 1), at 169; Kesler, *Federalist 10*, in Kesler, supra note 230 (ch. 1), at 22.

158. Id., at 113 (No. 16) (Hamilton). See also Richard, supra note 6 (ch. 1), at 105; Sirico, supra note 4 (pr.), at 446–51.

159. Id., at 122 (No. 17) (Hamilton).

160. Id., at 122 (No. 18) (Madison (with Hamilton)).

161. Id., at 125.

162. Id., at 122–23.

163. Id., at 123. See also Gottfried Dietze, THE FEDERALIST: A CLASSIC ON FEDER-ALISM AND FREE GOVERNMENT, at 180–84 (Baltimore: Johns Hopkins Press, 1960).

164. See Richard, supra note 6 (ch. 1), at 106.

165. See John Dickinson, LETTERS OF FABIUS V, reprinted in Ford, PAMPHLETS, supra note 46 (ch. 2), at 188, 191–93 n.*.

166. FEDERALIST, at 124–25 (No. 18) (Madison (with Hamilton)).

167. Id., at 125.

168. Id., at 125–26 (emphasis in original). See also Dietze, supra note 163, at 184–85.

169. FEDERALIST, at 128 (No. 18) (Madison (with Hamilton)). See also John Dickinson, LETTERS OF FABIUS V, reprinted in Ford, PAMPHLETS, supra note 46 (ch. 2), at 188, 194 (quoting Polybius' observation that the Romans feared the rising power of the Achaeans).

170. FEDERALIST, at 128 (No. 18) (Madison (with Hamilton)). See also Dietze, supra note 163, at 191.

171. FEDERALIST, at 123 (No. 18) (Madison (with Hamilton)).

172. For Dickinson's earlier views, see Gummere, supra note 6 (ch. 1), at 180.

173. John Dickinson, LETTERS OF FABIUS V, reprinted in Ford, PAMPHLETS, supra note 46 (ch. 2), at 188, 191.

174. Id., at 193. See also Natelson, Dickinson, supra note 158 (ch. 1), at 445–47.

175. FEDERALIST, at 275 (No. 43) (Madison) (quoting Montesquieu).

176. Id., at 290 (No. 45) (Madison).

177. U.S. Const. Art. VI, cl. 2.

178. FEDERALIST, at 204 (No. 33) (Hamilton) ("But it is said that the laws of the Union are to be the SUPREME LAW of the land. But what inference can be drawn from this, or what would they amount to, if they were not to be supreme? It is evident they would amount to nothing. A LAW, by the very meaning of the term, includes supremacy. It is a rule which those to whom it is prescribed are bound to observe. This results from every political association. If individuals enter into a state of society, the laws of that society must be the supreme regulator of their conduct. If a number of political societies enter into a larger political society, the laws which the latter may enact, pursuant to the powers intrusted to it by its constitution, must necessarily be supreme over

those societies, and the individuals of whom they are composed.") (emphasis in original).

179. U.S. Const., Art. I, § 8, cl. 18. Hamilton acknowledged that this was "affectedly called" the "sweeping clause." FEDERALIST, at 203 (No. 33) (Hamilton).

180. See 3 Elliot, at 218. ("There is a general power given to [the national government] to make all laws that will enable them to carry their powers into effect. There are no limits pointed out. They are not restrained or controlled from making any law, however oppressive in its operation, which they may think necessary to carry their powers into effect."); 3 id., at 436 (remarks of Patrick Henry) ("If [members of Congress] think any law necessary for their personal safety, after perpetrating the most tyrannical and oppressive deeds, cannot they make it by this sweeping clause?").

Even James Madison acknowledged that "few parts of the Constitution had been assailed with more intemperance than" the Sweeping Clause. FEDERALIST, at 284 (No. 44) (Madison). See also J. Randy Beck, *The New Jurisprudence of the Necessary and Proper Clause*, 2002 U. ILL. L. REV. 581; Gary Lawson and Patricia B. Granger, *The "Proper" Scope of Federal Power: A Jurisdictional Interpretation of the Sweeping Clause*, 43 DUKE L. J. 267, 270–71 (1993).

181. FEDERALIST, at 285 (No. 44) (Madison).

182. 2 WORKS OF JAMES WILSON, supra note 123 (ch. 1), at 829.

183. See Wilson's speech to the Pennsylvania ratifying convention, 2 Elliot, at 422.

184. 1 WORKS OF JAMES WILSON, supra note 123 (ch. 1), at 248.

185. See 2 Elliot, at 187 (Oliver Ellsworth's remarks); 4 id., at 293 (Robert Barnwell's comment before the South Carolina ratifying convention that "the Amphictyonic council of the Greeks . . . was the palladium of their united liberties . . . [and] the cornerstone of their federal union.") (Jan. 16–17, 1788).

186. 1 WORKS OF JAMES WILSON, supra note 123 (ch. 1), at 248.

187. Id., at 249.

188. Id.

189. See id., at 264 ("Thus Greece was ruined, when the kings of Macedon obtained a seat among the Amphyctions."). See also John Dickinson, LETTERS OF FABIUS VII, reprinted in Ford, PAMPHLETS, supra note 46 (ch. 2), at 188, 201 (as for the Amphictyonic Council "it was not entirely an assembly of strictly democractical republics. Besides, it wanted a sufficiently close connection of its parts.").

190. Id., at 265.

191. Id., at 250.

192. John Dickinson, LETTERS OF FABIUS V, reprinted in Ford, PAMPHLETS, supra note 46 (ch. 2), at 188, 192.

193. 3 Elliot, at 210 (June 10, 1788).

194. Id.

195. 1 WORKS OF JAMES WILSON, supra note 123 (ch. 1), at 250, 253 (citing different translations of Tacitus). See also Mayer, supra note 136 (ch. 1), at 13–14, 19–20 (for influence of Tacitean depictions of Briton and Teutonic self-government on Whig historians and the Framing Generation); 5 CAF 38 (*Essays by a Farmer*, No. IV) (March 21, 1788) (quoting Tacitus, *Germania* xi. 1, in describing popular assemblies of Teutonic tribes).

196. See, for example, Edward A. Freeman, 1 History of Federal Government: History of the Greek Federations, at 123–26 (London: MacMillan 1863); Reinhold, Classica Americana, supra note 6 (ch. 1), at 103–04; Richard, supra note 6 (ch. 1), at 104–05.

197. Abbé Mably, Observations sur l'Histoire de la Grèce, at 9–10 (Paris, 1766). See also Nelson, supra note 93 (ch. 1), at 176–83.

198. Federalist, at 126 (No. 18) (Madison (with Hamilton)).

199. 2 Works of James Wilson, supra note 123 (ch. 1), at 762. See also Reinhold, Classica Americana, supra note 6 (ch. 1), at 104.

200. 2 Elliot, at 224.

201. See, for example, Geoffrey P. Miller, *The Song of Deborah: A Legal-Economic Analysis*, 144 U. Pa. L. Rev. 2293 (1996).

202. See J. A. O. Larsen, Representative Government in Greek and Roman History, at 130–44 (Berkeley: University of California Press, 1955) (description of the Commonality of the Three Gauls).

203. See Bederman, supra note 29 (ch. 2), at 124–34, 154–71; Georg Busolt, Griechische staatskunde (Heinrich Swoboda, ed., 3rd ed.; Munich: Beck, 1920–26); Gabriel Herman, Ritualized Friendship and the Greek City (Cambridge, UK: Cambridge University Press, 1987); J. A. O. Larsen, Greek Federal States (Oxford: Clarendon Press, 1968); Luigi Moretti, Ricerche sulle leghe greche (1962).

204. See Sir Frank Adcock and D. J. Mosley, Diplomacy in Ancient Greece, at 229 (London: Thames & Hudson, 1975). For the origins of the Greek word *amphictyony*, as a derivation of the phrase for "neighbor," see Coleman Phillipson, 2 The International Law and Custom of Ancient Greece and Rome, at 3 (London: MacMillan, 1911) (glossing Homer, 1 The Odyssey, at 41 (A. T. Murray transl. 1919; Loeb Classical Library, 1919) (passage ii.65) and Homer, 1 The Iliad, at 354, 391 (A. T. Murray transl., 1921; Loeb Classical Library reprint, 1929) (passages xviii. 212, xix. 104, and 109)). See also Lord Arundell of Wardover, Tradition Principally with Reference to the Mythology of the Law of Nations, at 361–63 (London: Burns & Oates, 1872).

205. See Adcock and Mosley, supra note 204, at 185–86, 229–31. See also 2 Phillipson, supra note , at 2–3.

206. See Thomas A. Walker, A History of the Law of Nations, at 39–40 (Cambridge, UK: Cambridge University Press, 1899).

207. See Bederman, supra note 29 (ch. 2), at 168–69 (discussing sources).

208. See Aeschines, supra note 129, at 357 (*Against Ctesiphon*, line 124). There is some authority for suggesting that there may have been a distinction between these two types of delegates to the amphictyonic council. See 2 Phillipson, supra note 204, at 6. The Council may have also had a permanent secretary and herald. See id. See also Georges Roux, L'Amphictinoie, Delphes et le temple d'Apollon au IVᵉ siècle (Lyon: 1979).

209. See Aeschines, supra note 129, at 399 (*Against Ctesiphon*, line 116).

210. See Adcock and Mosley, supra note 204, at 230 (discussing appointment of the Athenian orator, Aeschines, to plead causes before the Council).

211. See Aeschines, supra note 129, at 245, 393 (passages ii.115, iii.109–10). See also Freeman, supra note 196, at 129.

212. See 2 Phillipson, supra note 204, at 9.
213. See id., at 9–10; John Hosack, *On the Rise and Growth of the Law of Nations* 11 – 12 (London, 1882) (rep., 1982). For a vigorous debate on these events, compare N. G. L. Hammond, *Philips Actions in 347 and Early 346 BC*, 44 CQ 367 (1994), with John Buckler, *Reply*, 46 CQ 380 (1996). For more on the Third Sacred War, see John Buckler, *Thebes, Delphoi, and the Outbreak of Third Sacred War*, in LA BÉOTIE ANTIQUE, at 237 (P. Roesch and G. Argord eds.; Paris: Editions du Centre national de la recherche scientifique, 1985).
214. See Plutarch, 4 MORALIA, at 247–49 (Frank Cole Babbitt, transl., 1936) (Loeb Classical Library reprint, 1972) (*Quaest. Graec.*, passage 59).
215. See 2 Phillipson, supra note 204, at 10.
216. See 2 Cicero, supra note 180 (ch. 2), at 235 (*De inventione*, passage ii.23).
217. See John Hosack, ON THE RISE AND GROWTH OF THE LAW OF NATIONS, at 11–12 (London, 1882; rep., Littleton: F. B. Rothman, 1982).
218. See Adcock and Mosley, supra note 204, at 186; Phillipson, supra note 204, at 11; Sir Paul Vinogradoff, *Historical Types of International Law*, in 1 BIBLIOTECA VISSERIANA DISSERTATIONUM IUS INTERNATIONALE ILLUSTRANTIUM, at 1, 21–22 (1923).
219. Georg Grote, 2 HISTORY OF GREECE, at 176 (London: J. Murray, 1872).
220. Vinogradoff, supra note 218, at 22. See also Freeman, supra note 196, at 123–43.
221. See A. E. R. Boak, *Greek Interstate Associations and the League of Nations*, 15 AM. J. INT'L L. 375, 382 (1921).
222. See Elie Bikerman, *Remarques sur le droit des gens dans la Grèe classique*, 4 RIDA (ser. 1), at 99, 99–106 (1950); Victor Martin, LA VIE INTERNATIONALE DANS LA GRÈCE DES CITÉS, at 138–41, 176–78 (Paris: Recueil Sirey, 1940); Georges Ténékidès, *Droit International et Communautés Fédérales dans la Grèce des Cités*, 90 RECUEIL DES COURS DE L'ACADEMIE DE DROIT INTERNATIONALE DE LA HAYE, at 469, 549–49 (1956-II) (who considers some hegemonic *symmachies* to be termed as *synedria*, or "congresses").
223. See Larsen, supra note 203, at xiv–xv. See also Irwin L. Merker, *The Ptolemaic Officials and the League of the Islanders*, 19 HISTORIA 141 (1970); William P. Merrill, TO PLETHOS in a Treaty Concerning the Affairs of Argos, Knossos and Tylissos, 41 CQ 16 (1991).
224. Little is actually known about the Delian league, formed by Athens after the pan-Hellenic coalition against Persia began to disintegrate in the 470s BCE. See Adcock and Mosley, supra note 204, at 189; G. E. M. de Ste. Croix, THE ORIGINS OF THE PELOPONNESIAN WAR, at 303–07 (Ithaca: Cornell University Press, 1972); Noel D. Roberston, *The True Nature of the "Delian League," 478–461 BC*, 5 AM. J. ANCIENT HIST. 64, 110 (1980); E. M. Walker, *The Confederacy of Delos, 478–463 B.C.*, 5 CAMBRIDGE ANCIENT HISTORY 40–41 (Cambridge, UK: Cambridge University Press, 1970).
225. See, generally, Adcock and Mosley, supra note 204, at 244–46 (comparing Second Athenian League with Macedon's League of Corinth). See also John Buckler, *Theban Treaty Obligations in IG II² 40: A Postscript*, 20 HISTORIA 506 (1971).
226. See Adcock and Mosley, supra note 204, at 244–45.
227. See id., at 245.

228. See Larsen, supra note 203, at xvii–xix. See also scholarship on an Athenian inscription honoring one of the *proëdroi*. L. Robert, *Adeimantos et la Ligue de Corinthe*, 2 HELLENICA 15 (1946). For a general treatment on the League of Corinth (or Hellenic League), see Adcock and Mosley, supra note 204, at 244–46, 261–62 (for a translation of the oath taken by members of the league). See also S. Perlman, *Greek Diplomatic Tradition and the Corinithian League of Philip of Macedon*, 34 HISTORIA 153 (1985).

229. The translation of the inscription can be found in Boak, supra note 221, at 379.

230. See Martin, supra note 222, at 186–89, 242–44, 253–54 (on the operation of the league council), 262–65 (on admission of new members).

231. See id.

232. See also Henri Francotte, LA POLIS GRECQUE, at 151 (Paderborn: F. Schöningh, 1907). For a brief historiography of scholarship on questions of Greek citizenship, see Larsen, supra note 203, at xxviii n.2.

233. Larsen, supra note 203, at xiv.

234. See Robert J. Buck, A HISTORY OF BOEOTIA (Edmonton: University of Alberta Press, 1979); Paul Roesch, THESPIES ET LA CONFÉDÉRATION BÉOTIENNE (Paris: E. de Boccard, 1965). Our primary source for the early history of the Boeotian Confederacy comes from the *Hellenica Oxyrhynchia*, a papyrus that was only discovered in 1906, and was thus unknown to the Framing generation. See HELLENICA OXYRHYNCHIA, at 83 (P. R. McKechnie and S. J. Kerns, transl.; Warminister: Aris & Phillips, 1988).

235. See, generally, Freeman, supra note 196, at 323–51; Larsen, supra note 203; Boak, supra note 221, at 382. See also 2 Phillipson, supra note 204, at 63–64 (describing a "complete" alliance between Hierapythna and Priansus in the third century BCE).

236. Larsen, supra note 203, at xxi.

237. See id., at xxi–xxvii, 209.

238. See Robert J. Buck, *The Hellenistic Boiotian League*, 7 ANCIENT HIST. BULL. 100, 103–04 (1993).

239. See Hellenica Oxyrhynchia, supra note 234, at 83; Larsen, supra note 203, at 34–35.

240. See Freeman, supra note 196, at 155–84; Larsen, supra note 203, at 36, 175–80.

241. FEDERALIST, at 127 (No. 18) (Madison (with Hamilton)).

242. See 10 Livy, supra note 148 (ch. 1), at 97–111 (passages xxxv.33–36); 5 Polybius, supra note 51 (ch. 2), at 211 (passage xx.1).

243. See Larsen, supra note 203, at 209–12.

244. Id., at 214.

245. See Strabo, GEOGRAPHY, at 311–13 (Horace Leonard Jones transl., 1929) (Loeb Classical Library reprint, 1989) (passage xiv.664).

246. See id., at 313–15 (passage xiv.665). See also Larsen, supra note 203, at 254–56. See also Freeman, supra note 196, at 208–17; Richard Bernstein, *A Congress Buried in Sand, Inspired One on a Hill*, NEW YORK TIMES, Sept. 19, 2005, at A1, col. 1 (describing excavations at Patara, seat of the Lycian League).

247. Larsen, supra note 203, at 215. See also Freeman, supra note 196, at 254–322.

248. See 1 Polybius, supra note 51 (ch. 2), at 347 (passages ii.43.1–2). See also Walbank, supra note 56 (ch. 2), at 235.

249. See Larsen, supra note 203, at 221–23.

250. See id., at 223–31.

251. See 1 Polybius, supra note 51 (ch. 2), at 337 (passage ii.38.6); 6 id., 85 (passages xxix.24.6–8) (indicating that all men over age 30 could vote in the Achaean league assemblies, although there may have also been a property qualification for certain offices or civic responsibilities).

252. See 1 Polybius, supra note 51 (ch. 2), at 333–35 (passages ii.37.7–11).

253. See 11 Livy, supra note 148 (ch. 1), at 101 (passage xxxviii.30.3).

254. See 6 Polybius, supra note 51 (ch. 2), at 431 (passage xxxviii.18.3).

255. See McDonald, supra note 214 (ch. 1), at 277–79; Rosen, supra note 164 (ch. 1), at 102–03.

256. 2 Elliot 403 (July 2, 1788).

257. FEDERALIST, at 107–08 (No. 15) (Hamilton).

258. *Saenz v. Roe*, 526 U.S. 489, 504, n. 17 (1999) (citing *U.S. Term Limits, Inc. v. Thornton*, 514 U.S. 779, 838 (1995) (Kennedy, J., concurring)) ("The Framers split the atom of sovereignty. It was the genius of their idea that our citizens would have two political capacities, one state and one federal, each protected from incursion by the other.").

259. 1 DEBATES ON THE CONSTITUTION, supra note 239 (ch. 2), at 196 (Madison's letter to Jefferson of Oct. 24, 1787).

260. See McDonald, STATES' RIGHTS, supra note 155, at 1–2, 19–25.

261. U.S. Const. Art. VIII ("The Ratification of the Conventions of nine States, shall be sufficient for the Establishment of this Constitution between the States so ratifying the Same.").

262. U.S. Const. Art. V (requiring ratification by three-fourths of the States – whether by their legislatures or by constitutional conventions – in order for an amendment to enter force).

263. U.S. Const., Amend. 10.

264. See McDonald, STATES' RIGHTS, supra note 155, at 24–25.

265. See THOMAS JEFFERSON: AN ANTHOLOGY, at 135 (Peter S. Onuf, ed.; New York, 1999).

266. See Susan Ford Wiltshire, GREECE, ROME AND THE BILL OF RIGHTS, at 176–81 (Norman: University of Oklahoma Press, 1992) (analogizing Tenth Amendment federalism with the autonomy of provinces in the Roman Empire).

267. See Gummere, supra note 6 (ch. 1), at 187; Kopff, supra note 318 (ch. 1), at 80.

268. See Worden, Nedham, in REPUBLICANISM, LIBERTY, supra note 3 (pr.), at 56.

269. See, for example, James D. Barnett, *The Bicameral System in State Legislation*, 9 AM. POL. SCI. REV. 449, 451 (1915); Matthew J. Herrington, *Popular Sovereignty in Pennsylvania, 1776–1791*, 67 TEMPLE L. REV. 575 (1993); John P. Senning, THE ONE-HOUSE LEGISLATURE, at 75–77 (New York: McGraw Hill, 1937); Alvin W. Johnson, THE UNICAMERAL LEGISLATURE, at 19–44 (London: Oxford University Press, 1938); Banning, supra note 164 (ch. 1), at 224–25; Wood, supra note 3 (pr.), at 227–37.

270. Cf. FEDERALIST 465 (No. 78) (Hamilton) (describing the Judiciary as "the least dangerous branch").

     For English political writings advocating bicameralism, see Bailyn, supra note 337 (pr.), at 39–40; Bolingbroke, supra note 141 (ch. 2) (*A Dissertation*

Upon Parties); Harrington, supra note 138 (ch. 2), at 174 (*Commonwealth of Oceana*, referring to an upper legislative house as a "senat"); David Hume, IDEA OF A PERFECT COMMONWEALTH (1777), in ESSAYS, MORAL, POLITICAL AND LITERARY, at 512, 515 (Eugene F. Miller, ed., rev. ed.; 1987). See also Banning, supra note 164 (ch. 1), at 204 (for Hume's influence on Madison's FEDERALIST (No.10)).

271. See Aristotle, ATHENIAN CONSTITUTION, supra note 175 (ch. 2), at 121–29 (passages xliii–xlv).

272. See Machiavelli, supra note 113 (ch. 2), at 34–35.

273. See Montesquieu, supra note 124 (ch. 2), at 65.

274. Id., at 145–46.

275. See James Harrington, THE COMMONWEALTH OF OCEANA AND A SYSTEM OF POLITICS (J. G. A. Pocock ed.; Cambridge, UK: Cambridge University Press, 1992).

276. See id., at 25–28, 141–42.

277. See id., at 28–29, 142.

278. See id., at 29, 143.

279. See id., at 29.

280. See id., at 29, 143.

281. See id., at 37–38.

282. See id., at 28–29, 142.

283. See id., at 25–28, 141–41. See David Hume, *On Some Remarkable Customs* (1777), in Hume, supra note 151 (ch. 2), at 368–69; Blair Worden, *Republicanism and Restoration*, in REPUBLICANISM, LIBERTY, supra note 3 (pr.), at 139, 162.

284. Harrington, supra note 275, at 143.

285. See id.

286. See id., at 155 (glossing Machiavelli, i.6). See also Nelson, supra note 93 (ch. 1), at 87–126; Rahe, *Jefferson's Machiavellian Moment*, in REASON AND REPUBLICANISM, supra note 134 (ch. 2), at 61.

287. See Sellers, supra note 85 (ch. 1), at 24–26, 40; S. B. Benjamin, *The Significance of the Massachusetts Convention of 1780*, 70 TEMPLE L. REV. 883, 895–901 (1997).

288. 4 PAPERS OF JOHN ADAMS, supra note 321 (ch. 1), at 88.

289. See Bailyn, BEGIN THE WORLD, supra note 11 (pr.), at 136–40; Douglas Dakin, TURGOT AND THE ANCIEN RÉGIME IN FRANCE (New York: Octagon Books, 1965); Malcolm Hill, STATESMAN OF THE ENLIGHTENMENT: THE LIFE OF ANNE-ROBERT TURGOT (London: Othila Press, 1999); Thompson, supra note 35 (ch. 1), at 128–29.

290. See 4 WORKS OF JOHN ADAMS, supra note 87 (ch. 1), at 273–74 (editor's preface), at 278–81 (text of Turgot's letter).

291. Id., at 279.

292. Id., at 444 (original emphasis omitted). See also Nelson, supra note 93 (ch. 1), at 225–30.

293. See 4 WORKS OF JOHN ADAMS, supra note 87 (ch. 1), at 445–47.

294. Id., at 447–48. For a critique of Adams's political theory, see Wood, supra note 3 (pr.).

295. See CITIZEN OF AMERICA [NOAH WEBSTER], AN EXAMINATION, reprinted in Ford, PAMPHLETS, supra note 46 (ch. 2), at 31 ("This fact suggests the

expediency of dividing the powers of legislation between the two bodies of men" and noting that "even in a small republic, composed of men, equal in property and abilities, and all meeting for the purpose of making laws, like the old Romans in the field of Mars, a division of the body into two independent branches, would be a necessary step to prevent disorders. . . . ").

296. FEDERALIST, at 206 (No. 34) (Hamilton) (original emphasis). See also Galston, supra note 230 (ch. 1), at 50.

297. 1 WORKS OF JAMES WILSON, supra note 123 (ch. 1), at 290 (*Lectures on Law*).

298. Id., at 291.

299. 1 Farrand, at 347 (June 20) (Yates's notes).

300. It is not clear whether the very selection of this name – unlike section 47 of the 1776 Pennsylvania Constitution's creation of the office of "the Council of Censors," which was charged with meeting every seven years to review the compliance of government organs with the state constitution, and to propose amendments – was intended to have classical evocations. See Gummere, supra note 6 (ch. 1), at 186–87; Herrington, supra note 269, at 588–92; Eidelberg, supra note 7 (pr.), at 106–65. See also VT. CONST. OF 1777, § XLIV (-providing for the authority of the Council of Censors).

301. 1 Farrand, at 151–52 (June 7) (Madison's notes).

302. 1 Farrand, at 153 (June 7) (Madison's notes).

303. FEDERALIST, at 384 (No. 63) (Madison). To similar effect is Hamilton's speech before the New York Ratifying Convention. See 2 Elliot, at 302 ("The history of ancient and modern republics had taught them that many of the evils which these republics suffered arose from the want of a certain balance and mutual control indispensable to a wise administration.").

304. Id., at 385. See also Epstein, supra note 253 (ch. 2), at 167–71; Kesler, *Federalist 10*, in Kesler, supra note 230 (ch. 1), at 39.

305. John Dickinson, *Fabius V*, in Ford, PAMPHLETS, supra note 46 (ch. 2), at 189–90.

306. CITIZEN OF AMERICA [NOAH WEBSTER], AN EXAMINATION, reprinted in Ford, PAMPHLETS, supra note 46 (ch. 2), at 38.

307. See 3 Elliot, at 175–76.

308. See Lintott, supra note 227 (ch. 1), at 34.

309. See 2 Elliot, at 62 (Massachusetts Convention) (Jan. 21, 1788) (Martin Kinsley); id., at 68 (Jan. 22, 1788) (Joseph Willard); 6 CAF 19 (*Essays by Cincinnatus, No. IV*) (Nov. 22, 1787).

310. 2 id., at 69. See also Sellers, supra note 85 (ch. 1), at 186.

311. 2 Elliot, at 253–54.

312. See Clinton, supra note 6 (pr.), at 905.

313. See Richard, supra note 6 (ch. 1), at 116–17; Eidelberg, supra note 7 (pr.), at 78–92.

314. See 1 Farrand, at 454 (June 28) (Yates's notes) (Luther Martin's remark that "The basis of all ancient and modern confederacies is the freedom and the independency of the States composing it. The states forming the amphyctionic council were equal, though Lacedemon, one of the greatest states, attempted the exclusion of three of the lesser States from this right. The plan reported, it is true, only intends to diminish those rights, not to annihilate them – It was the ambition and power of the great Grecian states which at last ruined this

respectable council."). See also id., at 459 (Paterson's notes) (recording that Martin quoted from volume 4 of Rollins' Ancient History (at page 79)). See also Chinard, supra note 77, at 228; 2 CAF 284 (Letters from a Federal Farmer No. X) (Jan. 7, 1788) (proposing a senate of more than a hundred members, as were the Roman and Punic bodies of that name).

315. U.S. Const. Art. V. For criticisms of this provision, see William N. Eskridge, Jr., *The One Senator, One Vote Clause*, 12 CONST. COMMENT. 159 (1995); Suzanna Sherry, *Our Unconstitutional Senate*, 12 CONST. COMMENT. 213 (1995).

316. FEDERALIST, at 279 (No. 43) (Madison). See also 4 Elliot, at 177 (North Carolina) (statement by James Iredell).

317. 2 Farrand, at 290 (Aug. 14) (Madison's notes).

318. 2 Farrand, at 290–92 (Aug. 14) (Daniel Carroll). See also Rakove, supra note 164 (ch. 1), at 171.

319. U.S. Const. Art. II, § 2.

320. Id., Art. I, § 3, cl. 6.

321. U.S. Const. Art. II, § 2.

322. U.S. Const Art. I, § 2, cl. 5.

323. U.S. Const. Art. I, § 7, cl. 1.

324. U.S. Const. Art. II, § 1, cl. 3 and Amend. 12.

325. 2 Farrand, at 235 (August 9) (Madison's notes). Ultimately, the Framers adopted a rule that Senators had to be at least citizens for 9 years. See U.S. Const. Art. I, § 3, cl. 3.

326. FEDERALIST, at 402–03 (No. 66) (Hamilton) (emphasis in original).

327. See Larsen, supra note 203, at 296–97.

328. See MacDowell, supra note 291 (ch. 2), at 27–29; Manville, supra note 285 (ch. 2), at 74–77. See also 1 Plutarch, supra note 112 (ch. 1), at 455–57 (*Solon*, xix).

329. See Chapter 2, at Notes 176–79 with text. The Roman senate was actually created under the regime of the kings, before their overthrow and the establishment of the republic. See Lintott, supra note 227 (ch. 2), at 67. For the functioning of the Roman senate at later periods, see Richard Talbert, THE SENATE OF IMPERIAL ROME (Princeton: Princeton University Press, 1984); C. E. V. Nixon, *The rôle of the Roman Senate in the Early Empire*, 23 ANCIENT HISTORY 95 (1993).

330. See Chapter 2, at Notes 98–102 with text.

331. N. Hooke, OBSERVATIONS ON I. THE ANSWER OF M. L'ABBÉ DE VERTOT TO THE LATE EARL STANHOPE'S INQUIRY, CONCERNING THE SENATE OF ANCIENT ROME: DATED DECEMBER 1719. II. A DISSERTATION UPON THE CONSTITU-TION OF THE ROMAN SENATE, BY A GENTLEMAN: PUBLISHED IN 1743. III. A TREATISE ON THE ROMAN SENATE, BY DR. CONYERS MIDDLETON: PUB-LISHED IN 1747. IV. AN ESSAY ON THE ROMAN SENATE, BY DR. THOMAS CHAPMAN: PUBLISHED IN 1750. BY MR. HOOKE (London, 1758).

332. CITIZEN OF AMERICA [NOAH WEBSTER], reprinted in Ford, PAMPHLETS, supra note 46 (ch. 2), at 37–39 n.* (on the number and election of Roman senators).

333. See 6 Polybius, supra note 303 (ch. 2), at 263–65 (passage xxxiii.1.5); 6 Plutarch, supra note 112 (ch. 1), at 455 (*Aemilius Paulus*, xxxviii) (censor acted to designate

"first senator"). See also 1 Brennan, supra note 307 (ch. 2), at 111 –29; Greenidge, supra note 84 (ch. 2), at 202–04, 268–69.

334. See Lintott, supra note 227 (ch. 1), at 84–85.

335. U.S. Const. Art. I, § 3, cl. 4.

336. 3 Polybius, supra note 51 (ch. 2), at 303–05 (passage vi.15.5) ("For it is obvious that the legions require constant supplies, and without the consent of the senate, neither corn, clothing, nor pay can be provided; so that the commander's plans come to nothing, if the senate chooses to be deliberately negligent and obstructive."); 5 Plutarch, supra note 112 (ch. 1), at 163–65, 177–85 (*Pompey*, xx, xxv–xxvii) (funding of campaign against pirates). See also Greenidge, supra note 84 (ch. 2), at 286–87.

337. See 12 Livy, supra note 148 (ch. 1), at 147 (passage xl.46.16); 13 id., at 143 (passage xliv.16.9); 5 Plutarch, supra note 112 (ch. 1), at 439–41 (*Marcellus*, ii) (impeachment of Capitolinus as aedile); at 497–501 (*Marcellus*, xxiii) (Marcellus acquitted in impeachment proceeding).

338. See Lintott, supra note 227 (ch. 1), at 19; Greenidge, supra note 84 (ch. 2), at 277–78.

339. Lintott, supra note 227 (ch. 1), at 101. See also Brennan, supra note 93 (ch. 2), at 388–403; Greenidge, supra note 84 (ch. 2), at 199–205, 285–86. See also 5 Plutarch, supra note 112 (ch. 1), at 267–73 (*Pompey*, lviii–lix); 8 id., at 339–41 (*Cato the Younger*, xliii).

340. See Lintott, supra note 227 (ch. 1), at 9–15, 19–20. See also 9 Plutarch, supra note 112 (ch. 1), at 401 –07 (*Pyrrhus*, xviii–xix) (senate's consideration of peace terms with Pyrrhus of Epiros). See also J. Linderski, *Ambassadors go to Rome*, in Les Relations internationales: Astes du Collque de Strasbourg, 15–17 Juin 1993 (Strasbourg: University of Science and the Humanities Press, 1995); J. W. Rich, Declaring War in the Roman Republic in the Period of Transmarine Expansion (Brussels: Collection Latomus, 1976). See also Walbank, supra note 56 (ch. 2), at 680–81. In the Roman republic, although the Senate was charged with deliberating on issues of war and peace, actual declarations of war were made by the citizen assemblies and by the college of fetials.

341. Federalist, at 391 (No. 64) (Jay).

342. Thirty years old, as indicated at U.S. Const. Art. I, § 3, cl. 3. For more on the age requirements in the Roman senate, see Lintott, supra note 227 (ch. 1), at 69–70.

343. Art. Confed. IX, para. 5.

344. See, generally, Jennings Bryan Sanders, Evolution of executive departments of the Continental Congress, 1774–1789 (Gloucester, Mass.: Peter Smith, 1971) (rep., 1935).

345. Art. Confed. IX, para. 5.

346. See, generally, Edmund Cody Burnett, The Continental Congress (New York: W. W. Norton, 1964); Calvin C. Jillson, Congressional dynamics: structure, coordination, and choice in the first American Congress, 1774–1789 (Palo Alto: Stanford University Press, 1994); Max B. May, The Continental Congress, 1775 to the surrender of Cornwallis: its organization, and its direct control of the diplomatic

AND MILITARY AFFAIRS OF THE COUNTRY DURING THE REVOLUTION (Cincinnati, 1900); Jack N. Rakove, THE BEGINNINGS OF NATIONAL POLITICS: AN INTERPRETIVE HISTORY OF THE CONTINENTAL CONGRESS (Baltimore: Johns Hopkins University Press, 1982); Jennings Bryan Sanders, THE PRESIDENCY OF THE CONTINENTAL CONGRESS, 1774–89; A STUDY IN AMERICAN INSTITUTIONAL HISTORY (2nd rev. ed.; Chicago: 1930).

347. Art. Confed. IX, para. 5.

348. Id., Art. X.

349. Clinton, BRIEF HISTORY, supra note 6 (pr.), at 895.

350. See id., at 894–95 and sources cited at note 326 supra. See also Clinton L. Rossiter, CONSTITUTIONAL DICTATORSHIP (Princeton: Princeton University Press, 1948); Mansfield, Taming, supra note 134 (ch. 2).

351. Machiavelli, supra note 113 (ch. 2), at 94.

352. Id., at 95. See also Mansfield, MACHIAVELLI, supra note 113 (ch. 2), at 110–26.

353. Machiavelli, supra note 113 (ch. 2), at 96. For a brief intellectual history of the influence of the Roman institution of dictatorship, see Mansfield, TAMING, supra note 134 (ch. 2), at 82–85. For an ancient Athenian analogy of dictatorship – the *aisymnetai* – see id., at 312 n.25 (citing Aristotle, POLITICS, supra note 96 (ch. 1), at 251, 325 (passages 1285a29–42 and 1295a11–17)).

354. See 5 Plutarch, supra note 112 (ch. 1), at 177–79 (*Pompey*, xxv). See also Robert Harris, *Pirates of the Mediterranean*, NEW YORK TIMES, Sept. 30, 2006, at A23, col. 1.

355. 7 Plutarch, supra note 112 (ch. 1), at 575 (*Caesar*, lvii).

356. 1 Livy, supra note 148 (ch. 1), at 277, 313–15 (passages ii.18–30); 2 id., at 71–73, 315, 341–43, 441 (passages iii.20.8; iv.17.8; iv.26.6; and iv.56.8); 3 id., 327 (passage vi.38.3); 4 id., at 121–23 (passage viii.32.3).

357. See Lintott, supra note 227 (ch. 1), at 109–10; Greenidge, supra note 84 (ch. 2), at 191–96. See also 3 Livy, supra note 148 (ch. 1), at 453–55 (passages vii.28.7–8); 4 id., at 73 (passages viii.18.12–13); 4 id., at 273 (passage ix.28.6). See also Jolowicz and Nicholas, supra note 177 (ch. 2), at 55–56; Kunkel, supra note 100 (ch. 2), at 17.

358. See Cicero, DE LEGIBUS, supra note 325 (ch. 1), at 467 (passage iii.9); 2 Livy, supra note 148 (ch. 1), at 99 (passage iii.29.7); 6 id., 73–77 (passages xxiii.22.2–11); 5 Plutarch, supra note 112 (ch. 1), at 259 (*Pompey*, liv) (Pompey elected sole consul); 505 (*Marcellus*, xxiv) (suggesting that dictators could only be appointed by consuls or praetors); 7 id., at 513 (*Caesar*, xxviii) (Pompey's election as sole consul "a more legal sort of monarchy ... [than] the dictatorship"). See also Lintott, supra note 227 (ch. 1), at 110–11; 2 Mommsen, supra note 177 (ch. 2), at 147–49, 160–61; 1 William E. Heitland, THE ROMAN REPUBLIC § 150 (Cambridge, UK: Cambridge University Press, 1923).

359. See Jolowicz and Nicholas, supra note 177 (ch. 2), at 36; Greenidge, supra note 84 (ch. 2), at 193–95; Lintott, supra note 227 (ch. 1), at 111. See also Cicero, DE OFFICIIS, supra note 293 (ch. 1), at 219–21 (passage ii.49–50); 1 Livy, supra note 148 (ch. 1), at 277 (passage ii.18.8); 1 id., at 315 (passage ii.30.5); 2 id., at 71–73 (passage iii.20.8); JUSTINIAN'S DIGEST 1.2.2.18 (Pomponius). But see 3

Dionysius of Halicarnassus, supra note 23 (ch. 2), at 211–27 (passages v.70–74) (suggesting that consul's or senate's appointment of dictators was intended to infringe the power of the popular assemblies and tribunes); Mansfield, TAMING, supra note 134 (ch. 2), at 84–85.

360. See Machiavelli, supra note 113 (ch. 2), at 107–12 (for an extended discussion of the *decemvirs*, and their rise to power and fall).

361. See 2 Livy, supra note 148 (ch. 1), at 117–23 (passages iii.36–37) (likening decemvirs to dictators in this respect).

362. Id., at 97. See also Mansfield, MACHIAVELLI, supra note 113 (ch. 2), at 126–39.

363. See Brennan, supra note 307 (ch. 2), at 49–53. See also 2 Plutarch, supra note 112 (ch. 1), at 95 (*Camillus*, i) (on the institution of military tribunes).

364. See Millar, POLITICAL THOUGHT, supra note 306 (ch. 2), at 129.

365. Montesquieu, supra note 124 (ch. 2), at 182. For a gloss on this text, see Saikrishna B. Prakash and Michael D. Ramsey, *Foreign Affairs and the Jeffersonian Executive: A Defense*, 89 MINN. L. REV. 1591, 1609–10, 1633–34 (2005); Carrithers, in MONTESQUIEU'S SCIENCE, supra note 327 (ch. 1), at 139–41.

366. Montesquieu, supra note 124 (ch. 2), at 193.

367. See id., at 192–93.

368. Id., at 185.

369. Id., at 188.

370. See Aristotle, ATHENIAN CONSTITUTION, supra note 175 (ch. 2), at 125–27 (passage xliv) (Board of Presidents), at 151–63 (passages lv–lx) (nine archons); 2 Dionysius of Halicarnassus, supra note 23 (ch. 2), at 497 (passage iv.73.4) (discussing dual kingship as key to Spartan constitution). See also MacDowell, supra note 291 (ch. 2), at 24–27.

371. See Larsen, supra note 203, at 217 (discussing Polybius' account).

372. Montesquieu, supra note 124 (ch. 2), at 189.

373. Id., at 190. See also Mansfield, TAMING, supra note 134 (ch. 2), at 214–46.

374. See Montesquieu, supra note 124 (ch. 2), at 193.

375. Mentioned in Aristotle's REPUBLIC, at passage ii. 10.

376. See Montesquieu, supra note 124 (ch. 2), at 191 and n.14 (citing 6 Dionysius of Halicarnassus, supra note 23 (ch. 2), at 45–51 (passage ix.37.3) (Genucius the tribune's action against former consuls).

377. See id., at 191–92.

378. See James Harrington, THE COMMONWEALTH OF OCEANA AND A SYSTEM OF POLITICS, at 67–77, 121, 241–65 (J. G. A. Pocock, ed.; Cambridge, UK: Cambridge University Press, 1992).

379. Id., at 122.

380. Id.

381. Id., at 171–72.

382. Id., at 172.

383. See Bolingbroke, POLITICAL WRITINGS, at 167–68 (David Armitage, ed.; Cambridge, UK: Cambridge University Press, 1997).

384. See id., at 129.

385. Id., at 130.

386. See id.

387. See id. (institution of dictatorship "suspended" or "endangered" the Roman constitution).
388. Mansfield, Taming, supra note 134, at 247–78. See also Sirico, supra note 4 (pr.), at 459–63 (discussing the *Federalist*'s consideration of the decemvirs).
389. 1 Farrand, at 74 (June 1) (Pierce's notes).
390. See 1 Farrand, at 244 (June 15) (Madison's notes) (referring to "persons" serving as Executive).
391. Id., at 254 (June 16) (Madison's notes). See also Galston, supra note 230 (ch. 1), at 51; Kennedy, supra note 87 (ch. 1), at 133; Rahe, supra note 3 (pr.), at 607–09; Richard, supra note 6 (ch. 1), at 115. For more on Wilson's classical view on this subject, see R. M. Gummere, *Classical Precedents in the Writings of James Wilson*, 32 Transactions of the Colonial Society of Massachusetts 534 (1937).
392. See Harold J. Krent, *Conditioning the president's conditional pardon power*, 89 Cal. L. Rev. 1665 (2001); Gregory C. Sisk, *Suspending the pardon power during the twilight of a presidential term*, 67 Mo. L. Rev. 13 (2002).
393. These functions were neatly summarized in Justice Hugo Black's observation that the President's "functions in the law-making process" include "the recommending of laws he thinks wise and the vetoing of law he thinks bad." *Youngstown Sheet & Tube Co. v. Sawyer*, 343 U.S. 579, 587 (1952). See also Vasan Kesavan and J. Gregory Sidak, *The Legislator-in-Chief*, 44 Wm. and Mary L. Rev. 1 (2002).
394. See U.S. Const. Art. II, §§ 2 and 3. See also Saikrishna Bangalore Prakash, *Hail to the chief administrator: the Framers and the president's administrative powers*, 102 Yale L. J. 991 (1993).
395. Citizen of America [Noah Webster], Debates on the Constitution, supra note 239 (ch. 2), at 136.
396. Id.
397. U.S. Const. Art. II, § 1, cl. 5.
398. Id., Art. I, § 2, cl. 2; Art. I, § 3, cl. 3.
399. See 3 Livy, supra note 148 (ch. 1), at 513 (passage vii.42.2); 4 id., at 405 (passage x.13.8); 9 Plutarch, supra note 112 (ch. 1), at 493 (*Gaius Marius*, xii). See also Jolowicz and Nicholas, supra note 177 (ch. 2), at 79; Lintott, supra note 227 (ch. 1), at 145; Greenidge, supra note 84 (ch. 2), at 186.
400. 2 CAF 311.
401. Taylor, supra note 173 (ch. 2), at 187–88.
402. See Federalist, at 167 (No. 25) (Hamilton) ("It was a fundamental maxim of the Lacedaemonian commonwealth, that the post of admiral should not be conferred twice on the same person. The Peloponnesian confederates, having suffered a severe defeat at sea from the Athenians, demanded Lysander, who had before served with success in that capacity, to command the combined fleets. The Lacedaemonians, to gratify their allies, and yet preserve the semblance of an adherence to their ancient institutions, had recourse to the flimsy subterfuge of investing Lysander with the real power of admiral, under the nominal title of vice-admiral." Hamilton concluded that "nations pay little regard to rules and maxims calculated to run counter to the necessities of society."). See also Walling, supra note 131 (ch. 1), at 133–34.

403. See George Anastalpo, The Constitution of 1787: A Commentary 106 (Baltimore: Johns Hopkins University Press, 1989); Bruce Ackerman, The Failure of the Founding Fathers: Jefferson, Marshall, and the Rise of Presidential Democracy (Cambridge, Mass.: Harvard University Press, 2005); Theodore J. Lowi, The Personal President: Power Invested, Promise Unfulfilled (Ithaca: Cornell University Press, 1985).

404. See U.S. Const. Art. I, § 7.

405. See 1 Farrand, at 432 (June 26) (Yates's notes) (remarks by Hamilton) ("What was the tribunitial power of Rome? It was instituted by the plebeians as a guard against the patricians. But was this a sufficient check? No – The only distinction which remained at Rome was, at last, between the rich and the poor.").

406. See New York Ratification Debates, reprinted in 2 Debates on the Constitution, supra note 239 (ch. 2), at 768 (June 21, 1788).

407. Id., at 774.

408. See Christopher N. May, Presidential Defiance of "Unconstitutional" Laws: Reviving the Royal Prerogative, at 11–15 (Westport: Greenwood Press, 1998).

409. See 3 Polybius, supra note 51 (ch. 2), at (passage vi.16.5) ("the tribunes are always obliged to act as the people decree and to pay every attention to their wishes."). See also Lintott, supra note 227 (ch. 1), at 207–08.

410. See Lintott, supra note 227 (ch. 1), at 122–28.

411. See id., at 106–07 (noting the difficulty of restraining consuls in office).

412. See id., at 123–24. The tribune's power of coercion against citizens was based on statute. See 1 Crawford, Roman Statutes, supra note 193 (ch. 2), at 7 (lex lat. Bant.), at 13 (lex osca. Bant.); 2 id., at 46 (Lex Silia).

413. The Independent Freeholder [Alexander White?], Jan. 18, 1788, reprinted in 8 Documentary Histrory, supra note 320 (ch. 1), at 311.

414. Federalist, at 423 (No. 70) (Hamilton).

415. Id., at 425. See also Walling, supra note 131 (ch. 1), at 129; Anastalpo, supra note 403, at 110, 113; Epstein, supra note 253 (ch. 2), at 171–76; Harvey C. Mansfield, Jr., *Republicanizing the Executive*, in Kesler, supra note 230 (ch. 1), at 168; Sirico, supra note 4 (pr.), at 453–59.

416. See 1 Farrand, at 74 (June 1) (Pierce's notes) (Wilson's comment), 254 (June 16) (Madison's notes) (Wilson's comments). See also Gummere, supra note 6 (ch. 1), at 185–86. See also Thornton Anderson, Creating the Constitution: The Constitutional Convention of 1787 and the First Congress, at 168 (University Park, Pa.: Pennsylvania State University Press, 1993); S. E. Finer, The Man on Horseback: The Role of the Military in Politics (2nd ed.; Boulder: Westview Press, 1988).

417. See 12 Papers of Thomas Jefferson, supra note 280 (ch. 1), at 351, 440–41.

418. See 2 Works of James Wilson, supra note 123 (ch. 1), at 446–48 (discussion of ancient Egyptian tribunals and the Athenian Areopagus), at 494–95 (Roman courts).

419. See Chapter 1, at Notes 320–27 with text. See especially the sources indicated id., at Note 325.

420. U.S. Const. Amend. 9.

421. See 1 WORKS OF JAMES WILSON, supra note 123 (ch. 1), at 152 and n.q (quoting Cicero, DE LEGIBUS (passage ii.4), for the notion "That first and final law... is the mind of God, who forces or prohibits everything by reason.").

422. Id., at 145 (quoting Cicero, DE RE PUBLICA (passage i.3)).

423. See Wiltshire, supra note 266, at 169–75.

424. 1 ANNALS OF CONGRESS, at 456 (1834) (debate of 1790).

425. 1 THE BILL OF RIGHTS: A DOCUMENTARY HISTORY, at 616 (Bernard Schwartz, ed.; New York: Chelsea House, 1971) (Madison letter to Jefferson of Oct. 17, 1788).

426. For more on which, see Raoul Berger, *Natural law and judicial review: reflections of an earthbound lawyer*, 61 U. CIN. L. REV. 5 (1992); Joseph C. Cascarelli, *Is judicial review grounded in and limited by natural law?*, 30 CUMB. L. REV. 373 (2001); Robert P. George, *Natural law, the Constitution, and the theory and practice of judicial review*, 69 FORDHAM L. REV. 2269 (2001); Helen K. Michael, *The role of natural law in early American constitutionalism: did the founders contemplate judicial enforcement of 'unwritten' individual rights?* 69 N.C.L. REV. 421 (1991).

427. See Lintott, supra note 227 (ch. 1), at 107–09; Greenidge, supra note 84 (ch. 2), at 204–08. See also 5 Plutarch, supra note 112 (ch. 1), at 123–25 (*Pompey*, iv) (prosecution for public defalcation); 8 id., at 341–43 (*Cato the Younger*, xliv) (praetor review of election corruption).

428. See MacDowell, supra note 291 (ch. 2), at 27–29.

429. See Rahe, supra note 3 (pr.), at 174–75. See Aristotle, POLITICS, supra note 96 (ch. 1), at 145 (passages 1271a6–8); 177–79 (passages 1275b8–10); Xenophon, CONSTITUTION OF THE LACADAEMONIANS, supra note 69 (ch. 2), at 163 (passage viii.4)

430. See Clinton, BRIEF HISTORY, supra note 6 (pr.), at 895.

431. FEDERALIST, at 465–66 (No. 78) (Hamilton) (emphasis in original). See also Carrese, supra note 127 (ch. 2); Epstein, supra note 253 (ch. 2), at 185–92.

432. U.S. Const., Art. I, § 9, cl. 3; art. I, § 10, cl. 1.

433. FEDERALIST, at 282 (No. 44) (Madison). See also *United States v. Brown*, 381 U.S. 437, 442 (1965) ("the Bill of Attainder Clause was intended not as a narrow, technical... prohibition, but rather as an implementation of the separation of powers, a general safeguard against legislative exercise of the judicial function, or more simply – trial by legislature.").

434. See Montesquieu, supra note 124 (ch. 2), at passage xii. 19. See also *Special Project, The Collateral Consequences of a Criminal Conviction*, 23 VAND. L. REV. 929, 941–42 (1970) (discussing ancient history of disenfranchisement and loss of other political rights).

435. See Cicero, DE LEGIBUS, supra note 325 (ch. 1), at 471, 511 (passages iii.11 and iii.44); Cicero, DE RE PUBLICA, supra note 325 (ch. 1), at 175 (passage ii.61). See also Lintott, supra note 227 (ch. 1), at 151. *Privlegium* was also the practice by later Roman emperors to grant anomalous rights (called *favorable privilegium*) or impose irregular obligations (odious) on an individual. BLACK's LAW DICTIONARY, at 1079 (5th ed.; 1979).

436. Id., at 466–68 (No. 78) (Hamilton) (emphasis in original). See also Carrese, supra note 127 (ch. 2), at 197–207 (for a gloss on FEDERALIST (No. 78));

Eidelberg, supra note 7 (pr.), at 202–46; James Stoner, *Constitutionalism and Judging in* The Federalist, in Kesler, supra note 230 (ch. 1), at 203, 210–16.

437. *Calder v. Bull,* 3 U.S. (3 Dall.) 386, 388 (1798) (Chase, J.) (emphasis in original) (and in describing "the very nature of our free Republican governments," is quoting (without attribution) from book XI of Montesquieu's *Spirit of the Laws*). But see id., at 398, 398–99 (Iredell, J., concurring) (for a critique of the application of natural law in the context of *ex post facto* legislation).

438. See Wood, supra note 3 (pr.), at 154–156, 407–08; Mary Patterson Clarke, PARLIAMENTARY PRIVILEGE IN THE AMERICAN COLONIES, 49–51 (New Haven: Yale University Press, 1943); *Judicial Action by the Provincial Legislature of Massachusetts,* 15 HARV. L. REV. 208 (1902) (collecting documents from 1708–1709).

439. FEDERALIST, at 484 (No. 81) (Hamilton). See also Carrese, supra note 127 (ch. 2), at 190–210.

440. U.S. Const. Art. III, § 1.

441. FEDERALIST, at 465 (No. 78) (Hamilton).

442. U.S. Const. Art. III, § 2.

443. Compare *Anastasoff v. United States,* 223 F.3d 898 (8th Cir. 2000) (holding that *stare decisis* is a constitutional restraint on court action), with *Hart v. Massanari,* 266 F.3d 1155 (9th Cir. 2001) (ruling that it was not a constitutional doctrine). For recent scholarly commentary, see R. Ben Brown, *Judging in the Days of the Early Republic: A Critique of Judge Richard Arnold's Use of History in* Anastasoff v. United States, 3 J.APP. PRAC. AND PROCESS 355, 375, 383 (2001); Thomas Healy, *Stare Decisis as a Constitutional Requirement,* 104 W. VA. L. REV. 43, 54–55 (2001); Thomas R. Lee, *Stare Decisis in Historical Perspective: From the Founding Era to the Rehnquist Court,* 42 VAND. L. REV. 647, 662–66 (1999); Henry Paul Monaghan, *Stare Decisis and Constitutional Adjudication,* 88 COLUM. L. REV. 723, 754–55 (1988); Polly J. Price, *Precedent and Judicial Power After the Founding,* 42 B. C. L. REV. 81 (2000).

444. FEDERALIST, at 471 (No. 78) (Hamilton).

445. Brutus, *Essay XII,* NEW YORK JOURNAL (Feb. 7 and 14, 1788), reprinted in 2 DEBATES ON THE CONSTITUTION, supra note 239 (ch. 2), at 171, 173.

446. William Cranch, *Preface,* 5 U.S. (1 Cranch) iii (1804).

447. See Carleton Kemp Allen, LAW IN THE MAKING, at 170–77 (7th ed.; Oxford: Clarendon Press, 1964); Carrese, supra note 127 (ch. 2), at 150–77.

448. William Blackstone, 1 COMMENTARIES *73.

449. 1 WORKS OF JAMES WILSON, supra note 123 (ch. 1), at 334.

450. See 2 id., at 502 ("*Stare decisis* may prevent the trouble of investigation; but it will prevent also the pleasure and the advantages of improvement.").

451. See Robert Johnson Bonner, EVIDENCE IN ATHENIAN COURTS (1905) (rep., New York: Arno Press, 1979); Edward M. Harris, *Law and Oratory,* in PERSUASION: GREEK RHETORIC IN ACTION, at 130, 132–40 (Ian Worthington, ed.; London: Routledge, 1994); Adriaan Lanni, *Precedent and Legal Reasoning in Classical Athenian Courts: A Noble Lie?,* 43 AM. J. LEG. HIST. 27, 41–51 (1999).

452. See 2 Brennan, supra note 93 (ch. 2), at 441–75; Jolowicz and Nicholas, supra note 177 (ch. 2), at 199–232; Kunkel, supra note 100 (ch. 2), at 84–94; A. Arthur Schiller, ROMAN LAW: MECHANISMS OF DEVELOPMENT, at 402–41

(The Hague: Mouton, 1978); Alan Watson, LAW MAKING IN THE ROMAN REPUBLIC, at 31–62 (Oxford: Oxford University Press, 1974).

453. See Dig. 1.2.2.6 (Pomponius). See also Bederman, CLASSICAL CANONS, supra note 51 (ch. 1), at 68–99.

454. See, for example, Dig. 24.3.66.pr (Javolenus) (indicating a series of juristic citations). Montesquieu specifically criticized the Roman imperial use of rescripts. See Montesquieu, supra note 124 (ch. 2), at 290–91 (passage xxix.17)

455. See Lintott, supra note 227 (ch. 1), at 147–62.

456. See Allen, supra note 447, at 174–76.

457. See Code Just. 7.45.13 ("No judge or arbitrator is to deem himself bound by juristic opinions [consutationes] which he considers wrong; still less by the decisions of learned prefects or other judges. For if an erroneous decision has been given, it ought not to be allowed to spread and so to corrupt the judgement of other magistrates. Decisions should be based on laws, not precedents").

458. U.S. Const., Art. III, § 2, cl. 3 ("The Trial of all Crimes, except in Cases of Impeachment, shall be by Jury."); Amend. 5 (grand jury requirement); Amend. 6 (right to "impartial jury of the State and district wherein the crime shall have been committed"); Amend. 7 (right to jury in civil cases "at common law" where the value in controversy exceeds $20).

459. See Clinton, BRIEF HISTORY, supra note 6 (pr.), at 910. This worry was manifest because the Constitution allowed federal appellate courts to review lower court decisions "both as to Law and Fact. . . . " U.S. Const. Art. III, § 2, cl. 2. See FEDERALIST, at 489 (No. 81) (Hamilton) ("If, therefore, the re-examination of a fact once determined by a jury, should in any case be admitted under the proposed Constitution, it may be so regulated as to be done by a second jury, either by remanding the cause to the court below for a second trial of the fact, or by directing an issue immediately out of the Supreme Court.").

460. 3 Elliot, at 595.

461. 3 CAF 19 (Letters from a Federal Farmer, No. VIII) (Jan. 3, 1788); 4 id., 213 (A Farmer, No. III) (June 6, 1788) ("Rome, Sparta, and Carthage, at the times when their liberties were lost, were strangers to the trial by jury"). In actuality, under the Spartan constitution, the gerousia sat as a jury in capital or infamous cases. See 2 Pausanias, DESCRIPTION OF GREECE, at 29 (W. H. S. Jones and H. A. Ormerods, transl., 1926) (Loeb Classical Library reprint, 1993) (passage iii.5.3); Aristotle, POLITICS, supra note 96 (ch. 1), at 179 (passage 1275b10).

462. See 2 WORKS OF JAMES WILSON, supra note 123 (ch. 1), at 510.

463. See MacDowell, supra note 291 (ch. 2), at 30–33. For civil matters, juries of 201 citizens were used for disputes at which 1,000 drachmae were at issue, and 401 dicasts sat when more was at issue. See Aristotle, ATHENIAN CONSTITUTION, supra note 175 (ch. 2), at 145 (passage liii.3).

464. See id., at 34–35, 170. See Aristotle, ATHENIAN CONSTITUTION, supra note 175 (ch. 2), at 81 (passage xxvii.4); 1 Plutarch, supra note 112 (ch. 1), at 451 (Solon, xviii). See also Robert J. Bonner, LAWYERS AND LITIGANTS IN ANCIENT ATHENS, at 37 (Chicago: University of Chicago Press, 1927).

465. See 2 WORKS OF JAMES WILSON, supra note 123 (ch. 1), at 511.

466. See Wolfgang Kunkel, Untersuchungen zur Entwicklung des römischen Kriminalverfahrens in vorsullanischer Zeit (München: Verlag der Bayerischen Akademie der Wissenschaften, 1962); Lintott, supra note 227 (ch. 1), at 154–56. See also 10 Plutarch, supra note 112 (ch. 1), at 209 (*Gaius Gracchus*, v) (reforms to allow plebians and equites to sit on juries). See also Walbank, supra note 56 (ch. 2), at 695–96; Greenidge, supra note 84 (ch. 2), at 245–50; Lintott, supra note 227 (ch. 2), at 108–09.

467. See Brennan, supra note 93 (ch. 2), at 441–75; Lintott, supra note 227 (ch. 1), at 155–61. See also Jolowicz and Nicholas, supra note 177 (ch.2), at 305–20; Kunkel, supra note 100 (ch. 2), at 66–69.

468. See Lintott, supra note 227 (ch. 1), at 161.

469. Id., at 229 (No. 37) (Madison). To the same effect was Madison's remark that "The experience of ages, with the continued and combined labors of the most enlightened legislatures and jurists, has been equally unsuccessful in delineating the several objects and limits of different codes of laws and different tribunals of justice. The precise extent of the common law, and the statute law, the maritime law, the ecclesiastical law, the law of corporations, and other local laws and customs, remains still to be clearly and finally established in Great Britain, where accuracy in such subjects has been more industriously pursued than in any other part of the world." Id., at 228.

470. Id., at 496 (No. 83) (Hamilton).

471. Id., at 468 (No. 78) (Hamilton). See also Walling, supra note 131 (ch. 1), at 81 (discussing Hamilton's use of classical canons in the 1784 *Rutgers v. Wadlington* litigation); Julius Goebel, 1 The Law Practice of Alexander Hamilton 311, 352 (New York: Columbia University Press, 1964) (quoting Cicero for the proposition that "when two laws clash, that which relates to the most important subject ought to be preferred").

472. Id., at 470. See also Robert J. Pushaw, Jr., *Justiciability and Separation of Powers: A Neo-Federalist Approach*, 81 Cornell L. Rev. 393, 425, and n. 151 (1996).

473. 2 Works of James Wilson, supra note 123 (ch. 1), at 478.

474. Id., at 486.

475. Cicero, De Inventione (H. M. Hubbell transl.; Loeb Classical Library reprint, 1949).

476. [Cicero], Rhetorica ad Herennium (Harry Caplan, transl., 1954; Loeb Classical Library reprint, 1981). The attribution of this work (dated to about 85 BCE) to Cicero is now known to be spurious.

477. Quitilian, Institutio Oratorio (H. E. Butler, transl.; Loeb Classical Library reprint, 1920). This work has been dated to about 95 CE. See also Bederman, Classical Canons, supra note 51 (ch. 1), at 22–45.

478. See 1 Blackstone, Commentaries on the Laws of England *59–61.

479. See Bederman, Classical Canons, supra note 51 (ch. 1), at 103–51. See also Clinton, supra note 332 (ch. 1), at 228–29; Jonathan T. Molot, *The Judicial Perspective in the Administrative State: Reconciling Modern Doctrines of Deference with the Judiciary's Structural Role*, 53 Stan. L. Rev. 1, 37–41 (2000).

480. See Clinton, supra note 332 (ch. 1), at 229. See also Robert Lowry Clinton, *Classical legal naturalism and the politics of John Marshall's constitutional jurisprudence*, 33 J. Marshall L. Rev. 935 (2000).

481. Art. Confed. IX, para. 1. See also Edling, supra note 3 (pr.), at 73–81.
482. See, for example, Anne-Marie Burley, *The Alien Tort Statute and the Judiciary Act of 1789: A Badge of Honor*, 83 Am. J. Int'l L. 461 (1989); Anthony D'Amato, *The Alien Tort Statute and the Founding of the Constitution*, 82 Am. J. Int'l L. 62, 64 (1988); Stewart Jay, *The Status of the Law of Nations in Early American Law*, 42 Vand. L. Rev. 819, 839–46 (1989); Beth Stephens, *Federalism and Foreign Affairs: Congress's Power to "Define and Punish . . . Offenses Against the Law of Nations,"* 42 Wm. and Mary L. Rev. 447, 465–68 (2000); Douglas J. Sylvester, *International Law as a Sword or Shield? Early American Foreign Policy and the Law of Nations*, 32 N.Y.U. J. Int'l L. and Pol. 1 (1999). See also *Sosa v. Alvarez-Machain*, 542 U.S. 692, 715–18 (2004) (discussing problems of foreign relations during the Articles of Confederation period).
483. See 28 Cont. Cong. 314.
484. See 34 id., at 111.
485. 2 CAF 88 (Oct, 10, 1787).
486. U.S. Const. preamble.
487. See Walling, supra note 131 (ch. 1), at 142–47.
488. See 3 Polybius, supra note 51 (ch. 2), at 383 (passage vi.50).
489. Machiavelli, supra note 113 (ch. 2), at 32.
490. Federalist, at 53 (No. 5) (Jay).
491. Id., at 57 (No. 6) (Hamilton).
492. See, for example, the remarks of delegate Henry at the Virginia Ratifying Convention: "In making a dictator [George Washington], we followed the example of the most glorious, magnanimous, and skillful nations. . . . Rome has furnished us an illustrious example." Hugh Blair Grigsby, The History of the Virginia Federal Convention of 1788, at 154–55 (Richmond: Virginia Historical Society, 1890).
493. Machiavelli, supra note 113 (ch. 2), at 315. See also Mansfield, Machiavelli, supra note 113 (ch. 2), at 189–97; Mansfield, Taming, supra note 134 (ch. 2), at 135–36, 142–49.
494. Id., at 316.
495. 1 Farrand, at 290 (June 18) (Madison's notes).
496. Federalist, at 257 (No. 41) (Madison).
497. 1 Montesquieu, supra note 124 (ch. 2), at 194.
498. Id., at 193–94. See also Curtis A. Bradley and Martin S. Flaherty, *Executive Power Essentialism and Foreign Affairs*, 102 Mich L. Rev. (2004); Lois G. Schwoerer, "No Standing Armies!" The Antiarmy Ideology in Seventeenth-Century England (Baltimore: Johns Hopkins University Press, 1974); John Philip Reid, In Defiance of the Law: The Standing-Army Controversy, the Two Constitutions, and the Coming of the American Revolution (Chapel Hill: University of North Carolina Press, 1981).
499. 1 Farrand, at 465 (June 29) (Madison's notes).
500. Brutus, Essay X (Jan. 24, 1788), reprinted in 2 Debates on the Constitution, supra note 239 (ch. 2), at 86. See also Citizen of America [Noah Webster], reprinted in Ford, Pamphlets, supra note 46 (ch. 2), at 51–52; 3 CAF 76 (A Federal Republican) (Oct. 28, 1787); 3 id., 190 (*The Impartial Examiner*, No. II) (May 28, 1788).

501. 3 Elliot 494. See also the remarks of Samuel Nason at the Massachusetts ratifying convention: "Was it not with [a standing army] that Ceasar passed the Rubicon, and laid prostrate the liberties of his country." S. B. Harding, THE CONTEST OVER THE RATIFICATION OF THE FEDERAL CONSTITUTION IN THE STATE OF MASSACHUSETTS (1896). See also Bailyn, BEGIN THE WORLD, supra note 11 (pr.), at 114–15.

502. See Rakove, supra note 164 (ch. 1), at 184–86.

503. 1 Farrand, at 112 (June 4) (Mason's speech).

504. See Kennedy, supra note 87 (ch. 1), at 124–25; Edling, supra note 3 (pr.), at 90–128.

505. FEDERALIST, at 68–69 (No. 8) (Hamilton).

506. See 3 Polybius, supra note 51 (ch. 2), at 311–17 (passages vi.19–21), at 327–29 (passage vi.26). See also Ernst Badian, ROMAN IMPERIALISM IN THE LATE REPUBLIC (Oxford: Oxford University Press, 1967); Holland, supra note 194 (ch. 2), at 162, 255, 295, 371 (for more on the agrarian myth of citizen armies and the Roman republic's safeguards against standing armies); William V. Harris, WAR AND IMPERIALISM IN REPUBLICAN ROME, 370–327 B.C. (Oxford: Clarendon Press, 1979).

507. See Michael M. Sage, WARFARE IN ANCIENT GREECE (London: Routledge, 1996); Antonio Santosuosso, SOLDIERS, CITIZENS, AND THE SYMBOLS OF WAR: FROM CLASSICAL GREECE TO REPUBLICAN ROME, 500–167 B.C. (Boulder: Westview Press, 1997).

508. See Aristotle, POLITICS, supra note 96 (ch. 1), at 121, 209–11 (passages 1267b29–33 and 1279b23–37).

509. See Jonathan Turley, *The Military Pocket Republic*, 97 N.W. U. L. REV. 1, 14–24 (2002); Wiltshire, supra note 266, at 134–42.

510. U.S. Const. Art. I, § 8, cl. 12.

511. FEDERALIST, at 171–73 (No. 26) (Hamilton) (emphasis in original).

512. See U.S. Const. Art. I, § 8, cls. 15 and 16 ("The Congress shall have power.... To provide for calling forth the Militia to execute the Laws of the Union, suppress Insurrections and repel Invasions; To provide for organizing, arming, and disciplining, the Militia, and for governing such Part of them as may be employed in the Service of the United States, reserving to the States respectively, the Appointment of the Officers, and the Authority of training the Militia according to the discipline prescribed by Congress.").

513. Id., Art. II, § 2, cl. 1.

514. FEDERALIST, at 185–86 (No. 29) (Hamilton) (original emphasis).

515. See, for example, *Perpich v. Department of Defense*, 496 U.S. 334, 353–54 (1990). See also Alan Hirsch, *The militia clauses of the Constitution and the National Guard*, 56 U. CIN. L. REV. 919 (1988); Patrick Todd Mullins, Note, *The militia clauses, the National Guard, and federalism: A constitutional tug of war*, 57 GEO. WASH. L. REV. 328 (1988); Edling, supra note 3 (pr.), at 74, 105–08.

516. See David C. Williams, *Civic republicanism and the citizen militia: The terrifying Second Amendment*, 101 YALE L. J. 551 (1991); Edling, supra note 3 (pr.), at 89–128.

517. See 3 Polybius, supra note 51 (ch. 2), at 301 (passages vi.14.3–4). See also Lintott, supra note 227 (ch. 1), at 20–21.

518. U.S. Const. Art. II, § 2, cl. 1.

519. Id., Art. I, § 8, cl. 11.

520. See Treanor, supra note 259 (ch. 1), at 740–52. See also Prakash and Ramsey, supra note 365, at 1609–10, 1633–34; Michael D. Ramsey, *Textualism and War Powers*, 69 U. Chi. L. Rev. 1543 (2002); John C. Yoo, *War and the Constitutional Text*, 69 id., at 1639.

521. Federalist, at 54–55 (No. 6) (Hamilton) (citing to Plutarch's *Life of Pericles*) (emphasis in original).

522. Art. Confed. IX, para. 6.

523. Federalist, at 261 (No. 41) (Madison).

524. This was reflected in Congressional control over the issuance of letters of marque and reprisal, the authority given to privateers to engage in captures of enemy ships and cargoes. See U.S. Const. Art. I, § 8, cl. 11. See also David I. Lewittes, *Constitutional Separation of War Powers: Protecting Public and Private Liberty*, 57 Brooklyn L. Rev. 1083, 1177–84 (1992); Jules Lobel, *Covert War and Congressional Authority: Hidden War and Forgotten Power*, 134 U. Pa. L. Rev. 1035 (1986); Jules Lobel, *"Little Wars" and the Constitution*, 50 U. Miami L. Rev. 61 (1995); C. Kevin Marshall, *Putting Privateers in their Place: The Applicability of the Marque and Reprisal Clause to Undeclared Wars*, 64 U. Chi. L. Rev. 953 (1997); Ramsey, supra note 520, at 1613–18. For the ancient Greek practice of *androlepsia* (literally "man seizure"), sanctioned private reprisals for belligerent conduct, see Bederman, supra note 29 (ch. 2), at 122–29.

525. See Ramsey, supra note 520, at 1605. See also Federalist, at 165 (No. 25) (Hamilton) ("As the ceremony of a formal denunciation of war has of late fallen into disuse. . . . ").

The Framing Generation would have also been familiar with the writings of Grotius and Emmerich de Vattel, who wrote about the Roman fetial procedure for declaring war. See Emmerich de Vattel, The Law of Nations (*Le Droit des Gens*), at 314–20 (T. and J. W. Johnson, eds., 1863) (Joseph Chitty, ed., 1758); Hugo Grotius, The Rights of War and Peace (*De Jure Belli ac Pacis*) 456 (London 1682) (William Evarts, transl., 1625).

526. See Rahe, supra note 3 (pr.), at 167, 169, 173. See also 3 Thucydides, supra note 24 (ch. 2), at 69–71 (passages v.36–38); 341–53 (passages vi.88.7–93.3).

527. See 1 Thucydides, supra note 24 (ch. 2), at 91 (passage i.53). See also Adcock and Mosley, supra note 204, at 153–54, 202–03 (for more on this incident).

528. See Robert A. Bauslaugh, The Concept of Neutrality in Ancient Greece (Berkeley: University of California Press, 1991); Bederman, supra note 29 (ch. 2), at 212–22; S. Séfériadès, *La Conception de la Neutralité dans l'ancienne Greece*, 16 Revue de droit internbational et de legislation comparée 641 (1935).

529. U.S. Const. Art. I, § 8, cl. 17. See also Federalist, at 273 (No. 43) (Madison) (noting why such installations had to be under the control of the federal government, not the States).

530. See Lewittes, supra note 524, at 1132–52. Cf. Art. Confed. IX, para. 5 (placing substantial restrictions on Congress' ability to raise troops).

531. 2 Farrand, at 341 (Aug. 20) (Madison's notes).

532. See 3 Polybius, supra note 51 (ch. 2), at 303 (passage vi.15.5). But see id., at 299 (passage vi.12.8) (suggesting that consuls could freely draw money from the treasury, through the quaestors). See also Jolowicz and Nicholas, supra note 177 (ch. 2), at 37–40; Lintott , supra note 227 (ch. 1), at 17.

533. Aristotle, ATHENIAN CONSTITUTION, supra note 175 (ch. 2), at 165–69 (passage lxi) (on the elections of ranks of officers).

534. FEDERALIST, at 42–43 (No. 3) (Jay) (emphasis in original).

535. Cicero, DE OFFICIIS, supra note 293 (ch. 1), at 37–39 (passages i.11.34–36). The institution of the fetials can be traced to the early days of the Roman kingdom. See 1 Plutarch, supra note 112 (ch. 1), at 347–51 (*Numa*, xii).

536. See Bederman, supra note 29 (ch. 2), at 231–41 ; Robert Morstein Kallet-Marx, HEGEMONY TO EMPIRE: THE DEVELOPMENT OF THE ROMAN IMPERIUM IN THE EAST FROM 148 TO 62 B.C. (Berkeley: University of California Press, 1995); William R. Nifong, *Promises Past: Marcus Atilius Regulus and the Dialogue of Natural Law*, 49 DUKE L. J. 1077, 1093–1113 (2000); Rich, supra note 340; Valerie M. Warrior, THE INITIATION OF THE SECOND MACEDONIAN WAR: AN EXPLICATION OF LIVY BOOK 31 (Stuttgart: Franz Steiner Verlag, 1996); Alan Watson, INTERNATIONAL LAW IN ARCHAIC ROME: WAR AND RELIGION (Baltimore: Johns Hopkins University Press, 1993).

537. See Jolowicz and Nicholas, supra note 177 (ch. 2), at 40–42; Kunkel, supra note 100 (ch. 2), at 12; Greenidge, supra note 84 (ch. 2), at 243–45, 282–84. Cf. Arthur Eckstein, SENATE AND GENERAL: INDIVIDUAL DECISIONMAKING AND ROMAN FOREIGN RELATIONS, 264–194 BC (Berkeley: University of California Press, 1987).

538. See 4 Livy, supra note 148 (ch. 1), at 5–7 (passages viii.2.1–4), 153–55 (passages viii.39.10–14), 163–65 (passages ix.1.1–10), 191 (passage ix.8.6).

539. 4 WORKS OF JOHN ADAMS, supra note 87 (ch. 1), at 438 (discussing 3 Polybius, supra note 51 (ch. 2), at 303 (passage vi.14.10). See also Walbank, supra note 56 (ch. 2), at 687–88.

540. See Nifong, supra note 536, at 1113–16.

541. U.S. Const. Art. I, § 8, cl. 10.

542. FEDERALIST, at 42 (No. 3) (Jay).

543. Id., at 476 (No. 80) (Hamilton). See also id., at 265 (No. 42) (Madison) ("The power to define and punish piracies and felonies committed on the high seas, and offenses against the law of nations, belongs with equal propriety to the general government, and is a still greater improvement on the articles of Confederation. These articles contain no provision for the case of offenses against the law of nations; and consequently leave it in the power of any indiscreet member to embroil the Confederacy with foreign nations.").

544. The Framers tended not to refer directly to the "ius gentium" or "jure gentium" or "ius inter gentes," although Blackstone's Commentaries did. See 1 Blackstone, COMMENTARIES, at *247–48 ("if an embassador makes a contract which is good jure gentium, he shall answer for it here"); at 411–13 (concerning the status of slavery). For some exceptions, see *Fairfax's Devisee v. Hunter's Lessee*, 11 U.S. (7 Cranch) 603, 620 (1813) (Story, J.) ("it was adjudged that a bequest to an alien enemy was good, and, after a peace, might be enforced.

Indeed, the common law in these particulars seems to coincide with the Jus
Gentium."); *De Lovio v. Boit*, 7 F. Cas. 418, 443 (C.C.D. Mass. 1815) (Story, J.)
(citing Cicero "Frag. de Repub. lib. 3 (Editio Bost. 1817, tom. 17, p. 186).").

545. See *Alden v. Maine*, 527 U.S. 706, 767 (1999) ("The doctrine that the sovereign
could not be sued by his subjects might have been thought by medieval civil
lawyers to belong to jus gentium, the law of nations, which was a type of
natural law; or perhaps in its original form it might have been understood
as a precept of positive, written law.") (Souter, J., dissenting); *Sosa v. Alvarez-
Machain*, 542 U.S. 692, 712–15 (2004); *The sally*, 12 U.S. (8 Cranch) 382, 384
(1814); Jeremy Waldron, *Foreign Law and the Modern* Ius Gentium, 119 Harv.
L. Rev. 129 (2005); Genc Trnavci, *The Meaning and Scope of the Law of Nations
in the Context of the Alien Tort Claims Act and International Law*, 26 U. Pa. J.
Int'l Econ. L. 193 (2005).

This debate is actually quite old. See Sir Henry Maine, Ancient Law Tucson:
University of Arizona Press 1986) (1861) (Maine's discussion of *ius gentium* was
intended primarily as a rebuttal to the notion that it was later transformed into
the modern law of nations). For the same view, see Henry Wheaton, History
of the Law of Nations in Europe and America, at 26 (New York: Gould
Banks & Co. 1845).

546. 17 U.S. (4 Wheat.) 122, 151 (1819) (argument of counsel).

547. See 1 Works of James Wilson, supra note 123 (ch. 1), at 162–67.

548. See also Onuf and Onuf, supra note 113 (ch. 2), at 97–144; Alfred P. Rubin,
Ethics and Authority in International Law, at 70–82 (Cambridge, UK:
Cambridge University Press, 1997).

549. 1 Works of James Wilson, supra note 123 (ch. 2), at 166.

550. Id., at 167 (spelling modernized).

551. Id., at 165 (citing U.S. Const. Art. I, § 10).

552. The Constitution grants Congress the authority to "regulate Commerce with
foreign Nations," "establish [a] uniform Rule of Naturalization," art. I, § 8,
while the President may appoint ambassadors subject to Senate approval, see
art. II, § 2, cl. 2, and "receive Ambassadors and other public Ministers," id., § 3.
The states, however, are prohibited from entering into "any Treaty, Alliance,
or Confederation," granting "Letters of Marque and Reprisal," or, without
the consent of Congress, "lay[ing] any Duty of Tonnage, keep[ing] Troops, or
Ships of War in time of Peace, enter[ing] into any Agreement or Compact with
another State, or with a foreign Power, or engag[ing] in War, unless actually
invaded, or in such imminent Danger as will not admit of delay." Id., Art. I,
§ 10.

553. U.S. Const. Art. II, § 2, cl. 2.

554. See Louis Henkin, Foreign Affairs and the U.S. Constitution, at 443–
44 (2nd ed.; Oxford: Clarendon Press, 1996); Arthur Bestor, *Respective Roles of
the Senate and President in Making and Abrogation of Treaties – The Original
Intent of the Framers and the Constitution Historically Examined*, 55 Wash. L.
Rev. 1 (1979).

555. Federalist, at 450–51 (No. 75) (Hamilton) (emphasis in original).

556. See id., at 453 ("This consideration seems sufficient to determine our opinion,
that the convention have gone as far in the endeavor to secure the advantage

of numbers in the formation of treaties as could have been reconciled either with the activity of the public councils or with a reasonable regard to the major sense of the community. If two thirds of the whole number of members had been required, it would, in many cases, from the nonattendance of a part, amount in practice to a necessity of unanimity. And the history of every political establishment in which this principle has prevailed, is a history of impotence, perplexity, and disorder. Proofs of this position might be adduced from the examples of the Roman Tribuneship, the Polish Diet, and the States–General of the Netherlands, did not an example at home render foreign precedents unnecessary.") See also Bradley and Flaherty, supra note 498; Howard R. Sklamberg, *The Meaning of "Advice and Consent": The Senate's Constitutional Role in Treatymaking*, 18 MICH. J. INT'L L. 445 (1997).

557. FEDERALIST, at 390–91 (No. 64) (Jay).
558. See Henkin, supra note 554, at 177–78, 445–47. See also Stephan Riesenfeld and Kenneth Abbott, *The Scope of Senate Control over Conclusion and Operation of Treaties*, 67 CHI.-KENT L. REV. 571 (1991); Bradley and Flaherty, supra note 498. Contra Prakash and Ramsey, supra note 365, at 1672–83 (summarizing Washington Administration practices).

For a contemporary account of President Washington's dealings with the senate on treaty negotiations, see 3 THE PAPERS OF GEORGE WASHINGTON; PRESIDENTIAL SERIES, at 521–27 (W. W. Abbott and Dorothy Twohig, eds.; Charlottesvile: University Press of Virginia, 1987–2005).

CHAPTER 4. MODERN RESONANCES

1. See, for example, *Plaut v. Spendthrift Farm, Inc.*, 514 U.S. 211 (1995) (Congress violated constitutional separation of powers principles by instructing federal courts to reopen final judgments); *Metropolitan Wash. Airports Auth. v. Citizens for the Abatement of Aircraft Noise*, 501 U.S. 252 (1991) (Congress' conditioning of transfer of District of Columbia area airports to local authority upon creation of Board of Review composed of congressmen and having veto power over decisions of local authority's directors violated separation of powers); *Mistretta v. United States*, 488 U.S. 361 (1989) (formation of Commission, including sitting judges, to develop sentencing guidelines was constitutional); *Morrison v. Olson*, 487 U.S. 654 (1988) (independent counsel statute, creating a prosecutor not subject to the President's control, did not violate separation of powers); *INS v. Chadha*, 462 U.S. 919 (1983) (Congress' century-long practice of allowing legislative vetoes of Presidential implementation of statutes violated separation of powers).

2. See, for example, the following works, Raoul Berger, EXECUTIVE PRIVILEGE: A CONSTITUTIONAL MYTH (Cambridge, Mass.: Harvard University Press, 1974); Raoul Berger, FEDERALISM: THE FOUNDERS' DESIGN (Norman: University of Oklahoma Press, 1987); John Hart Ely, WAR AND RESPONSIBILITY: CONSTITUTIONAL LESSONS OF VIETNAM AND ITS AFTERMATH (Princeton: Princeton University Press, 1993); Robert M. Hardaway, THE ELECTORAL COLLEGE AND THE CONSTITUTION: THE CASE FOR PRESERVING FEDERALISM

(Westport: Praeger, 1994); Clyde E. Jacobs, THE ELEVENTH AMENDMENT AND SOVEREIGN IMMUNITY (Westport: Greenwood Press, 1972); John T. Noonan, NARROWING THE NATION'S POWER: THE SUPREME COURT SIDES WITH THE STATES (Berkeley: University of California Press, 2002); Martin S. Sheffer, THE JUDICIAL DEVELOPMENT OF PRESIDENTIAL WAR POWERS (Westport: Praeger, 1999).

3. See the discussion in the Preface, at Note 13 with text.
4. See U.S. Const. Art. I, § 3, cl. 1.
5. See id., Art. I, § 2, cl. 1; Art. II, § 1, cl. 2 ("Each State shall appoint, in such Manner as the Legislature thereof may direct, a Number of Electors. . . . ").
6. See id., Art. I, § 8.
7. See id., Art. VI, § 2.
8. See id., Art. I, § 10.
9. See id., Art. I, § 1 ("All legislative Powers *herein granted* shall be vested in a Congress. . . . ") (emphasis added).
10. Id., Amend. 10.
11. FEDERALIST 243–46 (No. 39) (Madison) (emphasis in original).
12. Id., at 245.
13. 1 Farrand, at 323 (June 19) (Madison's notes).
14. Id.
15. 1 Farrand, at 157 (June 7) (Yates's notes).
16. See Chapter 3, at Notes 8–48 and accompanying text. See also Rakove, supra note 164 (ch. 1), at 65. For an earlier English assessment of these sources, see Harrington, supra note 275 (ch. 2), at 227 (quoting Sigonius i.1, and Cicero, *In Verrem* ii.13).
17. 1 Farrand, at 135 (June 6) (Madison's notes) (spelling and punctuation modernized) (discussing also Swiss and Dutch confederacies).
18. See U.S. Const. Art. I, § 8, cl. 9.
19. 1 Farrand, at 125 (June 5) (Madison's notes) (spelling modernized). See also Rosen, supra note 164 (ch. 1), at 111–13.
20. For more on the question of whether the national government preexisted that of the independent states, see Berger, FEDERALISM, supra note 2, at 21–47; Rakove, supra note 164 (ch. 1), at 163–76.
21. But see Berger, FEDERALISM, supra note 2, at 31–34 (suggesting that there was a consensus that the states had preexisting sovereignty).
22. 1 Farrand, at 471 (June 29) (Yates's notes).
23. See 3 Farrand, at 522.
24. Art. Confed. II.
25. See, for example, *Nathan v. Virginia*, 1 Dall. 77 (Pa. Ct. Common Pleas 1781). See also Jacobs, supra note 2, at 11–13.
26. See the *Vanstophorst v. Maryland* case, docketed in the Supreme Court in February 1791, discussed in Jacobs, supra note 2, at 43–46.
27. 2 U.S. (2 Dall.) 419 (1793).
28. See Doyle Mathis, Chisholm v. Georgia: *Background and Settlement*, 54 J. AM. HIST. 19 (June 1967).
29. 2 U.S. (2 Dall.) at 424 (argument of counsel) (citing, for information on the Amphictyonic Council, "Anacharis, 3 Vol. p. 300.").

30. See U.S. Const. Art. III, § 2, cl. 1 ("The Judicial Power shall extend to....
Controversies . . . between a State and Citizens of another State . . . and between
a State . . . and foreign States, Citizens or Subjects.").

31. See 2 U.S. (2 Dall.) at 471–72 (Jay, C. J.). See also Jacobs, supra note 2, at 53–
55.

32. See 2 U.S. (2 Dall.) at 453 (Wilson, J.).

33. Id., at 455 (citing "Som, Sup. c. 3."). The actual citation is to Cicero, DE RE
PUBLICA, supra note 325 (ch. 1), at 265–67 (passage vi.13). See Hoffman, supra
note 138 (ch. 1), at 61, 79.

34. See 2 WORKS OF JAMES WILSON, supra note 123 (ch. 1), at 497–98. See also
Jacobs, supra note 2, at 52 and n.46.

35. 2 U.S. (2 Dall.) at 459.

36. Id. See also Hoffman, supra note 138 (ch. 1), at 78–80.

37. 2 U.S. (2 Dall.) at 463 (original emphasis) (citing "Iliad, I., 2. v. 54.").

38. See Introduction, WORKS OF JAMES WILSON, supra note 123 (ch. 1), at 32–35
(commenting on the significance of Wilson's opinion in Chisholm, despite its
prolixity).

39. 2 WORKS OF JAMES WILSON, supra note 123 (ch. 1), at 497. See also 2 Elliot, at
443 (for Wilson's speech at the Pennsylvania ratifying convention).

40. FEDERALIST, at 289–90 (No. 45) (Madison). See also Dietze, supra note 163
(ch. 3), at 181–85.

41. See Larsen, supra note 203 (ch. 3), at xxii , 20, 277–78.

42. See id., at 233, 271.

43. U.S. Const. Amend. 11. See also Jacobs, supra note 2, at 64–74.

44. "It is inherent in the nature of sovereignty not to be amenable to the suit of an
individual *without its consent.* This is the general sense and the general practice
of mankind; and the exemption, as one of the attributes of sovereignty, is now
enjoyed by the government of every State of the Union. Unless, therefore, there
is a surrender of this immunity in the plan of the convention, it will remain
with the States. . . . " FEDERALIST, at 487–488 (No. 81) (Hamilton) (emphasis in
original). See also *Alden v. Maine*, 527 U.S. 706, 730 (1999).

45. See *Fed. Mar. Comm'n v. S. C. State Ports Auth.*, 535 U.S. 743 (2002); *Alden
v. Maine*, 527 U.S. 706 (1999); *Seminole Tribe of Fla. v. Florida*, 517 U.S. 44
(1996). See, for example, John J. Gibbons, *The Eleventh Amendment and State
Sovereign Immunity: a Reinterpretation*, 83 COLUM. L. REV. 1889 (1983); William
A. Fletcher, *A Historical Interpretation of the Eleventh Amendment: A Narrow
Construction of an Affirmative Grant of Jurisdiction Rather than a Prohibition
Against Jurisdiction*, 35 STAN. L. REV. 1033 (1983); Lee, *Eleventh Amendment*,
supra note 100 (ch. 3); Caleb Nelson, *Sovereign Immunity as a Doctrine of Personal
Jurisdiction*, 115 HARV. L. REV. 1559 (2002); Susan Randall, *Sovereign Immunity
and the Uses of History*, 81 NEB. L. REV. 1 (2002).

46. FEDERALIST, at 245 (No. 39) (Madison).

47. Alden, 527 U.S., at 714.

48. Id., at 729.

49. See id., at 763 (Souter, J., dissenting).

50. See id., at 766–68, 797.

51. Id., at 798.

52. Id., at 768, n.6 (citing 1 The Digest of Justinian 13 (T. Mommsen and P. Krueger, eds., A. Watson transl.; 1985); Brian Tierney, *The Prince Is Not Bound by the Laws: Accursius and the Origins of the Modern State*, 5 Comparative Studies in Society and History 378 (1963); Kenneth Pennington, The Prince and the Law, 1200–1600: Sovereignty and Rights in the Western Legal Tradition, at 77–79 (Berkeley: University of California Press, 1993)).

53. Id., at 803, n.35 (citing and quoting "Digna Vox, Justinian's Code 1.4.14 ('Digna vox maiestate regnantis legis alligatum se principem profiteri') ('It is a statement worthy of the majesty of the ruler for the Prince to profess himself bound by the laws').").

54. For elements of this debate, derived from Herbert Wechsler's famous article, *The Political Safeguards of Federalism: The Role of the States in the Composition and Selection of the National Government*, 54 Colum. L. Rev. 543 (1954); see Bradford R. Clark, *Putting the Safeguards Back into the Political Safeguards of Federalism*, 80 Tex. L. Rev. 327 (2001); Marci A. Hamilton, *Why Federalism Must be Enforced: A Response to Professor Kramer*, 46 Vill. L. Rev. 1069 (2002); Larry D. Kramer, *Putting the Politics Back into the Political Safeguards of Federalism*, 100 Colum. L. Rev. 215 (2002); Saikrishna B. Prakash and John C. Yoo, *The Puzzling Persistence of Process-Based Federalism Theories*, 79 Tex. L. Rev. 1459 (2001).

55. Compare *Garcia v. San Antonio Metro. Transit Auth.*, 469 U.S. 528 (1985) (holding such disputes to be nonjusticiable), overruling *National League of Cities v. Usery*, 426 U.S. 833 (1976).

56. 521 U.S. 898 (1997).

57. Id., at 921, n.11 (quoting Federalist, at 138 (No. 20) (Madison (with Hamilton)); and *United States v. Lopez*, 514 U.S. 549, 575 (1995) (Kennedy, J., concurring) (citing Friendly, *Federalism: A Forward*, 86 Yale L. J. 1019 (1977))). See also Bailyn, Begin the World, supra note 11 (pr.), at 128–30 (commentary on the Justices' use of *The Federalist Papers* in the *Printz* case).

58. U.S. Const. Art. I, § 6, cl. 1.

59. See *Kilbourn v. Thompson*, 103 U.S. 168, 202–204 (1880); *United States v. Johnson*, 383 U.S. 169, 178 (1966). "[T]he central role of the Speech or Debate Clause [is] to prevent intimidation of legislators by the Executive and accountability before a possibly hostile judiciary." *Gravel v. United States*, 408 U.S. 606, 617 (1972).

60. See U.S. Const. Art. III, § 1.

61. See Federalist, at 465–72 (No. 78) (Hamilton).

62. See Johnson, 383 U.S., at 177–79.

63. U.S. Const. Art. II, § 1, cl. 1.

64. But see id., Art. II, § 1, cl. 7. ("The President shall, at stated Times, receive for his Services, a Compensation, which shall neither be increased or diminished during the Period for which he shall have been elected. . . .")

65. 2 Elliot, at 480.

66. U.S. Const. Art. II, § 3, cl. 4.

67. See Berger, Executive Privilege, supra note 2, at 53–55; Edwards S. Corwin, The President: Office and Powers, 1787–1948, at 2–17 (New York: New York University Press, 1948).

68. See Lintott, supra note 227 (ch. 1), at 96; Greenidge, supra note 84 (ch. 2), at 152–53. See also 6 Plutarch, supra note 112 (ch. 1), at 363 (*Aemilius Paulus*, iv) (number of lictors due to consuls and praetors).

69. See Lintott, supra note 227 (ch. 1), at 122–25, 129. See also Greenidge, supra note 84 (ch. 2), at 173–76, 208–09, 234. See also 4 Plutarch, supra note 112 (ch. 1), at 157–63 (*Coriolanus*, xvii–xviii).

70. See *United States v. Nixon*, 418 U.S. 683, 703–707 (1974). See also Corwin, supra note 67, at 136–45.

71. See *Nixon v. Fitzgerald*, 457 U.S. 731 (1982).

72. See *Clinton v. Jones*, 520 U.S. 681 (1997).

73. See Berger, Executive Privilege, supra note 2, at 60–140, 216–24.

74. Compare U.S. Const. Art. I, § 8, cl. 11 ("Congress shall have Power. . . . to declare War. . . . ") with U.S. Const. Art. V ("The Congress, whenever two thirds of both Houses shall deem it necessary, shall propose Amendments to this Constitution. . . . "). But see Pacificus No. 1, in 15 Hamilton Papers, supra note 155 (ch. 1), at 42 (Hamilton indicating that the President could veto a declaration of war).

75. See Treanor, supra note 259 (ch. 1), at 724–29. Contra Gregory Sidak, *To Declare War*, 41 Duke L. J. 27, 84 (1991); John C. Yoo, *Clio at War: Misuse of History in the War Powers Debate*, 70 U. Colo. L. Rev. 1169, 1214 (1999); Praksah and Ramsey, supra note 365 (ch. 3), at 1609–10, 1633–34.

76. Annals of Cong., 5th Cong., 2117 (July 1798) ("The House know[s] that, by the distribution of powers under this Government, it is only competent for Congress to declare the country in war; therefore, until that declaration is made by this department, the Executive and Judiciary cannot act in the same way as if the country was at war."). See also id., at 1321 (Congressman Baldwin: "[T]he subject seemed to be placed wholly in the hands of the Legislature."); id., at 1324 (referring to statement of Congressman Nicholas: "[H]e had never heard it doubted that Congress had the power over the progress of what led to war, as well as the power of declaring war."); id., at 1336 (referring to statement of Congressman Pinckney: "Mr. P. agreed that this was Legislative power, and not Executive.").

77. James Madison, A Proclamation (June 12, 1812), 2 A Compilation of the Messages and Papers of the Presidents, at 497 (James D. Richardson, ed.; 1897).

78. 3 Polybius, supra note 51 (ch. 2), at 303 (passages vi.14.9–11).

79. See Lintott, supra note 227 (ch. 1), at 62.

80. See Bederman, supra note 29 (ch. 2), at 231–41.

81. See Titus Livius, 1 The History of Rome, at 403 (Bangs, Brother, & Co., 1855) (George Baker, transl.) (initiation of Second Punic War against Carthage); 2 id., 95 (initiation of war with Philip of Macedon).

82. For more on which, see Michael J. Gerhardt, The Federal Impeachment Process: A Constitutional and Historical Analysis (2nd ed.; Chicago: University of Chicago Press, 2000); Goldwin Smith, A Constitutional and Legal History of England, at 348 (1955).

83. 1 Farrand, at 300 (June 18) (Yates's notes).

84. Federalist, at 242 (No. 39) (Madison).

85. 1 Works of James Wilson, supra note 123 (ch. 1), at 425.
86. See id. (citing "Tacitus, Germanicus, ch. 12"). See also 4 Works of John Adams, supra note 87 (ch. 1), at 561–67.
87. See 3 Herodotus, supra note 47 (ch. 2), at 231 (passage vi.82); 1 Thucydides, supra note 24 (ch. 2), at 221 (passage i.131). See also H. W. Parke, *The Deposing of Spartan Kings*, 39 CQ 106 (1945).
88. See Aristotle, Athenian Constitution, supra note 175 (ch. 2), at 31 (passage viii.4).
89. See Aristotle, Politics, supra note 96 (ch. 1), at 165–67, 227 (passages 1274a, 1281b). We know much of Athenian impeachment procedure from the surviving speeches of Hyperides. See Hyperides, Forensic Speeches (David Whitehead transl.; New York: Oxford University Press, 2000). See also Mogens Herman Hansen, Eisangelia: the sovereignty of the people's court in Athens in the fourth century B.C. and the impeachment of generals and politicians (Odense: Odense Universitetsforlag, 1975).
90. See Jennifer Tolbert Roberts, Accountability in Athenian Government, at 14–15 (Madison: University of Wisconsin Press, 1982).
91. See 1 Thucydides, supra note 24 (ch. 2), at 375 (passages ii.65.3–4). See also 2 A. W. Gomme, A Historical Commentary on Thucydides, at 183 (Oxford: Clarendon Press, 1970).
92. See 1 Xenophon, Hellenica, at 67–85 (Carleton L. Brownson, transl.; Loeb Classical Library reprint, 1932) (passage i.7).
93. See Aristotle, Athenian Constitution, supra note 175 (ch. 2), at 135 (passage xlviii.4) ("The Council also elect by lot ten of their own body as Accountants, to keep the accounts of the officials for each presidency. Also they elect by lot Auditors, one for each tribe, and two Assessors for each Auditor. . . . and if anyone wishes to prefer a charge, of either a public or private nature, against any magistrate who has rendered his accounts before the jury-count . . . he writes on a tablet his own name and that of the defendant, and the offence of which he accuses him, adding whatever he thinks suitable, and gives it to the Auditor; and the Auditor takes it and reads it, and if he considers the charge proved, he hands it over, if a private case, to those jurymen in the villages who introduced this tribe, and if a public suit, he marks it to the Legislators. And the Legislators, if they receive it, introduce this audit again before the jury-court, and the verdict of the jurymen holds good.").
94. See id., at 127–29 (passage xlv.2). See also Rhodes, supra note 291 (ch. 2), at 147–62.
95. See 2 A. R. W. Harrison, The Law of Athens, at 208 (London: Duckworth, 1998); Deirdre Dionysia von Dornum, *The Straight and the Crooked: Legal Accountability in Ancient Greece*, 97 Colum. L. Rev. 1483, 1496 (1997).
96. See Aristotle, Athenian Constitution, supra note 175 (ch. 2), at 147 (passage liv.2). See also MacDowell, supra note 291 (ch. 2), at 170–71; von Dornum, supra note 95, at 1496.
97. See Aristotle, Athenian Constitution, supra note 175 (ch. 2), at 135 (passages xlviii.4–5), id., at 163 (passage lix.2).
98. See 2 Demosthenes, Speeches, at 232–42, 247 (C. A. Vince and J. H. Vince, transl., 1926) (Loeb Classical Library reprint, 1971); Roberts, supra note 90, at 49–54.

99. See 2 Plutarch, supra note 112 (ch. 1), at 223 (*Aristides*, iv.3).
100. See Aristotle, Athenian Constitution, supra note 175 (ch. 2), at 79 (passage xxviii.1); 2 Plutarch, supra note 112 (ch. 1), at 449 (*Cimon*, xiv–xv).
101. Cited in MacDowell, supra note 291 (ch. 2), at 172. n. 394.
102. See Rudi Thomsen, THE ORIGINS OF OSTRACISM (Copenhagen: Gyldendal, 1972). See also 2 Plutarch, supra note 112 (ch. 1), at 17, 33 (*Themistocles*, v and xi) (ostracism of Aristides and his return).
103. See Aristotle, ATHENIAN CONSTITUTION, supra note 175 (ch. 2), at 123 (passage xliii.5).
104. See Mogens Herman Hansen, THE ATHENIAN ASSEMBLY IN THE AGE OF DEMOSTHENES, at 144 (Oxford: Basil Blackwell, 1987).
105. See 4 Livy, supra note 148 (ch. 1), at 265 (passage ix.26.17); 1 ROMAN STATUTES, supra note 193 (ch. 2), at 65 (lines 8–9). See also Gummere, supra note 6 (ch. 1), at 186.
106. See 12 Livy, supra note 148 (ch. 1), at 349–55 (passages xlii.21–22) (recall of Popilius Laenas in 172 BCE); Cicero, De Legibus, supra note 325 (ch. 1), at 483 (passage iii.20) (investigation of D. Iunius Brutus in 138 BCE); 3 Plutarch, supra note 112 (ch. 1), at 357–59 (*Crassus*, xvi) (audit of Crassus in 55 BCE); 4 Plutarch, supra note 112 (ch. 1), at 337 (*Sulla*, v) (abortive prosecution of Sulla for financial irregularities as pro-praetor). See also Walbank, supra note 56 (ch. 2), at 682.

    Cicero won his first major case prosecuting an ex-governor of Sicily, Verres, for corruption in office. See CICERO THE ADVOCATE, at 29–36, (Jonathan Powell and Jeremy Patterson, eds.; Oxford: Oxford University Press, 2004); Andrew Lintott, *Legal Procedure in Cicero's Time*, in id., at 61–78.

107. Cicero, PHILIPPICS, supra note 180 (ch. 2), at 291 (passage v.34); id., at 377 (passage viii.14); 7 Plutarch, supra note 112 (ch. 1), at 119 (*Cicero*, xv). See also Lintott, supra note 227 (ch. 1), at 89–93 (on these so-called final decrees); Greenidge, supra note 84 (ch. 2), at 278–81.
108. See 1 Mommsen, supra note 177 (ch. 2), at 136–52.
109. See Lintott, supra note 227 (ch. 1), at 111–12.
110. See U.S. Constitution, Art. I, § 9, cl. 2. ("The Privilege of the Writ of Habeas Corpus shall not be suspended, unless when in cases of Rebellion or Invasion the public Safety may require it.")
111. See 6 ANNALS OF CONGRESS, at 403–15 (Jan. 26, 1807) (statement of Mr. Elliott) ("We can suspend the writ of habeas corpus only in a case of extreme emergency; that alone is *salus populi* which will justify this *lex suprema*. And is this a crisis of such awful moment? Is it necessary, at this time, to constitute a dictatorship, to save the people from themselves, and to take care that the Republic shall receive no detriment? What is the proposition? To create a single Dictator, as in ancient Rome, in whom all power shall be vested for a time?"); id. (statement of Mr. Eppes) ("I consider the provision in the Constitution for suspending the habeas corpus as designed only for occasions of great national danger. Like the power of creating a Dictator in ancient Rome, it prostrates the rights of your citizens and endangers public liberty.").
112. U.S. Const. Art. II, § 4.
113. 1 Farrand, at 230.

114. 2 Farrand, at 64, 172, 186, 495, 545, 550.
115. See id.
116. 1 WORKS OF JAMES WILSON, supra note 123 (ch. 1), at 426.
117. See FEDERALIST, at 399 (No. 65) (Hamilton) ("The punishment which may be the consequence of conviction upon impeachment, is not to terminate the chastisement of the offender. After having been sentenced to a perpetual ostracism from the esteem and confidence, and honors and emoluments of his country, he will still be liable to prosecution and punishment in the ordinary course of law").
118. See Raoul Berger, IMPEACHMENT: THE CONSTITUTIONAL PROBLEMS, at 53–102, 193–213 (Cambridge, Mass.: Harvard University Press, 1973).
119. U.S. Const. Art. I, § 3, cl. 7.
120. FEDERALIST, at 416 (No. 69) (Hamilton).
121. See id., at 242 (No. 39) (Madison).
122. See, for example, Michael J. Gerhardt, THE FEDERAL IMPEACHMENT PROCESS: A CONSTITUTIONAL AND HISTORICAL ANALYSIS, at 79–81 (Princeton: Princeton University Press, 1996); id., The Constitutional Limits to Impeachments and Its Alternatives, 68 TEX. L. REV. 1, 94–97 (1989); Brian C. Kalt, The Constitutional Case for the Impeachability of Former Federal Officials: An Analysis of the Law, History and Practice of Late Impeachment, 6 TEX. REV. OF L. AND POL. 13 (2001).
123. CONG. GLOBE, 29th Cong., 1st Sess. 641 (1846) (statement of J. Q. Adams).
124. Joseph Story, COMMENTARIES ON THE CONSTITUTION OF THE UNITED STATES § 400, at 284 (R. Rotunda and J. Nowak eds.; 1987) (explaining that the United States, unlike England, confined impeachment to officeholders because citizens, who are relatively defenseless against the government's impeachment power, should be secure from reprisal "for their conduct in exercising their political rights and privileges").
125. See Paul Bestor, Impeachment, 49 WASH. L. REV. 255, 277–79 (1973) (reviewing Raoul Berger, IMPEACHMENT: THE CONSTITUTIONAL PROBLEMS); Ronald D. Rotunda, An Essay on the Constitutional Parameters of Federal Impeachment, 76 KY. L. REV. 707, 716–17 (1987).
126. FEDERALIST, at 398–99 (No. 65) (Hamilton).
127. See Mitchell Franklin, Romanist Infamy and the American Constitutional Concept of Impeachment, 23 BUFFALO L. REV. 313 (1974). See also 10 Plutarch, supra note 112 (ch. 1), at 193 (Gaius Gracchus, iv) (Roman law that those removed from public office were barred from holding subsequent positions).
128. U.S. Const. Art. I, § 7, cl. 3.
129. Id., Art. I, § 9, cl. 7.
130. 524 U.S. 417 (1998).
131. 110 Stat. 1200 (1996).
132. See 524 U.S., at 438–39.
133. Id., at 439–40 (quoting Chadha, 462 U.S., at 951 and quoting 33 WRITINGS OF GEORGE WASHINGTON, at 96 (J. Fitzpatrick ed.; 1940)). See also May, supra note 408 (ch. 3), at 32.
134. See 524 U.S., at 473–80 (Breyer, J., dissenting).
135. Id., at 483.

136. See id. ("Nor can one say that the Act's basic substantive objective is constitutionally improper, for the earliest Congresses could . . . and often did, confer
on the President this sort of discretionary authority over spending. . . . "); Cf.
J. W. Hampton, 276 U.S., at 412 (Taft, C. J.) ("[C]ontemporaneous legislative
exposition of the Constitution when the founders of our Government and the
framers of our Constitution were actively participating in public affairs . . . fixes
the construction to be given to its provisions").").

137. See 524 U.S., at 471, 472 (quoting *McCulloch v. Maryland*, 17 U.S. (4 Wheat.)
316, 415 (1819)).

138. FEDERALIST. at 359 (No. 58) (Hamilton).

139. 3 Polybius, supra note 51 (ch. 2), at 299 (passage vi.13.3). See also Walbank,
supra note 56 (ch. 2), at 677–79; Greenidge, supra note 84 (ch. 2), at 212–16.

140. See 13 Livy, supra note 148 (ch. 1), at 287–89 (passage xlv.13.12); Rhetorica ad
Herennium, supra note 476 (ch. 3), at 39 (passage i.21); 8 Plutarch, supra note
112 (ch. 1), at 269–79 (*Cato the Younger*, xvi–xviii) (Cato as quaestor). See also
Lintott, supra note 227 (ch. 1), at 136–37.

141. See 1 ROMAN STATUTES, supra note 193 (ch. 2), at 65 (Lex repetendarum, lines
57–69); id., at 113 (Lex agraria, lines 46–47, 74).

142. See Robert C. Byrd, THE SENATE OF THE ROMAN REPUBLIC: ADDRESSES ON
THE HISTORY OF ROMAN CONSTITUTIONALISM, Sen. Doc. 103–23, as autho-
rized to be published in S. Cong. Res. 68, 103d Cong., 2d Sess. (Washington,
DC: U.S. GPO, 1995).

143. See Neil A. Lewis, *Byrd's Eloquent Voice Continues to Fight to Honor Tradition
in the Senate*, NEW YORK TIMES, Nov. 29, 1997, at A7, col. 1.

144. See 146 Cong Rec. S2914 (Apr. 26, 2000) (debate on a Victim's Compensation
constitutional amendment) ("We are acquainted with [Montesquieu's] 'Spirit
of the Laws' and with his 'Persian Letters,' but perhaps we are not so familiar
with the fact that he also wrote an analysis of the history of the Romans and the
Roman state. This essay, titled 'Considerations on the Causes of the Greatness
of the Romans and their Decline,' was produced in 1734. Considering the fact
that Montesquieu was so deeply impressed with the ancient Romans and their
system of government, and in further consideration of his influence upon
the thinking of the Framers and upon the thinking of educated Americans
generally during the period of the American Revolution, let us consider the
Roman system as it was seen by Polybius. . . . "); 140 id., S2049 (March 1, 1994)
(Balanced Budget amendment); 139 id., S5724 (May 11, 1993).

145. See 146 Cong. Rec. S2915–16 (Apr. 26, 2000). ("The theory of a mixed constitution had had its great measure of success in the Roman Republic. It is not
surprising then, that the Founding Fathers of the United States should have
been familiar with the works of Polybius, or that Montesquieu should have been
influenced by the checks and balances and separation of powers in the Roman
constitutional system, a clear and central element of which was the control over
the purse, vested solely in the Senate in the heyday of the Republic. Were the
Framers influenced by the classics? Every schoolchild and student in the universities learned how to read and write Greek and Latin. Those were required
subjects. The founders were steeped in the classics, and both the Federalists
and the Antifederalists resorted to ancient history and classical writings in their

disquisitions. Not only were classical models invoked; the founders also had their classical 'antimodels' – those individuals and government forms of antiquity whose vices and faults they desired to avoid. Classical philosophers and the theory of natural law were much discussed during the period prior to and immediately following the American Revolution. It was a time of great political ferment, and thousands of circulars, pamphlets, and newspaper columns displayed the erudition of Americans who delighted in classical allusions.")

146. See Byrd, supra note 142, at 29–31, 34, 44, 97.

147. See id., at 22–23.

148. See id., at 96. See also Greenidge, supra note 84 (ch. 2), at 274–77.

149. See Byrd, supra note 142, at 99–101.

150. See Lintott, supra note 227, at 143–44. See also Cicero, DE LEGIBUS, supra note 325 (ch. 1), at 499 (passage iii.34); 10 Plutarch, supra note 112 (ch. 1), at 159–69 (*Tiberius Gracchus*, viii.10); 207–09 (*Gaius Gracchus*, v). For the text of the Gracchi's agrarian statute, see ANCIENT ROMAN STATUTES: A TRANSLATION, WITH INTRODUCTION, COMMENTARY, GLOSSARY, AND INDEX, at 50 (Allan Chester Johnson, Paul Robinson Coleman-Norton, and Frank Card Bourne, eds.; Austin: University of Texas Press, 1961).

151. See 14 Livy, supra note 148 (ch. 1), at 61–63 (passage lviii); 10 Plutarch, supra note 112 (ch. 1), at 177–79, 181–83 (*Tiberius Gracchus*, xi, xiv.5–8; xv.2–4). For a full account of Roman disputes on agrarian reform, see Nelson, supra note 93 (ch. 1), at 49–68; A. H. Bernstein, TIBERIUS GRACCHUS: TRADITION AND APOSTASY (Ithaca: Cornell University Press, 1978); David Stockton, THE GRACCHI (Oxford: Clarendon Press, 1979).

152. See Byrd, supra note 142, at 91–92 (senatorial adoption of a dictatorial decree, aimed at curbing the influence of the Gracchi). See also J. Linderski, *The Pontiff and the Tribune: The Death of Tiberius Gracchus*, 90(2) ATHENAEUM 339 (2002).

153. 3 Polybius, supra note 51 (ch. 2), at 307 (passage vi.16.5). For a gloss on Montesquieu's discussion of this account, see Carrese, supra note 127 (ch. 2), at 58.

154. Cicero, DE LEGIBUS, supra note 325 (ch. 1), at 483 (passage iii.20). See also Nelson, supra note 93 (ch. 1), at 57–59.

155. 139 Cong. Rec. S8160 (June 29, 1993). See also Byrd, supra note 142, at 101.

156. See id.

157. But see 139 Cong. Rec. S5839 (May 12, 1993) (remarks of Sen. McCain) ("[L]et me compliment Senator BYRD. I can think of no individual in the Senate who could so eloquently and with such heartfelt passion discuss the Roman Empire and its relation to the line-item veto").

158. See May, supra note 408 (ch. 3), at 3–8.

159. See U.S. Const. Art. II, § 3, cl. 3.

160. See 3 Elliot, at 657–63 (Virginia debates); 3 id., at 226, 242–52 (North Carolina).

161. See May, supra note 408 (ch. 3), at 25 (James Madison's views).

162. *United States v. Smith*, 27 F. Cas. 1192, 1230 (C.C.D. N.Y. 1806) (No. 16,342).

163. Id., at 1229–30.

164. Id., at 1231.

165. See, for example, David W. Abbott and James P. Levine, Wrong Winner: The Coming Debacle in the Electoral College (New York: Praeger, 1991); Judith Best, The choice of the people?: debating the electoral college (Lanham: Rowman & Littlefield, 1996); Alexander M. Bickel, Reform and Continuity: The Electoral College, The Convention and the Party System (New York: Harper & Row, 1971); John D. Feerick, *The Electoral College – Why It ought to be Abolished*, 37 Fordham L. Rev. 1 (1968); Michael J. Glennon, When No Majority Rules: The Electoral College and Presidential Succession (Washington, DC: Congressional Quarterly, 1992); Robert M. Hardaway, The Electoral College and the Constitution: The Case for Preserving Federalism (Westport: Praeger, 1994); Tadahisha Kuroda, The Origins of the Twelfth Amendment: The Electoral College in the Early Republic, 1787–1804 (Westport: Greenwood Press, 1994); Lawrence D. Longley and Real R. Peirce, The Electoral College Primer 2000 (New Haven: Yale University Press, 1999); Securing Democracy – Why we Have an Electoral College (Gary L. Gregg, II, ed.; Wilmington, Del.: ISI Books, 2001).

166. See Eidelberg, supra note 7 (pr.), at 169–91; Jack Rakove, *The Accidental Electors*, New York Times, Dec. 19, 2000, at A35.

167. 2 Farrand 501 (Sept. 4) (Madison's notes). See also Paul A. Rahe, *Moderating the Political Impulse*, in Gregg, supra note 165, at 55, 59–62; Daniel Patrick Moynihan, *The Electoral College and the Uniqueness of America*, in id., at 87, 88–96.

168. See 1 Farrand, at 68 (June 1).

169. Illustrative were the views of Elbridge Gerry, see 2 Farrand, at 57 (July 19) ("The popular mode of electing the Chief Magistrate would certainly be the worst of all.... [T]he people are uninformed, and would be misled by a few designing men.").

170. Akhil Reed Amar, *A Constitutional Accident Waiting to Happen*, 12 Const. Comment. 143, 143–44 (1995).

171. See 2 Farrand, at 30, 32 (remarks of Charles Pinckney and Hugh Williamson) (July 17). See also Paul Finkelman, *The Proslavery Origins of the Electoral College*, 23 Cardozo L. Rev. 1145 (2002); Victor Williams and Alison M. Macdonald, *Rethinking Article II, Section I and its Twelfth Amendment Restatement: Challenging Our Nation's Malapportioned, Undemocratic Presidential Election Systems*, 77 Marq. L. Rev. 201, 205–10 (1994); Wills, Negro President, supra note 61 (ch. 3).

172. See Clinton, Brief History, supra note 6 (ch. 1), at 905.

173. See 1 Farrand, at 77.

174. See 2 id., at 57 (July 19). For more on what was the understanding of the role of state legislatures in this process, see Hayward H. Smith, *History of the Article II Independent State Legislature Doctrine*, 29 Fla. St. U. L. Rev. 731 (2001).

175. U.S. Const. Art. II, § 1, cl. 2.

176. See id.

177. 1 Works of James Wilson, supra note 123 (ch. 1), at 439. See also U.S. Const. Art. II, § 1, cls. 3 and 4 ("Congress may determine the Time of chusing the

Electors; and the Day on which they shall give their Votes; which Day shall be the same throughout the United States.").

178. See id., Art. II, § 1, cl. 3.
179. See id. The individual receiving the next highest level of electoral college votes was to become Vice President, if that person had a majority of the electoral ballots, otherwise the Convention ultimately decided the Senate would make the vice presidential selection. See id. This scheme was altered by the Twelfth Amendment, adopted in 1804 after the debacle of the 1800 election in which Thomas Jefferson and Aaron Burr, running on the same party ticket, tied for electoral votes, and it was only after much balloting and wrangling that Jefferson was selected by the House. See Doris Faber and Harold Faber, We The People: The Story of the United States Constitution Since 1787, at 74–87 (New York: Schribner's, 1987).
180. See Art. II, § 1, cl. 3. See also Clinton, Brief History, supra note 6 (ch. 1), at 908.
181. Federalist, at 244 (No. 39) (Madison). See also Mansfield, Republicanizing the Executive, in Kesler, supra note 230 (ch. 1), at 175–78.
182. 1 Works of James Wilson, supra note 123 (ch. 1), at 438.
183. See Luis Fuentes-Rohwer and Guy-Uriel Charles, *The Electoral College, The Right to Vote, and Our Federalism: A Comment on a Lasting Institution*, 29 Fla. St. U. L. Rev. 879 (2001).
184. See, for example, 1 Farrand, at 290 (June 18) (Madison's notes); id., 300 (June 18) (Yates's notes). See also Federalist, at 206 (No. 34) (Hamilton) ("It will be readily understood that I allude to the comitia centuriata and the comitia tributa. The former, in which the people voted by centuries, was so arranged as to give a superiority to the patrician interest; in the latter, in which numbers prevailed, the plebian interest had an entire predominancy. And yet these two legislatures coexisted for ages, and the Roman republic attained to the utmost height of human greatness."); id., 425 (No. 70) (Hamilton). See also Sirico, supra note 4 (pr.), at 469–73.
185. Noah Webster, An Examination into the Leading Principles of the Federal Constitution (Oct. 10, 1787), reprinted in Ford, Pamphlets, supra note 46 (ch. 2), at 35.
186. Id.
187. Id., at 36. Webster may well have been criticizing James Harrington's favorable discussion of the voting in Roman popular assemblies. See Harrington, supra note 275 (ch. 2), at 73–77.
188. See lex Gabinia, 1 Roman Statutes, supra note 193 (ch. 2), at 345; lex Malacitana (55 BCE).
189. See Lintott, supra note 227 (ch. 1), at 10–11 (although noting that in the late republic, consular elections often occurred in July); Greenidge, supra note 84 (ch. 2), at 189.
190. See Nicolet, supra note 22 (ch. 2), at 246–50; Taylor, Voting Assemblies, supra note 16 (ch. 3), at 78–83. See also 9 Plutarch, supra note 112 (ch. 1), at 471–73 (*Gaius Marius*, v).
191. See Nicolet, supra note 22 (ch. 2), at 250–58; Taylor, Voting Assemblies, supra note 16 (ch. 3), at 44.

192. See Rhetorica ad Herennium, supra note 476 (ch. 3), at 405–09 (passage iv. 68); 6 Livy, supra note 148 (ch. 1), at 197 (passage xxiv.8); 6 id., 345–47 (passage xxv.2.6–8) (Scipio Africanus's election as aedile in 213 BCE). See also 5 Plutarch, supra note 112 (ch. 1), at 443–51, 463–67 (*Marcellus*, iv–vi, xii) (unfavorable auspices for consular elections); 7 id., at 471–73 (*Caesar*, xiii) (personal appearance of consular candidates required).

193. See Nicolet, supra note 22 (ch. 2), at 258–67; Taylor, Voting Assemblies, supra note 16 (ch. 3), at 81–82. See also 8 Plutarch, supra note 112 (ch. 1), at 335–39 (*Cato the Younger*, xlii).

194. See Taylor, Voting Assemblies, supra note 16 (ch. 3), at 84–88. See also Greenidge, supra note 84 (ch. 2), at 258–60.

195. Cicero, De Re Publica, supra note 325 (ch. 1), at 149 (passage ii.39).

196. 1 Livy, supra note 148 (ch. 1), at 153 (passage i.43.10).

197. See 2 Dionysius of Halicarnassus, supra note 23 (ch. 2), at 337 (passage iv.21.3) (describing the reform as more "democratic"). See also Taylor, Voting Assemblies, supra note 16 (ch. 3), at 84, 87–88; Walbank, supra note 56 (ch. 2), at 683–87.

198. See 4 Works of John Adams, supra note 87 (ch. 1), at 498–505 (Achaean Confederation), at 515 (Boeotian Confederation).

199. In the Boeotian Confederacy, the archon was a mere figurehead. Real power resided in the board of seven boeotarchs. See Larsen, Representative Government, supra note 202 (ch. 3), at 73.

200. See Aymard, Achaean Assemblies, supra note 122 (ch. 3), at 253; Larsen, supra note 203 (ch. 3), at xxi–xxiii. See also 3 Polybius, supra note 51 (ch. 2), at 77 (passage v.30.7) (election of Aratus as strategos in 217 BCE).

201. See Larsen, Representative Government, supra note 202 (ch. 3), at 83–84.

202. See 2 Polybius, supra note 51 (ch. 2), at 309 (passage iv.5.8) ("By these arguments and others in the same sense, [Dorimachus of the Aetolians] made Scopas and his friends so eager for the enterprise that without waiting for the General Assembly of the Aetolians, without taking the Special Council into their confidence, without in fact taking any proper steps, but acting solely as their own passion and their private judgement dictated, they made war all at once on the Messenians, Epirots, Achaeans, Acarnanians, and Macedonians.").

203. See, for example, 2 Polybius, supra note 51 (ch. 2), at 297–509; 3 id., 3–267 (passages iv–v); 7 Livy, supra note 148 (ch. 1), at 3–197 (passage xxvi).

204. See Federalist, at 425 (No. 70) (Hamilton). ("The experience of other nations will afford little instruction on this head. As far, however, as it teaches any thing, it teaches us not to be enamoured of plurality in the Executive. We have seen that the Achaeans, on an experiment of two Praetors [strategos], were induced to abolish one.")

205. See Bush v. Palm Beach County Canvassing Bd., 531 U.S. 70 (2000) (per curiam); Bush v. Gore, 531 U.S. 98 (2000) (per curiam).

206. See Chapter 2, at Notes 214–69 with text.

207. U.S. Const. Art. IV, § 4.

208. William W. Wiecek, The Guarantee Clause of the U. S. Constitution 1 (Ithaca: Cornell University Press, 1972).

209. John R. Vile, *John C. Calhoun on the Guarantee Clause*, 40 S. CAR. L. REV. 667, 667 (1989).
210. John Adams to Mercy Warren, July 20, 1807, reprinted in *Correspondence between John Adams and Mercy Warren relating to her "History of the American Revolution,"* in 4 MASSACHUSETTS HISTORY SOCIETY COLLECTIONS (5th series), at 352 (Boston, 1878). See also Anastalpo, supra note 403 (ch. 3), at 172–75.
211. See, for example, 2 Farrand 47 (July 18) (Madison's notes) ("The Resoln. has 2. objects. 1. to secure Republican Government. 2. to suppress domestic commotions. He urged the necessity of both these provisions.") (Randolph's remarks); FEDERALIST, at 274–77 (No. 43) (Madison).
212. See U.S. Const. Art. IV, § 1 (Full Faith and Credit Clause); § 2, cl. 1 ("The Citizens of each State shall be entitled to all Privileges and Immunities of Citizens in the several States"); § 2, cl. 2 (inter-state extraditions); § 3 (admission of new states and Congressional authority over federal property and facilities).
213. For more on this view, see Charles L. Black, Jr., *On Worrying About the Constitution*, 55 U. COLO. L. REV. 469 (1984); Arthur E. Bonfield, *The Guarantee Clause of Article IV, Section 4: A Study in Constitutional Desuetude*, 46 MINN. L. REV. 513 (1962); Deborah Jones Merritt, *The Guarantee Clause and State Autonomy: Federalism for a Third Century*, 88 COLUM. L. REV. 1 (1988).
214. See Vile, supra note 209, at 679–80 (for John C. Calhoun's views in 1843). See also *South Carolina v. United States*, 199 U.S. 437 (1905); *Duncan v. McCall*, 139 U.S. 449 (1891).
215. James Madison, *Vices of the Political System of the United States* (1787), reprinted in Madison's POLITICAL THOUGHT, supra note 172 (ch. 2), at 57.
216. See Edmund Randolph, LETTER ON THE FEDERAL CONSTITUTION, reprinted in Ford, PAMPHLETS, supra note 46 (ch. 2), at 267.
217. 1 Farrand, at 22 (May 29) (Madison's notes).
218. See Wiecek, supra note 208, at 53–54.
219. 2 id., at 317 (Aug. 17) (Madison's notes).
220. 1 id., at 227 (draft proposal that a state's "republican constitution, and it's [sic] existing laws, ought to be guaranteed . . . by the United States.").
221. 2 id., at 47, 220 (criticism of the lack of a constitution for Rhode Island). See also id., at 47 ("Mr. HOUSTON was afraid of perpetuating the existing Constitutions of the States. That of Georgia was a very bad one, and he hoped would be revised & amended. It may also be difficult for the Genl. Govt. to decide between contending parties each of which claim the sanction of the Constitution.").
222. 2 id., 47 ("Mr. WILSON moved as a better expression of the idea, 'that a Republican form of Governmt. shall be guarantied to each State & that each State shall be protected agst. foreign & domestic violence.' This seeming to be well received, Mr. MADISON & Mr. RANDOLPH withdrew their propositions & on the Question for agreeing to Mr. Wilson's motion, it passed nem. con.").
223. 2 Documentary History, supra note 240 (ch. 2), at 437 (Pennsylvania ratifying convention) (Nov. 30, 1787).
224. 2 Elliot 168 (remarks of Rev. Samuel Stillman).

225. See Merritt, supra note 213, at 33–36.
226. IMPARTIAL EXAMINER No. 1, Feb. 20, 1788, reprinted in 8 DOCUMENTARY HISTORY, supra note 240 (ch. 2), at 393.
227. Adams to Mercy Warren, July 20, 1807, reprinted in *Correspondence between John Adams and Mercy Warren relating to her "History of the American Revolution,"* in 4 MASSACHUSETTS HISTORY SOCIETY COLLECTIONS (5th series) 352 (Boston, 1878).
228. FEDERALIST, at 241 (No. 39) (Madison) (emphasis in original).
229. Id., at 146 (No. 22) (Hamilton).
230. 2 U.S. (2 Dall.) 419, 457 (1793) (Wilson, J.).
231. See 2 Elliot, at 195–97 (Oliver Ellsworth at the Connecticut convention: "In republics, it is a fundamental principle that the majority govern, and that the minority comply with the general voice."); 3 id., at 46 (Patrick Henry at the Virginia convention observing that minority rule is inconsistent with republicanism); 4 id., 237 (William Davie at the North Carolina convention: "A majority is the rule of republican decisions.").
232. FEDERALIST, at 81 (No. 10) (Madison).
233. Id., at 82. See also Pangle, supra note 102 (ch. 1), at 153–58.
234. 3 Elliot, at 396.
235. 2 Farrand, at 48 (July 18) (Madison's notes) (spelling modernized).
236. FEDERALIST, at 139–40 (No. 21) (Hamilton). See also Richard D. Brown, *Shay's Rebellion and the Ratification of the Federal Constitution in Massachusetts*, in Beyond Confederation, supra note 61 (ch. 3), at 113.
237. Id., at 275–77 (No. 43) (Madison) (emphasis in original). See Wiecek, supra note 208, at 63–67.
238. FEDERALIST, at 242 (No. 39) (Madison).
239. Id., at 126 (No. 18) (Madison).
240. 2 Elliot, at 31, 85–88, 145–47 (Jan. 17, 1787, Jan. 23, 1788 & Feb. 4, 1788) (remarks of James Bowdoin, Thomas Thacher, and Charles Turner).
241. FEDERALIST, at 274–75 (No. 43) (Madison) (quoting Montesquieu, *Spirit of the Laws*, book ix).
242. 1 WORKS OF JAMES WILSON, supra note 123 (ch. 1), at 264.
243. See 3 Elliot 209–11 (James Monroe at the Virginia convention); 4 id., at 195 (James Iredell at the North Carolina convention).
244. See 2 CAF 146 (Samuel Bryan, Letters of Centinel No. II); 2 id., 157 (No. III) (Nov. 8, 1787); 6 CAF 185 (speech by George Clinton before the New York Ratifying Convention, July 11, 1788).
245. Pelatiah Webster, THE WEAKNESS OF BRUTUS EXPOSED, Nov. 4, 1787, reprinted in Ford, PAMPHLETS, supra note 46 (ch. 2), at 130.
246. U.S. Const. Art. IV, § 1.
247. Id., Art. IV, § 2, cl. 1.
248. See Larry D. Kramer, *Same-Sex Marriage, Conflict of Laws, and the Unconstitutional Public Policy Exception*, 106 YALE L. J. 1965, 2006 (1997).
249. See *Minor v. Happersett*, 88 U.S. (21 Wall.) 162 (1874).
250. See Vile, supra note 209, at 680 (noting Calhoun's admonition that the Guarantee Clause had to be viewed as to "the forms of the governments of the several States, composing the Union, as they stood at the time of their admission,

are the proper standard, by which to determine whether any after change, in any of them, makes its form of government other than republican.") (quoting Calhoun's letter to William Smith (July 3, 1843), reprinted in 17 THE PAPERS OF JOHN C. CALHOUN, at 277 (C. Wilson, ed.; 1986).

251. FEDERALIST, at 323 (No. 51) (Madison).

252. Id., at 423, 425 (No. 70) (Hamilton).

253. *Bauers v. Heisel*, 361 F.2d 581, 588–89 (3d Cir. 1966) (citing "The FEDERALIST, pp. 236, 303–305, 488 et seq., 494 et seq.").

254. *In re Interrogatories Propounded by the Senate Concerning House Bill 1078*, 536 P.2d 308 (Colo. 1975).

255. *Vansickle v. Shanahan*, 511 P.2d 223 (Kan. 1973).

256. See 536 P.2d at 316–18. See also *State v. Lehtola*, 198 N.W. 2d 354 (Wis. 1972).

257. FEDERALIST, at 241 (No. 39) (Madison).

258. Id., at 275 (No. 43) (Madison).

259. 511 P.2d at 241.

260. See Wiecek, supra note 208, at 86–110. See Also Arthur May Mowry, THE DORR WAR: THE CONSTITUTIONAL STRUGGLE IN RHODE ISLAND (New York: Chelsea House rep., 1970).

261. 48 U.S. (7 How.) 1 (1849).

262. Id., at 42 (Taney, C. J.).

263. See Wiecek, supra note 208, at 60, 76–77.

264. See L. Rex Sears, *Punishing the States for their "Peculiar Institution": Congress on the Constitutional Dilemmas*, 2001 UTAH L. REV. 581, 605–06.

265. In 1996, of the more than seventeen thousand laws adopted by those twenty-four states allowing citizen initiatives, only forty-five were enacted by referenda, a paltry 0.3 percent of all laws passed. Jeff Jacoby, *Ballot Initiatives Keep Democracy on Track*, BOSTON GLOBE, June 5, 2000. See also Akhil Reed Amar, *The Central Meaning of Republican Government: Popular Sovereignty, Majority Rule, and the Denominator Problem*, 65 U. COLO. L. REV. 794 (1994).

266. See Hardy Myers, *The Guarantee Clause and Direct Democracy*, 34 WILLAMETTE L. REV. 659 (1998); Robin Charlow, *Judicial Review, Equal Protection and the Problem with Plebiscites*, 79 CORNELL L. REV. 527 (1994); Louis J. Sirico, Jr., *The Constitutionality of the Initiative and Referendum*, 65 Iowa L. Rev. 637 (1980); W. A. Coutts, *Is a Provision of the Initiative and Referendum Inconsistent with the Constitution of the United States?*, 6 MICH. L. REV. 304, 306 (1907). But see for example, William T. Mayton, *Direct Democracy, Federalism & the Guarantee Clause*, 2 GREEN BAG 2D 269 (1999) (for the opposite view).

267. See *Pacific States Telephone & Telegraph Co. v. Oregon*, 223 U.S. 118 (1912) (holding that such a challenge was nonjusticiable in federal court; only Congress could determine such a matter).

268. See, for example, *Margolis v. District Court*, 638 P.2d 297 (Colo. 1981); *Westberg v. Andrus*, 757 P.2d 664 (Idaho 1988); *In re Initiative Petition No. 348, State Question No. 640*, 820 P.2d 772 (Okla. 1991); *Kadderly v. City of Portland*, 74 P. 710, 719 (Or. 1903). See also Robert G. Natelson, *A Republic, Not a Democracy? Initiative, Referendum, and the Constitution's Guarantee Clause*, 80 TEX. L. REV. 807, 811 n.19 (2002) (collecting case citations).

269. The only such case appears to be *Rice v. Foster*, 4 Del. (4 Harr.) 479, 487 (1847) ("To guard against these dangers and the evil tendencies of a democracy, our republican government was instituted by the consent of the people. The characteristic which distinguishes it from the miscalled republics of ancient and modern times, is, that none of the powers of sovereignty are exercised by the people; but all of them by separate, co-ordinate branches of government in whom those powers are vested by the constitution. These co-ordinate branches are intended to operate as balances, checks and restraints, not only upon each other, but upon the people themselves; to guard them against their own rashness, precipitancy, and misguided zeal; and to protect the minority against the injustice of the majority.").

270. See Natelson, supra note 268, at 812–14 (discussing recent cases and commentary).

271. See id., at 834–40.

272. 4 WORKS OF JOHN ADAMS, supra note 87 (ch. 1), at 471 (Adams reporting that the single dissenting vote of a senator would send an issue for popular determination).

273. 4 id., at 481–83 (on the Athenian assembly).

274. 4 id., at 523–41.

275. 4 id., at 551–55.

276. 4 id., at 482. See also MacDowell, supra note 291 (ch. 2), at 48–49.

277. 4 id., at 552. See also Rahe, supra note 3 (pr.), at 136–38, 183–85.

278. 4 id., at 523, 526, 534. See also Taylor, ROMAN VOTING ASSEMBLIES, supra note 16 (ch. 3), at 5 (chart facing), 59–64; Walbank, supra note 56 (ch. 2), at 676.

279. See Wiecek, supra note 208, at 18–19.

280. See Natelson, supra note 268, at 840 ("The modern *plebis scitum* is, of course, the plebiscite. It is one of the delicious oddities of legal literature, born clearly of historical ignorance, that some legal writers continue to contend earnestly that all or certain plebiscites are not 'republican.' Yet plebiscites originated in the state that the Founders viewed as the grandest republic of all! One might as well contend that pizza is not Italian.") (citations omitted).

281. See also Taylor, Roman Voting Assemblies, supra note 16 (ch. 3), at 59–64 (discussing proper interpretation of the Lex Hortensia (287 BCE) and other statutes); Greenidge, supra note 84 (ch. 2), at 123–26, 158–59, 234–55.

CHAPTER 5. THE CLASSICAL CONSTITUTION

1. Wood, supra note 3 (Pr.), at 558–63.

2. See the sources noted in the Preface, at Notes 3–10, with accompanying text.

3. See Richard, supra note 6 (ch. 1), at 233. See also Chapter 1, at notes 310–11 and accompanying text.

4. See Sellers, supra note 85 (ch. 1), at 240, 245.

5. 4 WORKS OF JOHN ADAMS, supra note 87 (ch. 1), at 295.

6. Quoted in Paul M. Spurlin, MONTESQUIEU IN AMERICA, 1760–1801, at 261 (University, La.: Louisiana State University Press, 1940).

7. See also Sellers, supra note 85 (ch. 1), at 233–36.

8. See Richard, supra note 6 (ch. 1), at 239.
9. U.S. Const. Art. I, § 2, cl. 2; Art. I, § 3, cl. 3; Art. II, § 1, cl. 5.
10. U.S. Const. Art. I, § 3; Art. II, § 2.
11. U.S. Const. Art. II, § 1.
12. U.S. Const. Art. I, § 8, cl. 11.
13. U.S. Const. Art. I, § 8, cl. 10.
14. U.S. Const. Art. I, § 3, cl. 4.
15. U.S. Const. Art. II, § 2, cl. 1.
16. U.S. Const. Art. I, § 3, cl. 7.
17. U.S. Const. Art. IV, § 1.
18. U.S. Const. Art. I, § 9, cl. 3; Art. I, § 10, cl. 1.
19. U.S. Const. Art. I, § 9, cl. 2.
20. U.S. Const. Art. IV, § 4.
21. See H. Trevor Colbourn, THE LAMP OF EXPERIENCE: WHIG HISTORY AND THE INTELLECTUAL ORIGINS OF THE AMERICAN REVOLUTION (Chapel Hill: University of North Carolina Press, 1965).
22. 2 Farrand, at 393–94 (Aug. 13) (Madison's notes). See also M. E. Bradford, "A Better Guide than Reason": The Politics of John Dickinson, 21 MODERN AGE 47 (Winter 1977); Richard, supra note 6 (ch. 1), at 242.
23. FEDERALIST 57 (No. 6) (Hamilton).
24. Id., 138 (No. 20) (Madison (with Hamilton)).
25. Patrick Henry, Speech in Virginia Convention (Richmond, Virginia, Mar. 25, 1775), quoted in, William Wirt, SKETCHES OF THE LIFE AND CHARACTER OF PATRICK HENRY (Philadelphia, 1818).
26. See, for example, Robert W. Gordon, Foreword: The Arrival of Critical Historicism, 49 STAN. L. REV. 1023 (1997); Alfred Kelly, Clio and the Court: An Illicit Love Affair, 1965 SUP. CT. REV. 119; Richard A. Posner, Post-Dependency, Pragmatism, and Critique of History in Adjudication and Legal Scholarship, 67 U. CHI. L. REV. 573 (2000); John Phillip Reid, Law and History, 27 LOY. L. A. L. REV. 193 (1993); Neil M. Richards, Clio and the Court: A Reassessment of the Supreme Court's Uses of History, 13 J. L. AND POL. 809 (1997); Randall T. Shepard, The Importance of Legal History for Modern Lawyering, 30 IND. L. REV. 1 (1997).
27. See Martin S. Flaherty, History "Lite" in Modern American Constitutionalism, 95 COLUM. L. REV. 523 (1995).
28. See Meyer, MADISON'S POLITICAL THOUGHT, supra note 172 (ch. 2), at 533–34, 548–49.
29. Richard, supra note 6 (ch. 1), at 240–41.
30. See Rahe, supra note 3 (pr.), at 604.
31. Clarence Thomas, Francis Boyer Lecture, American Enterprise Institute (Feb. 13, 2001), reprinted at http://www.aei.org/boyer.thomas.htm.
32. Antonin Scalia, Originalism: The Lesser Evil, 57 U. CIN. L. REV. 849 (1989).
33. See Yoo, supra note 75 (ch. 4), at 1173–74 (arguing that the views of the ratifiers matter more in any analysis of original intent). See also RATIFYING THE CONSTITUTION 1–23 (Michael Allen Gillespie and Michael Lienesch, eds.; Lawrence: University Press of Kansas, 1989).

34. See, for example, Robert H. Bork, THE TEMPTING OF AMERICA 143–60 (New York: Free Press, 1990); Rakove, supra note 164 (ch. 1), at 259.
35. 521 U.S. 898, 921 n.11 (1997) (quoting FEDERALIST 138 (No. 20) (Madison (with Hamilton)); and *United States v. Lopez*, 514 U.S. 549, 575 (1995) (Kennedy, J., concurring) (citing Friendly, *Federalism: A Forward*, 86 YALE L. J. 1019 (1977)).
36. 3 POLYBIUS, supra note 51 (ch. 2), at 271 (passage vi.2.9).

INDEX